# Virtue Ethic

# VIRTUE ETHICS

**Edited by**
**Daniel Statman**

EDINBURGH UNIVERSITY PRESS

*For Yael*

© The Contributors, 1997
© Chapters 1, 5, 6, 13,
Edinburgh University Press, 1997

Transferred to digital print 2009

Edinburgh University Press Ltd
22 George Square, Edinburgh

Reprinted 2003

Typeset in Garamond by
Bibliocraft, Dundee,
Printed and bound in Great Britain by
CPI Antony Rowe, Chippenham and Eastbourne

A CIP record for this book is
available from the British Library

ISBN 0 7486 0898 2 (hardback)

ISBN 0 7486 0896 6 (paperback)

# CONTENTS

# CONTRIBUTORS

Daniel Statman is a professor of philosophy at Bar-Ilan University, Israel. He is author of *Moral Dilemmas*, co-author of *Religion and Morality* and editor of *Moral Luck*.

Harold Alderman is Professor of Philosophy at Sonoma University, California. He is author of a book on Nietzsche, as well as many articles on a variety of philosophical topics, including ethics and continental philosophy.

Rosalind Hursthouse is Head of the Philosophy Department at the Open University in Britain. She is author of *Beginning Live*, is co-editor of *Virtues and Reasons: A Festschrift for Philippa Foot* and has written extensively in the area of virtue theory.

Robert B. Louden is Professor of Philosophy at the University of Southern Maine. He is author of *Morality and Moral Theory: A Reappraisal and Reaffirmation*, editor of *The Greeks and Us: Essays in Honor of Arthur Adkins*, and is currently working on a book manuscript entitled *Kant's Impure Ethics: The Application of A Priori Moral Theory to Empirical Circumstances*.

Phillip Montague is Professor of Philosophy at Western Washington University. He is author of *In the Interest of Others: An Essay in Moral Philosophy* and of *Punishment as Societal Defense*.

Gerasimos X. Santas is Associate Professor of Philosophy at the University of California at Irvine. He is the author of *Socrates* and of *Plato and Freud: Two Theories of Love*.

Peter Simpson is Associate Professor of Philosophy and Classics at the Graduate School, City University of New York, and also at the College of Staten Island. He is author of *Goodness and Nature: A Defense of Ethical Naturalism*, and of a new translation to and commentary of Aristotle's *Politics*.

Michael Slote is Professor of Philosophy at the University of Maryland, College Park. He is the author of many articles and books on ethics, including *Good and Virtues, Beyond Optimizing: A Study of Rational Choice* and *From Virtue to Morality*.

David Solomon is Professor of Philosophy at Notre Dame University.

Robert C. Solomon is Quincy Lee Centennial Professor of Business and Philosophy at the University of Texas at Austin and the author of many books and articles including *The Passions, In the Spirit of Hegel, About Love* and *Ethics and Excellence*.

Michael Stocker is Guttag Professor of Ethics and Political Philosophy at Syracuse University, New York, and Reader in Philosophy at La Trobe University, Melbourne. He is author of *Plural and Conflicting Values*, co-author of *Valuing Emotions* and author of many articles on moral and political philosophy.

Christine Swanton is Professor of Philosophy at Auckland University, New Zealand. She is author of *Freedom: A Coherent Theory* and of a variety of articles in ethics and political philosophy.

Gregory Velazco y Trianosky is Associate Professor of Philosophy at Olivet College in Michigan. He has published articles on supererogation, virtue ethics and the history of ethics. He is currently working on issues in the philosophy of race and racism that involve the notion of *mestizaje* or mixed-race identity. He is also at work on a book manuscript on compassion and the altruistic virtues.

Gary Watson is Associate Professor of Philosophy at the University of California at Irvine. He specialises in moral and political theory and in the philosophy of agency. Among his major publications are 'Free Agency', 'Free Action and Free Will' and 'Two Faces of Responsibility'.

# PREFACE

In recent years, virtue ethics has become the focus of growing interest by moral and political philosophers. Yet there is no work which collects under one cover a systematic introduction to this topic and an assembly of the central essays in the field. This volume is an attempt to fill this gap.

Most of the essays collected here are reprints of work published elsewhere. Harold Alderman, Gerasimos Santas and Christine Swanton took advantage of the opportunity to revise their essays. Two essays, Rosalind Hursthouse's (Chapter 5) and Michael Stocker's (Chapter 6), appear here for the first time. I am grateful to all the contributors for their kind cooperation and encouragement and for their enthusiasm in the project.

My work on this project was made possible thanks to the excellent conditions and generous stipend I received from the Institute for Advanced Study in Princeton, as a member of the School of Social Science in the academic year 1994–5. I am very grateful for the opportunity that was afforded me. If there is any place in the academic world that is close to Paradise, that place is the Institute.

Finally, I want to pay tribute to Jane Feore, my editor at Edinburgh University Press, who was always helpful and encouraging. It was a pleasure to work with her and with the rest of the EUP staff.

Danny Statman
Ramat-Gan, Israel
July 1996

# ACKNOWLEDGEMENTS

I thank the following for their generous permission to use copyrighted material:

*American Philosophical Quarterly* for permission to reprint Robert B. Louden, 'On Some Vices of Virtue Ethics', Vol. 21 (1984); Gregory Velazco y Trianosky, 'What is Virtue Ethics All About?', Vol. 27 (1990); and Phillip Montague, 'Virtue Ethics: A Qualified Success Story', Vol. 29 (1992).

*Business Ethics Quarterly* for permission to reprint Robert C. Solomon, 'Corporate Roles, Personal Virtues: An Aristotelean Approach to Business Ethics' (1992).

Cambridge University Press for permission to reprint Robert B. Louden, 'Kant's Virtue Ethics', *Philosophy* 61 (1986).

*The Journal of Philosophy* for permission to reprint a revised version of Christine Swanton, 'Satisficing and Virtue', Vol. 90 (1993).

The MIT Press for permission to reprint Gary Watson, 'On the Primacy of Character', from *Identity, Character, and Morality*, ed. Flanagan and Rorty (1990).

Oxford University Press for permission to reprint extracts from Michael Slote's *From Morality to Virtue* (1992).

*Philosophical Inquiry* for permission to reprint Gerasimos X. Santas, 'Does Aristotle Have a Virtue Ethics?', Vol. 15 (1993).

Princeton University Press for permission to reprint Rosalind Hursthouse, 'Virtue Theory and Abortion', *Philosophy and Public Affairs*, Vol. 20 (1992).

*The Review of Metaphysics* for permission to reprint Harold Alderman, 'By Virtue of a Virtue', Vol. 36 (1982); and Peter Simpson, 'Contemporary Virtue Ethics and Aristotle', Vol. 46 (1992).

University of Notre Dame Press for permission to reprint David Solomon, 'Internal Objections to Virtue Ethics', from *Midwest Studies in Philosophy*, Vol. 13 (1988).

# 1

# INTRODUCTION TO VIRTUE ETHICS

## *Daniel Statman*

### CONTENTS

The most conspicuous development in contemporary ethics is the growing interest in virtue ethics (VE). While only several years ago it seemed as though VE would not manage to get off the ground, it is now recognised almost everywhere as a serious rival to traditional moral theories, utilitarianism and deontology. This fast change in the status of VE is manifest in the varying evaluations of VE in the literature of recent years. In his 1988 paper (reprinted in this volume), David Solomon argues that 'the most striking feature of virtue ethics is the near universality of its rejection in contemporary ethical theory and in modern ethics generally'. Only three years later, in a paper included here, Rosalind Hursthouse notes that '[VE] is now quite widely recognized as at least a possible rival to deontological and utilitarian theories'. In the space of another three years, Christopher Cordner argues that 'VE is prominent, if not pre-eminent, in contemporary moral philosophy',[1] while John Cottingham confirms that 'the revival of [virtue theory] seems to be one of the most promising recent developments in philosophical ethics'.[2]

This growing attraction of VE is due not only to the positive features of virtue theory, which is just taking its first steps,[3] but also to growing dissatisfaction with some central features of modern ethical theories. The shift to VE reflects the hope that this new outlook will provide a way out of the difficulties that current ethical theory faces. But the interest in VE in not merely a theoretical one. At times a return to the virtues expresses, implicitly or explicitly, dissatisfaction with some basic aspects of modern (Western) society, and thus, by opting for VE, one might be said to be opting ultimately for a different kind of society and for different relationships among its members.[4]

My introduction offers a systematic orientation to the field of VE. I start by explaining the main difficulties in the prevailing moral outlooks which have led some philosophers to opt for VE. I proceed by presenting the main versions of VE and explaining its basic features, and I point to the relation between VE and other developments in moral and political theory. I then turn to present the objections levelled against VE and the common strategies utilised by VE to meet these objections. I conclude by indicating how discussions on VE have inspired a fresh study of some major aspects in the history of ethics, especially in the philosophy of Aristotle and Kant.

## 1. DIFFICULTIES IN MODERN ETHICAL THEORY

Any attempt to speak about the difficulties in 'modern ethical theory' might sound like a gross simplification, one which disregards the fact that there are several modern ethical theories, with significant differences between them. Yet most critics believe that these theories resemble one another more than they differ, and that their shared assumptions and structures are vulnerable to the same kind of criticism. In particular, the differences between utilitarianism and deontology are considered relatively insignificant from the point of view of many of the objections. Thus, for these critics, ethical theory offers two main alternatives: 1. an ethics of virtue (sometimes referred to as 'agent-ethics'[5]); 2. an ethics of duty (sometimes referred to as 'an ethics of principles',[6] 'rule ethics'[7] or 'act-ethics'[8]). To simplify, I will sometimes use 'Duty Ethics (DE)' to refer to all non-VE theories, including both utilitarianism and Kantianism. This way of dividing the camps in contemporary ethics might seem odd, in particular the piling together of utilitarianism and Kantianism. Yet these two approaches do share some essential characteristics, all of which are denied by VE: that all human beings are bound by some universal *duties* (which are either prior to or derivative from some notion of the good); that moral reasoning is a matter of applying *principles*; and that the value of the virtues is derivative from the notion of the right or of the good.

### *Moral duty*

What, then, are these fundamental notions which come under attack? The most important one is that of a *moral duty*, which is central to both utilitarianism and deontology. The first major attack against this notion in contemporary ethics is made by Elizabeth Anscombe in her celebrated 1958 essay 'Modern Moral Philosophy'.[9] It is further developed by Alasdair MacIntyre,[10] and given its clearest formulation by Richard Taylor (1985, 1988). Let's call this attack the 'anti-duty' thesis. It comprises two arguments, one conceptual, the other historical, which together seek to establish the above thesis.

The conceptual argument is based on the idea that 'to say that a given action is *obligatory* is to say . . . that some rule, law, or principle requires that it be done'.[11] Thus, for example, to say there is an obligation to pay a 6 per cent tax on a purchase is to imply that there is a legal rule requiring one to do so, just as to say that people ought to go to church on Sundays implies that there is a religious law requiring it. Duties, obligations, all the 'oughts' always presuppose the existence of a set of laws put down by some kind of authority – be it the King, Parliament or God. This characteristic of duties is expressed in the response of children (and of some adults too) to the claim that they ought to do such and such. They say, 'Why? *Who said so?*', implicitly recognising that 'oughts' must be laid down by some person who has the authority to do so. However, the argument continues, when we turn to the so-called '*moral* ought', we are surprised to find that no such reference to a person-made law is made. The moral ought does not refer to the legal system, because we often use morality to criticise this system. Nor can we interpret it as referring to divine law, since this law, too, is often judged from the perspective of morality. The moral ought thus seems to be 'free floating and unsubscribed', to use Philippa Foot's words,[12] in a way that simply makes it unintelligible. The concept of a moral obligation, as different from and superior to all other sorts of obligation, is, according to Taylor, 'an empty concept'.[13]

If 'moral obligation' is an empty concept, how is it that it is taken so seriously by the vast majority of people in the Western world? Some error theory is needed to answer this question, and this is where the historical argument comes in. According to this argument, the concept of a special 'moral' obligation did not exist in ancient ethics, where the focus was on questions concerning the good life for human beings and the traits of character necessary for obtaining this good life. Thus, for the Greek philosopher, asking what we *morally* ought to do, apart from what we legally ought to do or what would best contribute to our welfare, would be meaningless. A dramatic change in the ethical outlook came about under the influence of Christianity.[14] Through the idea of a divine lawgiver, Christianity implies the existence of a law which is above all human institutions and laws, and which takes the form of an obligation incumbent on all human beings. In this manner, prohibitions such as murder and adultery are regarded as universally valid irrespective of any individual desires or ends, and as especially powerful relative to any human-made law. This view of certain types of behaviour did not fade out even when religious belief was abandoned by most of Western society. People still regard moral obligations as universally valid and as overriding, although they deny the very frame of thought that gave sense to this view. Hence the emptiness of the concept.[15]

That the concept of a moral obligation is closely connected to a religious framework has also been argued recently by moral philosophers with a different orientation; divine command theorists. Robert Adams, for instance, has argued that a divine command theory of morality provides the best account for the essential features of moral obligation, and, therefore, this theory should be preferred to competing theories.[16] Thus, while Adams and Taylor agree that we cannot understand the concept of moral obligation without recognising its religious contexts, they disagree about the conclusions to be derived from this fact. According to Adams, the conclusion is that we should anchor the concept of moral obligation back in its religious framework. According to Taylor, the conclusion is that we should reject this concept altogether and opt for a new (or a renewed) approach to ethics.

The charge that the concept of a moral obligation is an empty one is similar to another charge often made by proponents of VE, that, *contra* Kant, moral judgments do not express categorical imperatives. According to Philippa Foot, the prevalent idea that there are some things that we morally *must* do (or refrain from doing) relies on 'an illusion'.[17] Recognising this illusion means recognising that moral reasons do not derive their force from some transcendental law binding upon us, but from 'something the agent wants or which it is in his interest to have'.[18]

## The problem of moral luck

The focus of traditional theories on the concept of duty has encouraged a legalistic view of morality, assigning great importance to the notion of the voluntary. Duties apply to agents only insofar as the agents have the ability to execute these duties ('ought' implies 'can'), and, in general, the boundaries of our responsibilities are determined by what is under our control. Yet this view leads into the paradox of moral luck.[19] The difficulties generated by this paradox play an important role in Williams' rejection of the 'peculiar institution' of morality[20] in favour of an approach to ethics similar to that of ancient ethics, and, more explicitly, in Slote's arguments for preferring VE over most other contemporary ethical outlooks (see Chapter 7).[21] The paradox results from two incompatible assumptions; the first is that we are responsible only for what is within our control, that is, for what is not a matter of luck, and the second is that in fact we are not in control of our lives for luck governs almost every aspect of our being and our actions. Within the framework set by DE there seems to be no solution to this paradox, because we cannot give up the idea – so central to Kantian morality – that morality is immune to luck, yet neither can we deny the obvious fact that the immunity condition cannot be fulfilled.

## Self-other asymmetry

Michael Slote develops another criticism of common theories of moral duty, based on what he calls the 'self-other asymmetry' (see Chapter 7);[22] while we have a duty to enhance the happiness of others, we have no such duty with regard to our own happiness (at the most, taking care of our own happiness is permissible). This asymmetry is problematic not only from an aesthetic point of view, but because of its disturbing moral implications, namely, the devaluation of moral agents. From a moral point of view, what matters is only (or mostly) what agents do for others, not what they do for themselves. The agents' own wellbeing is given no positive moral value. To put it crudely, from a moral point of view, the agents are viewed as mere tools for helping others. This conclusion is somewhat surprising within a Kantian outlook which puts such great emphasis on the intrinsic and equal value of each individual. Yet in light of the above asymmetry, this emphasis turns out to be rather superfluous. Though all individuals are intrinsically valuable, some (my self) seem to be less valuable than others.

## Principles and rules

The second notion under attack in traditional morality is that of moral *principles*, or moral *rules*. Ethical theories see it as their primary task to formulate principles, often referred to as 'rational', that should guide human behaviour. According to these theories, when we face a practical quandary, we are supposed to go through this list of principles, determine which principle applies to the particular case, and 'apply' it. When we face a conflict of considerations we are supposed to turn to some higher-order principle to resolve the conflict. In this manner, the ideal person is one whose principles govern everything he or she does, and the best theory is the one that provides the most comprehensive and consistent system of principles. This 'obsession' with principles[23] is shared by both utilitarianism and deontology, which differ only regarding the content of these principles.[24]

The problem with this approach – according to proponents of VE – is simply that it has failed. As Watson notices, a main impetus for the interest in VE 'is the sense that the enterprise of articulating principles of right has failed'.[25] In spite of the enormous amount of material in applied ethics dealing with attempts to apply principles to solve practical dilemmas, many feel that '[m]odern moral philosophy generally has not been much help in terms of putting its theoretical contributions to work on practical matters'.[26] Defenders of VE contend that principles are just too abstract to provide helpful guidance in the complicated situations met in everyday ethics. These situations typically involve conflicting considerations, to which principle-ethics either offers no solution, or formulates higher-order principles of preference, which, again, are too abstract and vague to offer any real help. In the final analysis, moral philosophers, armed with their sophisticated principles, do not seem to be better equipped to solve practical problems than doctors, police officers, and other professionals, to whom moral philosophy presumes to offer advice.

If principles are insufficient to guide our behaviour and cannot simply be 'applied' to concrete situations, some other factor must be at work in real-life decision-making. This factor, according to VE, is character. Whether or not the advice offered by some people in hard cases is reasonable depends ultimately not on their system of principles, but on their moral character. If one already has a high moral character and is a sensitive and a compassionate human being, then one will do the right thing anyway, i.e. without the aid of principles. Principles thus seem to be neither necessary, nor sufficient, for right behaviour. In short, principles seem to be redundant.

## The problem of 'schizophrenia'

Yet redundance is not the only problem with principles. The more disturbing problem is that such a view leads to what Michael Stocker calls a 'schizophrenia' of modern ethical theory.[27] The schizophrenia is caused by the unbridgeable gap between justification and motivation in modern ethics. If we made the justificatory principles of these theories into our motives, the result would be destructive to the moral life and to the relationships between human beings. No friendship would exist if we helped our friends merely 'out of duty', or because we thought that such help was needed for the maximisation of happiness. Under the tyranny of principles, to borrow an expression from Toulmin, the person seems to disappear. Living according to utilitarianism and deontology would mean caring about principles, rules and obligations, not about real human beings. Continuing to correct this still widespread view is the main purpose of Stocker's contribution to this volume (Chapter 6).[28]

The focus of DE on principles and on obligations has a further unwanted result; it incites the thought that the only important thing from the moral point of view is to fulfil our duties. Yet it is surely possible, and indeed often the case, that people who violate no duty nevertheless behave in an inhumane and a disgusting manner.[29] A similar problem arises with regard to the concept of rights: the focus on our rights, so typical to contemporary moral and political thought, leads people to think that they are allowed to do whatever they want provided they do not violate some other agent's rights. Needless to say, this is a rather damaging way of thinking from a moral point of view.

Some of these difficulties, such as moral luck and moral asymmetry, apply only to deontology and leave open the utilitarian option. This option, however, suffers from other problems which were pointed out by proponents of VE, and which I cannot go into here.[30] To these various objections against DE developed by virtue ethicists, one might want to add the arguments levelled against deontology and utilitarianism from other directions,[31] the result of all of them being that these ethical theories are in serious trouble. In the next sections we shall see whether VE offers a way out of this trouble.

## 2. THE BASIC IDEA: THE PRIMACY OF CHARACTER

The expressions 'virtue theory' and 'virtue ethics' have been used in a rather broad and undefined sense. At times they refer to that area of ethics whose subject matter is the nature and the value of virtues. At other times they refer to the general complaint which argued that ethical theories do not assign enough importance to the virtues within ethical theory. Only since the late 1980s has the meaning of VE become more or less fixed. It now refers to a rather new (or renewed) approach to ethics, according to which *the basic judgments in ethics are judgments about character*.[32]

As Trianosky notes,[33] this basic assumption embodies two main theses: 1. at least some judgments about the value of character traits are independent of judgments about the rightness or wrongness of actions; and 2. the notion of virtue justifies that of right conduct, that is, in Watson's terms (see Chapter 3), the concept of virtue is explanatory prior to that of right conduct.

Both theses run against a widespread view of the relation between virtue and rightness, a view shared by both deontologists and utilitarians. According to this view, the value of character traits is dependent on the value of the conduct that these traits tend to produce, and it is the concept of right behaviour that is theoretically prior, not that of virtue. In reversing the order of justification, VE is calling for a real revolution in ethical thought, for what might be described in Kuhnian terms, a change in a paradigm. Shifting our focus from actions to virtues within ethical theory is no minor change.[34]

If the virtues are not justified in terms of right behaviour, one naturally asks wherein their justification lies. The prevalent answer to this question is that according to VE the virtues are justified in terms of their essential role in the wellbeing of the agent. Virtues are viewed as necessary conditions for, or as constitutive elements of, human flourishing and wellbeing.[35] Understood in this manner, the primary concept in ethics would be that of human flourishing, from which we could somehow derive the virtues, and then proceed to infer judgments about actions. However, as I show later, this link between virtues and wellbeing is not assumed by all proponents of VE and I believe it should not be regarded as essential to VE. What is essential is the idea that aretaic judgments, i.e. judgments about character, are prior to deontic judgments, i.e. judgments about the rightness or wrongness of actions.

The focus of VE on virtue and character makes VE more congenial than DE to explorations of the importance of people and their differences, of subjectivity, human relations and emotions (see Stocker, Chapter 6). The better accounts of VE in these areas might be a mere historical accident, as Hursthouse argues with respect to VE's account of the emotions (Chapter 5), and other ethical theories might be able to incorporate VE's insights. If and when they do so, the result will be a reduction of the differences between these competing moral outlooks, a point to which I shall return later.

### Extreme and moderate versions

Different versions of VE disagree as to how far we should take the claim about the dominance of the notion of virtue. Moderate versions contend that though judgments of character are independent of judgments of actions, at least some judgments of acts are similarly independent of judgments of character. Some actions are wrong, indeed abhorrent, irrespective of who carries them out and of what his or her motivation is. Slote, for instance, argues that 'the ethical status of acts is not *entirely derivative* from that of traits, motives, or individuals, even though traits and individuals are the *major focus* of the ethical views being offered'.[36] According to such moderate versions, ethical theory has (at least) two parts which are irreducible to each other, one dealing with the morality of acts, the other dealing with the morality of character. Objection to reduction is a central conclusion of Louden's essay on VE (Chapter 10), which suggests we 'see the ethics of virtue and the ethics of rules as adding up, rather than as cancelling each other'. Different versions of VE, however, take a more unitary view, according to which there are no judgments of acts which are independent of judgments of virtue, since right conduct is defined in terms of virtue. Such a view can be found, for example, in Alderman (Chapter 8) and in Solomon (Chapter 9).

Within this more unitary view, as Montague shows,[37] we can once more distinguish between two versions. One contends that 'act appraisals are explicable in terms of more basic person appraisals',[38] that is to say, we can and should use deontic concepts such as rightness and obligatoriness, provided we remember that they are derivative from aretaic concepts. I shall call this version 'the reductionist view'. The second version, which represents the most extreme interpretation of VE, contends that we should get rid of the deontic notions altogether; 'the rightness, wrongness, obligatoriness, etc., of acts are either incoherent or pernicious, and should be ignored entirely by ethical theory' (ibid.). This view, which Watson calls 'the replacement thesis', is ascribed by Montague to Anscombe, Stocker, Williams, Taylor and MacIntyre.[39] Of these, the philosophers who most certainly hold the replacement view are Taylor[40] and Anscombe,[41] who, as we saw in section 1., deny the very intelligibility of the concept of a moral obligation. The picture is less clear with regard to the other philosophers on Montague's list.[42]

Note that one can hold a replacement thesis without holding VE, if the replacing notions are not virtue notions. For instance, one might suggest that we replace the abstract 'moral ought' with 'thick' moral terms, such as 'just' or 'honest'. According to Watson, this is the view held by Anscombe.[43] It is partially held by Slote, who proposes to replace 'right' and 'wrong' with 'admirable' and 'deplorable', but does not hold that all judgments of admirability and deplorability are grounded in terms of character; some acts are deplorable, irrespective of any considerations about virtue.[44]

We can now see how judgments of character become the focus of ethical theory in all versions of VE. In the moderate version, though some actions can be evaluated independently of questions of virtue, most of morality is connected with character. In the reductionist version, all judgments of rightness are reducible to judgments of character. Finally, in the replacement version, the aretaic notions gain priority by way of default, as Watson nicely puts it,[45] after the deontic concepts have been eliminated from the scene. Note, however, that even the replacement version does not eliminate *all* non-aretaic concepts. As Hursthouse rightly observes, VE relies on many significant moral concepts: 'Charity or benevolence, for instance, is the virtue whose concern is the *good* of others; that concept of *good* is related to the concept of *evil* or *harm*, and they are both related to the concepts of the *worthwhile*, the *advantageous* and the *pleasant*'.[46] That VE does not propose a new understanding of all our moral notions is not surprising; objections levelled by VE against DE do not entail such a sweeping destruction of our moral concepts either.[47]

To further clarify the difference between the above versions of VE on the one hand, and DE, on the other, let us consider the relation between the notion of a virtuous person and that of right behaviour. According to both VE and DE, virtuous persons fulfil their obligations, but each theory offers a different explanation for why this is so. According to DE, the explanation lies in the terms in which virtue is defined, as a disposition to do what is right. In contrast, in VE, what is right is defined in terms of virtue. As Santas puts it, 'the issues concern what is prior in the Aristotelian sense of priority of definition'. Contrary to both these views, according to the replacement thesis, we cannot say that virtuous persons fulfil their moral obligations, simply because no such obligations exist.[48]

Finally, all of these versions of VE should be distinguished from Audi's proposal (1995) to regard VE as a theory of *moral worth* rather than as a meta-ethical theory concerning the conceptual priority of some moral notions. As a theory of moral worth, VE holds that virtue is the sole ground of moral goodness, even though it is not the ground of moral rightness or of obligatory conduct. As Audi notes, this view is consistent both with Kantianism and with other views commonly contrasted with VE.

## *The notion of a paradigmatic character*

VE is often formulated through the idea of a paradigmatic character and developing such an understanding of VE is the main point in Alderman's essay (Chapter 8).[49] According to Hursthouse, reference to such a character is part of the formal definition of VE, which starts with the principle, 'An action is right if it is what a virtuous agent would do in the circumstances'.[50] While this idea might not be a necessary part of VE (Slote, for example, does not use it), we can see its attraction. VE does not offer us any principles to define the exact meaning of the virtues or to help us in applying them to real-life cases: 'If VE means anything, it must mean that the clue to character is something other than acting on the basis of principles'.[51] Therefore, appealing to some paradigmatic personality who exemplifies the virtues in an extraordinary way appears to be the only available way to understand and apply the virtues. To find out what is required by friendship, for example, in some specific situation, would be to imagine an ideal friend and try to figure out how this friend would behave. Through the idea of this character we also get a deeper understanding into the relation between the various virtues, a task which is hard to carry out if we focus on particular virtues separated one from the other.

From a systematic point of view, however, it is important to note that according to most versions of VE[52] and according to DE too, 'the moral goodness of persons is determined by the virtues they possess':[53] some people are admirable *because* they have some desirable traits of character, and not the other way round, that some traits of character are desirable and admirable because they are possessed by certain people. The notion of an ideal character might be epistemically prior to that of virtue (cf. Schneewind), but it does not provide a justification for it.[54]

## *VE and the deontological/teleological division*

Where does VE fit in the common division of ethical theories into deontological and teleological (or consequentialist) ones? Both Trianosky (Chapter 2) and Watson (Chapter 3) argue that VE indeed does not fit this division very well, a fact that helps us realise that this division might not have been very helpful in the first place.[55] Consider Aristotle. On the one hand, he seems to hold a teleological view, since in his ethics the concept of good is primary. On the other hand, since in teleological views 'the right is defined as that which maximizes the good',[56] Aristotle cannot be said to hold this view, because 'for Aristotle, the virtuous person is not one who is out to maximize anything, nor is virtue itself defined as a state that tends to promote some independently definable good'.[57] Thus, according to Watson, we should understand Aristotle's view as both teleological and nonconsequentialist, and interpret VE in the same way. That is to say, while in VE the concept of good is prior, VE utilises no notion of maximisation.[58]

A different division is put forward by Trianosky, who suggests that we distinguish two basic types of VE: teleological and non-teleological (or deontological). In a teleological view of VE, the virtues are explained in terms of some good that is defined independently of the virtues. In a non-teleological view, 'the basic judgments about virtuous traits can be grounded without appeal to any independently-formulated account of the good'.[59] Such a view is held by Aristotle, because he regards virtue as 'a constitutive element of the human good rather than merely a means to its attainment'.[60] Trianosky is certainly right in observing that many writers on VE defend some sort of a teleological, if not specifically utilitarian view, when they argue, in different ways, for the usefulness of the virtues.[61] Yet this teleological framework obscures the unique nature of VE, because it makes it hard to distinguish between VE and (a rich notion of) utilitarianism. Indeed, according to Watson, only non-teleological views of the virtues can be regarded as genuine instances of VE.

Such a non-teleological view of the virtues is held by Slote, who argues that we admire certain traits of character 'not for their results, as instrumentalities, but in large measure because of their intrinsic character'.[62] Thus, Slote rejects the idea that the virtues should be explained in terms of their contribution to, or their being part of, the agent's wellbeing.[63] Such non-teleological views of VE seem to face a serious problem in justifying the virtues, and I shall return to this issue in sections 4–5. At any rate, it is important to notice (1.) that VE is not necessarily tied to the notion of wellbeing; and (2.) that according to some philosophers, VE is necessarily, or at least typically, of a *non*-teleological nature.

### 3. OTHER ASPECTS OF VE

#### *Normative position*

In the last section, I argued that the main thrust of VE is the reversal of the order of the aretaic and deontic notions in ethical theory. Does this meta-ethical difference between VE and DE suggest any normative difference too? Hursthouse answers this question in the affirmative, arguing that 'with respect to a number of familiar examples, virtue ethicists and deontologists tend to stand shoulder to shoulder against utilitarianism'.[64] The non-utilitarian character of VE is developed and defended by Christine Swanton in Chapter 4. According to Swanton, choosing less than the best amongst enumerated and evaluated options is rationally permissible if it stems from a desire to be a certain sort of person. Thus, for instance, an agent might realise that the optimific action is to betray her friend, but refuse to do so because of not wanting to be the sort of person who betrays friends in order to maximise possible results. Being a good friend means acting in ways that express the friendship even when those ways do not promote overall utility. To be sure, within VE, loyalty to one's friends, or responsibility to one's children, do not always outweigh the promotion of overall good, but there would have to be a significant amount of good at stake to justify betraying these relationships, much higher than that required in a consequentialist framework. Thus, in contrast to the utilitarian, a virtuous person acts first and foremost out of virtues, and not out of a concern for the maximisation of the good, and does so even when it is clear that, by such acts, less than optimal good would be achieved.[65] The question of whether agent-based reasons permit (or, at times, commit) us not to act in the best available way has been largely disputed in recent years,[66] and in this dispute VE 'turns out to be a friend of agent centered normative conceptions'.[67] A related point is made by Stocker (124–7) who argues that emotions that show one to be a good person need not be proportional to the amount of value which is the object of the emotion. Though atrocities in wars are much worse than the death of an aged parent, it would be perfectly appropriate for the virtuous person to react more strongly to the latter case than to the first, and sometimes *in*appropriate to react otherwise. The emotional and behavioural reactions of a virtuous character are thus not a simple mirror of the amount of value to which he or she reacts.

The focus of VE on virtue and character in ancient ethics is part of an elitist view of human excellence; only a small group of people are capable of reaching true *arete*. This view is closely connected to the importance of the intellectual virtues, without which one cannot have moral virtue. As the intellectual virtues are pretty hard to achieve, moral virtue is also much rarer than assumed nowadays. The point is made by Amelie Rorty in her essay on the intellectual virtues,[68] who notes the oddity of current VE, which follows the Greeks regarding the centrality of virtue but follows Kant with regard to the egalitarian character of virtue. If Rorty – and Aristotle – are right about the necessity of the intellectual virtues for moral *arete*, VE might lead to quite a different view about the equality of human beings than the one we inherited from Kant.[69]

## *Moral motivation*

Following Stocker, Swanton argues that acting for a reason does not necessarily mean acting for the sake of a reason, namely, with some future goal in mind. When we act 'for friendship', we often do not mean 'for the sake of friendship' (this particular friendship, or friendship in general), but *out of* friendship.[70] According to VE, if Joan is my friend, she helps me because she likes me and cares about me, indeed because she is my *friend*, and not because she thinks she morally ought to do so.[71] That the actions of the virtuous person *express* her virtues helps us to see how VE evades the 'schizophrenia' problem I considered in section 1. No schizophrenia emerges because the desired motivation in VE does not stem 'out of duty' (especially on the replacement thesis), but derives from the virtues.

According to Marcia Baron, the issue of motivation is the main point of disagreement between VE and DE. While, according to DE, a necessary condition for perfect moral personhood is that the perfect person 'be governed by the concept of duty', VE denies this condition and regards the perfect person as someone 'with morally right desires but with no commitment to seeing to it that they remain right and (typically) with no conception of them as right'.[72] Thus, according to Baron, the dispute between DE and VE is mainly a dispute about the nature of the morally good person, and not about the nature and the justification of our basic moral notions.[73]

## *Education*

Since, according to VE, rules don't play a role in moral motivation, they play only a marginal role (if at all) in moral education. Becoming a good person is not a matter of learning or 'applying' principles, but of imitating some models. We learn to be virtuous the same way we learn to dance, to cook, and to play football – by watching people who are competent in these areas, and trying to do the same (see especially Alderman, Chapter 8). According to VE, education through moral exemplars is more effective than education focused on principles and obligations, because it is far more concrete.[74] If these exemplars and their virtues are portrayed in an attractive way – as they surely can be – the motivation to imitate them will be strong.

## *Account of the right*

As I indicated in section 1, the focus of DE on principles that determine the deontic status of acts encourages viewing morality as a sort of a legal system.[75] Especially relevant for our present concern is the assumption widely made by both DE and legal systems, that only one right answer exists to practical quandaries: either you owe Tom the money or you do not, either abortion in some case is right or it is wrong. Since 'right' and 'wrong' are generally considered as contraries, the very use of these terms encourages the thought that every act is either right or wrong. By contrast, according to VE, especially in the replacement thesis, the recommended method in ethics would be an Aristotelian one, in the sense that we can expect no precise answer to practical questions. Just as in medical issues, there is often no one right answer to the question of what we ought to do in order to be healthy, in ethics too there is often no one right answer to whether some particular action is right or wrong.

Thus, while virtuous people surely agree on many matters, and consequently, according to VE, there is one answer with respect to how we should behave, at times even virtuous people disagree, with the result that we have two (or more) answers to the same practical question. Hursthouse[76] intentionally formulates VE to allow for such a possibility, namely, 'that two virtuous agents, faced with the same choice in the same circumstances, may act differently', and, nevertheless, both be right.[77] VE is thus more favourable to the conclusion reached by many writers on moral dilemmas, who argue, from a different perspective, that it is false to assume that only one uniquely right answer exists to every moral quandary.[78] It is not surprising then to find that some prominent supporters of the reality of moral dilemmas also support a kind of VE.[79]

The issue of moral dilemmas also bears on the specific version of VE that one chooses. As Watson notes, if one assumes that 'right' and 'wrong' are contraries, then, assuming that these notions are explained in terms of virtues and vices, this commits VE to a kind of harmony among the virtues: 'If it were possible for someone to act in accordance with one virtue while acting contrary to another, one's conduct would in that case be both right and wrong'.[80] If one rejects the idea of such a harmony,[81] two other options are available. One is to adopt the replacement thesis, according to which disharmony among the virtues would entail no logical inconsistency between judgments of rightness, simply because the notion of rightness would be eliminated. The second option is to reject the idea that 'right' and 'wrong' are contraries, a move that could rely on a central position in the debate over moral dilemmas: I mean the position that an act can be both right and wrong at the same time.[82]

### VE *and the notion of the voluntary*

Ceasing to think of ethics as a kind of legal system has another implication, one which assigns less importance to the distinction between the voluntary and the non-voluntary. This distinction is crucial in legal or quasi-legal systems, because to impose responsibility for wrong behaviour we must presuppose voluntariness. If we abandon this framework and focus instead on the evaluation of character traits, voluntariness becomes much less important. We would not withdraw our admiration for some person only because we found out that his or her being such a person was not a result of voluntary choice. The problem of moral luck thus does not arise within VE, because it does not share with DE the assumption that moral evaluation depends on immunity to luck.[83] According to VE, judgments of character, such as, 'Barbara is a friendly woman', 'Tom is unbearably arrogant', are not touched by the discovery that these traits are a result of genes, education and circumstances, over which the agent has very limited control. In this sense, judgments of character are like aesthetic judgments, and indeed we often use aesthetic predicates to evaluate character ('She is such a beautiful human being'), in accordance with the Greek use of *kalon* in both ethical and aesthetic contexts. Indeed the analogy with aesthetics becomes so natural here that proponents of VE need to explain in what way ethical judgments are nevertheless different from aesthetic ones.[84]

As the idea of immunity to luck is almost built into the modern concept of morality, giving up this idea naturally leads to giving up the idea of the 'moral' as a separate category, as opposed to the 'non-moral'. Williams is especially strict with regard to this point, arguing that invoking the category of the 'moral' 'achieves absolutely nothing'.[85] Yet a more important reason exists for the redundancy of the moral/non-moral distinction within VE, namely, that when we evaluate character, we are not concerned only with 'moral' traits, but with all aspects of character.[86] This is particularly so in those versions of VE that tie the virtues to human flourishing, since the answer to the question of what constitutes the most successful way of life is much wider than the answer to the limited question of what our moral obligations are. The revolutionary nature of VE thus manifests itself on the terminological level in the rejection of the basic term that has dominated DE for so many years, i.e. that of 'morality'. This term, argues Robert Solomon, 'has been so distorted by a century or two of conflation with a very specialized and overly principled conception of morals and confusion with very narrow questions of behavior . . . that it is, perhaps, no longer a useful term for understanding the subtleties of social harmony' (219). The preferred term is 'ethics', which is regarded as much wider, and one which does not imply the various difficulties in DE mentioned above.[87]

## VE and culture

By this point, the reader might feel that something very fundamental is missing in my description of VE, namely, the connection between VE and culture. John Cottingham, for instance, believes that:

> one of the key insights of virtue theory is that the good life consists in a structured pattern of living . . . whose fundamentals have to be rooted in a civic culture, a culture in which the right pathways of emotion and action have been laid down in infancy and fostered by long habits of training and upbringing.[88]

Such views of VE are inspired by the last chapters of *After Virtue*,[89] where MacIntyre argues that the concept of virtue is secondary to that of a role-figure, where the latter is always defined by some particular tradition and culture. The virtues admired in the Homeric era, for instance, are those connected to the primary role in that culture, that of the warrior king, while the virtues admired in Christianity are those required by the role of the sinful worshipper standing before God. Thus, VE conceives of human beings as being rooted in particular cultural traditions, and not as abstract individuals governed by a universal concept of obligation. Viewed in this manner, 'opting for VE, one might indeed opt for a return to a closed, traditional society'.[90] That is to say, the adoption of VE signifies not merely a theoretical change, but a social change too, or, more precisely, a desire that such a change take place.[91] Many writers regard the notions of roles and practices as essential to VE, and assume that part of VE is MacIntyre's definition of virtues as qualities 'the possession and exercise of which tends to enable us to achieve those goods which are internal to practices'.[92] This view of VE has been influential especially in attempts to apply VE to the domain of business ethics.[93]

Nevertheless, the connection between these notions and VE is not so simple. First, prominent supporters of VE such as Slote, Hursthouse and Alderman, do not in any way rely on them. Second, VE is not committed to the view that virtues are culture- or role-relative, but is consistent with regarding the virtues as universal.[94] Third, assuming a necessary connection between virtues and the attainment of internal goods entails a teleological version of VE which would be hard to distinguish from a rich notion of utilitarianism.[95]

## VE as 'naturalistic'

Rather than attempt to summarise the many points I raised in the last two sections, let me try to spell out a claim often made by proponents of VE, that, unlike other ethical theories, VE is truly 'naturalistic'. In what sense might VE be said to meet this description? First, VE locates the ethical within this world, and 'requires no invocation of transcendence or other-worldliness'.[96] Second, having the virtues is necessary for living a characteristically human life, that is, for realising human nature in the best way.[97] Third, VE is said to be naturalistic by virtue of the connection between virtue and human flourishing, a view which, as we saw, is held by many proponents of VE. In this manner VE is naturalistic 'in the sense that virtuous agents individually, as well as the community they compose, benefit from virtue'.[98] And fourth, regarding moral motivation, the virtuous person does the right thing 'naturally', without having to fight with emotions, inclinations or traits of character, without being in any conflict between 'spirit' and 'body', or 'reason' and 'passion'.[99]

## 4. VE AND OTHER DEVELOPMENTS IN MORAL AND POLITICAL THEORY

In the previous sections, I suggested that the emergence of VE is connected to some perceived flaws in DE, and, at times, also to a desire for a deep revision in the social order. In this section, I point to the close relation between VE and other trends in contemporary moral and political thought, thereby providing a broader explanation for the current attractiveness of VE.

### *Anti-theory*

Since the 1980s, ethics has witnessed a new sort of moral scepticism, this time about the possibility of moral *theories*. By 'moral theory', anti-theorists mean a systematic or-ganisation of our principles and obligations, an organisation that provides a universally valid answer to every moral question.[100] Anti-theorists contend that the enterprise of formulating moral theories is misguided and has distorted our understanding of the moral (or the ethical) realm. Theories, as one writer puts it, 'are more threats to moral sanity and balance than instruments for their attainment'.[101] The important point for our present concern is that most of the dominant anti-theory writers also advocate some kind of VE, notably John Mcdowell, Bernard Williams, Martha Nussbaum and Annette Baier. VE is thus regarded by these writers as the cure for the ills caused by the idea of a moral theory. This feature of VE re-emphasises its radical nature, i.e. we are speaking of a new ethical position that, contrary to all other positions, explicitly does not regard itself as a *theory*. This means that VE should not have the features assigned by anti-theorists to ethical theories; in particular, that VE should avoid attempting to reach a systematic arrangement of the practical domain.[102]

Note, however, that not all proponents of VE share this negative attitude toward the idea of a moral theory. Slote explicitly detaches himself from this view, and argues that we should take seriously the idea of ethical theory, mainly to overcome the inconsistencies in our intuitive moral thinking. Such inconsistencies give us reason to pursue a systematic theory in ethics in the way it has been pursued in other areas of philosophy.[103] I suspect that the debate is not about moral theories 'as such', but about certain kinds of moral theories, or certain themes in moral theories. Any attempt to go beyond intuitions and say something about their justification, the way they should be universalised or how to apply them surely leads to *some* kind of a theory, which gets more and more complex and in need of systematisation once we try to spell out what exactly it means.

## Ethics of care

By an 'ethic of care' or 'relational ethics', I mean the view developed by Carol Gilligan, Nell Noddings, Annette Baier and others, according to which most of Western morality is distorted and should be replaced by a view that focuses on care and human relationships, rather than on principles. The main complaints of these writers against traditional morality are strikingly similar to those of VE against DE,[104] namely, that morality has focussed too much on the idea of universal principles, a focus which has obscured the value of direct relationships between human beings, and led to moral 'schizophrenia'. Accordingly, the alternative view put forward by proponents of relational ethics is very close to that developed by VE, especially in the value it assigns to certain traits of character and its view of the appropriate moral motivation (i.e. acting out of caring and not out of duty).[105]

The exact relation between VE and relational ethics is a project which is worth exploring for the benefit of both views.[106] Some first steps have been made by Daniel Putman, who argues that VE 'can help sort out some of the assumptions behind discussions of caring and relational ethics'.[107] Further research is still required in this area, and it strikes me as possible, and rather likely too, that the two approaches under discussion, VE and relational ethics, will finally integrate into one theory. One advantage of such an integration would be to distinguish the notion of care and that of virtues in general from issues of feminism. As Solomon puts it, 'the importance of emphasizing the virtues (including the so-called 'feminine' virtues) should not be held captive to gender distinctions'.[108] The question of whether an ethics of virtue/care presents a better framework than an ethics of duty should be kept separate from the question of whether these two outlooks express, respectively, a feminine and a masculine point of view.[109]

## Communitarianism

As indicated earlier, some writers contend that VE views the virtues as essentially tied to particular traditions which define the roles of individuals and, accordingly, their virtues. The connection between virtue and flourishing is not of a universal pattern, but must be worked out relative to every tradition and community. The good for some individual 'has to be the good for one who inhabits the roles' defined by his or her social structure and values.[110] These ideas come close to the ideas developed by communitarianism, and it is not surprising to find MacIntyre, for example, arguing for both views.[111] The importance of community within VE is especially emphasised by Robert Solomon in his essay included here. He regards business ethics as Aristotelian 'precisely because it is membership in a community, a community with collective goals . . . and a shared sense of *telos*'.[112]

One advantage of noticing the connections between VE and communitarianism is that by doing so we might gain a better understanding of the political implications of VE. If VE and communitarianism stem from similar complaints about the basic assumptions of DE, communitarianism might turn out to be the political aspect of VE. This whole issue concerning VE and political theory, however, has only just started to be explored.[113]

## Philosophy and literature

If VE focuses on the idea of a paradigmatic character, then, as Alderman explains, 'the appropriate structure of any possible substantively adequate moral philosophy must be more like the structure of a story than the structure of a formal system' (Chapter 8). Competing ethical theories refer to different narratives, each presuming to tell the human tale most fully. Thus understood, philosophy should broaden its traditional horizon and search for further material for these narratives, especially in literature (but also in real-life examples[114]). The fundamental texts of moral philosophy would then include not only Aristotle, but also 'Thomas à Kempis *On the Imitation of Christ*, Nietzsche's *Thus Spake Zarathustra*, and Thoreau's *Walden Pond*, to name but the most important' (Alderman, Chapter 8).

This essential interest of VE in literature accords well with the increasing interest of philosophers in literature in the last decade, an interest to which Nussbaum, a friend of VE, has contributed extensively.[115] If ethics is no longer preoccupied with principles, but rather with traits of character, we should do ethics by portraying these traits in the fullest and richest manner, and novelists appear to be more successful in this task than philosophers.

## Moral psychology

Finally, VE is closely connected to the growing research in moral psychology, research whose aim is to make use of psychological knowledge in reflecting on normative issues.[116] To be sure, all normative theorists should be concerned about psychological knowledge, so that their theories are not detached from reality.[117] The advantage of VE is that this concern is built into its fundamental assumptions, a fact that once more manifests the 'natural' character of VE in comparison to other moral theories.

It is always hard to determine the exact relation between different trends in a given culture, particularly to decide whether any causal relation exists between them, or whether they are merely different manifestations of one *zeitgeist*. It is hard to determine whether the anti-theory trend or the discussions about moral luck have been the actual cause for the rise of VE, or merely express, at a deeper level, the same basic shift from DE to VE. At any rate, it is clear that VE is deeply intertwined with other movements in contemporary thought.[118]

## 5. DIFFICULTIES IN VE

That VE offers itself as a cure to the diseases of Kantianism and utilitarianism does not mean that it has not got its own ailments. It certainly has, and in this section I shall elaborate on the most important ones. In the next section I shall present some of the tactics used by VE to overcome these difficulties.

## *Justification*

Having rejected the traditional way of justifying the virtues, i.e. as dispositions for right behaviour, VE seems to have two available routes to follow: either to ground the virtues in the idea of human flourishing, in a teleological manner, or to conceive them in a non-teleological manner, as in some sense worthy in themselves. Let's deal with these two options in turn.

I mentioned earlier Trianosky's observation that many writers on VE presuppose a teleological background, typically arguing that the virtues are necessary for human wellbeing or flourishing. The faults of this view are analysed by Conly[119] who argues as follows. To base VE on the idea of flourishing we need first to have an independent account of human flourishing, then we need to show how the virtues are necessary for it, and, finally, the result must more or less coincide with our intuitions about virtues and vices. An account of the virtues which implied that cruelty, for instance, was all right, would not be very attractive. Yet, argues Conly, no such account seems to work: if we define flourishing in terms of the virtues ('a fully successful human life is defined as a life in which the virtues are exercised'), we simply beg the question in favour of the virtues and provide no real explanation for their value. So the notion of flourishing must be prior to that of the virtues.

But what account of flourishing would be both plausible in itself, that is, irrespective of the concerns of VE, and could also provide the anchor to which to tie the virtue? One possibility would be to define flourishing in terms of one substantive feature, saying, for example, that the good life for humans is the life of theoretical contemplation, and then showing how the virtues are necessary conditions for living such a life. But, as Conly argues, it is hard to accept 'that any one activity, however well done, could capture all of what we see as constituting a good life and good character'.[120] Thus, such an account would not be very attractive as a general account of human wellbeing. A different possibility would be to adopt a broader definition of flourishing which refers to a plurality of goods and contends that human beings can flourish in various ways. What we end up with, however, is such a broad picture of flourishing, that 'it is hard to see what traits in particular will contribute to or detract from it'.[121] In other words, on a rich conception of human flourishing, both individuals and societies seem to be able to flourish without the virtues. Human history is full of people like Lorenzo the Magnificent, to borrow Conly's example, who were clearly unjust, but also clearly flourished.[122] Thus, either VE offers no account for the value of the virtues, in which case it lacks any explanatory force,[123] or it tries to account for them in terms of human flourishing, in which case the account is inadequate.[124]

The attempt to link VE to the notion of flourishing is also attacked, from a different direction, by Audi, who argues that this notion is a normative one, or at least embodies normative notions. For instance, philosophical contemplation which is viewed by Aristotle as part of the most fulfilling life, is clearly governed by logical and epistemic standards. Hence, concludes Audi, accepting the above link means that, conceptually speaking, virtue notions depend on other normative concepts.[125]

The problem of justification is especially troubling in Slote's VE, which is presented as 'common sense VE'. If the virtues are not tied to some larger theoretical framework, it is unclear how we can account for *mistaken* judgments and how, more generally, we can decide that some traits of character are desirable and others are not.[126] Also, since on the commonsense level the virtues are perceived as related to the deontic notions, it is hard to see what would be left of our common *virtue* concepts after we abandon the deontic ones.[127]

Finally, it is important to notice that the difficulties in justifying the virtues arise even within moderate versions of VE, which accept the existence of irreducible act-appraisals. These difficulties arise once one accepts the idea that virtues have a life of their own not entirely derivative from the deontic notions.

## Universality

A central point made by MacIntyre in *After Virtue* is that different cultures embody different virtues. Recognising this plurality of conceptions leads to the conclusion that an ethics based on virtues will necessarily be non-universalistic and will merely reflect some local set of virtues,[128] which has no claim upon individuals from other cultures.[129]

The problem of universality is, of course, connected to the problem of justification. If we could anchor the virtues in some general theory of human flourishing, we could thereby grant them universal application, assuming that such a theory would apply, more or less equally, to all human beings. Since, however, such an anchor is not available, we are left with changing intuitions about virtues and vices, upon which no universal claims can be made.

This criticism can be interpreted in two ways, as a meta-ethical argument, or as a normative one. The meta-ethical version is the claim that universality is a necessary property of any ethical theory and therefore VE, which fails in this respect, is not such a theory, and hence poses no alternative to genuine ethical theories. The normative version is the claim that the lack of any universal criterion for deciding between different conceptions of the virtues implies that there are no restraints on the virtues VE might recommend. Moreover, not only does VE allow us to be content with our local virtues, ugly as they might be, it suggests that we build our entire ethical view upon them.

## Applicability

According to proponents of VE, rules and principles might have their problems, but they do seem to be helpful when it comes to pragmatic guidance. Armed with these devices, we are able to analyse in a relatively clear manner the practical problems we face, and to reach conclusions. No such guidance seems to be provided by VE. Suppose I face the dilemma of whether or not to torture a terrorist in order to force him to reveal where he has placed a bomb. How should we decide such a case within the framework of VE? One possibility would be to work with notions such as caring, mercy or cruelty. Thus we might argue that torture is wrong because it is cruel. But not trying to save the lives of many innocent civilians who might be killed by the bomb also expresses a significant lack of caring, and VE provides us with no criterion to choose between these two options. Another way of approaching such dilemmas from the perspective of VE would be to try to figure out what a virtuous person would do in such a situation. But the directives we could get out of such a method are rather vague, to say the least.

If this complaint is justified, then VE will not be able to set itself up as a serious rival to utilitarianism and Kantianism, the two theories that have dominated discussions in applied ethics for the last decades. And since practical guidance is a central aim for any ethical theory, any failure of VE in this respect – if, indeed, it fails – would significantly weaken it in comparison to its rivals.[130]

## *Moral status of acts*

According to most versions of VE, act-appraisals are reducible to, or replaceable by, agent-appraisals, which means that actions are evaluated only as manifestations of character. This contention, however, is hard to swallow, as critics have pointed out in different ways. Van Inwagen complains that VE leaves out something essential, namely, the existence of a standard of behaviour which is prior to and independent of human character, in terms of which we evaluate the behaviour and the character of ourselves and of others. According to van Inwagen, it is not 'really possible for us to carry on the business of life using (in the final analysis) no moral predicates but those that apply to the characters of moral agents' (1990, 393).[131] Some support for the impossibility of such an enterprise can be found, he suggests, in the use of the term 'sick'. For a while, instead of saying that somebody did something wrong, we said that he or she was 'sick'. But very soon 'sick' came to express what we hitherto meant by 'wicked', and, more importantly, people began using it as a property of actions ('that was such a sick thing to do'). Thus, we probably just cannot get rid of some sort of act-appraisals which do not depend on the evaluations of their doers.

The same conclusion emerges from a different direction, the one taken by Louden (Chapter 10). According to VE, being a virtuous person is a sufficient (as well as a necessary) condition for doing the right thing. But this ignores, or rather denies, the possibility of moral tragedy, that is, of situations in which people of excellent character nevertheless do the wrong thing in some situation. VE forces us to say that, insofar as the hero has an excellent and stable character, his or her actions cannot be wrong.

The reason we find the position of VE unreasonable here is our belief, again alluded to by Louden, that some actions are not only bad, but intolerable and absolutely forbidden, irrespective of the motive or character of their doers. This belief goes back to Aristotle, who argues that some actions, such as adultery, theft and murder 'are themselves bad', and 'simply to do any of them is to do wrong'. That duties are created irrespective of facts about character is obvious, according to Montague, from the case of promises, which bind their makers irrespective of their motives or personality. VE's requirement that we give up these beliefs seems too high a price to pay.[132]

## 6. RESPONSE TO OBJECTIONS

How do friends of VE respond to these objections? Their main strategy is the 'partners in crime' one, namely, the argument that the objections apply to other ethical theories too and that VE can meet them no worse, and often better than other theories. Let us see how this strategy can be applied with regard to the main objections of the last section, starting with that of justification.

### *Justification and universality*

The justification of ethical theories involves more than logic and empirical knowledge. It involves relying on some basic moral intuitions which are not, and cannot be, proved, and which are taken by the theory as self-evident. Since ethical theories cannot account for all of our pre-reflective intuitions and at the same time advance their systematising aspirations, their aim is to reach the best possible balance between these intuitions and aspirations. In this manner, some proponents of VE, notably Slote, contend that although VE's fundamental notions cannot be justified in the formal sense of being derived from more basic notions or principles, they can be justified in a broader sense, namely, in the sense of cohering in the best way with our moral intuitions and theoretical concerns.

A different approach toward the justification of VE would be to try – notwithstanding the difficulties mentioned above – to anchor the virtues in the idea of human flourishing (within those views that ground the virtues in this idea). Though such an approach could make room for some of the virtues, I suspect it will leave out others, especially the 'moral' ones, such as justice and kindness. This might be a high price for most of us, though some writers, especially Richard Taylor, would probably not be too troubled by it. Whether or not this is a 'price' is related to the rather neglected question of whether VE suggests only a theoretical revolution, or whether it embodies a normative revolution too. While most friends of VE recommend VE precisely because it fits our current moral intuitions,[133] Taylor contends that releasing ourselves from the deontic tradition with its 'empty concept of obligation' entails a whole new view about the desired traits of character and the desired form of life. As I indicated earlier, Rorty's emphasis on the importance of the intellectual virtues also might bring VE to depart from some commonly accepted intuitions concerning the egalitarian character of the ethical domain.

Critics complain that in light of the plurality of conceptions about the virtues, VE is unable to make any universally valid claims, and is thus a bad, if not a harmful, ethical outlook. However, just as there is a plurality of virtues, there is also a plurality of moral rules, as advocates of relativism keep reminding us. Hence, if plurality is a problem for VE, it is no less a problem for rule-based theories.

One common way of responding to the relativistic charge is to argue that as a matter of fact the diversity is quite marginal, and that there is wide agreement on the core norms and values.[132] A similar move is often made by proponents of VE, for example by Alderman, who argues that 'what is most obvious about the paradigmatic individuals – as with the great moral theories – is that there is a common core of obvious behaviors endorsed by all of them' (p. 151). This claim goes back to Hume, who contended that benevolence is universally recognised as the most valuable trait of character.[133] Proponents of VE who tie the virtues to the idea of flourishing add the claim that the general conditions for having a successful human life apply to all individuals and societies.[134] The notion of flourishing refers to flourishing 'in this world in which we inevitably find ourselves, not in the particular culture or society we happen to find ourselves in'.[135]

With regard to the complaint that VE fails to explain the fact that certain acts are absolutely and unconditionally forbidden, VE might respond by saying that precisely the opposite is true. One of the main charges of Anscombe in her celebrated 1958 paper was that in all modern moral theories, killing an innocent person might in principle be permitted, a fact that shows that something has gone seriously wrong in moral theory. By contrast, VE might account for the intuition that some actions are absolutely wrong by relying on the idea of the paradigmatic character; some actions, such as intentionally killing innocent human beings, are so horrible that such a character would never commit them, and therefore, according to VE, they will be unconditionally forbidden.

## *Applicability*

Finally, I would like to deal with the objection concerning the applicability of VE. To accommodate it, friends of VE first try to show that in this respect VE is in no worse a situation than other theories, and second, to show in a more positive way how VE can help us deal with practical problems. Let's take these two methods in turn.

Easy moral quandaries constitute no serious problem, neither to DE, nor to VE. If I promised to do *x*, then unless there are strong reasons against doing so, I ought to do *x*, be it because I am under an obligation to do so (on DE), or because such behaviour manifests honesty (on VE). The problems start in more complex situations, especially when deep conflict emerges between different moral considerations. But it would be naive to think that in these more complex situations DE offers us anything like a principle to solve the problem, of the sort VE cannot provide. 'Applying' principles in these situations is not a simple exercise in logic, but a result of judgment. The point is that the right behaviour cannot be codified into a set of *a priori* principles, the following of which necessarily leads to right action. Thus, even on DE, the virtuous person is not the person who has excellent knowledge of some set of principles, meta-principles and meta-meta-principles, but the person who has right perception as to which rules should apply here and now. And this person must be, among other things, sensitive, compassionate and perceptive – the same features so praised in VE. Hence, it is false that with rules and principles we are better equipped to deal with the moral complexities of human reality than with virtues.[136]

Yet not only is the knowledge of rules insufficient for right decision, such knowledge might not even be necessary, as David Solomon seeks to show. Virtues, he argues, 'might fare better than rules or principles with regard to specificity and decisiveness',[137] and in this respect they are like the power of discernment typical of wine-tasters or art critics. Wine-tasters do not need principles to decide about the quality of the wine they taste, and, by the same token, the virtuous person does not need principles to reach the right decision. When we reflect on the way people deliberate about their actions, principles are rarely there, a point strongly made by Robert Solomon:

> The very idea that the good person is one who acts according to the right principles – be they categorical imperatives or the principle of utility – has always struck me as colossally out of tune with the manner in which ordinary people (and most philosophers) think about and judge themselves and their actions. As a matter of fact it makes my blood run cold.[138]

Yet even if principles are less important in real-life moral decisions than DE would like us to believe, they at least provide us with some framework within which to deliberate. No such framework is available within VE, which seems to imply that no room is left for deliberation; with regard to the excellent people, the right actions are supposed simply to 'flow' out of their character, while with regard to ordinary people all they can do is try to imagine how the paradigmatic character would behave. It would thus be helpful if friends of VE could show in a more positive manner what it means to approach practical problems from the perspective of VE, and how such an approach differs from the one suggested by DE.

Meeting this challenge is the main concern of Rosalind Hursthouse in her essay on VE and abortion (Chapter 13). In applying VE to the problem of abortion, Hursthouse seeks to illustrate the applicability of VE and to show how the use of the virtue and vice concepts transforms the discussion of such a practical problem.[139]

Most of the debate over abortion focuses on two issues, the mother's assumed right over her body, and the status of the foetus. From the point of view of VE, however, both of these questions are irrelevant to the rightness or wrongness of abortion. Whether or not a woman has a right to terminate her pregnancy is irrelevant, because it says nothing about the most crucial question, namely, whether, in having an abortion in such-and-such circumstances, the woman would be behaving virtuously or viciously. And the metaphysical question about the status of the foetus is irrelevant, because the more familiar – though often overlooked – facts are the relevant ones, for instance 'that human parents, both male and female, tend to care passionately about their offspring, and that family relationships are among the deepest and strongest in our lives – and, significantly, among the longest-lasting' (Chapter 13). Understanding these facts entails the conclusion that regarding abortion as morally neutral, as if it were no different than a haircut (as one writer put it), would be 'callous and light-minded, the sort of thing that no virtuous and wise person would do'.

That this is so is partially supported, argues Hursthouse, by our attitude towards spontaneous abortion, that is, miscarriage. Reacting to a woman's grief over miscarriage by saying, or even thinking, 'What a fuss about nothing!', would certainly be callous and light-minded, not (only) because the potential mother happened to want the child but because of the great significance of pregnancy and motherhood for (most) women. There is no reason to think that the case is different with artificial abortion. Another source of worry about abortion on the part of VE comes from VE's concern with the idea of *eudaimonia*, and the conditions for a good human life. On Hursthouse's view, parenthood in general, and motherhood in particular, are partially constitutive of a flourishing human life, and, therefore, opting for not being a mother 'may manifest a flawed grasp of what her life should be, and be about – a grasp that is childish, or grossly materialistic, or shortsighted, or shallow'. Thus, contrary to a common complaint, VE does have something to say about practical problems, in a way that far from being uselessly vague, presents a powerful alternative to the approach of utilitarianism and Kantianism.

VE is being used to advance our understanding of other areas in applied ethics too. In business ethics, VE is causing what Dobson recently called 'something of a paradigm shift'.[140] The shift is from a view that regards the figures on the 'bottom line' as the sole end of corporations to a view that regards corporations as 'real communities' (Solomon, Chapter 12), through which individuals can excel and flourish. Individuals find their identity and meaning only within communities, which, for most of us, are the companies or the institutions in which we work. Thus, being part of such communities is necessary for leading a successful and meaningful life. But 'being part of' means much more than 'getting a salary from' or 'making profits from'. It means identifying with the ends of the company, an identification which incorporates the virtues of loyalty, honesty, cooperativeness, decency and others. It also means perceiving one's colleagues as friends with a joint *telos*, who 'spend their days together in whatever they love most in life; for since they wish to live with their friends, they do and share in those things which give them the sense of living together' (Aristotle, *Nicomachean Ethics*, end of book IX). Working in companies where making money is the only goal is likely to cause disharmony, disintegration and alienation, whereas working in companies which appreciate the importance of individual virtue and integrity is likely to lead to a more successful life. Such companies would also be more humane in their recognition 'that people come before profits' (Solomon, Chapter 12).

The element of VE which particularly inspires such discussions in applied ethics is the connection made by many friends of VE between virtues and living a fully successful human life. MacIntyre's definition of virtues as qualities that enable us to achieve the internal goods of practices (see section 2 above) is often referred to in this context.[141] Loyalty, honesty and integrity might not be necessary for the achievement of the external goods of a corporation, namely more money, but they are essential to achieving and enjoying the internal goods of such activities, goods such as friendship, a sense of belonging, and self-realisation.[142]

In recent years VE has been applied to more and more areas; to animal ethics (Schollmeier) and vegetarianism (Shafer-Landau), medical ethics (Vitek), psychological ethics (Jordan & Meara), environmental ethics (Hill, Frasz), and political philosophy (Slote, Paden).[143] I cannot discuss the details of these various studies here,[144] but it seems to me that this growing literature by itself amounts to some refutation of the charge that VE is too vague to have any practical application.

## 7. VE AND THE HISTORY OF ETHICS

Notwithstanding the free and non-authoritative spirit of philosophy, new and radical ideas are often presented by philosophers not as innovations, but as re-formulations of old ideas. This holds true for friends of VE too, who ascribe the essence of their view to some great moral philosopher of the past, be it Plato,[145] the Stoics,[146] Hume[147] or, in most cases, Aristotle.[148] The history of moral philosophy also provides the current discussion with the assumed great enemy of VE, namely Kant,[149] and in this manner the whole debate is projected backwards as a debate between Aristotle and Kant. The work generated by these assumptions has produced a better understanding of VE through examining the extent to which Aristotle was a virtue ethicist and the extent to which Kant was an opponent of VE. The re-reading of Aristotle and Kant in the light of the notions alluded to by VE has incited richer and more balanced understandings of both Aristotle and Kant, the former being regarded as holding quite a moderate version of VE (if at all) and the latter being regarded as a rather moderate foe of VE. This general picture accords well with a conspicuous trend in current studies to view Aristotle as much less 'Aristotelian', and Kant as much less 'Kantian', with the implication that the differences between these alleged two great rivals has become rather marginal, or may have disappeared altogether; according to Christine Korsgaard, the apparent contrast 'does not reflect any ethical disagreement between the two philosophers at all'.[150]

It is beyond the scope of this introduction to discuss in detail these historical issues. I point briefly to the exegetic questions that VE incited with regard to Aristotle and to some arguments which contend that Aristotle is not a virtue ethicist. Then I turn to Kant and point to the type of observations that VE has stimulated in his respect.

### VE and Aristotle

In section 2 I mentioned the widespread view that in VE the virtues are explained and justified by their intimate connection to the notion of the human flourishing of the agent. This aspect of VE is frequently referred to as Aristotelian.[151] Did Aristotle really hold it? According to Peter Simpson (Chapter 14), the answer is clearly in the negative, a position which marks a crucial difference between Aristotle and contemporary VE. Aristotle defines *eudaimonia* as activity of the soul along with virtue, not the other way round, which means that 'the notion of virtue must be prior to the notion of *eudaimonia*'.[152] Yet if the virtues are not derived from the notion of flourishing, where are they derived from? From common opinion, or, more accurately, from the opinions of Athenian gentlemen, which Aristotle takes for granted with no proof.[153] While one of the chief concerns of virtue ethicists is to establish that the virtues really are virtues, or really are goods worth having, this is never a concern for Aristotle and, thus, he does not offer a good place for virtue ethicists to develop their theory.[154] The tying of the virtues to gentlemanly opinions and to gentlemanly politics is very far from the intentions of contemporary friends of VE,[155] whose theory 'is not, and could never be, Aristotelian . . . [VE] is not a continuation of something old. On the contrary, it is quite new'.[156]

A central question within VE is whether all act-appraisals are reducible to judgments about character, or whether an independent criterion for the value of acts exists. Alderman, who holds the former view, seems to ascribe it to Aristotle too. Slote, by contrast, who contends that the assessment of acts is not strictly derivative from the evaluation of persons or traits, also ascribes his view to Aristotle. What is at stake here is how to understand Aristotle's *phronimos*; is the *phronimos* the standard for appropriate behaviour so that an act is right because, and only because, the *phronimos* performs (or would perform) it, or does the *phronimos* perform it because he perceives its independent value?[157] That Aristotle holds the latter view is argued for by Slote[158] and Santas (Chapter 15). Santas shows that according to Aristotle it is (practical) reason that determines whether some act should be done, and not virtue, which merely enables one to do the act reason selects. Hence, in the Aristotelian context, it cannot be the case that the value of acts derives from the value of traits of character.

A closely related question is whether VE applies to all virtues, or only to some of them. According to Santas, the latter possibility is generally overlooked, though it is a vital one for any ethical theory. In fact, Santas seeks to show that this might have been the case with Aristotle who explicitly explains justice – unlike other virtues – in terms of law; 'what is just will be what is lawful and what is equal'.[159] Hence, concludes Santas, the belief that Aristotle had a virtue ethics 'is false of his analysis of justice, and perhaps false of his analyses of the other virtues'. A similar point is made by Stocker, who argues that Aristotle's emphasis on the importance of rules, laws and procedures fits poorly, if at all, with the ideal of virtuous people being the touchstone for right behaviour; 'an important part of administrative virtue has to do with dealing well with laws, procedures, precedents . . . – where these are not, in turn, developed or judged just . . . in terms of what virtuous people would determine'. However, unlike Santas, Stocker leaves open the possibility that VE could make recourse to rules, laws, and the like.

One of the aims of Santas is to suggest a different picture of the history of virtue than the one suggested by Schneewind. Schneewind sets out to rebut the habitual complaint made by friends of VE, that virtue is a neglected topic in modern moral philosophy. Schneewind shows that this topic was far from neglected in the seventeenth and eighteenth centuries, a fact which becomes clear once we notice that the vocabulary of virtue was replaced in this period by a different vocabulary, notably that of *imperfect duties*.[160] Thus, generosity, compassion, love and friendliness were not neglected at all but merely discussed under a different rubric – that of imperfect duties in Grotius, Pufendorf[161] and Kant, and that of 'natural duties' in Hume. The advantage of these modern thinkers over the ancient virtue ethicists, argues Schneewind, is that in addition to imperfect duties (i.e. virtues) they also recognise the existence of perfect duties, or duties of justice, which are essential for the existence of society, and whose value does not depend on the character or the motivation of the agent. Such a notion is absent in Aristotle, and thus 'classical virtue theory is of little or no use' in confronting the most urgent problems of society.[162] Against this picture Santas argues that Aristotle has the same concept of justice as the modern writers and that 'there is no relevant difference between his view and Locke's or Grotius' definitions of justice by appeal to law'.[163]

Santas and Schneewind agree that virtue was not neglected in modern moral philosophy and, if Santas is right in his analysis of justice in Aristotle, then the result of these two claims is, once again, a reduction of the gulf between ancient ethics and modern morality, or between Aristotle and Kant.

## VE and Kant

Probably every theory needs some opponent in contrast to whom it can identify itself, and for VE Kant is no doubt the standard enemy.[164] Kant allegedly assumes that virtues and emotions have no intrinsic moral value, a value which consists in obeying the principle of morality out of the proper motivation, namely, respect for the moral law. Yet this widespread view of Kant is incompatible with many Kantian texts – especially if we read past the *Grundlegung*.[165] Consider, for example, the following quotations from Kant cited by Louden:[166] 'Among moral attributes, true virtue alone is sublime'; 'Everything good that is not based on a morally good disposition . . . is nothing but pretence and glittering misery'. Surely, then, virtue has a much more important role in Kantian ethics than friends of VE would admit. Let me mention some of the points made by Louden in this respect.

First, we tend to overlook the fact that Kant opens the *Grundlegung* arguing for the unqualified goodness of the good will, not for the supreme value of duty or principle. And the good will 'is a will which steadily acts from the motive of respect for the moral law'.[167] But because of their inclinations, human beings are in a perpetual state of tension, and their good will is thus necessarily limited. Only a holy will possesses an absolutely good will, while human morality can be nothing more than virtue (*Tugend*). Thus, concludes Louden, 'if virtue is the human approximation to the good will, and if the good will is the only unqualified good, this does imply that moral virtue, for Kant, is foundational, and not a concept of derivative or secondary importance'.[168] Second, take Kant's notion of a maxim. Louden joins Onora O'Neill in arguing that by 'maxim' Kant does not mean a specific intention for some discrete act, but 'the *underlying intention* by which the agent orchestrates his numerous more specific intentions'.[169] One argument for this interpretation is that if maxims were specific intentions it would be possible to act with no maxim, when we act absent-mindedly, yet Kant says explicitly that we always act on some maxim. This interpretation of the notion of a maxim leads to a virtue reading of Kant, since our underlying intentions tie in directly with the sort of persons we are, namely, our characters. Third, Kant argues that we have two necessary ends: our own perfection, namely, to achieve the purest state of virtue, and the happiness of others, and the former conditions the latter. Since what is basic to all duties is the concept of binding oneself, we cannot have a duty to others unless we create one, by realising a state of virtue in our character as the basis of all action. In this sense, virtue 'is not only the heart of the ethical for Kant; it also has priority in morals considered as a whole'.[170]

These sorts of considerations have led some scholars, notably O'Neill, to argue that Kant 'offers primarily an ethic of virtue rather than an ethic of rules'.[171] Louden contends that this is an exaggeration which ignores the crucial role of the moral law in Kant's ethics. After all, the good will cannot be detached from the idea of obedience to moral law, our maxims should always be examined in light of the categorical imperative, moral personhood is defined in terms of obedience to law, and virtue itself 'remains conceptually subordinate to the moral law'.[172] Thus, in Louden's view, Kant presents us with a virtue ethics in which the 'rule of law' nevertheless plays the lead role. According to Louden, this combination of virtue and rule is the right approach for VE to take, as he argues at the end of his other chapter on VE included here (Chapter 10).

The last point I would like to discuss in regard to Kant and Aristotle concerns moral motivation. We saw earlier that VE rejects the idea that the virtuous person is the one who acts out of duty, or out of principle, and suggests instead that he or she acts out of virtue. Accordingly, Kant is portrayed as holding the former view, i.e. one who endorses acting strictly out of duty, while Aristotle is illustrated as holding the latter, more naturalistic, view of moral motivation. Yet, again, this interpretation is inaccurate both with respect to Aristotle and with respect to Kant. Aristotle explicitly distinguishes between 'natural virtue', which everybody might achieve, and 'virtue in the strict sense' (*NE*, Book 6, Chapter 13), which is the mark of the *phronimos*, whose actions are governed by reason. Of special importance to the present discussion is Aristotle's requirement that the good action is carried out 'for the sake of the noble (*to kalon*)'.[173] Hence, whatever the merits of VE's 'natural' motivation might be, Aristotle seems to hold a different and more 'Kantian' view of moral motivation. As for Kant, interpreting his view depends to a large extent on the way we understand the meaning of acting 'out of duty'. According to Louden, acting out of duty does not mean performing some specific act for the sake of a specific rule which prescribes it, 'but rather that one strives for a way of life in which all of one's acts are a manifestation of a character which is in harmony with moral law'.[174] In a similar vein Korsgaard argues that on Kant's view the purpose of the moral person is not 'to do their duty', but, for instance, 'to help', and they differ from amoral persons in the reflectiveness which accompanies their adoption of this purpose. While naturally sympathetic persons help others just because they want to do so, moral persons do so because that is what they are required to do.[175] Thus, in the final analysis Aristotle and Kant agree that the value of an action depends on how it is chosen, which means that it depends on the character of the agent.[176]

A further contribution to closing the gap between these two great thinkers is made by Hursthouse in Chapter 5. Hursthouse shows the superficiality of the widespread view according to which Aristotle and Kant have a fundamental disagreement about whether the good person is the one with full virtue (*arete*), who does the right thing naturally and enjoys doing it (Kant's happy philanthropist), or whether he/she is the self-controlled person (*enkrateie*), who does the right thing in spite of a desire to do otherwise (Kant's third philanthropist who helps others with no inclination to do so).

According to this view, Aristotle is assumed to hold the former view, while Kant is assumed to hold the latter. Hursthouse shows that the two philanthropists do not correspond to the *arete/enkrateie* distinction; Aristotle would not regard the happy philanthropist as having *arete*, because such a person does not act from reason, but neither would he regard the sorrowing philanthropist as having *enkrateie*, because his difficulties in helping others do not reflect his (lack of) virtue but rather reflect the difficult circumstances in which he finds himself.

These new readings of Aristotle and Kant – which are quite different from those usually ascribed to them by proponents of VE – reflect an interesting dialectical development. As I explained in section 1, the emergence of VE was motivated by dissatisfaction with some central elements in our modern moral outlook. This dissatisfaction led friends of the virtues to search for an alternative to this outlook, and Aristotle was the natural candidate. To help Aristotle suit the view attributed to him, the virtue elements in his ethics were overstated, at the expense of elements referring to *phronesis*, act-evaluations, and moral motivation. Accordingly, to make Kant fit the image of the great enemy of VE, the virtue elements in his view were downplayed, while the 'Kantian' elements were overstated. These interpretive proposals encouraged closer scholarly examination of Aristotle's and Kant's views in the above respects, the result of which has been to bring to light a surprising similarity between these two thinkers. To an extent, this result undermines the distinctiveness of VE, insofar as VE embodies the hope that we can overcome the difficulties in modern moral theories simply by replacing them with ancient ethics. As Julia Annas points out, this hope expresses a misplaced romantic nostalgia, that if only we released ourselves from our modern deontic notions and talked about friendship and the good life instead of about obligations and hard cases, 'ethics would be a kinder, gentler place'.[177]

That Aristotle does not hold the view some virtue ethicists ascribe to him does not, of course, prove that VE is mistaken. However, the fact that both Aristotle and Kant sought an integration of virtues and rules, and of emotion and reason, does lend some support to the thought that the more extreme versions of VE – like the more extreme versions of DE – will not work. In other words, the lesson from the above historical study is that VE might do better to reduce its 'revolutionary' inspirations and focus on more moderate versions, which emphasise the irreducible value of character, without denying the irreducible value of other moral notions.[178] Developing an ethical theory along these lines would mean taking the best out of both Aristotle and Kant and re-constructing a view which, as it were, both could accept. In Hegelian terms, such synthesis might indeed mark the highest stage of moral philosophy.[179]

## ENDNOTES

1. Christopher Cordner, 'Aristotelian Virtue and Its Limitations', *Philosophy* 69 (1994), 291.
2. John Cottingham, 'Religion, Virtue and Ethical Culture', *Philosophy* 69 (1994), 177.
3. The first (and to date, the only) full-length book to defend and develop an ethics of virtue is Slote 1992. For critical discussions of this book, see Stocker 1994, Richardson 1994, Darwall 1994 and Driver 1994.
4. See, for instance, Putnam 1988, 381, and the part on communitarianism in section 4. below.
5. See Louden, 288. Page numbers without publication year refer to this volume.

6. See Waide 1988.
7. Louden, 287.
8. Louden, 288.
9. According to Wallach 1992, 619, this paper has been 'the benchmark work for renewed philosophical interest in Aristotle'. For defences of Anscombe's thesis, see Diamond 1988 and Richter 1995.
10. See MacIntyre 1985, especially chapters 1–5. For MacIntyre's debt to Anscombe, see ibid., 53.
11. Richard Taylor, 'Ancient Wisdom and Modern Folly', in *Midwest Studies in Philosophy* (1988), Vol. 13, 61.
12. Foot 1978, 169, n. 15.
13. Taylor 1988, 63. See also Taylor 1985. For criticism of this argument, see Kurt Baier 1988, 127–9, and Pigden 1988, 30–2.
14. For criticism of this argument, see Pigden 1988, 37–40, who refers to Cicero as an example of a thinker who, in the pre-Christian period, employed a concept very close to that of the modern moral 'ought'.
15. Since obligations correlate to rights, the rejection of the former naturally leads to the rejection of the latter too. In this manner MacIntyre argues that no natural rights (i.e. rights not derived from any human-made law) exist, 'and belief in them is one with belief in witches and in unicorns' (1985, 69). For a defence of a VE-based account of natural and civil rights, see Hursthouse 1990–1.
16. Adams' view is analysed and discussed at length in Sagi and Statman 1995.
17. Foot 1978, 167.
18. Ibid., 179.
19. See Statman 1993.
20. See Williams 1985, Chapter 10, and also his articles 'Moral Luck' and 'Postscript' in Statman 1993.
21. The paradox of moral luck does not apply equally to all ethical theories; especially it does not endanger utilitarianism. To show the preferability of VE to utilitarianism Slote develops different arguments. See Slote 1992, Part 4.
22. Various versions of this argument were developed by other philosophers too, for instance, Stocker (1976b, 1984). Contrary to Slote, Stocker contends that the self-other asymmetry is foundational and should not be philosophically 'resolved' in favour of a symmetrical framework. See Stocker, 118, and also Stocker 1994.
23. See Robert Solomon, 211.
24. Cf. ibid., 211–12.
25. Watson, 60.
26. Vitek 1992, 174.
27. Michael Stocker, 'The Schizophrenia of Modern Ethical Theories', *Journal of Philosophy* 73 (1976a), 453–66.
28. For criticism of Stocker's argument, see Kurt Baier 1988, 129–32.
29. See Gregory Trianosky, 'Supererogation, Wrongdoing and Vice', *Journal of Philosophy* 83 (1986), 26–40.
30. See Williams 1973, Slote 1992 and Swanton, Chapter 4.
31. See, for example, Shelly Kagan's powerful criticism (1989) of deontology and commonsense morality.
32. For this characterization of VE, sometimes referred to as 'pure', or 'radical' VE, see Solomon, 165; Simpson, 245; Schneewind 1990, 43; Baier 1988, 127; Slote 1993, 15; van Inwagen 1990, 392; Dreier 1993, 34. See also McDowell 1979, 331, who says that on the view he proposes, the question, 'How should one live?' is approached via the notion of a virtuous person, so that a conception of right behaviour 'is grasped, as it were, from the inside in'.
33. Trianosky 1986, 336.
34. According to Savarino 1993, this shift necessitates a specific account of the virtues, i.e. viewing the virtues as *hexis* rather than as mere dispositions to do certain acts.
35. See, for instance, Hursthouse 1995, 68: 'A virtue is a character trait that human beings, given their physical and psychological nature, need to flourish (or to do and fare well)'.
36. Michael Slote, *From Morality to Virtue*, New York: Oxford University Press (1992), 89.
37. Montague, 195.

38. Ibid.
39. Shafer-Landau (1994, 97) uses the expression 'to abandon' to characterise this approach, instead of 'to replace', ascribing it to Anscombe and Slote (100, n. 7).
40. Cf. Watson, 68–9, n. 6.
41. For the claim that Anscombe supports a replacement thesis, cf. also Baier 1988, 127–9; Pence 1984, 281; and Solomon 1992, 33. Richter 1995, 70, correctly remarks that Anscombe's objection is not directed to all uses of 'ought', but only to what she calls the 'special "moral" sense' of this term.
42. From Stocker's celebrated 1976a essay on the schizophrenia of modern ethical theories one indeed might get the impression that for the schizophrenia to be cured we must abandon the framework and vocabulary of modern ethics altogether. Yet, as far as I know, Stocker nowhere draws this conclusion, and his more recent work – Stocker 1987, as well as the essay included here – does not support it either. As for Williams, in spite of his attacks on what he calls 'morality, the peculiar institution' (1985, Chapter 10) and on some basic concepts of traditional morality (see also Williams 1993), it is unclear whether this criticism leads Williams to adopt some version of the replacement thesis. Williams' emphasis on the plurality of moral considerations (see 1985, Chapter 1) provides a strong reason to doubt that he wishes to eliminate all the deontic notions. At any rate, I know of no place where Williams explicitly calls for such an elimination (for criticism of Williams' approach, see Darwall 1987 and Scheffler 1987). Finally, with regard to MacIntyre, it is unclear whether he wishes to eliminate the deontic concepts or merely to ground them in a different context from the one in which they originally belonged.
43. Watson, n. 6. It would seem to me however that Anscombe *is* seeking to justify thick moral notions in terms of character. See, for example, Anscombe 1958, 21: 'For a proof that an unjust man is a bad man would require a positive account of justice as a "virtue"'.
44. Cf. Richardson 1994, 704, who argues against Slote that the core element of his proposal, namely, replacing 'right' by 'admirable', 'has nothing especially to do with character or discernment'.
45. Watson, op. cit., 58.
46. Hursthouse, 230.
47. The paradox of moral luck, for example, does not apply to axiological concepts. See Statman 1993, 2.
48. By eliminating the idea of a moral obligation, VE appears to eliminate the meaning of moral guilt-feelings, which are typically tied to the recognition of wrongdoing. But see Greenspan 1994, who seeks to show that the moral significance of guilt is an important element of VE.
49. On the psychology of moral excellence and on why such excellence is worthy of admiration and aspiration, see Blum 1988.
50. This volume, Chapter 13. Cf. Frasz 1993, 260.
51. Solomon 1992, 32. Watson shows nicely that lack of principles is not strictly a corollary of VE, because once we accept that right action is acting in accordance with the virtues, 'it might turn out that some principle(s), even the principle of utility or the categorical imperative, characterizes what the virtues would lead a person to do' (59). However, Watson concludes, the relation between VE and the rejection of principles is not accidental, since a central motive for the interest in VE is the feeling that the enterprise of articulating principles has failed.
52. See Montague, 196–8. Montague ascribes to Plato the opposite view, namely, the view that the evaluation of the virtuous person is prior to and independent of the evaluation of his virtues.
53. Montague, 197.
54. The idea of a paradigmatic character is related to questions about the meaning and the possibility of ethical expertise. See, for instance, Weinstein 1994.
55. Cf. Korsgaard, n. 12. For the misleading results of the term 'deontology' in the understanding of Kant, see Herman's chapter 'Leaving Deontology Behind' in Herman 1993. Cf. also Louden (forthcoming).
56. Rawls 1971, 24, quoted by Watson, 450.
57. Cf. Cooper 1975, 88, quoted by Watson, n. 3, who argues that Aristotle's theory 'while decidedly not teleological in the modern sense, is also not deontological either'.
58. The notion of maximisation or promotion can apply to acts, to virtues, or to both, as emphasised by Swanton (1995). Aristotle does not hold a promotional view with

regard to either of these categories. Note also that the relation between the teleological character of a view and the notion of maximisation is more complicated than suggested above; a view could be teleological and non-maximising (see Swanton, Chapter 4).

59. Trianosky, op. cit., 47.
60. Ibid.
61. Cf. Elliot 1993, 329, who contends that 'some kind of teleological framework is the proper framework for a virtue ethics', and Terzis 1994, who takes VE to mean 'an ethics according to which how we ought to act . . . is explained in terms of how it is best for us to be, i.e., in terms of the ideal character traits on which our individual human flourishing depends' (360, n. 1).
62. Michael Slote, 'Precis of *From Morality to Virtue*', *Philosophy and Phenomenological Research* 54 (1994), 687.
63. Ibid. Cf. Swanton 1993, 42, who maintains that the connection between virtue and flourishing is 'not essential to virtue-based conceptions of rationality'. These two thinkers disagree, however, with regard to the notion of the good; Swanton takes this notion to be primary but believes that promotion is not the only response to it, while Slote rejects this primacy and contends that VE would do better without the notion of a good state of affairs (1992, 194–5).
64. Hursthouse (forthcoming), 'Normative Virtue Ethics', in Roger Crisp (ed.), *How Should One Live? Essays in the Philosophy of Virtue*, Oxford: Clarendon Press.
65. For a different view see Upton 1993, 192–3, who argues that VE has nothing unique to offer on the question of maximisation. If, for instance, I ought to be benevolent, it is unclear why, on VE, I am not required to be *very* benevolent, as benevolent as possible.
66. See, for instance, Williams 1973, in support of agent-based permissions and restrictions, and Kagan 1988 in sharp opposition to them. Also see Scheffler 1985 and Brook 1991.
67. James Dreier, 'Structures of Normative Theories', *Monist* 76 (1993), 35.
68. Amélie Rorty (forthcoming), 'From Exasperating Virtues to Civic Virtues', *American Philosophical Quarterly*.
69. Cf. Audi 1995, 465–6, who argues that as practical wisdom is required for a morally adequate life, the exercise of moral virtue alone is not sufficient for such a life.
70. For the rich and diverse forms of acting out of virtue, see Swanton 1995.
71. See also Louden, 288–9.
72. Marcia Baron, 'Varieties of Ethics of Virtue,' *American Philosophical Quarterly* 22 (1985), 47.
73. Baron makes it clear that all of what she says would be irrelevant if VE held that all value is agent-relative (52). As shown earlier, this indeed is the case with regard to many proponents of VE, even those holding moderate versions of VE.
74. For the advantages of VE to moral education, see Putman 1992a.
75. That DE is dominated by a 'legal metaphor' is argued by Waide 1988.
76. Hursthouse, 242, n. 1.
77. Schneewind (62) appears to disagree with Hursthouse when he argues that, according to Aristotle, 'if two allegedly virtuous agents strongly disagree, one of them (at least) must be morally defected'. Note, however, that Schneewind is referring to *serious* disagreement (ibid.), and he might agree that in cases of less serious disagreement it is possible that more than one right answer exists.
78. See, for instance, Hampshire 1983. The possibility of moral dilemmas within the framework of VE is explained at length by Hursthouse (forthcoming).
79. Williams and Nussbaum are good examples. See Williams 1978 for his view on dilemmas, and 1993a for his preference for the philosophical thought of the ancient world. For Nussbaum's view on dilemmas, see Nussbaum 1986, Chapter 2, and for her view on the virtues see Nussbaum 1988, 1992. See also Hursthouse (1995, 61–2), who argues with friends of moral dilemmas that one condition for the adequacy of a moral theory is that it allows for some cases to be *un*resolved. I am not of course arguing that these two theses necessarily go together. Nagel, for instance, a major supporter of the reality of moral dilemmas, does not endorse VE. For further discussion of these connections, see Statman 1995b, especially Chapter 3.
80. Watson, 59.
81. For the unity of the virtues problem, see Walker 1993, and the sources he refers to on p. 44, n. 1.

82. For the claim that 'ought' and 'ought not' are not, formally speaking, contraries, see, for instance, Sayre-McCord 1986, 181.

83. See Slote 1992, Chapter 7. But see Darwall 1994, 697, and Driver 1994, 508–12, who argue that in the final analysis Slote's VE does not evade the problem of moral luck.

84. See Slote 1992, 122–4.

85. Bernard Williams, 'Postscript', in *Moral Luck*, Daniel Statman (ed.) (1993), Albany, New York: State University of New York Press, 254.

86. Cf. also Gerrard 1994.

87. See Slote 1994b, 711; Williams 1985, 1993b. That ethics should be interpreted as concerned with all traits of character is argued by Hume 1966, Appendix IV, who also rejects the importance of the voluntary/non-voluntary distinction to ethics.

88. Cottingham, 'Religion, Virtue and Ethical Culture', 177.

89. Alasdair MacIntyre, *After Virtue*, London: Duckworth (1985, 2nd edn).

90. Putnam 1988, 381. Cf. the above quote from Cottingham 1994.

91. That VE is intimately related to the idea of a civic culture is, in Cottingham's view, a significant advantage. Yet – he continues to argue – precisely because of this relation VE is in trouble these days, as most of contemporary discourse is detached from an ethical culture that could grant it meaning and depth. Thus VE is right in linking morality to ethical culture, but due to the absence of such culture, it cannot work.

92. MacIntyre, op. cit., 191. Regarding VE as especially concerned with the attainment of internal goods is a major theme in Daniel Putman's writings on VE. By virtue of this concern he seeks to explain how VE is more successful than other theories in explaining why self-deception is a vice (Putman 1987), why VE is not an egoistic theory (Putman 1992b), and why VE provides a successful framework for students to address the question of what a good life is (Putman 1992a).

93. See Dobson 1994. With regard to the application of VE, I agree with Klein's evaluation (1989, 59) that MacIntyre is the most influential virtue ethicist.

94. Non-relativity does not necessarily imply universality. Aristotle did not believe that all virtues are universal (*megalopsychia*, for example, was not), but nor did he believe that virtues are relative to actual practices. I thank Christine Swanton for helping me see this point.

95. That something like the distinction between internal and external goods is supposed by Mill's distinction between 'higher' and 'lower' pleasures is argued by MacIntyre himself (1985, 199).

96. Cordner, ibid.

97. See especially Watson, 62–6, and also Swanton 1995, 60, who favours a pluralistic theory of virtue, because it is 'more expressive of our nature as human beings', and Solomon, 166, who takes VE to regard the virtues as necessary 'to reach the appropriate telos of human life'.

98. Jerome B. Schneewind, 'The Misfortunes of Virtue', *Ethics* 101 (1990), 43.

99. See, for instance, Swanton 1995, 47: 'What makes a character trait a virtue is that the trait facilitates or *makes natural* an agent's responding in various positive ways to value as opposed to disvalue' (italics added).

100. For a fuller account of what anti-theory sceptics take as the features of moral theory, see Louden 1992, Chapter 5. Louden criticises this scepticism and reaffirms the importance of (a rich conception of) moral theory.

101. Pincoffs 1986, quoted by Louden 1992, 85.

102. Cf. Stocker, 118, who says that 'if VE is a *theory* of ethics with all the weight we now attach to "theory"', then he would prefer to say that he is not an adherent of VE.

103. Slote 1992, 32–5, and Slote 1994a, 683.

104. Cf. Blum 1988a, who lists the contrasts between Gilligan and Kohlberg and then points out (483) that these contrasts also characterise the contrast between VE and its rivals.

105. Onora O'Neill (1983, 109, n. 3) explicitly refers to Gilligan as a virtue ethicist.

106. In light of the last section, it is also worth exploring the relation between the ethics of care and the anti-theory. Annete Baier, for example, a friend of the former, also endorses the latter (1985, 207).

107. Daniel Putman, 'Relational Ethics and Virtue Theory', *Metaphilosophy* 22 (1991b), 231.

108. Robert C. Solomon, 213.

109. At least with respect to VE, many of its supporters are males – Williams, Taylor, Slote, Stocker, Alderman, Solomon – which does not of course mean that VE is a masculine sort of theory.

110. MacIntyre, op. cit., 204.
111. It is noteworthy that O'Neill (1993, 109, n. 3) refers to Sandel as a virtue ethicist.
112. Robert Solomon, this volume, Chapter 12. Solomon, however, explicitly distances himself from what he see as 'the rather dangerous nostalgia for "tradition" and "community" that is expressed by Alasdair MacIntyre and Charles Taylor among others' (ibid., 212). Solomon believes that this nostalgia is purely imaginary and is often defined by a naive religious solidarity and unrealistic expectation of communal consensus. On the relation between VE and the importance of living in a community, cf. also Vitek 1992, 196 ff.
113. For some pioneering discussions, see Slote 1993 and the responses of Goodin 1993, Hursthouse 1993, and Swanton 1993.
114. According to Frasz 1992, 261, environmental VE involves the study of 'environmental heroes' such as Aldo Leopold and John Muir, and also the study of 'environmental villains' such as James Watt.
115. See Nussbaum 1990. For the close connection between philosophy and literature, see Williams 1993b, 12–20.
116. For discussions of what virtues are, see, for instance, Dent 1984, and the survey of Pence 1987.
117. See Flanagan and Rorty 1990, 1–2.
118. An analogous theory to VE has recently been discussed in epistemology, that of *virtue epistemology*. See, for instance, Greco 1993.
119. Sarah Conly, 'Flourishing and the Failure of the Ethics of Virtue', in *Midwest Studies in Philosophy* (1988), 83–96.
120. Ibid., 87.
121. Ibid., 90.
122. Cf. Watson, 462–3. Philippa Foot, who once believed in a necessary connection between virtue and self-interest, later changed her mind. See her Introduction to Foot 1978, especially xiii–xiv.
123. See Conly's criticism of Alderman on 95, n. 3.
124. For similar criticism, see Terzis 1994, who compares his criticism to that of Conly's on 341, n. 3.
125. Audi 1995, 467.
126. Cf. the criticism of Driver 1994.
127. See Darwall 1994, 696.
128. Cf. Nussbaum 1988, 33, who argues that for Foot, MacIntyre and Williams, the turn to VE also expresses a turn to a type of relativism, namely, to the idea that there are no trans-cultural criteria for moral goodness, and the criteria are 'internal to the traditions and practices of each local society or group that asks itself questions about the good'.
129. MacIntyre tries to solve this problem by arguing that in addition to the notion of virtue as tied to historically and culturally situated roles, there is a notion of the virtue which is tied to a human *telos* applying to all human beings. See MacIntyre 1985, Chapter 15, and his 'Postscript', ibid., 272–8. Yet this has attracted a lot of criticism, and many have argued that this universalistic claim is incompatible with MacIntyre historicism. See Putman 1987, and the sources he refers to on 99, n. 8.
130. For some difficulties in applying VE to moral problems in psychology, see Statman 1995a.
131. Peter van Inwagen, 'Response to Slote', *Social Theory and Practice* 16 (1990), 393.
132. For more arguments along this line, see Louden's chapter. For the claim that VE might even lead to morally wrong actions, see Veatch 1985, 334, and the response of Putman 1988. For a discussion of the charge that VE expresses an ego-centred outlook, see Putman 1992b.
133. Cf. Richardson's remark (1994, 703) that Slote's book does not seek to re-invent ethics but rather to offer 'a different basis for the life we already live'.
132. See, for instance, Rachels 1986, Chapter 2.
133. Hume 1966, Chapter 2. See also Putman 1992b, 118, who refers to the work of Kohlberg and of Gilligan to show that the criteria for human development are universal, and that 'the standard of excellence must somehow really exist'.
134. See especially Nussbaum 1992.
135. Hursthouse 1995. For Aristotle's view about the non-relativistic character of the virtues, see Nussbaum 1988. For further discussion about virtues and relativism, see Wong 1984, Chapter 9, and Perry 1992.

136. For various versions of this argument, see Pincoffs 1986, 24–5; Solomon, 174–7; Audi 1995, 468; Hursthouse (forthcoming), 13–14; Larmore 1987, 1–16; Paden 1993, 13. That ethical judgment is not a matter of rule-following is a central theme in McDowell's writings (1979, 1981).

137. David Solomon, 176.

138. Robert Solomon, 'Beyond Reason, The Importance of Emotion in Philosophy', in *Revising Philosophy*, James Ogilvy (ed.) (1992), Albany, New York: State University of New York Press, 32.

139. The example of abortion is used by Solomon 1992, 22–9, to make a similar point regarding the relevance of emotions to ethics.

140. John Dobson, 'Theory of the Firm: Beyond the Sirens', *Economics and Philosophy* 10 (1994), 83.

141. This definition has been applied in other areas too, for example in sexual morality; Daniel Putman (1991) seeks to show that virtues such as sensitivity and self-honesty contribute significantly to the practice of sex, and make it much more rewarding and enjoyable.

142. See especially Dobson 1994, 82–4. Albert Hirschman kindly referred me to some of his works in which similar concerns are expressed. See, for instance, Hirschman 1986.

143. I thus cannot agree with Terzis' evaluation that 'recent work in VE has largely ignored its earlier normative aspirations and has instead concentrated on meta-issues' (1994, 340). The work of Rosalind Hursthouse (Chapter 13, and also 1995 and forthcoming) is especially helpful in understanding the normative dimensions of VE.

144. For strong opposition to the application of VE in medical ethics, see Veatch 1985. See also Daniel Putman's response (1988), and Veatch's reply (1988). For responses to Slote's paper on VE and democratic values, see Goodin 1993, Hursthouse 1993, and Swanton 1993. For critical discussion of Jordan and Meara's essay on VE and psychological ethics (1990), see Statman 1995a.

145. According to Trianosky (43), Plato is an example of a 'pure virtue ethics', since on his view at least some aretaic judgments can be established without relying on judgments about the rightness or the wrongness of actions. Santas (n. 7) objects to this evaluation, pointing out that on Plato's view the notion of justice in the individual is not really primary but depends on the notion of social justice. According to Slote (1993, 32), though Plato's *procedure* is to go from social justice to justice within the individual, when we focus on what Plato says about individual justice itself, it is clear that he seeks to derive just action from an inner state of justice. To view Plato's virtue theory as more helpful, especially regarding questions of business ethics, see Klein 1989.

146. See Slote 1993, who seeks to defend a VE conception of social justice on the basis of Stoic ideas about *autarkeia*.

147. According to Putnam (1988, 379) Hume is an important model of a virtue ethicist, a fact which is often overlooked. MacIntyre (1985, 216) depicts Hume as holding that virtues are dispositions necessary for adopting the rules of morality. But see Schneewind's criticism of MacIntyre on 45, n. 13, and 50–4. Schneewind himself contends that Hume's view must be considered 'one of the misfortunes of virtue' (54).

148. See, for instance, Alderman, 63, n. 3., according to which Aristotle's view 'is *properly* to be construed as the first important virtue theory'. See also Stocker, 119 ('Aristotle's ethics – one of our pre-eminent theories of VE') and Hursthouse, Chapter 5. The return to Aristotelian ethics is sometimes supplemented by a return to what is presented as Aristotelian politics, see Salkever 1990 and Nussbaum 1992.

149. In Robert Solomon's view (211), 'Kant, magnificent as he was a thinker, has proved to be a kind of disease in ethics.'

150. Korsgaard (forthcoming), 3. Cf. also Annas 1992.

151. See, for instance, Putnam 1988, 380.

152. Simpson, 247–8. For references to Aristotle and to some modern commentators, see ibid., n. 11. The priority of *eudaimonia* over virtue seems to be assumed by Audi 1995, 466–7.

153. For the claim that Aristotle does not set himself to justify the virtues he recommends, see Simpson, op. cit.; Putnam 1988, 380.

154. Simpson, 250. That the identification of the excellent people is not regarded as problematic in Aristotle is probably connected to the fact that he lived in a small and relatively closed community in which there was shared recognition of such excellence. Cf. Schneewind, 62, and Putnam 1988, 380.

155. For this reason, Simpson argues that Hume cannot serve as historical inspiration for contemporary VE either, because of his 'evident' dependence on gentlemanly opinion.
156. Cf. Cordner 1994, who argues that 'most contemporary virtue ethicists fail to appreciate much of what is crucial to Aristotle's ethics because they read him as having, in effect, a proto-Christian outlook' (290). This is evident, argues Cordner, from the way Aristotle's *andreia*, originally referring mainly to valour in battle, has been interpreted as referring to moral courage. Note that even Slote, who is sympathetic to the views of Aristotle (1992, 89–93 and *passim*), makes it clear that we cannot simply return to Aristotle whose world 'is too different from ours'. What we need is a distinctively *modern* form of VE (1994b, 719). For the charge that virtue ethicists tend to tone down the political aspects of Kant's ethics, see Wallach, 619.
157. The reader may notice that a Euthyphro-type dilemma suggests itself here. I hope to discuss it elsewhere.
158. Slote, *From Morality to Virtue*, 89.
159. *Nicomachean Ethics*, 1129b, quoted by Santas, 277.
160. Elsewhere I argue that this 'translation' of virtues into the language of (imperfect) duties was not very successful. See Statman (1996).
161. See Schneewind 1987, especially section 3.
162. Schneewind, op. cit., 62.
163. Santas, 277. Alderman (n. 3) would probably agree with Schneewind that in Aristotle justice should be read without isolation from the other virtues, though, contrary to Schneewind, Alderman regards this as an advantage.
164. For references, see Louden, 286–7, and Schneewind 1990, 42.
165. Cf. Schneewind 1990, 61, who argues that 'if the misfortune is that virtue was neglected by moral philosophers, then part of the answer is that it was the *Groundwork*, not the *Metaphysics of Morals*, that until recently got most of the attention'.
166. Louden, 286.
167. Ibid., 289.
168. Ibid., 290.
169. O'Neill 1984, 394, quoted by Louden, 291.
170. Louden, 294.
171. Onora O'Neill, 'Kant After Virtue', *Inquiry* 26 (1984), 397.
172. Louden, 294.
173. Aristotle, *Nicomachean Ethics* (1122b6–7).
174. Louden, 295.
175. Christine M. Korsgaard (forthcoming), 'From Duty and for the Sake of the Noble, in *Rethinking Happiness and Duty*, S. Ergstrom and J. Whiting (eds), New York: Cambridge University Press.
176. Cf. Hudson 1990, 11, who argues that Kant and Aristotle 'held the same attitude about the ultimate justification for morality and the life it commends; namely, it is to become one's life because persons of moral excellence (virtue) would choose it . . . because it is commended by practical reason'. Barbara Herman's work (1993) has a central place in this re-reading of Kant. In her view, 'Kantian moral judgment depends on the availability of an articulated conception of value – in particular, *of the value of the fully embodied person*' (ix, italics added). Cf. Sherman 1993 and also Audi 1995, 450, who argues that 'Kantian actions from duty are often similar in important ways to Aristotelian actions from virtue'.
177. Julia Annas, 'Ancient Ethics and Modern Morality', in *Philosophical Perspectives* 6 (1992), 133.
178. Cf. Louden, Chapter 10; Klein 1989, 77–8. That VE can and should make room for rules and principles is emphasised by Hursthouse (forthcoming) and Watson, 451. According to Watson, to think that VE is opposed to principles or duties is a category mistake.
179. For helpful comments on earlier versions I am greatly indebted to Rosalind Hursthouse, Sam Fleischacker, Robert Louden, Helen Nissenbaum, Saul Smilanski, Michael Stocker and Christine Swanton. I also benefited from comments by an anonymous referee for EUP.

## BIBLIOGRAPHY

Annas, Julia (1992) 'Ancient Ethics and Modern Morality', in James E. Tomberlin (ed.), *Philosophical Perspectives* 6: 119–36.

Anscombe, Elizabeth (1958) 'Modern Moral Philosophy', *Philosophy* 33: 1–19. Reprinted in her *Ethics, Religion and Politics*, Oxford: Basil Blackwell, 1981.

Aristotle (1925) *The Nicomachean Ethics*. Trans. by David Ross. Oxford: Oxford University Press.

Audi, Robert (1995) 'Acting From Virtue', *Mind* 104: 449–71.

Baier, Annette (1985) *Postures of the Mind: Essays on Mind and Morals*. Minneapolis: University of Minnesota Press.

Baier, Annette (1986) 'Trust and Antitrust', *Ethics* 96: 231–60.

Baier, Annette (1989) 'Doing Without Moral Theory?', in Stanley Clark and Evan Simpson (eds), *Anti-Theory in Ethics and Moral Conversation*, Albany, New York: State University of New York Press, 29–48.

Baier, Kurt (1988) 'Radical Virtue Ethics', in French et al., 1988, 126–35.

Baron, Marcia (1985) 'Varieties of Ethics of Virtue', *American Philosophical Quarterly* 22: 47–53.

Blum, Lawrence (1988a) 'Gilligan and Kohlberg: Implications for Moral Theory', *Ethics* 98: 472–91.

Blum, Lawrence (1988b) 'Moral Exemplars: Reflections on Schindler, the Trocmes, and Others', in French et al., 1988, 196–221.

Brook, Richard (1991) 'Agency and Morality', *Journal of Philosophy* 88: 190–212.

Conly, Sarah (1988) 'Flourishing and the Failure of the Ethics of Virtue', in French et al., 1988, 83–96.

Cooper, John (1975) *Reason and Human Good in Aristotle*, Cambridge, Massachussetts: Harvard University Press.

Cordner, Christopher (1994) 'Aristotelian Virtue and Its Limitations', *Philosophy* 69: 291–316.

Cottingham, John (1994) 'Religion, Virtue, and Ethical Culture', *Philosophy* 69: 163–80.

Darwall, Stephen L. 1987. 'Abolishing Morality', *Synthese* 72: 71–89.

Dent, N. J. H. (1988) *The Moral Psychology of the Virtues*, Cambridge: Cambridge University Press.

Diamond, Cora (1988) 'The Dog that Gave Himself the Moral Law', in French et al., 1988, 161–79.

Dobson, John (1994) 'Theory of the Firm: Beyond the Sirens', *Economics and Philosophy* 10: 73–89.

Dreier, James (1993) 'Structures of Normative Theories', *Monist* 76: 22–40.

Driver, Julia (1994) 'A Critical Study of Michael Slote's *From Morality to Virtue*', *Nous* 28: 505–14.

Elliot, David (1993) 'The Nature of Virtue and the Question of Its Primacy'. *The Journal of Value Inquiry* 27: 317–30.

Flanagan, Owen and Rorty, Amelie (eds) (1990) *Identity, Character, and Morality: Essays in Moral Psychology*, Cambridge, Massachusetts: MIT Press.

Foot, Philippa (1978) *Virtues and Vices*, Berkeley: University of California Press.

Frasz, Geoffrey B. (1993) 'Environmental Virtue Ethics: A New Direction for Environmental Ethics', *Environmental Ethics* 15: 259–74.

French, Peter A., Uehling, Theodore E. Jr. and Wettstein, Howard K. (eds) (1988) *Midwest Studies in Philosophy*, Vol. 13. Notre Dame, Indiana: University of Notre Dame Press.

Gerrard, Steve (1994) 'Morality and Codes of Honour', *Philosophy* 69: 69–84.

Gilligan, Carol (1982) *In A Different Voice*. Cambridge, Massachusetts: Harvard University Press.

Goodin, Robert (1993) 'Independence in Democratic Theory: A Virtue? A Necessity? Both? Neither?', *Journal of Social Philosophy* 24: 50–6.

Greco, John (1993) 'Virtues and Vices of Virtue Epistemology', *Canadian Journal of Philosophy* 23: 413–32.

Greenspan, Patricia (1994) 'Guilt and Virtue', *Journal of Philosophy* 91: 57–70.

Hampshire, Stuart (1983) *Morality and Conflict*, Cambridge, Massachusetts: Harvard University Press.

Herman, Barbara (1993) *The Practice of Moral Judgment*, Cambridge, Massachusetts: Harvard University Press.

Hill, Thomas E. Jr. (1983) 'Ideals of Human Excellence and Preserving Natural Environment', *Environmental Ethics* 5: 211–24.

Hirschman, Albert (1986) 'Against Parsimony: Three Easy Ways of Complicating Some Categories of Economic Discourse', in his *Rival Views of Market Society and Other Recent Essays*, Viking: Elisabeth Sifton Books.

Hudson, Stephen (1990) 'What is Morality All About?', *Philosophia* 20: 3–13.

Hume, David (1964) *An Enquiry Concerning the Principles of Morals*, La Salle, Illinois: Open Court.

Hursthouse, Rosalind (1990–1) 'After Hume's Justice', *Proceedings of the Aristotelian Society* 91: 229–46.

Hursthouse, Rosalind (1993) 'Slote on Self-Sufficiency', *Journal of Social Philosophy* 24: 57–67.

Hursthouse, Rosalind (1995) 'Applying Virtue Ethics', in Rosalind Hursthouse, Gavin Lawrence and Warren Quinn (eds), *Virtues and Reason: Philippa Foot and Moral Theory*, Oxford: Clarendon Press, 57–75.

Hursthouse, Rosalind (Forthcoming) 'Normative Virtue Ethics', in Roger Crisp (ed.), *How Should One Live?: Essays in the Philosophy of Virtue*, Oxford: Clarendon Press.

Jordan, A. E. and Meara, N. M. (1990) 'Ethics and the Professional Practice of Psychologists: The Role of Virtues and Principles', *Professional Psychology* 21: 101–14.

Klein, Sherwin (1989) 'Platonic Virtue Theory and Business Ethics', *Business and Professional Ethics* 8: 59–82.

Korsgaard, Christine M. (Forthcoming) 'From Duty and for the Sake of the Noble', in Stephen Engstrom and Jennifer Whiting (eds), *Rethinking Happiness and Duty*, New York: Cambridge University Press.

Kruschwitz, R. & Roberts, R. (eds) (1987) *The Virtues: Contemporary Essays on Moral Character*, California: Wadsworth.

Larmore, Charles (1987) *Patterns of Moral Complexity*, Cambridge: Cambridge University Press.

Louden, Robert B. (1992) *Morality and Moral Theory: A Reappraisal and Reaffirmation*, New York: Oxford University Press.

Louden, Robert B. (Forthcoming) 'Toward a Genealogy of "Deontology"', *The Journal of the History of Philosophy*.

MacIntyre, Alasdair (1985) *After Virtue* (2nd edn), London: Duckworth.

McDowell, John (1979) 'Virtue and Reason', *Monist* 62: 331–50.

McDowell, John (1981) 'Non-Cognitivism and Rule-Following', in Holtzman and Leich (eds), *Wittgenstein: To Follow a Rule*, London: Routledge & Kegan Paul, 141–62.

Noddings, Nell (1984) *Caring: A Feminine Approach to Ethics and Moral Education*, Berkeley: University of California Press.

Nussbaum, Martha C. (1986) *The Fragility of Goodness: Luck and Ethics in Greek Tragedy and Philosophy*, Cambridge: Cambridge University Press.

Nussbaum, Martha C. (1988) 'Non-Relative Virtues: An Aristotelian Approach', in French et al., Chapter 3.

Nussbaum, Martha C. (1990) *Love's Knowledge: Essays on Philosophy and Literature*, New York: Oxford University Press.

Nussbaum, Martha C. (1992) 'Human Functioning and Social Justice: In Defense of Aristotelian Essentialism', *Political Theory* 20: 202–46.

O'Neill, Onora (1984) 'Kant After Virtue', *Inquiry* 26: 387–405.

O'Neill, Onora (1993) 'Duties and Virtues', in A. Phillips Griffiths (ed.), *Ethics*, Royal Institute of Philosophy Supp. 35; Cambridge: Cambridge University Press, 107–20.

Paden, Roger K. (1993) 'Virtue and Repression', *Contemporary Philosophy* 15: 12–15.

Pence, Gregory E. (1987) 'Recent Work on Virtues', *American Philosophical Quarterly* 21: 281–97.

Perry, Michael J. (1992) 'Virtues and Relativism', in John W. Chapman and William A. Galston (eds), *Virtue*. NOMOS 34. New York: New York University Press, 117–31.

Pigden, Charles (1988) 'Anscombe on "Ought"', *The Philosophical Quarterly* 38: 20–41.

Pincoffs, Edmund L. (1986) *Quandaries and Virtues*, Lawrence: University of Kansas Press.

Putman, Daniel (1987) 'Virtue and Self-Deception', *Southern Journal of Philosophy* 25: 549–57.

Putman, Daniel (1988) 'Virtue and the Practice of Modern Medicine', *Journal of Medical Ethics* 13: 433–43.

Putman, Daniel (1991a) 'Sex and Virtue', *International Journal of Moral and Social Studies* 6: 47–56.

Putman, Daniel (1991b) 'Relational Ethics and Virtue Theory', *Metaphilosophy* 22: 231–8.

Putman, Daniel (1992a) 'Virtue Theory in Ethics Courses', *Teaching Philosophy* 15: 51–6.

Putman, Daniel (1992b) 'Egoism and Virtue', *The Journal of Value Inquiry* 26: 117–24.

Putnam, Ruth Anna (1988) 'Reciprocity and Virtue Ethics', *Ethics* 98: 379–89.

Rachels, James (1986) *The Elements of Moral Philosophy*, Philadelphia: Temple University Press.

Rawls, John (1971) *A Theory of Justice*, Cambridge, Massachusetts: Harvard University Press.

Richardson, Henry S. (1994) 'Rescuing Ethical Theory', *Philosophy and Phenomenological Research* 54: 703–8.

Richter, Duncan (1995) 'The Incoherence of the Moral "Ought"', *Philosophy* 70: 69–86

Rorty, Amélie (Forthcoming) 'From Exasperating Virtues to Civic Virtues', *American Philosophical Quarterly*.

Sagi, Avi and Statman, Daniel (1995) *Religion and Morality*, Value Inquiry Book Series. Amsterdam: Rodopi.

Salkever, Stephen (1990) *Finding the Mean: Theory and Practice in Aristotelian Political Philosophy*, Princeton, New Jersey: Princeton University Press.

Savarino, Mary Ella (1993) 'Towards an Ontology of VE', *Journal of Philosophical Research* 18: 243–59.

Sayre-McCord, Geoffrey (1986) 'Deontic Logic and the Priority of Moral Theory', *Nous* 20: 179–97.

Scheffler, Samuel (1985) 'Agent-Centered Restrictions, Rationality and the Virtues', *Mind* 94: 409–19.

Scheffler, Samuel (1987) 'Morality Through Thick and Thin – A Critical Notice of *Ethics and the Limits of Philosophy*', *The Philosophical Review* 65: 411–34.

Schneewind, Jerome B. (1987) 'Pufendorf's Place in the History of Ethics', *Synthese* 72: 123–55.

Schneewind, Jerome B. (1990) 'The Misfortunes of Virtue', *Ethics* 101: 42–63.

Schollmeier, Paul (1992) 'Equine Virtue', *Between the Species* 8: 38–43.

Shafer-Landau, Russ (1994) 'Vegetarianism, Causation and Ethical Theory', *Public Affairs Quarterly* 8: 85–100.

Sherman, Nancy (1993) 'Wise Maxims/Wise Judging', *Monist* 76: 41–65.

Slote, Michael (1992) *From Morality to Virtue*, New York: Oxford University Press.

Slote, Michael (1993) 'Virtue Ethics and Democratic Values', *Journal of Social Philosophy* 24: 5–37.

Slote, Michael (1994a) 'Precis of *From Morality to Virtue*', *Philosophy and Phenomenological Research* 54: 683–7.

Slote, Michael (1994b) 'Reply to Commentators', *Philosophy and Phenomenological Research* 54: 709–19.

Solomon, Robert C. (1992) 'Beyond Reason: The Importance of Emotion in Philosophy', in James Ogilvy (ed.), *Revising Philosophy*, Albany, New York: State University of New York Press, 19–47.

Statman, Daniel (ed.) (1993) *Moral Luck*, Albany, New York: State University of New York Press.

Statman, Daniel (1995a) 'Virtue Ethics and Psychology', *The International Journal of Applied Philosophy* 9: 43–50.

Statman, Daniel (1995b) *Moral Dilemmas*, Value Inquiry Book Series. Amsterdam: Rodopi.

Statman, Daniel (1996) 'Who Needs Imperfect Duties?', *American Philosophical Quarterly*.

Stocker, Michael (1976a) 'The Schizophrenia of Modern Ethical Theories', *Journal of Philosophy* 73: 453–66.

Stocker, Michael (1976b) 'Agent and Other: Against Ethical Universalism', *Australasian Journal of Philosophy* 54: 206–20.

Stocker, Michael (1981) 'Values and Purposes: The Limits of Teleology and the Ends of Friendship', *Journal of Philosophy* 78: 747–65.

Stocker, Michael (1987) *Plural and Conflicting Values*, New York: Oxford University Press.

Swanton, Christine (1993) 'Commentary on Michael Slote's "Virtue Ethics and Democratic Values"', *Journal of Social Philosophy* 24: 38–49.

Swanton, Christine (1995) 'Profiles of the Virtues', *Pacific Philosophical Quarterly* 76: 47–72.

Taylor, Richard (1985) *Ethics, Faith, and Reason*, Englewood-Cliffs, New Jersey: Prentice-Hall.

Taylor, Richard (1988) 'Ancient Wisdom and Modern Folly', in French et al., 54–63.

Toulmin, Stephen (1981) 'The Tyranny of Principles; Regaining the Ethics of Discretion', *Hastings Center Reports* 11: 31–8.

Trianosky, Gregory (1986) 'Supererogation, Wrongdoing and Vice: On the Autonomy of the Ethics of Virtue', *Journal of Philosophy* 83: 26–40.

Upton, Hugh (1993) 'On Applying Moral Theories', *Journal of Applied Philosophy* 10: 189–99.

Van Inwagen, Peter (1990) 'Response to Slote', *Social Theory and Practice* 16: 385–95.

Veatch, Robert M. (1985) 'Against Virtue: A Deontological Critique of Virtue Theory in Medical Ethics', in Earl Shelp (ed.), *Virtue and Medicine: Explorations in the Character of Medicine*, Dordrecht: D. Reidel, 329–45.

Veatch, Robert M. (1988) 'The Danger of Virtue', *The Journal of Medicine and Philosophy* 13: 445–6.

Vitek, William (1992) 'Virtue Ethics and Mandatory Birth Control', in James M. Humber & Robert F. Almeder (eds), *Biomedical Ethics Reviews*, Totowa, New Jersey: Humana Press, 173–213.

Waide, John (1988) 'Virtues and Principles', *Philosophy and Phenomenological Research* 48: 455–72.

Walker, A. D. M. (1993) 'The Incompatibility of the Virtues', *Ratio* (New Series) 6: 44–62.

Wallach, John (1992) 'Contemporary Aristotelianism', *Political Theory* 20: 613–41.

Weinstein, Bruce D. (1994) 'The Possibility of Ethical Expertise', *Theoretical Medicine* 15: 61–75.

Williams, Bernard (1973) 'A Critique of Utilitarianism', in J. J. C. Smart and Bernard Williams, *Utilitarianism: For and Against*, Cambridge: Cambridge University Press.

Williams, Bernard (1978) 'Ethical Consistency', in Joseph Raz (ed.), *Practical Reasoning*, Oxford: Oxford University Press, 91–109.

Williams, Bernard (1985) *Ethics and the Limits of Philosophy*, London: Fontana Press.

Williams, Bernard (1993a) 'Postscript', in Statman 1993, 251–8.

Williams, Bernard (1993b) *Shame and Necessity*, Berkeley: University of California Press.

Wong, David B. (1984) *Moral Relativity*, Berkeley: University of California Press.

# 2

# WHAT IS VIRTUE ETHICS ALL ABOUT?

## Gregory Velazco y Trianosky

The past fifteen years have witnessed a dramatic resurgence of philosophical interest in the virtues. The charge that modern philosophical thought neglects the virtues (Becker 1975; Von Wright 1963; Taylor in French, Wettstein and Uehling 1988), once apposite, is by now outmoded; and the calls for a renewed investigation of virtue and virtue ethics are being answered from many quarters. What has been missing to date is any systematic guide to the plethora of issues, charges, claims and counter-claims raised in recent work on the virtues. This survey takes the first steps toward charting this vast and vastly exciting terrain.[1]

Interestingly, not all those who are engaged in the new investigations of virtue agree in endorsing an *ethics of virtue*, or for that matter any single substantive position. Instead concentration on the virtues has served as a rallying point for many writers opposed in different ways to the main tendencies of post eighteenth-century thinking in ethics. In particular, what unifies recent work on the virtues is its opposition to various central elements of a view which I will call *neo-Kantianism*.[2] This is not necessarily Kant's own view, as a number of able commentators have pointed out recently, although its elements are in their ancestry recognisably Kantian. Nor is it necessarily a view held in *toto* by any one contemporary moral philosopher. (See Donagan 1977; Darwall 1983; Gewirth 1978 for defences of important elements of neo-Kantianism.) Nor, finally, is it always a view whose component claims are either uniformly understood or carefully distinguished by its adversaries. Its tenets follow.

1. The most important question in morality is, 'what is it right or obligatory to do?'
2. Basic moral judgments are judgments about the rightness of actions.
3. Basic moral judgments take the form of general rules or principles of right action. Particular judgments of the right are always instances of these.

4. Basic moral judgments are universal in form. They contain no essential reference to particular persons or particular relationships in which the agent may stand.

5. Basic moral judgments *are not* grounded on some account of the human good which is itself entirely independent of morality.

6. Basic moral judgments are categorical imperatives. They have a certain 'automatic reason-giving [justificatory] force'[3] independently of their relation to the desires and/or interests of the agent.

7. It is possible for considerations about what is required by basic moral judgments to play some role in the actual motivation *of any agent*, independently of the operation of desire and emotion in him/her.

8. It is necessary that considerations about what is required by basic moral judgments play some role in the actual motivation of *the truly virtuous agent*, independently of the operation of desire and emotion in him/her.

9. The virtuousness of a trait is always derivative from some relationship it displays to what is antecedently specified as right action.

Nearly all contemporary writers on the virtues do agree in rejecting 1. Their work always shows and typically says that the emphasis in moral philosophy should shift from investigations of the right to investigations of virtue, the virtues, and the virtuous life (Taylor in French, Wettstein and Uehling 1988; Becker 1975; Anscombe 1958). Further, nearly every contemporary writer on the virtues rejects at least one more of these nine claims. Our study of recent work on the virtues will be the study of how the assaults on each of these nine claims are interrelated, both logically and dialectically.

## 1.

We may begin by considering one central contrast, that between the ethics of duty and the ethics of virtue. To speak roughly, in its pure form an ethics of duty holds that only judgments about right action are basic in morality, and that the virtuousness of traits is always derivative in some way from the prior rightness of actions.[4] Conversely, an ethics of virtue in its pure form holds that only judgments about virtue are basic in morality, and that the rightness of actions is always somehow derivative from the virtuousness of traits. The conjunction of neo-Kantian claims 2 and 9 constitutes an endorsement of one form of the pure ethics of duty and a rejection of its contrary, the pure ethics of virtue. The perceptual intuitionism endorsed by Prichard and Ross' Aristotle constitutes the endorsement of another form of the pure ethics of duty.

Formulated more precisely, a pure ethics of virtue makes two claims. First it claims that at least some judgments about virtue can be validated independently of any appeal to judgments about the rightness of actions. In Plato's *Republic* for example it appears to be simply the harmonious order of the just person's psyche which makes it good, and not, say, its aptness to produce right action.

Second, according to a pure ethics of virtue it is this antecedent goodness of traits which ultimately makes any right act right. For instance, Plato says that just actions are those which produce and maintain that harmonious condition of the psyche;[5]

and Aristotle might be read as saying that what one ought to do is what the virtuous person, or the person of practical wisdom, would do. In both these cases the rightness of action supervenes on some appropriate relation to what is antecedently established as virtue.

Obviously views about exactly what is to count as 'an appropriate relation' to virtue will vary. (Our discussion below in section 4 of the varieties of the ethics of duty should suggest by analogy some of the forms such views may take.) But in any case for the pure ethic of virtue the moral goodness of traits is always both independent of the rightness of actions and in some way originative of it as well. The same points may be made, *mutatis mutandis*, about the pure ethics of duty.

## 2.

The debate which inaugurated much of the renewed interest in the virtues began in Anscombe's well-known article, 'Modern Moral Philosophy' (1958). Anscombe challenges claim 6. She finds the notion of a universal moral law which is not the command of any deity, a 'special moral "ought" ', unintelligible (cf. Taylor 1985). It might remain to 'look for norms', she says, which are grounded in the facts about what we need in order to 'flourish'. And perhaps what it is for us to flourish, she suggests, is as Aristotle held to live a life informed by virtue.

The rejection of 6 is often equated with the embracing of this Aristotelian virtue ethic. In point of fact, linking them requires several controversial steps. Anscombe's own argument is a case in point. First she claims that there is no secularised moral 'ought' which has an intelligible application to all rational beings, or even to all human beings, independently of their interests and desires. Second, she claims that there is an 'ordinary' ought or norm, which applies in some version or other to every living creature. This is the 'ought' which instructs us about what is good for us. Third, there is the claim that the notion of our good is to be parsed in terms of what we 'need' or require in order to flourish. Finally, there is the characteristically Aristotelian claim that 'the flourishing of a man *qua* man consists in his being good . . . a man needs, or ought to perform, only virtuous actions'. Plainly one might reject 6, and endorse the first two of these claims, and yet reject the third and/or fourth. The movement to the Aristotelian ethic of virtue is a natural dialectical progression from the rejection of 6. But it is not a logical consequence of it, taken alone.

Foot's well-known 'Morality as a System of Hypothetical Imperatives' (1978) has also been influential in the rejection of 1 and 6, if not in the development of an ethics of virtue proper. She claims that although moral requirements may have a legitimate *application* to an agent independently of whether his desires and interests are served by conformity, these requirements do not give *reasons to act* which are independent of whether his desires and interests are thus served. Indeed, there are no such reasons.[6] Thus if a thoroughly wicked person has no desire or interest which is promoted by his or her being moral, he or she has no reason to be moral.[7] Foot concludes that the reason-giving force of moral requirements is always conditional. They constitute only hypothetical imperatives and not categorical ones.

Here again, no position on the issue of whether basic moral judgments are in Foot's sense categorical or hypothetical entails the rejection of claims 2 and 9, and the acceptance of any version of the ethics of virtue as we have defined it; nor conversely. Yet Foot's discussion reveals that larger questions about moral motivation are connected in a variety of ways to questions about the nature of the reasons there are to be moral.

For one thing, the dispute over 6 is linked with arguments over what sorts of moral motivation are possible or desirable by certain kinds of *internalist* suppositions. That is to say, writers on the virtues often hold (for differing reasons) that philosophical claims about the nature of moral requirement must somehow be modelled in the motivational structure of moral agents. Many neo-Kantians seem to agree. For example, they suppose that since moral requirements are categorical, 7 must be true: it must be at least possible for any moral agent to be motivated by a 'sense of duty', conceived as wholly distinct from desire (Darwall 1983). Moreover, a commitment to 7 is characteristically paired with a commitment to 4, the claim that basic moral principles are impartial in their content. 4 and 7 together imply that it is possible for moral agents to be motivated impartially, simply by considerations about what basic moral requirements dictate. Rejection of either the possibility or the worth (moral or otherwise) of such impartial motivation is a recurring theme in the work of contemporary writers on the role of character in ethics (Williams 1981; Stocker in Kruschwitz and Roberts 1987; Blum 1980, 142f; Wolf in Kruschwitz and Roberts 1987). It should be noted, however, that in many cases the arguments of these anti-Kantian writers go through only given much stronger formulations of internalist doctrines like 7 or 8 than the ones presented here. The work of Herman and Baron forcefully suggests that no such stronger formulations are entailed by 6, or by any other central Kantian thesis.

Disputes about the moral worth of various patterns of motivation enter the arena in yet another way in the discussion of 8. Suppose for a moment that we follow Foot and many others in identifying a core group of traits as *substantive virtues*. These are traits which involve a powerful and enduring concern for some morally valuable end like the wellbeing of others, the telling of the truth, or the keeping of agreements.[8] Then we might adopt a distinction of Prichard's which has had some influence in the contemporary literature on virtue (Frankena 1970). According to Prichard *moral goodness* involves the disposition to be motivated by a sense of duty, conceived as independent of desire. On the other hand a (substantive) *virtue* is simply a standing, intrinsic desire for some morally significant end, *where the end is described wholly in non-moral terms*. One can then think of the 'ethics of virtue' in the way that some claim Foot does (Baron 1983), as holding that the truly moral agent need only display the substantive 'virtues', and need not be 'morally good'. The 'ethics of virtue' will then hold up the ideal of a near-preternatural innocence as true virtue (Trianosky 1990). The 'ethics of duty', at least in its most well-known form, will be some version of the claim expressed in 8.

I think this use of virtue and duty terminology is infelicitous, but no real harm is done so long as we understand that the ethics of virtue as we initially defined it does not commit one to the 'ethics of virtue' as it is understood here. Ethics of virtue advocates could agree that some 'practical' element of responsiveness to basic moral principles must enter into the makeup of any truly virtuous agent. Of course they will tend to conceive this element as involving a responsiveness to considerations about (say) what a person of practical wisdom would do, rather than strictly to considerations about duty. This is not really a disagreement over 8, however, but instead over 2, and perhaps its frequent consort 3.

### 3.

Since its introduction into the contemporary discussion by Anscombe, the ethics of virtue has come to be seen as a 'third option', competing with both deontological and utilitarian views. On this way of looking at the matter, deontological theories take judgments about the right as basic; utilitarianism takes judgments about 'the desirability of certain states of affairs that [actions] produce' as basic; and the ethics of virtue 'derives the desirability of the act from the desirability of . . . motives or traits of character . . .'[9] (cf. Louden 1984).

This classificatory approach encourages one to overlook the radical alternatives which the utilitarian tradition can provide to the ethics of duty. To be sure, the most familiar utilitarian views characterise virtues either as dispositions (however complex) to do what would be in fact right by act-utilitarian standards (Hare 1981); or as traits which maximise the probability that we will do what would be right by such standards.[10] But recent work by Brandt and Adams describes forms of trait- and motive-utilitarianism in which the relation between moral character and utility is not thus mediated by an account of the right. On one such view, for instance, what makes a trait a virtue is simply that its general possession would maximise utility. No reference to any theory of the right, utilitarian or otherwise, is presupposed by this view of virtue.

I suggest that we may more perspicuously divide ethical theories along two distinct and orthogonal lines. First, they may be divided into the ethics of virtue and the ethics of duty in the manner indicated at the outset. This distinction divides ethical theories on the question of what sort of *moral* judgments they take to be basic. Next, each of these ethics may take either a teleological or a non-teleological, 'deontological' form. This second distinction divides ethical theories on the question of whether they take the basic moral judgments themselves to be autonomous or derivative. Pure *teleological* theories hold that basic moral judgments are to be grounded on some account of the good, where the good is conceived as describable *independently of any reference either to moral rightness or to virtue*: pleasure, the satisfaction of desire, or the obtaining of various intrinsically desirable states of affairs, for example. Pure teleological theories deny that ethics is autonomous because they hold that all judgments about moral value, if I may use this as a generic term for rightness and moral virtue, must ultimately be grounded in this way on judgments about *non-moral* value. Non-teleological or 'deontological' theories disagree, holding instead that basic moral judgments, whether about virtue or about duty, are not grounded on considerations about the (non-moral) good. In this way pure non-teleological theories hold that moral value is autonomous, or not dependent for its philosophical justification on any claims about non-moral value (Scanlon 1982). 5, one of the central propositions of neo-Kantian ethics, embodies the non-teleological claim, albeit in a comparatively weak form. So, as I will indicate below, do the writings of certain virtue theorists.

(I have used the label 'teleological' to advertise that the range of views here is not limited to strictly utilitarian theories. What is characteristic of utilitarianism is its insistence that the rightness of actions or the virtuousness of traits depends on their *causal* relation to the good. But the relation between an action or a trait and the good may be intentional rather than causal. The act or trait may *aim* at human wellbeing, for example, rather than simply helping to promote it. Neither of these necessarily implies the other. Non-utilitarian teleological theories might measure the rightness of acts or the virtuousness of traits not by their effects but simply by the extent to which they take the good as their intentional object. Thus Frances Hutcheson, for example, famously says that 'benevolence is the whole of virtue', because he takes a virtuous person to be one who aims at the good.)

Now it should be clear that the sorts of issues which lie between the ethics of duty and the ethics of virtue as we have characterised them will be quite different from those raised by the 'deontology-teleology' debate. Moreover, it follows from this way of understanding things that just as there are both teleological and deontological forms of the ethics of duty, familiar from long-standing debates in this and the previous two centuries, so also there are both teleological and non-teleological or (as it were) 'deontological' forms of the ethics of virtue. Many of these last are only now beginning to be explored again.

Non-teleological ethics of virtue are theories which maintain against all forms of utilitarianism that the basic judgments about virtuous traits *can* be grounded without appeal to any independently-formulated account of the good. Like the familiar deontological views in the ethics of duty, these theories hold that basic moral judgments, however conceived, may be justified *autonomously*. The most familiar non-teleological theories are perfectionist ones like Aristotle's, on which virtue is a constitutive element (if not the central element) of the human good rather than merely a means, however indispensable, to its attainment.[11]

This way of drawing distinctions suggests that the relationship between utilitarianism and contemporary writers on the virtues is likely to be an ambiguous one, and so it is. On the one hand, utilitarians as I have described them plainly reject 5. But given the distinctions I have drawn, no position on 5 will follow from a virtue theorist's rejection of 2 and 9 and the acceptance of a pure ethics of virtue. Indeed, perfectionist versions of the non-teleological ethic of virtue will endorse 5 as it is written.

Nonetheless, one of the greatest and most widespread sources of dissatisfaction among contemporary writers on virtue is the way in which the Kantian tradition does take morality to be autonomous in the extreme, cut off entirely from the human good at its base. Neo-Kantians typically will endorse not only 5 but the stronger thesis that basic moral principles are not to be grounded on any account of the human good at all, whether independent of morality or not (Donagan 1977; Darwall 1983). Advocates of a perfectionist ethic of virtue will join utilitarians in rejecting this stronger thesis;

for they all agree against such neo-Kantians that some conception of the human good must figure centrally in our account of moral value. The renewed interest in Aristotle so familiar in the writings of virtue theorists is but one sign of this widely-held conviction.

Plainly, the crucial issue for writers on the virtues who wish to affirm a close relation between virtue and the good is thus whether such a conception of the good can be described independently of reference to moral virtue. Teleological virtue theorists like the motive- and trait-utilitarians say 'yes'. Non-teleological, perfectionist virtue theorists say 'no'. What is surprising is how many of the most influential writers on the virtues today in fact defend some sort of teleological if not specifically utilitarian answer. Von Wright's[12] remark is representative: 'Virtues . . . are needed in the service of the good of man. This usefulness of theirs is their meaning and [natural] purpose' (cf. Wallace 1978; Warnock 1971; Geach 1977; MacIntyre 1981).[13]

To be sure, what distinguishes many of these writers most sharply from more brazenly utilitarian writers like Hare or Smart is that their conception of the good is far richer. They are not hedonists, nor satisfaction-of-desire theorists. They speak instead of human flourishing or wellbeing, or of practices, traditions, and narratives. This enrichment of our philosophical repertoire of conceptions of the good is without question a very important contribution to modern moral philosophy. But utilitarian ism is one kind of teleological doctrine about the foundations of ethics. It holds that the right and the virtuous must somehow promote the (non-moral) good. It is not necessarily committed to any particular substantive theory of that good. Hence writers on the virtues cannot avoid a commitment to utilitarianism by offering a more sophisticated theory of the good.

The possibility of a non-teleological ethics of virtue which seek to retain a close relation between virtue and the human good is precisely what Elizabeth Anscombe suggested (1958).[14] This suggestion has set the agenda for the future for many writers on the virtues. The difficulty for some of these has been how to adopt some more or less Aristotelian notion of human flourishing without Aristotelian metaphysical commitments, but at the same time without abandoning the search for an alternative to utilitarianism.[15] Others (Taylor 1985; Nussbaum in French, Uehling and Wettstein 1988) seem willing simply to endorse Aristotle's claim that our function is a life of rational activity despite whatever metaphysical difficulties may attend it.

Despite the great deal of work that remains to be done on them, non-teleological ethics of virtue offer important advantages over any other view. They do justice to two guiding intuitions which seem at first to be irreconcilably at odds. The first is the minimal Kantian idea, expressed in 5, that morality is autonomous. The second is the idea that, as utilitarians have always insisted, morality is essentially connected with the human good. Defenders of the non-teleological ethics of virtue can accept this latter utilitarian idea, for they can maintain that virtue is a constitutive element of the human good. By the same token, although they reject any extreme neo-Kantian version of 5, they can accept 5 as I have formulated it.

We may close this section by noting that here we have discovered one final connection between a non-teleological ethic of virtue and the debate over reasons for action which was the focus of 6. One may combine a perfectionist view of the human good with the claim made by both Anscombe and Foot that one always has reason to do what is in one's interest. Taken together these entail that moral virtue is a form of *human excellence*, or a state of character which there is reason to pursue for its own sake as a constituent of one's good. I believe this is the position that Anscombe was suggesting and that Foot is working towards. It is certainly a position which any admirer of Aristotle's ethics should take seriously.

## 4.

I remarked at the outset that not all writers on the virtues defend the ethics of virtue as I have defined it. Indeed, when one comes to examine prevalent views about what the virtues are and what makes them virtues, it becomes clear that many of these writers still operate within the framework of an ethic of duty. Seeing how this is so will demonstrate some of both the merits and the limitations of recent work on the virtues.

Earlier we made a distinction between two kinds of teleological theories: causal or utilitarian theories and intentional theories. They differed in their account of what the proper relation was between morality and the (non-moral) good. This distinction cut across the ethics of duty/ethics of virtue distinction with which we began. Here we may make yet another similar distinction within the ethics of duty, having to do with the view of the virtues taken by such an ethic. Despite the similarities of structure, this new distinction will be orthogonal to both the previous distinctions.

Recall that the ethics of duty took judgments about the right to be fundamental in morality. Moreover, it held that the virtuousness of traits was always wholly derivative, in one way or another, from the prior rightness of actions.

Whether its criterion of rightness happens to be deontological or teleological, therefore, we might say that an ethic of duty always affirms that virtue consists in *a proper orientation towards the right*. But this notion of proper orientation towards the right typically has been interpreted in one of two distinct ways. On the one hand, it has often been understood as involving a disposition to *choose for the sake of* what is antecedently established as right. (Gert (1981) and Brandt (1981) offer quite different perspectives on what it is to have such a disposition.) The radical Kantian view suggested by certain familiar passages in the *Groundwork*, that only the concern to do what is right *as such* constitutes true virtue, is a limiting case of the general idea that all the virtues are substantive concerns of this sort. A surprising number of contemporary authors seem to agree with this general idea (Rawls 1970; Brandt in French, Wettstein and Uehling 1988; Warnock 1971; Gert 1981), even if they do not agree with Kant's specific contention that all the virtues are varieties of the sense of duty. (Cf. Wallace, 1978, on the virtues of conscientiousness *versus* the virtues of benevolence.) These writers thus all offer an account of the virtues which is entirely compatible with the ethics of duty.

On the other hand, the notion of being properly oriented towards the right has been interpreted in causal terms. The virtues have then been understood as whatever traits generally serve to enable human beings *better to pursue their commitment to* what is antecedently identified as right. So understood, the virtues may be quite a heterogeneous lot, or they may all be traits of the same kind (Von Wright 1963; Roberts in Kruschwitz and Roberts 1987). But to conceive the virtues as enablers of this sort is again to deny no tenet of the ethics of duty. Moreover, as I have suggested, within the ethics of duty both deontologists and teleologists may endorse either of these conceptions of virtue.

Certain current writers on the virtues hold the moderately pluralistic view that some virtues are substantive dispositions to choose what is right, while the rest are traits which enable right action.[16] Here again, of course, this moderate pluralism remains entirely consistent with the central ethics of duty claim, that the moral worth of virtuous traits is wholly derivative from the rightness of the actions to which they are somehow related.

One of our earlier distinctions can now be shown to be extensionally equivalent to a version of this same substantive virtue/enabling virtue dichotomy, at least within the comparatively restricted domain of the *teleological ethics of virtue*. Now a teleological ethic of virtue conceives of the virtues as consisting in proper orientation towards *the* (non-moral) *good*, rather than towards the right. But recall the distinction in section 3 between two broad teleological conceptions of the relation between morality and that good: on the one hand morality may be understood as involving some suitable *intentional* orientation towards the good; or on the other hand it may be understood as involving a suitable *causal* orientation towards the good. If one defends a teleological ethics of virtue, then in the former case the virtues may again be interpreted as involving substantive dispositions to choose for the sake of what is good. In the latter case, correspondingly, they may be interpreted as traits which generally enable the pursuit of the good. Indeed, teleological virtue theorists have generally conceived of the virtues on one of these two models; although naturally teleological duty theorists have not (Adams 1976). Our earlier distinction between two types of teleological theories is thus extensionally equivalent to a version of the distinction between the conception of virtue as substantive and the conception of virtue as enabling, but only within the realm of teleological virtue ethics. Within the realm of teleological duty ethics the two distinctions remain orthogonal.

A less modest and even more reasonable pluralism about the virtues would amalgamate all these various conceptions of virtue, and hold the mixed ethics of duty/ethics of virtue view that virtues must all be species of proper orientation towards *either* the right *or* some independently conceived non-moral good; and that such a proper orientation could in each case be interpreted as involving either a substantive disposition to choose or some enabling trait.[17]

However, even this more reasonable pluralism commits one to rejecting a non-teleological ethic of virtue, in which autonomous judgments of virtue are fundamental. Hence it makes it difficult, though not impossible, to accept the Aristotelian position I mentioned at the end of section 3, on which virtues are conceived as human excellences (Frankena 1980).´

It is also too modest in a more intramural respect. For one thing, there may be a variety of significant causal relationships between traits and the good or the right besides the enabling-relation between trait and action. (One's wisdom may win the respect of others and so make them more responsive to one's advice, for example; and one's willingness to abide by one's agreements may allow others in the community better to pursue their ends.) Analogously, there are many intentional states which are not fundamentally dispositions to behave, to choose, or to deliberate. Yet surely one's attitudes and emotions about the right or the good, for example, may be either appropriate or inappropriate. One may venerate the moral law, or one may obey its dictates resentfully. One may love the good wholeheartedly, or one may take a secret pleasure in what is evil. A full appreciation of the richness of the intuitive idea that virtue consists in proper orientation towards the right and/or the good thus awaits further exploration of the great variety of intentional states which may take the right or the good – or for that matter the bad or the wrong – as their objects (Dent 1985; Trianosky 1988); as well as the variety of causal relations which may obtain between traits and moral value.

## 5.

Perhaps the most frequently-heard objection to virtue ethics is that '[it] is structurally unable to say much of anything' about what people ought to do. 'What can a virtues and vices approach say about specific moral dilemmas', critics ask (Louden in Kruschwitz and Roberts 1987). The real force of this objection is properly directed against a pure ethics of virtue, or perhaps against a position which proposes to substitute a theory of virtue for a theory of right action. Much of what is being written about the virtues involves an endorsement neither of such a pure position nor of such a substitution; and there is certainly no denying that writers on the virtues have begun to take great interest in concrete moral issues (e.g. Foot 1978; Hursthouse 1987). Moreover, here as in section 2 some form of internalist supposition is operating. Here it seems to be the assumption that any theory of the virtue-making characteristics of traits and actions must at the same time constitute an account of valid moral decision procedures. In general, however, this sort of internalist supposition about theories of moral value seems questionable (Smith 1988; Railton 1984); and typically no argument is given for why virtue theorists in particular must be committed to it.

Perhaps not surprisingly, Pincoffs (1986) and many other virtue theorists seem implicitly to accept the relevant internalist supposition. They handle the objection by instead rejecting the supposition that the central business of moral theories is to help us resolve 'moral quandaries'. But even if resolving moral quandaries is not the premier task of an ethical theory, there still remains the question of what the ethics of virtue can say about that aspect of the moral life which does involve choosing courses of action.

One answer to this question seeks to reject claim 3, replacing rules and principles with a different sort of standard for right action. The suggestion is that some personal moral ideal is to guide one's decision-making (Cua 1978; Pincoffs 1986, 24; Moravcsik 1980). Personal moral ideals are understood here as articulating some conception of virtuous character. Interestingly, however, the advocates of this suggestion usually conceive ideals as operating subject to constraints imposed by 'the big rules', as Moravcsik calls them,[18] or 'the minimal requirements' of universalisability, as Pincoffs calls them.[19] Even in MacIntyre's argument for a complete reorientation of our understanding of ourselves and our lives towards the virtues, there is a 'morality of law' which is not just coordinate with the 'morality of virtue', but which seems to impose basic constraints on how decisions are to be made.[20] Hence this answer seems entirely compatible with a commitment to the pure ethics of duty.

A more radical *tu quoque* response against the ethics of duty is that no theory of the right can constitute a complete guide to action without being supplemented by a theory of virtue. This response has been defended on several levels. First, it has sometimes been pointed out that rules or principles of right action must be applied, and conflicts between them adjudicated. But the rules themselves do not tell us how to apply them in specific situations, let alone how to apply them well, or indeed when to excuse people for failing to comply with them. For these tasks, it is claimed, an account of the virtues is required (Cua 1978; Becker 1975; Moravcsik 1980).

Next, it has been argued that much of right conduct cannot be codified in rules or principles (McDowell 1979). Moral situations are too complex; moral rules too general and simplistic. Instead, various substantive virtues like benevolence, honesty, justice and generosity may each be seen as embodying a form of responsiveness to some range of moral considerations about helping others, truth-telling, and so on. Enabling virtues like sensitivity and empathy operate to ensure that one does not overlook relevant considerations in the particular case. On this model there will be no fixed rules or decision procedures which tell one how to weigh these competing considerations once they are identified (Pincoffs 1986). Moreover, except when one can look to some morally exemplary or paradigmatic individual (Cua 1978), the extent to which one decides well will depend largely on the extent to which one has already developed a virtuous character.

What makes an act right in these instances will instead be simply that it is the particular choice endorsed by thoughtful judgment or practical wisdom, informed by virtuous concern. In these instances at least judgments of virtue will be primary and judgments of rightness derivative. (Whether it follows that the pure ethics of duty defended in claim 9 is mistaken depends on whether these judgments of virtue in turn are basic, or whether they are themselves derivative from even more fundamental principles of the right. For example, it is consistent with the conclusion of the *tu quoque* argument as I have formulated it that a complete account of the nature of practical wisdom in turn requires essential reference to some fundamental principles of the right. Hence it is consistent with that conclusion that both the ethics of duty and the ethics of virtue, taken on their own, are incomplete as action guides.)

In any case it certainly follows that insofar as an ethics of duty is committed to claim 3, it must be incomplete as an action guide. A significant portion of the account of right action will be formulable only in the language of virtue, and not in the language of rules or principles of duty.

It is perhaps out of a desire to show that the judgments of virtue involved here are indeed basic and not derivative from other principles of the right that writers on the virtues characteristically resist the sometimes-suggested translation of statements about virtue into the idiom of rules of duty (Warnock 1971). They maintain that typically there is no codifiable rule or principle of the right which covers just that set of actions characteristic of a given virtue. That set will be describable solely by reference to the virtue itself. (Blum 1980, 142; Von Wright 1963; Burnyeat 1971; Dent 1985, 29–30; Pincoffs 1986, 77–78. But see Trianosky 1987.)[21]

If the *tu quoque* argument succeeds then there is at least one powerful reason to study the virtues. But whether it succeeds or not, perhaps the most persuasive argument in favour of studying the virtues is simply that they are the stuff of which much of the moralities of everyday life are made (Sabini and Silver 1982; Thomas 1989). If we are to give moral experience precedence over moral theorising, we must study the rich and subtle phenomena of moral character.

## ENDNOTES

1. Pence (1984) is the only other survey of recent work on the virtues of which I am aware. It is less systematic and more oriented towards thumbnail sketches of the canonical texts. Because it is readily available, I have given less space to summary and more space to systematising the issues addressed by writers on the virtues. Kruschwitz and Roberts (1987) contains a fairly comprehensive bibliography of recent work on the virtues, including work on particular virtues like generosity, courage, humility and mercy. Card and Hunt (1991) includes a large number of excellent articles on particular virtues.
2. Lawrence Blum, *Friendship, Altruism, and Morality*, London: Routledge & Kegan Paul (1980), 1–3.
3. Philippa Foot, *Virtues and Vices*, Berkeley: University of California Press (1978), 161.
4. See, for example, Alan Gewirth, 'Rights and Virtues', *Review of Metaphysics*, Vol. 38 (1985), 751.
5. Plato, *Republic*, 443e.
6. Foot, op. cit., 179, 148–56.
7. Ibid., 161.
8. Ibid., 165–6, 154–5.
9. N. J. H. Dent, *The Moral Psychology of the Virtues*, Cambridge: Cambridge University Press (1984), 32–4.
10. Cf. Peter Railton, 'Alienation, Consequentialism and the Demands of Morality', *Philosophy and Public Affairs*, Vol. 13 (1984), 152–6.
11. Charles E. Larmore, *Patterns of Moral Complexity*, Cambridge: Cambridge University Press (1987), 30–6.
12. G. H. von Wright, *The Varieties of Goodness*, London: Humanities Press (1963), 140.
13. Perfectionist virtue theorists will reject even MacIntyre's sophisticated utilitarian conception of virtues like truthfulness, justice and courage: '[The virtues are] those dispositions which . . . sustain us in the relevant quest' for the good, by enabling us to overcome the harms, dangers, temptations and distractions which we encounter. 'The good life for man is the life spent in seeking for the good life for man, and the virtues necessary for the seeking are those which will enable us to understand what more and what else the good life for man is' (1981, 204).
14. Cf. Peter Geach, *The Virtues*, Cambridge: Cambridge University Press (1977), 9–12.
15. Cf. James Wallace, *Virtues and Vices*, Ithaca: Cornell University Press (1978), 34; Alasdair MacIntyre, *After Virtue*, Notre Dame: University of Notre Dame Press (1981), 187–9.
16. Foot, op. cit., 1–18; Richard M. Hare, *Moral Thinking*, Oxford: Oxford University Press (1981).
17. W. D. Ross, *The Right and the Good*, Oxford: Oxford University Press (1930), 134.
18. Julius Moravscik, 'On What We Aim At and How We Live', in David J. Depew (ed.), *The Greeks and the Good Life*, Fullerton: Department of Philosophy, California State University (1980), 219–20.
19. Edmund Pincoffs, *Quandaries and Virtues*, Lawrence: University Press of Kansas (1986), 35.
20. MacIntyre, op. cit., 141–3, 187.
21. An earlier and much longer version of this paper was presented to MAPPS, the newly-formed Orange County Moral and Political Philosophy Society, in December 1988. I am very grateful for the comments of Society members, especially David Estlund, Craig Ihara, Alan Nelson

and Gary Watson. I am also very grateful for the comments of Rachel Cohon, Amy Gutman, Brad Hooker, Joel Kupperman, Michael Slote and a number of others.

## BIBLIOGRAPHY

Adams, Robert M. (1976) 'Motive-Utilitarianism', *Journal of Philosophy*, Vol. 73, 467–81.
Anscombe, G. E. M. (1958) 'Modern Moral Philosophy', *Philosophy*, Vol. 33, 1–19.
Baron, Marcia (1983) 'On De-Kantianizing the Perfectly Moral Person', *Journal of Value Inquiry*, Vol. 17, 281–93.
Baron, Marcia (1984) 'The Alleged Moral Repugnance of Acting from Duty', *Journal of Philosophy*, Vol. 81, 197–220.
Becker, Lawrence (1975) 'The Neglect of Virtue', *Ethics*, Vol. 85, 110–22.
Blum, Lawrence (1980) *Friendship, Altruism, and Morality*, London: Routledge & Kegan Paul.
Brandt, Richard B. (1981) 'W. K. Frankena and Ethics of Virtue', *Monist*, Vol. 64, 271–92.
Burnyeat, M. F. (1971) 'Virtues in Action', in *The Philosophy of Socrates*, Gregory Vlastos (ed.), New York: Doubleday Anchor Books.
Card, Claudia and Hunt, Lester (eds) (1991) *Character: Essays in Moral Psychology*, Ithaca: Cornell University Press.
Cua, Antonio (1978) *Dimensions of Moral Creativity*, University Park: Pennsylvania State University Press.
Darwall, Stephen L. (1983) *Impartial Reason*, Ithaca: Cornell University Press.
Darwall, Stephen L. (1986) 'Agent-Centered Restrictions From the Inside Out', *Philosophical Studies*, Vol. 50, 291–319.
Dent, N. J. H. (1984) *The Moral Psychology of the Virtues*, Cambridge: Cambridge University Press.
Donagan, Alan (1977) *The Theory of Morality*, Chicago: University of Chicago Press.
Flanagan, Owen and Rorty, Amelie (eds) (1990) *Identity, Character, and Morality*, Cambridge: MIT Press.
Foot, Philippa (1978) *Virtues and Vices*, Berkeley: University of California Press.
Frankena, William K. (1970) 'Prichard and the Ethics of Virtue', *Monist*, Vol. 54, 1–17.
Frankena, William K. (1980) 'The Carus Lectures of William Frankena: Three Questions About Morality', *Monist*, Vol. 63, 3–47.
French, Peter A., Uehling, Theodore E. and Wettstein, Howard K. (1988) *Midwest Studies in Philosophy*, Vol. XIII, *Character and Virtue*, Notre Dame: University of Notre Dame Press.
Geach, Peter (1977) *The Virtues*, Cambridge: Cambridge University Press.
Gert, Bernard (1981) *The Moral Rules*, New York: Harper Torchbook.
Gewirth, Alan (1985) 'Rights and Virtues', *Review of Metaphysics*, Vol. 38, 739–62.
Gewirth, Alan (1978) *Reason and Morality*, Chicago: University of Chicago Press.
Hare, Richard M. (1981) *Moral Thinking*, Oxford: Oxford University Press.
Herman, Barbara (1981) 'On the Value of Acting from the Motive of Duty', *Philosophical Review*, Vol. 90, 359–82.
Hudson, Stephen D. (1985) *Human Character and Morality*, London: Routledge & Kegan Paul.
Hursthouse, Rosalind (1987) *Beginning Lives*, Oxford: Basil Blackwell Ltd.
Kruschwitz, Robert B. and Roberts, Robert C. (eds) (1987) *The Virtues: Contemporary Essays in Moral Character*, Belmont, California: Wadsworth Publishing.
Larmore, Charles E. (1987) *Patterns of Moral Complexity*, Cambridge: Cambridge University Press.
Louden, Robert B. (1984) 'On Some Vices of Virtue Ethics', *American Philosophical Quarterly*, Vol. 21, 227–36.
Louden, Robert B. (1986) 'Kant's Virtue Ethics', *Philosophy*, Vol. 61, 473–89.
McDowell, John (1979) 'Virtue and Reason', *Monist*, Vol. 62, 331–50.
MacIntyre, Alasdair (1981) *After Virtue*, Notre Dame: University of Notre Dame Press.
Moravcsik, Julius (1980) 'On What We Aim At and How We Live', in David J. Depew (ed.), *The Greeks and The Good Life*, Fullerton: Department of Philosophy, California State University.
O'Neill, Onora (1983) 'Kant After Virtue', *Inquiry*, Vol. 26, 387–405.
Pence, Gregory E. (1984) 'Recent Work on Virtues', *American Philosophical Quarterly*, Vol. 21, 281–97.
Pincoffs, Edmund (1986) *Quandaries and Virtues*, Lawrence: University Press of Kansas.
Railton, Peter (1984) 'Alienation, Consequentialism, and the Demands of Morality', *Philosophy and Public Affairs*, Vol. 13, 134–71.

Rawls, John (1970) *A Theory of Justice*, Cambridge: Harvard University Press.

Ross, W. D. (1930) *The Right and The Good*, Oxford: Oxford University Press.

Sabini, John and Silver, Maury (1982) *Moralities of Everyday Life* Oxford: Oxford University Press.

Scanlon, Thomas M. (1982) 'Contractarianism and Utilarianism', in Amartya Sen and Bernard Williams (eds), *Utilitarianism and Beyond*, Cambridge: Cambridge University Press.

Slote, Michael (1983) *Goods and Virtues*, Oxford: Oxford University Press.

Smith, Holly M. (1988) 'Making Moral Decisions', *Nous*, Vol. 22, 89–108.

Taylor, Richard (1985) *Ethics, Faith, and Reason*, Englewood Cliffs, New Jersey: Prentice-Hall.

Thomas, Lawrence (1989) *Living Morally: A Psychology of Moral Character*, Philadelphia: Temple University Press.

Trianosky, Gregory (1987) 'Virtue, Action, and the Good Life: Toward a Theory of the Virtues', *Pacific Philosophical Quarterly*, Vol. 68, 124–47.

Trianosky, Gregory (1988) 'Rightly Ordered Appetites: How to Live Morally and Live Well', *American Philosophical Quarterly*, Vol. 25, 1–12.

Trianosky, Gregory (1990) 'Natural Affection and Responsibility for Character: A Critique of Kantian Views of the Virtues', in Owen Flanagan and Amelie Rorty (eds) *Identity, Character, and Morality*, Cambridge: MIT Press.

Von Wright, G. H. (1963) *The Varieties of Goodness*, London: Humanities Press.

Wallace, James (1978) *Virtues and Vices*, Ithaca: Cornell University Press.

Warnock, Geoffrey (1971) *The Object of Morality*, London: Methuen Press.

Williams, Bernard (1981) 'Persons, Character, and Morality', in *Moral Luck*, Cambridge: Cambridge University Press.

# 3

# ON THE PRIMACY OF CHARACTER

## Gary Watson

## 1.

John Rawls taught us to think of moral theory as treating primarily three concepts: the concept of right (wrong, permissible), the concept of good, and the concept of moral worth. Of these concepts, however, he takes the latter to be derivative: 'The two main concepts of ethics are those of the right and the good; the concept of a morally worthy person is, I believe, derived from them. The structure of an ethical theory is, then, largely determined by how it defines and connects these two basic notions'.[1] Thus Rawls recognises two types of theories: those that 'define' the right in terms of the good and those that do not. Rawls' own theory illustrates the second type. An example of the first is classical utilitarianism, which 'defines' right action as maximising human happiness (or the satisfaction of rational desire), which is taken to be the intrinsic or ultimate good.

On either of the types of theory that Rawls recognises, the concept of moral worth (which includes that of virtue) will be subordinated to one of the other concepts. For example, on Rawls' theory (as well as on broadly Kantian theories generally), virtues are construed as 'strong and normally effective desires to act on the basic principles of right'.[2] Some versions of utilitarianism may accept this construal as well, or else define virtues directly in terms of the good that certain traits or dispositions will do.

Recently a number of philosophers have expressed dissatisfaction with this kind of scheme on the grounds that it precludes from the outset views that give to virtue a more central place (such as those by and large of the ancients). My aim is to investigate whether or not this dissatisfaction is well grounded. The alleged alternative has not, in my opinion, been sufficiently, or even roughly, articulated. I wish, then, to explore the structure of 'ethics of virtue', as they are usually called, to determine whether they indeed constitute theories of a third kind.

## 2.

Rawls' twofold scheme corresponds to another prevalent division of theories into 'teleological' and 'deontological'. These theories are ways of relating the two concepts that Rawls takes to be basic. In teleological views 'the good is defined independently from the right, and then the right is defined as that which maximizes the good'.[3] Teleological theories are, in a word, consequentialist. The contrasting conception is defined negatively as what is not teleological. As a result, all moral theories are construed as either consequentialist or deontological.

The awkwardness of this taxonomy can be seen by applying it to the case of Aristotle. Rawls considers Aristotle a teleologist (of the perfectionist variety). This classification would have us think of Aristotle's view as differing from utilitarianism only in its conception of what is to be maximised. But that is very doubtful. For Aristotle, the virtuous person is not one who is out to maximise anything, nor is virtue itself defined as a state that tends to promote some independently definable good (these being the two ways in which virtue can be treated in a broadly consequentialist theory).

So Aristotle's theory is deontological if that just means nonconsequentialist. But this classification seems equally inapt.[4] For a concept of good *is* primary in Aristotle's view. Thus if teleological theories are those in which the (or a) concept of the good is primary, then Aristotle's theory is rightly said to be teleological. It is a mistake, however, to think that the only way of asserting the primacy of the good is consequentialism. We should recognise the possibility of a view that is at once teleological and nonconsequentialist. An ethics of virtue, I shall suggest, is a theory of this kind.[5]

We can avoid some unfortunate conflations by replacing this distinction as Rawls draws it with the threefold distinction that his discussion originally suggests: an ethics of requirement, an ethics of consequences, and an ethics of virtue or character. This classification enables us to observe that while both ethics of consequences and ethics of virtue are teleological insofar as they are guided fundamentally by a notion of the good, Aristotle is nonetheless closer to Kant than to Bentham on the question of consequentialism. It also enables us to consider what it means to take the concept of virtue as fundamental.

## 3.

Before I go on to consider this question more fully, I should note that the phrase 'ethics of virtue' is often used in a different way from the way in which it will be used here. Some writers use this phrase to indicate something to live by, such as Frankena, a certain moral outlook that calls for exclusive moral attention to questions about character and the quality of one's whole life. The contrast here is supposed to be with an 'ethics of duty or principle', in which the fundamental moral questions are about what one's duty is and how to do it.

This is not at all the contrast that concerns me in this chapter. In the sense that concerns me, an ethics of virtue is not a code or a general moral claim but a set of abstract theses about how certain concepts are best fitted together for the purposes of understanding morality. To claim that we should give exclusive moral attention either to questions of duty or to questions of character seems to me a very special and suspect position. A morally admirable person will, for example, acknowledge her duties as a teacher to read her students' work carefully and promptly, acknowledge her obligation to repay a loan, and acknowledge the principle never to take bribes as a juror. No doubt we will disagree in some cases about what duties there are and what they involve (whether a democratic citizen has a duty to vote, for instance) and about the importance of certain duties relative to one another and to other considerations. Nonetheless, to say that questions of duty or principle never take moral precedence (or always do) seems morally incorrect.

To think that an ethics of virtue in my sense is opposed to duty is a category mistake. Duties and obligations are simply factors to which certain values, for example, fidelity and justice, are responsive. They do not compete with virtue for moral attention.

## 4.

While it might have implications for how one lives, an ethics of virtue is not, like an ethics of love or liberation, a moral outlook or ideal but a claim that the concept of virtue is in some way theoretically dominant. On an ethics of virtue, how it is best or right or proper to conduct oneself is explained in terms of how it is best for a human being to be. I will call this the *claim of explanatory primacy*.

Explanatory primacy can be realised in different ways by different theories. One straightforward way, for example, is to explain right conduct as what accords with the virtues.[6] To be explanatory, of course, virtue must be intelligible independently of the notion of right conduct. That requirement would be violated by the Rawlsian definition of the virtues as attachments to the principles of right.

But I have formulated the thesis too narrowly, for it should also encompass terms of appraisal besides 'right'. It should include more generally the concepts that fall under the heading of 'morally good conduct'. An ethics of virtue is not a particular claim about the priority of virtue over right conduct but the more general claim that action appraisal is derivative from the appraisal of character. To put it another way, the claim is that the basic moral facts are facts about the quality of character. Moral facts about action are ancillary to these.

Indeed, some recent writers have been deeply distrustful of the general notions of moral right and wrong; they question whether there *are* any facts about right and wrong of the kind that moral philosophers want to explain. They recommend the *replacement* of talk about moral right and wrong with talk about the virtues. As G. E. M. Anscombe puts it, 'It would be a great improvement if, instead of "morally wrong," one always named a genus such as "untruthful," "unchaste," "unjust." We should no longer ask whether doing something was "wrong," passing directly from some description of an action to this notion; we should ask whether, e.g., it was unjust; and the answer would sometimes be clear at once'.[7]

I shall extend the interpretation of the thesis of explanatory priority to accommodate replacement views. This is admittedly a stretch, since on the most radical view, virtue concepts achieve priority by default. (Unless otherwise noted, when I speak of the claim of explanatory primacy hereafter I mean to include both the reductionist and the replacement interpretations.)

## 5.

If 'right' and 'wrong' are contrary predicates, then the thesis of explanatory primacy commits ethics of virtue (in their nonreplacement versions) to a kind of harmony among the virtues. If it were possible for someone to act in accordance with one virtue while acting contrary to another, one's conduct would in that case be both right and wrong. This implication can be avoided if no virtue can be exercised in a way that is contrary to another. In this way, ethics of virtue is naturally led to embrace a historically controversial thesis.[8]

The controversy is avoided altogether by rejecting the idea that 'right' and 'wrong' are contraries. It might also be avoided by a sufficiently radical replacement view. The view would have to replace not only 'right' and 'wrong' but also 'proper' and 'improper', 'licit' and 'illicit', for these too seem to be contraries.

## 6.

Another tenet often associated with ethics of virtue is uncodifiability, that is, that there are no formulas that can serve as exact and detailed guides for action. Aristotle expresses this idea in the following passage: 'How far and how much we must deviate to be blamed is not easy to define in an account; for nothing perceptible is easily defined, and [since] these [circumstances of virtuous and vicious actions] are particulars, the judgment about them depends on perception' (*Nicomachean Ethics* 1109a21f).[9] I shall confine myself to three general remarks on this idea.

First, this thesis is difficult to evaluate because codifiability seems to be a matter of degree. On the one hand, there are true moral generalizations about conduct, as even the proponents of uncodifiability should agree; on the other hand, the most rigid codifiers should concede that judgment is necessary for interpreting and applying any rules and principles. The uncodifiability thesis is supposed to be opposed to classical utilitarian and Kantian formulas, although these are far from exact and detailed. So it is unclear what counts as too much codification.

In the second place, uncodifiability is not strictly a corollary of an ethics of virtue. It is not incompatible with explanatory primacy to suppose that right action could be determined according to a clear and definite general criterion. If it could be shown that some principle of right action could somehow be derived from and explained by the conditions for being a virtuous human being, then the resulting view would still deserve to be called an ethics of virtue. Such a derivation would be perfectly consistent with the claim of explanatory primacy. Right action is acting in accordance with the virtues, but it might turn out that some principle(s), even the principle of utility or the categorical imperative, characterises what the virtues would lead a person to do.

In this connection, it is sometimes said that in an ethics of principles or duties, it is the principles or duties that tell you what to do, whereas in an ethics of virtue, it is virtue that tells you what to do. So it might be supposed that if such principles were available (if morality were codifiable), virtue would lose this distinctive role. This thought seems to me to be somewhat confused. In the sense in which a principle can tell one what to do, namely by expressing or implying a prescriptive conclusion about action, a virtue cannot tell anything. A virtue is not a proposition one can consult or apply or interpret; it does not in the same sense prescribe any course of action. Only something like a principle can do that. On the other hand, one's virtues may enable one to endorse, apprehend, correctly apply, or disregard some principle of action. But they will also have this role in an ethics of consequences or requirement. The principle of utility may tell agents what to do, but it is their virtue that leads them to listen, interpret, and to follow.

I conclude that the uncodifiability thesis is not something to which every version of an ethics of virtue is committed. Nonetheless (and this is my third point), the relation between uncodifiability and ethics of virtue is not merely an accidental association. One of the main impetuses for the recent resurgence of interest in ethics of virtue, I suspect, is the sense that the enterprise of articulating principles of right has failed. On the Rawlsian view, that failure leaves the concept of virtue (as attachment to the right) altogether at sea. The content of virtue, if it has any, would have to come from somewhere else. One of the appeals of ethics of virtue, I conjecture, is that it promises a nonsceptical response to the failure of codification.

## 7.

An alternative response to the failure of codification is traditional intuitionism. We have just seen that uncodifiability is not necessarily a tenet of an ethics of virtue. Since that thesis is compatible with the right being prior to the good, it is even more clearly not sufficient for an ethics of virtue. Some intuitionists may think of virtue(s) as attachment(s) to right conduct, as intuitively apprehended in particular circumstances, or perhaps better as capacities for discernment and commitment to right conduct. More generally, if intuitionism is defined as any nonsceptical view of right conduct that rejects codifiability, then some ethics of virtue are species of intuitionism.[10] More familiar members of the genus would be distinguished by their acceptance of a different direction of priority between the concepts of right and virtue.

Because of the preferred direction of priority of an ethics of virtue, its theoretical power clearly depends upon its theory of virtue. Once more, the concept of proper or right conduct will be well understood only if the concept of virtue is. Though some will hold that we can understand what the virtues are and how they are expressed without the benefit of any general theory,[11] the thesis of explanatory primacy will then be quite gratuitous. If the alleged priority cannot be established by an account, in this case a theory of virtue, then the distinction between virtue intuitionism and act intuitionism seems merely to be nominal. I question whether 'prior' has any sense here whatever.

To be interesting and, I suspect, even to be meaningful, the priority claim has to occur as part of a theory of virtue. I shall take it, then, that an ethics of virtue will have two components:

(a)  Some version of the claim of explanatory primacy

(b)  A theory of virtue

My aim in the remainder of this chapter is to explore some of the difficulties of developing (b) in a way that does not compromise the distinctive character of an ethics of virtue.

## 8.

The most familiar versions of (b) are theories of an Aristotelian kind.[12] An Aristotelian ethics of virtue will look something like this:

(1) *The claim of explanatory primacy*  Right and proper conduct is conduct that is contrary to no virtue (does not exemplify a vice). Good conduct is conduct that displays a virtue. Wrong or improper conduct is conduct that is contrary to some virtue (or exemplifies a vice).

(2) *The theory of virtue*  Virtues are (a subset of the) human excellences, that is, those traits that enable one to live a characteristically human life, or to live in accordance with one's nature as a human being.

I shall not pause to consider the content of (2). It is, of course, the merest gesture towards a certain type of naturalism. What interests me at this point is the contrast with another theory in which (2) is replaced with (2′):

(1)  As before

(2′)  A virtue is a human trait the possession of which tends to promote human happiness more than the possession of alternative traits.

As with (2), this formulation is oversimplified. The view it oversimplifies is often called *character utilitarianism*.[13] This theory has the same structure as the Aristotelian one. The only difference comes from the second component. Is it too an ethics of virtue?

## 9.

But if character utilitarianism is an ethics of virtue, we have not succeeded in identifying an ethics of a third kind. To see this, recall my earlier suggestion that the three central concepts of moral philosophy correspond to the three distinct types of theory that take one of these as basic: ethics of requirement, ethics of consequences, and ethics of virtue or character. Plainly, character utilitarianism belongs in the second category.[14] Even though character utilitarianism differs from its cousins in not taking the consequences of actions as the direct standard of appraisal for those actions – and hence is not consequentialist in Rawls' sense[15] – the value of the outcome of possessing and exercising certain traits is the ultimate standard of all other value. It shares with act utilitarianism the idea that the most fundamental notion is that of a good consequence or state of affairs, namely, human happiness. For these reasons, it seems better to call this general class of theories *ethics of outcome*.

In these terms the problem will be to see how to avoid classifying ethics of virtue as a species of ethics of outcome. For will not the ultimate standard of appraisal on Aristotelian theories be the idea of living properly as a human being, that is, flourishing, from which the value of virtue is derived?

The three types of theories are distinguished by what they take the fundamental moral facts to be: facts about what we are required to do, about the intrinsic or ultimate value of possible outcomes, or about people's desires, ends and dispositions. An ethics of virtue, at least of the Aristotelian kind I have considered, will have a theory that explains the significance of various constituents of character by reference to certain necessities and desiderata of human life, in which case the basic moral facts would be facts about what is constitutively and instrumentally needed for that way of life, facts, in short, about flourishing.

The problem, then, appears to be this: any ethics of virtue that lacks a theory of virtue will be nonexplanatory[16] but any ethics of virtue that has such a theory will collapse into an ethics of outcome. If that is so, then Rawls' classification has not been seriously challenged.

The independence of an ethics of virtue as a type of theory distinct from character utilitarianism and other ethics of outcome must depend on the special character of its theory of good. I shall consider two proposed accounts of this special character. On the first explanation, what distinguishes the Aristotelian view from character utilitarianism is its conception of virtues as constitutive of, not merely instrumental to, flourishing. This difference is conspicuous, but on the second account the difference is deeper. It is not merely that an ethics of virtue employs a different theory of what is ultimately good from that of character utilitarianism; it is that an ethics of virtue does not have that kind of theory of good at all.

## 10.

On the first account, what distinguishes an ethics of virtue from character utilitarianism is that it takes human excellence to be at least partially constitutive of flourishing, not just instrumental. Now if there were other constituents of flourishing, it would be arbitrary to make the theory the namesake of virtue. (It should then be called an ethics of virtue plus whatever else constitutes flourishing.) Thus virtue must be construed as the sole or somehow primary constituent of flourishing, as it was by Socrates. The resultant theory construes the basic moral facts to be facts about virtue.

Here the proposed contrast turns on the theory of value rather than on the claim of explanatory primacy. As I have construed it so far, the claim of explanatory primacy asserts the primacy of virtue over action appraisal. The theory as a whole must also establish the primacy of virtue over other values. On character utilitarianism, virtues are so identified because of their relation to independent values such as happiness. According to the first account, then, an ethics of virtue must imply, in all of its components, that human excellence is the sole or at least primary constituent of what is intrinsically valuable.

## 11.

This is an appealing account of the difference. And such a view is naturally called an ethics of virtue. Nevertheless, I doubt that this account succeeds in identifying a theory of the third kind, that is, of a kind that contrasts with both an ethics of requirement and an ethics of outcome.

Character utilitarianism is disqualified as an ethics of virtue because the facts it takes to be morally basic are not facts about virtue. However, it is not enough just to meet this qualification. For consider a restricted version of what Rawls calls perfectionism, which enjoins us to promote the development and exercise of virtue, these being intrinsically good.[17] This view meets the above qualifications, but if it is an ethics of virtue, it is so only in the way in which utilitarianism is an ethics of happiness or welfare. What fills in the blank in 'an ethics of –' merely indicates the kinds of intrinsically valuable facts or states of affairs that are taken as basic. Different terms yield different versions of ethics of outcome.

Thus if the view I have been investigating is an ethics of virtue because it takes virtue as the ultimate value, then so is perfectionism, which is an ethics of outcome. To be sure, perfectionism differs from what I have been calling an ethics of virtue in its rejection of the claim of explanatory primacy. And so it might be suggested that both an 'areteic' theory of value and an 'areteic' theory of right are necessary and sufficient for an ethics of virtue. According to this suggestion, an ethics of virtue stands to perfectionism as character utilitarianism stands to act utilitarianism: each pair has the same theory of good but a different theory of right.

To disqualify perfectionism as an ethics of virtue because it does not hold the claim of explanatory primacy is superficial. For unlike character utilitarianism, which in its theory of virtue goes against the grain of the primacy of virtue, the perfectionist theory of right and theory of good both hold virtue supreme. Taken together, they enjoin the fullest realisation of virtue in character and action. A consequentialist theory of right is only a schema without a theory of good. When that theory is areteic, so is the theory of right. Questions of classification are, of course, relative to purpose. But for the reasons just mentioned, the kinship of perfectionism and Aristotelianism (as conceived on the first account) seems to me much closer than the relationship of character utilitarianism to either.

## 12.

Unlike perfectionism, of course, an ethics of virtue as so far conceived is not consequentialist (in the prevalent narrow sense). But nor, as we have seen, is character utilitarianism. Consequentialist theories in the narrower sense belong to a wider class of theories that share a certain scheme of value according to which the ultimate standard of appraisal is provided by states of affairs or outcomes deemed to be intrinsically good or desirable on their own. I have been calling this wider class of theories ethics of outcome, which are characterised neither by their theories of right (which may or may not be consequentialist) nor by the specific content of their theories of good (which may range from pleasure to excellence of character) but by their appeal to this kind of scheme.

The first account of an ethics of virtue makes it a kind of ethics of outcome that is like perfectionism in its appraisal of outcomes but like character utilitarianism in the form of its conception of right conduct. I now turn to the second account, which holds that an ethics of virtue is not an ethics of outcome at all.

## 13.

We may depict the appraisal of conduct on an (Aristotelian) ethics of virtue with the following schema:

1. Living a characteristically human life (functioning well as a human being) requires possessing and exemplifying certain traits, $T$.
2. $T$ are therefore human excellences and render their possessors to that extent good human beings.
3. Acting in way $W$ is in accordance with $T$ (or exemplifies or is contrary to $T$).
4. Therefore, $W$ is right (good or wrong).

Here there is an appeal to several notions of good: to functioning well as a human being, to being a good human being, to being a human excellence (perhaps also to being good for one as a human being). But at no stage need there be an essential appeal to the idea of a valuable state of affairs or outcome from which the moral significance of everything (or anything) else derives.

To be sure, a concern for outcomes will be internal to certain virtues. For instance, the benevolent person will be concerned that others fare well. But the moral significance of this concern stems from the fact that it is part of a virtue, not from the fact that misery and wellbeing are intrinsically or ultimately bad and good respectively. To put it another way, it will follow from an ethics of virtue that virtuous people care about certain things (and outcomes) for their own sakes (as final ends in themselves). There is no further commitment, however, to the idea that these concerns are virtuous ones because their objects are inherently valuable or desirable for their own sakes.[18]

Nor, more generally, is there a foundational role for the idea that living a characteristic human life is intrinsically good. Perhaps it will follow from the theory that the virtuous person *will* desire to live such a life for its own sake, and in that sense such a life can be said to be desirable for its own sake (the virtuous person being the standard), but that will be because such a desire is part of human excellence, rather than the other way around. That appraisal is made from the standpoint of virtue and is not its basis.

It may be useful to compare a theory of excellence for a nonhuman animal. The judgment that a lack of attention to her cubs is an imperfection in a mother tiger (though not in the father) is based upon a notion of a good specimen of tiger. This idea in turn depends upon what is normal for or characteristic of tigers. None of these judgments is mediated by any notion of the value of a tiger's living a life characteristic of its species. On an ethics of virtue, the same goes for people. The specific excellences will be different, of course. Moreover, for us but not for tigers there may be a point to a distinction between virtues and other excellences.

What is liable to be confusing on this account is that faring well, for example, plays a double role in this view, first in the theory of virtue, where virtues are identified in part by their contribution to a characteristic human life, and second in the theory of good, where living such a life may be among the final ends of morally admirable individuals. The distinctive feature of an ethics of virtue on the second account is that the evaluation of such a life as a final end is derivative from, rather than foundational to, the theory of virtue. On the first account, the theory of virtue is dependent on a theory of the ultimate good. On the second account, the theory of ultimate good is dependent on the theory of virtue.[19] (Hence, the fact that virtues are identified as such by their 'instrumental' properties does not make them of instrumental value.)

Whatever one may think of the prospects for an ethics of virtue, this last point seems to me to be of some importance for moral philosophy. For it shows the way in which one can assert a systematic connection between virtues and other goods without undermining the autonomy of virtue. In an outcome ethics that recognises these goods, it is notoriously difficult to explain satisfactorily why they should not be of paramount moral concern (at least ideally), that is, how there can properly be restrictions on consequentialist reasoning. On an outcome ethics, such restrictions can never seem fully enlightened. (Hence the appearance of paradox or irrationality in 'indirect' forms of consequentialism.) On an ethics of virtue, however, there is not even the appearance of a problem, for the value of virtue is not said to come from the value of anything else at all. Although it is a teleological view, an ethics of virtue can acknowledge 'deontological' reasons without paradox, because it is not an ethics of outcome.[20]

In summary, on the first account, an ethics of virtue is a species of ethics of outcome, distinguished from character utilitarianism by the fact that it takes virtue and its exercise to be the sole ultimate value and from perfectionism by the fact that it does not give a consequentialist definition of right action. On this view, Rawls is right in the end to think that moral theories come in two fundamental kinds, namely (in my terminology) ethics of requirement and ethics of outcome. What his scheme overlooks is that ethics of outcome can take both a consequentialist and nonconsequentialist form.

On the second account, what Rawls' scheme overlooks is more significant. Ethics of virtue contrast importantly with both ethics of outcome and ethics of requirement. The first two are teleological in that the primary notion is a notion of goodness, but they differ in the kind of theory of good that is employed. On the first account, act utilitarianism, character utilitarianism, perfectionism and ethics of virtue are merely structural variations of an ethics of outcome. But on the second account, it is not that ethics of virtue have a different view of what outcomes are good but rather that they do not employ this notion at the foundation of the theory. The result is a teleological theory that has not received much attention or even recognition. For this reason, only the second account seems to me to identify a distinctive, third kind of moral theory.

Furthermore, only the second account yields a theory that is at bottom truly naturalistic. Admittedly, what is valuable on the first account is the natural (what belongs to human nature). But so long as the theory relies upon a primitive idea of the intrinsically or ultimately valuable outcome, the conception of value remains ungrounded. In contrast, valuable outcomes are understood on the second account by reference to the concerns of those who exemplify human nature.

## 14.

By rejecting outcomes as the foundational standards of appraisal, ethics of virtue are, of course, allied with ethics of requirement. I complained in section 2 that the identification of teleological and consequentialist theories forces us wrongly to classify ethics of virtue as deontological. What we have now seen is that if teleological theories are those in which appraisals are guided ultimately by some notion of the good, then there are (at least) two kinds of teleological theory: those based on the notion of a good outcome and those based on the notion of good of (and for) a kind.

As I have remarked, ethics of virtue will, of course, be deontological on Rawls' negative characterisation, namely, as nonconsequentialism. But if a deontological view holds more positively that 'it is sometimes wrong to do what will produce the best available outcome overall',[21] then it will not do to think of an ethics of virtue as deontological. For on this characterisation, deontological views share with consequentialism the assumption that there is a coherent and acceptable way of defining 'best available outcome overall' independently of the notion of right and wrong action. But an ethics of virtue is not committed to this assumption.[22]

Nor need an ethics of requirement accept this assumption. Kant, for one, would have rejected it, though he is the first to come to most people's minds when they think of 'deontologists'. For Kant, it may indeed turn out to be wrong to do what would in the circumstances produce the greatest overall satisfaction of desire (or to maximise any specified kind of effect), but that will not be, for Kant, a case in which acting wrongly would produce the best overall outcome. The satisfaction of desire has no value whatever when it conflicts with the moral law.

Instead of defining 'deontological theory' in either of the ways just considered, it seems best simply to use it synonymously with 'ethics of requirement', a usage that is in accordance with its etymology. This type of theory, as I have said, is one that takes the notion of requirement as primary to the concepts of virtue and valuable outcome. But what this means more precisely remains to be clarified. Presumably, Kant's moral philosophy, which attempts to understand moral phenomena in terms of the requirements stemming from the conditions on free agency, is to be included, as is the minimal theory of Prichard, according to which we intuitively apprehend facts about duties and obligations. One would also expect contractualism to fall under this heading. It construes moral phenomena in terms of the requirements implicit in the conditions for mutually acceptable social life. But perhaps all that these views have in common is that they are *not* teleological in either of the two ways I have identified. Is there another way? Until we understand these theories better, we cannot say.[23]

## 15.

Despite a renewal of interest in Aristotelian ideas, ethics of virtue continue to prompt a lot of resistance. Perhaps it is worthwhile briefly to indicate why.

Many of our modern suspicions can be put in the form of a dilemma. Either the theory's pivotal account of human nature (or characteristic human life) will be morally indeterminate, or it will not be objectively well founded. At best, an objectively well-founded theory of human nature would support evaluations of the kind that we can make about tigers – that this one is a good or bad specimen, that that behaviour is abnormal. These judgments might be part of a theory of *health*, but our conception of morality resists the analogy with health, the reduction of evil to defect. (This resistance has something to do, I suspect, with a conception of free will that resists all forms of naturalism.) An objective account of human nature would imply, perhaps, that a good human life must be social in character. This implication will disqualify the sociopath but not the Hell's Angel. The contrast is revealing, for we tend to regard the sociopath not as evil but as beyond the pale of morality. On the other hand, if we enrich our conception of sociality to exclude Hell's Angels, the worry is that this conception will no longer ground moral judgment but rather express it.

A related but distinct complaint concerns moral motivation. Even if we grant that we can derive determinate appraisals of conduct from an objective description of what is characteristic of the species, why should we care about those appraisals? Why should we care about living distinctively human lives rather than living like pigs or gangsters? Why is it worthwhile for us to have those particular virtues at the cost of alternative lives they preclude? There are two sorts of scepticism here.

1. Can an objective theory really establish that being a gangster is incompatible with being a good human being?
2. If it can, can it establish an intelligible connection between those appraisals and what we have reasons to do as individuals?

To answer 2 by saying 'Because we are human beings' is obscure. For we are (or can be) these other things as well. 'Our humanity is inescapable,' it might be replied, 'whereas we can choose whether or not to be a Hell's Angel'.[24] The force of this reply is unclear, however, for we *can* choose whether to live a *good* (that is, characteristic) human life.

However, the point might be that we are human beings *by nature* and not these other things, and our nature determines what descriptions are essential. A good gangster is a bad human being and for that reason fails to fare well. Defective or non-virtuous human beings are worse off for that. They are not merely bad human beings but *they* are badly off as individuals, and if they acquired virtue, they would not only be better human beings but also be better off than they would have been otherwise. Whether we are flourishing depends on who (what) we are by nature. Since we are essentially human, the description 'bad human being' dominates the description 'good gangster' in appraisals of wellbeing.

Such evaluational essentialism does not sit well with modern notions. Just as God is dead, it will be said, so the concept of human nature has ceased to be normative. We can no more recover the necessary-world view of the ancients than we can revitalise the Judeo-Christian tradition. But an ethics of virtue need not take this essentialist line. It could say instead that we care about being good human beings because or insofar as we are good human beings. Insofar as we are not, we don't (at least in the virtuous way). If we don't, then we will not flourish as human beings, though we might do very well as thieves. There is no further question to be answered here about wellbeing.

These seem to me to be the main worries and issues that must be faced before we can determine the prospects for an ethics of virtue. There is much to be said about what an objective account of human nature is supposed to be, as well as about the supposed disanalogies with health and about issues of motivational internalism.[25] In this section I have tried merely to indicate some of the more troublesome questions.[26]

## 16.

I began with a complaint about one of Rawls' distinctions. I shall conclude by endorsing another. In 'The Independence of Moral Theory' Rawls characterises moral theory as the systematic comparison of moral conceptions, in other words, 'the study of how the basic notions of the right, the good, and moral worth may be arranged to form different moral structures'.[27] He rightly emphasises the importance of such a study quite independent of the question of which moral conception is correct. He believes that 'the further advance of moral philosophy depends upon a deeper understanding of the structure of moral conceptions' and urges that 'all the main conceptions in the tradition of moral philosophy must be continually renewed: we must try to strengthen their formulation by noting the criticisms that are exchanged and by incorporating in each the advances of the others, so far as this is possible. In this endeavor the aim of those most attracted to a particular view should be not to confute but to perfect'.[28]

This chapter is intended to be a contribution to 'moral theory' in Rawls' sense. My complaint has been that Rawls' twofold classification stymies the recently renewed examination of ethics of virtue by obscuring its distinctive character. We should not be indifferent to this consequence, even if we suspect that nowadays an ethics of virtue is not something that we are going to be able to live with philosophically. For the distinctive features of this moral conception (or set of conceptions) might reveal theoretical possibilities that will help us eventually to fashion something in which we can feel more at home.[29]

## ENDNOTES

1. J. Rawls, *A Theory of Justice*, Cambridge, Massachusetts: Harvard University Press (1971), 24.
2. Ibid., 436.
3. Ibid., 24. If maximising is understood causally, as Rawls pretty clearly construes it, then the independence clause is implied by the definition. $E$ cannot be said to maximise or produce $G$ unless $G$ is definable independently from $E$.
4. I agree with John Cooper: 'In Aristotle's theory, human good *consists* (partly) in virtuous action, so his theory, while decidedly not teleological in the modern [consequentialist] sense, is also not deontological either' (1975, 88). See Note 24 for a further discussion of Aristotle.
5. Rawls' treatment of the three main concepts of moral theory might seem infelicitous in another way. The concept of moral worth is the concept of a kind of goodness of persons. If it is derivative at all, how could this concept fail to be derived from the concept of the good, since it is an instance of that concept? The answer, I think, is that here Rawls is thinking of the concept of the good needed for consequentialist theories, the concept of a good state of affairs or outcome. See Note 17.
6. At least the negative half of the primacy thesis – that wrong action is to be construed as behaviour that exemplifies a vice or is contrary to a virtue – is endorsed by James Wallace:

'It is a plausible thesis generally that the faulty actions philosophers lump under the heading of "morally wrong" are actions fully characteristic of some vice' (1978, 59).

The relation between action appraisal and character appraisal is complicated and is different for different terms of appraisal. My formulations of the primacy claim suggests that the rightness or wrongness of an action depends upon its explanation (in the person's motive or character). However, we often appraise a prospective action as the right or wrong thing to do without appraising anyone's character. We need not refer to someone's motives or character to judge that it would be wrong for her not to return a lost wallet. This observation indicates the oversimplifications of the formulations of the primacy thesis in the text. An adequate formulation would distinguish, for example, between the appraisals '*P* acted rightly or wrongly in doing *a*', and 'It would be wrong (for *P*) to do *a*' or 'What *P* did was the right (or wrong) thing', and it would show how all of these appraisals are implicated with standards of virtue. It might show, for example, that the standard for the right thing to do is what the morally good person would do but also that whether one acts rightly or wrongly in doing the right thing depends on one's reasons and hence on the explanation of one's behaviour (or what it displays about one's character). When particular formulations of the primacy thesis are given in the text, the reader should bear these complications in mind.

A mixed view is also possible here: that priority holds in the case of some virtues and not others. I shall ignore this possibility.

7. Anscombe 1981, 33. I do not assert here that Anscombe is adopting an ethics of virtue. One could hold a version of the replacement thesis – that 'right' and 'wrong' should be replaced by 'unjust', 'cowardly' etc. – without holding that the latter terms can be explained in terms of character. In several forums Richard Taylor has recommended a radical version of the replacement thesis. He advanced this view in his lecture at the Conference on Virtue at the University of San Diego, February 1986. See also Taylor 1985.

8. This commitment is not peculiar to ethics of virtue. If the explanatory relation between virtue and right conduct were reversed, if, for example, a virtue were a kind of sensitivity to proper conduct within a certain sphere, then arguably the harmony thesis would follow as well. For this kind of argument, see McDowell 1979.

9. Aristotle, *Nicomachean Ethics* (1109a21f).

10. Radical replacement theories neither accept nor reject codifiability, since this question presupposes the applicability of the concepts they wish to abandon.

11. In the lecture referred to in Note 6 Taylor opposes theory of this kind.

12. For the most part my discussion will be confined to roughly Aristotelian versions. See Note 24 for a brief discussion of a non-Aristotelian alternative.

13. See Adams 1976. One glaring oversimplification is this. Virtues are obviously only a subset of optimising traits. Another point is that optimising traits cannot be determined in isolation from other traits possessed by the agent. This last point is not so easily met.

14. My concern, of course, is not with utilitarianism in particular but with consequentialism in general. There are as many different theories of this kind as there are kinds of valuable consequences that virtue(s) might foster.

15. The limits of Rawls' taxonomy is further revealed in its application to this case. Because of (1) and because character utilitarianism does not define the right as what maximises the good, Rawls' scheme counts that view (along with all nonact forms of consequentialism) as deontological.

16. To charge intuitionism with being nonexplanatory is not an honest objection to this view, for the 'objection' is precisely what intuitionism asserts: that there are no explanations of the kind we seek. This is no problem for the theory if the theory is true. So the charge begs the question. It is a 'problem' only for those who wish more. So this charge (as a charge) has to be seen as an expression of one's conviction that this assertion is unreasonable. The burden will be on one who makes this charge to produce the relevant account.

17. Rawls' scheme cannot accommodate perfectionism as readily as Rawls supposes. The theory that we are to maximise excellence (where virtues are understood as human excellences) is clearly a teleological view. But it is not one in which the concept of moral worth is derived from the other concepts of the good and the right. Unlike other forms of consequentialism, perfectionism cannot accept Rawls' definition of virtues as 'normally effective desires to act on the basic principles of right' (1971, 436). To avoid circularity (virtue is a commitment to maximise virtue) and to yield a teleological theory, virtues must be independently defined.

On the other hand, perfectionism is not a view in which the concept of virtue is derived from the good. On this view, virtue *is* the good.

18. Christine Korsgaard (1983) has pointed out the importance of the difference between the concept of the intrinsically good and the concept of what is desirable in itself. For my purposes here, however, I do not think it matters which way I put it. An ethics of outcome may be stated either way. On the second account, an ethics of virtue has no use for the former and explains the latter by appeal to the desires of the virtuous person.

19. This constitutes my reply to a problem posed at the end of section 9 above. Insofar as virtues must in the end be characterised by their contribution to the good for human beings, that notion of the good will be primary relative to virtue. But there would still be a point to thinking of the theory under consideration as an ethics of virtue, since virtue remains basic relative to concepts of right and a good state of affairs. In the classification to which I refer at the beginning, I suspect that Rawls understands the concept of the good in that context as what is ultimately worth choosing, aiming at, seeking – that is, in effect, as the finally good outcome. So understood, on the theory I am trying to describe, virtue is prior to *that* notion, and so the priority claim is maintained. See Note 4.

20. For more on deontological reasons, see the next section. My discussion here is obviously influenced by the work of Philippa Foot (1985). Foot urges that the basic feature of consequentialism is that it employs the idea of 'the best overall state of affairs'. While I know of no work in which she characterises the distinctive features of ethics of virtue as I suggest here, this characterisation fits well with the writings I have seen.

21. Scheffler 1982, 2. This is his initial characterisation of 'standard deontological views'. He goes on to say, 'In other words, these views incorporate what I shall call "agent-centred restrictions": restrictions on action which have the effect of denying that there is any non-agent-relative principle for ranking overall states of affairs from best to worst such that it is always permissible to produce the best available state of affairs so characterised'. What follows 'in other words' is not equivalent to what precedes it. An ethics of virtue will be deontological in the former sense but not in the latter.

22. See once again Foot 1985.

23. It follows from my discussion that one cannot tell whether a theory belongs to one of these types by consulting the content of its requirements or proscriptions. Conceivably, a particular version of an ethics of virtue may conclude that there is but a single virtue, the concern to produce the greatest good for the greatest number or to act only on maxims that could become universal laws for all rational beings. The same goes for contractualism; it could be argued that utilitarianism or Kantianism gives the content of the basic agreement. Moreover, many an ethics of outcome has argued for a role for 'deontological constraints' in vouchsafing their favourite states of affairs. What makes these theories what they are is not their practical implications but their premises.

24. For this reply, see Wallace 1978, 43–4.

25. Foot has recently explored these questions in an illuminating set of lectures, which remain, as far as I know, unpublished.

26. Did Aristotle have an ethics of virtue in the sense I have been after? The text intimates in several places that he did have, that since his theory does not comply with Rawls' scheme, it is a model for the third kind of theory I have been seeking. Surely my formulation of the second component of the theory is rightly named after Aristotle, but there is textual evidence that he did not countenance the first component, that is, the claim of explanatory primacy. The evidence I have in mind comes from the doctrine of the mean. That doctrine is a thesis about what a virtue is, namely, a state of character that is 'a mean between two vices, one of excess and one of deficiency'. The trouble arises when Aristotle goes on to say that this state is a mean '*because* it aims at the intermediate condition in feelings and action' (*Nicomachean Ethics* 1109a22–32). Again, 'Virtue is a mean insofar as it aims at what is intermediate' (1106b28).

Such passages as these show how an intuitionist such as W. D. Ross could have found Aristotle's views so congenial. If these remarks on the mean are put together with Aristotle's remarks on uncodifiability, we get the basic intuitionist picture. If Aristotle held an ethics of virtue, one would have expected him to have said that action and desire are 'intermediate', when they are, in that (because) they manifest a medial disposition. (So Aristotle is construed by Urmson, who does not consider these contrary texts.) What he said instead implies that states of character are virtues, when they are, because of the qualities of the actions and desires in which they issue.

In view of the complexity of Aristotle's texts, I do not find these passages to be conclusive. The issue must be discussed in the context of a reading of Aristotle's work as a whole. The bearing of Aristotle's treatment of *eudaimonia* in *Nicomachean Ethics*, Book 1, and of the discussion of practical reason in Book 6 are also important to consider. It is not clear, for instance, how to think of the aim of practical reason on an ethics of virtue. Doesn't the practically wise individual *get it right*, and can we make sense of this without reference to a standard independent of virtue? What does the individual get right, according to an ethics of virtue? (I am grateful to Gloria Rock for pressing this point in conversation.)

Meanwhile, it is somewhat disconcerting not to be able to adduce here a single clear instance of a historically important ethics of virtue in the sense I have identified. (Of course, Aquinas should be considered in this connection as well.)

My second question is this. In view of the problems engendered by the appeal to human nature, are there alternatives to Aristotelian versions of ethics of virtue? Aristotelian formulations are most familiar, but there are also hints in contemporary discussions of the possibility of a *tradition-based* theory, a theory in which the concept of tradition somehow does the work that the concept of human nature does in the Aristotelian view. (See, for example, Larmore 1987; MacIntyre 1981; Wallace 1988. As far as I can tell, none of these writers explicitly adopts the view I sketch below.) Let me consider briefly some of the questions raised by this idea.

The idea of a tradition-based view might be expressed as follows. Morality is radically underdetermined by the abstract and universal notion of human nature employed in Aristotelian views. To be sure, nature places boundary conditions on culture, but by itself it yields no definite content for the moral life. That content can come only from particular cultures and traditions. (Although they are clearly not synonymous, I will use 'culture' and 'tradition' interchangeably here.) To put it another way, what is characteristically human is to be initiated into a shared way of life. Human nature must be made determinate by socialisation.

So far these ideas do not suffice for an ethics of virtue. To do so, they have to be conjoined with something like the following thesis: that proper behaviour (acting, feeling and thinking properly) is acting in accordance with the virtues as these are specified and interpreted in a person's ideals that are implicit in the culture.

I am not prepared to pursue this matter further here. I shall confine myself to two observations. First, most obviously, culture-based and nature-based views need not be exclusive. Nature might determine the sorts of things that are virtues for human beings, while culture determines the specific content. This conception would allow for cultural variation within a general nature-based ideal of the human being. (See Hampshire 1983.)

The second observation is this. It may be illuminating to subsume ethics of virtue, in either a culture-based or a nature-based version, under 'self-realisation' ethics. That is to say, acting properly is acting in accordance with those traits that express or realise one's self, nature or identity. Whether one is faring well depends, as I said, upon what one is. Nature-based and tradition-based views can be seen at the extremes as giving different answers to the question of what is central to human identity. On a nature-based view, one's identity is cast by one's 'species-being', so to speak, whereas on the tradition-based version, the self is more particular to its culture. As I just suggested, however, this is a false opposition on the sensible view that human nature is bound up with culture. If human nature is to live in and in accordance with a tradition, then tradition-based ethics of virtue is a form of nature-based ethics of virtue.

27. J. Rawls, 'The Independence of Moral Theory', *Proceedings and Addresses of the American Philosophical Association* 48 (1975), 5.

28. Ibid., 22.

29. This chapter originated in a brief panel presentation at a conference on virtue theory at the University of San Diego in February 1986. I am grateful to the director, Lawrence Hinman, for inviting me. I am also grateful to members of the Moral and Political Philosophy Society of Southern California and to the Philosophy Department at the University of California at Riverside for helpful discussions of earlier drafts of the paper, in particular, to David Estlund, Craig Ihara, Gloria Rock, Gerry Santas and Paul Weithman. Thanks are also due, finally, to Owen Flanagan and to Amélie Rorty.

## BIBLIOGRAPHY

Adams, E. M. (1975) *Philosophy and the Modern Mind*, Chapel Hill: University of North Carolina Press. (Reprinted by University Press of America, Washington, DC, 1985.)

Adams, R. M. (1976) 'Motive utilitarianism', *Journal of Philosophy* 73: 467–81.

Adams, R. M. (1985) 'Involuntary sins', *Philosophical Review* 94: 3–31.

Amir, M. (1971) *Patterns in Forcible Rape*, Chicago: University of Chicago Press.

Annis, David B. (1987) 'The meaning, value, and duties of friendship', *American Philosophical Quarterly* 24, 4: 349–56.

Anscombe, G. E. M. (1981) 'Modern moral philosophy', in *The Collected Philosophical Papers of G. E. M. Anscombe* (Vol. 3), Minneapolis: University of Minnesota Press (first published 1958).

Ardal, P. (1966) *Passion and Value in Hume's Treatise*, Edinburgh: Edinburgh University Press.

Aristotle (1925) *Nicomachean Ethics*, translated by W. D. Ross, London: Oxford University Press.

Aristotle (1962) *The Nicomachean Ethics*, translated by M. Ostwald, New York: Library of Liberal Arts.

Aristotle (1963) *Nicomachean Ethics*, Oxford: Oxford University Press.

Aristotle (1984) *Politics* (revised Oxford translation), Princeton: Princeton University Press.

Aristotle (1985) *Nicomachean Ethics*, translated by T. Irwin, Indianapolis: Hackett.

Austin, J. (1873) *Lectures on Jurisprudence*, London: John Murray.

Axelrod, R. (1984) *The Evolution of Cooperation*, New York: Basic Books.

Badhwar, N. K. (1985) 'Friendship, justice, and supererogation', *American Philosophical Quarterly* 22: 123–31.

Baier, A. (1978) 'Hume's analysis of pride', *Journal of Philosophy* 75: 27–40.

Baier, A. (1985a) 'What do women want in a moral theory?' *Noûs* 19: 53–63.

Baier, A. (1985b) *Postures of the Mind: Essays on Mind and Morals*, Minneapolis: University of Minnesota Press.

Baier, A. (1986) 'Trust and antitrust', *Ethics* 96: 231–60.

Baier, A. (1987a) 'Hume, the women's moral theorist?' in E. F. Kittay and D. T. Meyers (eds), *Women and Moral Theory*, Totowa, New Jersey: Littlefield, Adams.

Baier, A. (1987b) 'The need for more than justice', in M. Hanen and K. Nielsen (eds), *Science, Morality, and Feminist Theory*, Calgary: University of Calgary.

Baier, A. (1988) 'Critical notice of C. Taylor', *Philosophy and the Human Sciences: Philosophical Papers*, Vol. 2, *Canadian Journal of Philosophy* 18: 589–94.

Baron, M. (1984) 'The alleged moral repugnance of acting from duty', *Journal of Philosophy* 81: 197–219.

Baron, M. (1988) 'Remorse and agent-regret', in P. A. French, T. E. Uehling and H. K. Wettstein (eds), *Midwest Studies in Philosophy*, Vol. 13, *Ethical Theory: Character and Virtue*, Notre Dame: Notre Dame University Press.

Bellah, R., Madsen, R., Sullivan, W., Swidler, A. and Tipton, S. (1985) *Habits of the Heart: Individualism and Commitment in American Life*, Berkeley: University of California Press.

Benedict, R. (1934) 'Anthropology and the abnormal', *Journal of General Psychology* 10: 59–82.

Bennett, J. (1974) 'The conscience of Huckleberry Finn', *Philosophy* 49: 123–34.

Berger, P. L. and Luckmann, T. (1966) *The Social Construction of Reality: A Treatise in the Sociology of Knowledge*, New York: Doubleday.

Blum, L. (1980) *Friendship, Altruism, and Morality*, London: Routledge & Kegan Paul.

Blum, L. (1986) 'Iris Murdoch and the domain of the moral', *Philosophical Studies* 50: 343–67.

Blum, L. (1987) 'Particularity and responsiveness', in J. Kagan and S. Lamb (eds), *The Emergence of Morality in Young Children*, Chicago: University of Chicago Press.

Blum, L. (1988a) 'Gilligan and Kohlberg: Implications for moral theory', *Ethics* 98: 472–91.

Blum, L. (1988b) 'Moral exemplars: Reflections on Schindler, the Trocmes, and others', *Midwest Studies in Philosophy*, Vol. 13, *Ethical Theory: Character and Virtue*, Notre Dame: University of Notre Dame Press.

Blum, L. (1991) 'Altruism and the moral value of rescue: Resisting persecution, racism, and genocide', in L. Baron, L. Blum, D. Krebs, P. Oliner, S. Oliner and Z. Smolenska, *Embracing the Other: Philosophical, Psychological, and Historical Perspectives on Altruism*, New York: New York University Press.

Bok, S. (1978) *Lying: Moral Choice in Public and Private Life*, New York: Pantheon Books.
Bowen, M. (1978) *Family Therapy in Clinical Practice*, New York: Jason Aronson.
Bradley, F. H. (1927) *Ethical Studies* (2nd edn), Oxford: Oxford University Press.
Brandt, R. B. (1964) 'The concepts of duty and obligation', *Mind* 73: 373–93.
Brandt, R. B. (1984) 'Utilitarianism and moral rights', *Canadian Journal of Philosophy* 14: 1–19.
Bratman, M. (1985) 'Davidson's theory of intention', in E. LePore and B. McLaughlin 1985.
Brink, D. O. (1986) 'Utilitarian morality and the personal point of view', *Journal of Philosophy* 83: 417–38.
Brink, D. O. (1988) 'Legal theory, legal interpretation, and judicial review', *Philosophy and Public Affairs* 17: 105–48.
Brink, D. O. (1989) *Moral Realism and the Foundations of Ethics*, New York: Cambridge University Press.
Brink, D. O. (1991) 'Sidgwick and the rationale for rational egoism', in B. Schultz (ed.), *Essays on Sidgwick*, New York: Cambridge University Press.
Bruch, H. (1988) *Conversations with Anorexics*, D. Czyzewski and M. A. Suhr (eds), New York: Basic Books.
Buchanan, A. (1977) 'Categorical imperatives and moral principles', *Philosophical Studies* 31: 249–60.
Burton, J. H. (1846) *Life and Correspondence of David Hume* (2 vols), Edinburgh: William Tait.
Burton, R. (1977) *The Anatomy of Melancholia*, New York: Vintage.
Butler, J. (1859) *Bishop Butler's Ethical Discourses and Essay on Virtue*, J. T. Champlin (ed.), Boston: J. P. Jewett & Co.
Butler, J. (1950) *Fifteen Sermons Preached at the Rolls Chapel*, New York: Bobbs Merrill. (Reprinted in S. Darwall (ed.), *Five Sermons*, Hackett, Indianapolis, 1983. First published 1749.)
Butler, S. (1970) *Characters*, Cleveland: Press of Case Western Reserve University.
Card, C. (1972) 'On mercy', *Philosophical Review* 81: 182–207.
Card, C. (1988a) 'Gratitude and obligation', *American Philosophical Quarterly* 25: 115–27.
Card, C. (1988b) 'Lesbian battering', *American Philosophical Association Newsletter on Feminism and Philosophy* 88: 3–7. (Review essay on Lobel 1986.)
Card, C. (1989) 'Defusing the bomb: Lesbian ethics and horizontal violence', *Lesbian Ethics* 3: 91–100.
Card, C. (1990) 'Intimacy and responsibility: What lesbians do', in Martha Fineman and Nancy Thomadsen (eds), *At the Boundaries of Law: Feminism and Legal Theory*, London: Routledge & Kegan Paul.
Card, C. (Unpublished) 'Virtues and moral luck', read at the 1985 Western Division Meetings of the American Philosophical Association.
Card, C. (Unpublished) 'Responsibility and moral luck: Resisting oppression and abuse', read at the 1989 Eastern Division Meetings of the American Philosophical Association.
Care, N. S. (1984) 'Career choice', *Ethics* 94: 283–302.
Care, N. S. (1987) *On Sharing Fate*, Philadelphia: Temple University Press.
Cavalli-Sforza, L. L. and Bodmer, W. F. (1971) *The Genetics of Human Populations*, San Francisco: W. H. Freeman and Co.
Charles, D. (1983) 'Rationality and irrationality', *Proceedings of the Aristotelian Society* 83: 191–212.
Charlton, W. (1988) *Weakness of Will: A Philosophical Introduction*, Oxford: Basil Blackwell.
Chaucer, G. (1985) *Canterbury Tales*, Oxford: Oxford University Press.
Cherniak, C. (1986) *Minimal Rationality*, Cambridge, Massachusetts: MIT Press.
Chodorow, N. (1978) *The Reproduction of Mothering: Psychoanalysis and the Sociology of Gender*, Berkeley: University of California Press.
Churchill, L. (1989) 'Reviving a distinctive medical ethic', *Hastings Center Report* 19, no. 3: 28–34.
Conee, E. (1982) 'Against moral dilemmas', *Philosophical Review* 91: 87–97 (reprinted in Gowans 1987).
Cooper, J. (1975) *Reason and Human Good in Aristotle*, Cambridge: Harvard University Press.
Cottingham, J. (1983) 'Ethics and impartiality', *Philosophical Studies* 43: 83–99.
Darwall, S. L. (1983) *Impartial Reason*, Ithaca: Cornell University Press.
Darwin, C. (1916) *The Expression of Emotion in Man and Animals*, New York: D. Appleton (first published 1872).
Davidson, D. (1963) 'Actions, reasons, and causes', *Journal of Philosophy* 60: 685–700 (reprinted in Davidson 1980).
Davidson, D. (1969) 'How is weakness of the will possible?' in J. Feinberg (ed.), *Moral Concepts*, Oxford University Press (reprinted in Davidson 1980).

Davidson, D. (1976) 'Hume's cognitive theory of pride', *Journal of Philosophy* 73: 744–56.

Davidson, D. (1980) *Essays on Actions and Events*, Oxford: Oxford University Press.

Dennett, D. (1984) *Elbow Room: The Varieties of Free Will Worth Wanting*, Cambridge, Massachusetts: MIT Press.

Dennett, D. (1988) 'Why everyone is a novelist', *Times Literary Supplement* 4, no. 459.

Dent, N. J. H. (1984) *The Moral Psychology of the Virtues*, Cambridge: Cambridge University Press.

De Sousa, R. (1987) *The Rationality of Emotion*, Cambridge, Massachusetts: MIT Press.

De Vos, G. (1973) *Socialization of Achievement*, Berkeley: University of California Press.

Dewey, J. (1960) *Theory of the Moral Life*, New York: Holt, Rinehart and Winston (original version, 1908; revised 1932).

Dworkin, R. (1986) *Law's Empire*, Cambridge, Massachusetts: Harvard University Press.

Earle, J. (1811) *Microcosmography*, London: White and Cochrane.

Emmet, D. (1966) *Rules, Roles, and Relations*, New York: St. Martin's Press.

Epicurus (1988) *Kuriai Doxa*, in *Hellenistic Philosophy: Introductory Readings*, translated by B. Inwood and L. Gerson, Indianapolis: Hackett.

Erikson, E. H. (1968) *Identity: Youth and Crisis*, New York: W. W. Norton.

Feinberg, J. (1970a) 'What is so special about mental illness?', in *Doing and Deserving: Essays in the Theory of Responsibility*, Princeton: Princeton University Press.

Feinberg, J. (1970b) 'Justice and personal desert', in *Doing and Deserving: Essays in the Theory of Responsibility*, Princeton: Princeton University Press.

Feinberg, J. (1970c) 'Crime, clutchability, and individual treatment', in *Doing and Deserving: Essays in the Theory of Responsibility*, Princeton: Princeton University Press.

Festinger, L. (1965) *Theory of Cognitive Dissonance*, Stanford: Stanford University Press.

Fingarette, H. (1967) *On Responsibility*, New York: Basic Books.

Fingarette, H. (1988) *Heavy Drinking: The Myth of Alcoholism as a Disease*, Berkeley: University of California Press.

Fischer, J. M. (ed.) (1986) *Moral Responsibility*, Ithaca: Cornell University Press.

Flanagan, O. (1986) 'Admirable immorality and admirable imperfection', *Journal of Philosophy* 83: 41–60.

Flanagan, O. (1991) *Varieties of Moral Personality: Ethics and Psychological Realism*, Cambridge, Massachusetts: Harvard University Press.

Flanagan, O. and Jackson, K. (1987) 'Justice, care, and gender: The Kohlberg-Gilligan debate revisited', *Ethics* 97: 622–37.

Foot, P. (1978a) *Virtues and Vices*, Berkeley: University of California Press.

Foot, P. (1978b) 'Hume on moral judgment', in Foot 1978a.

Foot, P. (1978c) 'Virtues and vices', in Foot 1978a.

Foot, P. (1978d) 'Morality as a system of hypothetical imperatives', in Foot 1978c.

Foot, P. (1985) 'Utilitarianism and the virtues', *Mind* 94: 196–209.

Frankena, W. K. (1970) 'Prichard and the ethics of virtue', *Monist* 54: 1–17.

Frankfurt, H. (1969) 'Alternate possibilities and moral responsibility', *Journal of Philosophy* 66: 828–39.

Frankfurt, H. (1971) 'Freedom of the will and the concept of the person', *Journal of Philosophy* 68: 5–20. (Reprinted in H. Frankfurt, 1988, *The Importance of What We Care About*, Cambridge: Cambridge University Press. Also reprinted in Watson 1982.)

Frankfurt, H. (1982) 'The importance of what we care about', *Synthese* 53: 257–72. (Reprinted in H. Frankfurt, *The Importance of What We Care About*, Cambridge, Cambridge University Press, 1988.)

Freud, S. (1961) 'Some psychical consequences of the anatomical distinction between the sexes', in *The Standard Edition of the Complete Psychological Works of Sigmund Freud* (Vol. 19), translated by J. Strachey, London: Hogarth (first published in 1925).

Fried, C. (1970) *An Anatomy of Values: Problems of Personal and Social Choice*, Cambridge, Massachusetts: Harvard University Press.

Friedman, M. (1987a) 'Beyond caring: The de-moralization of gender', in M. Hanen and K. Nielsen (eds), *Science, Morality, and Feminist Theory*, Calgary: University of Calgary.

Friedman, M. (1987b) 'Care and context in moral reasoning', in E. F. Kittay and D. T. Meyers (eds), *Women and Moral Theory*, Totowa, New Jersey: Littlefield, Adams.

Fuller, L. L. (1964) *The Morality of Law*, New Haven: Yale University Press.

Gardiner, P. (1963) 'Hume's theory of the passions', in *David Hume, A Symposium*, London: Macmillan.

Gauthier, D. (1986) *Morals by Agreement*, Oxford: Oxford University Press.

Geertz, C. (1973) 'Person, time, and conduct in Bali', in *The Interpretation of Cultures*, New York: Basic Books.

Geertz, C. (1984) 'From the native's point of view: On the nature of anthropological understanding', in R. Shweder and R. Levine (eds), *Culture Theory: Essays in Mind, Self, and Emotion*, Cambridge: Cambridge University Press.

Gewirth, A. (1978) *Reason and Morality*, Chicago: University of Chicago Press.

Gewirth, A. (1989) 'Ethical universalism and particularism', *Journal of Philosophy* 85: 283–302.

Gies, M., with Gold, A. L. (1987) *Anne Frank Remembered*, New York: Simon and Schuster.

Gilligan, C. (1982) *In a Different Voice: Psychological Theory and Women's Development*, Cambridge, Massachusetts: Harvard University Press.

Gilligan, C., Ward, J. V. and Taylor, J. M., with Bardige, B. (eds) (1988) *Mapping the Moral Domain: A Contribution of Women's Thinking to Psychological Theory and Education*, Cambridge, Massachusetts: Harvard University Press.

Glass, B. and Li, C. C. (1953) 'The dynamics of racial admixture – An analysis of the American negro', *American Journal of Human Genetics* 5: 1–20.

Glover, J. (1983) 'Self-creation', *Proceedings of the British Academy* 69: 445–71.

Gordon, R. (1987) *The Structure of Emotion*, Cambridge: Cambridge University Press.

Gowans, C. W. (ed.) (1987) *Moral Dilemmas*, Oxford: Oxford University Press.

Green, T. H. (1969) *Prolegomena to Ethics*, New York: Crowell (first published 1883).

Greenspan, P. S. (1978) 'Behavior control and freedom of action', *Philosophical Review* 87: 225–40.

Greenspan, P. S. (1988) *Emotions and Reasons*, New York: Routledge, Chapman and Hall.

Haksar, V. (1964) 'Aristotle and the punishment of psychopaths', *Philosophy* 39: 323–40.

Hampshire, S. (1983) 'Two theories of morality', in *Morality and Conflict*, Cambridge, Massachusetts: Harvard University Press.

Hare, R. M. (1952) *The Language of Morals*, Oxford: Oxford University Press.

Hare, R. M. (1963) *Freedom and Reason*, Oxford: Oxford University Press.

Harman, G. (1975) 'Moral relativism defended', *Philosophical Review* 84: 3–22.

Harman, G. (1986) *Change in View: Principles of Reasoning*, Cambridge, Massachusetts: MIT Press.

Harrison, R. (ed.) (1979) *Rational Action*, Cambridge: Cambridge University Press.

Hart, H. L. A. (1961) *The Concept of Law*, Oxford: Oxford University Press.

Held, V. (1984) *Rights and Goods: Justifying Social Action*, New York: Free Press/Macmillan.

Held, V. (1987a) 'Feminism and moral theory', in E. F. Kittay and D. T. Meyers (eds), *Women and Moral Theory*, Totowa, New Jersey: Littlefield, Adams.

Held, V. (1987b) 'Non-contractual society', in M. Hanen and K. Nielsen (eds), *Science, Morality, and Feminist Theory*, Calgary: University of Calgary.

Heller, M. (1984) 'Temporal parts of four dimensional objects', *Philosophical Studies* 46: 323–34.

Hendel, C. W., Jr. (1925) *Studies in the Philosophy of David Hume*, Princeton: Princeton University Press.

Herman, B. (1981) 'On the value of acting from the motive of duty', *Philosophical Review* 90: 359–82.

Herman, B. (1983) 'Integrity and impartiality', *Monist* 66: 233–50.

Herman, B. (1984a) 'Rules, motives, and helping actions', *Philosophical Studies* 45: 369–77.

Herman, B. (1984b) 'Mutual aid and respect for person', *Ethics* 94: 578–602.

Herman, B. (1985) 'The practice of moral judgment', *Journal of Philosophy* 82: 414–36.

Herman, B. (1990) 'What happens to the consequences', in P. Guyer and T. Cohen (eds), *Pursuit of Reason*, Lubbock: Texas Tech University Press.

Herman, B. (Unpublished) 'Moral deliberation and the derivation of duties'.

Hoagland, S. L. (1988) *Lesbian Ethics*, Palo Alto, California: Institute for Lesbian Studies.

Hobson, L. (1947) *Gentleman's Agreement*, New York: Grosset & Dunlap.

Holmes, O. W. (1959) 'The path of law', in C. Morris (ed.), *The Great Legal Philosophers*, Philadelphia: University of Pennsylvania Press (first published 1895).

Horney, K. (1942) *Self-Analysis*, New York: W. W. Norton.

Houston, B. (1987) 'Rescuing womanly virtues: Some dangers of reclamation', in M. Hanen and K. Nielsen (eds), *Science, Morality, and Feminist Theory*, Calgary: University of Calgary.

Hudson, S. (1986) *Human Character and Morality*, Boston: Routledge & Kegan Paul.

Hume, D. (1846) 'Letters, Hume to Hutcheson, Hume to Henry Home', in Burton (ed.), *Life and Correspondence of David Hume* (2 vols), Edinburgh: William Tait.

Hume, D. (1889) *A Dissertation on the Passions*, in T. H. Green and T. H. Grose (eds), *Essays Moral, Political, and Literary*, London: Longhan, Green and Co. (first published 1757).

Hume, D. (1957a) *An Inquiry Concerning the Principles of Morals*, C. Hendel (ed.), New York: Library of Liberal Arts (first published 1751).

Hume, D. (1965) 'Of the standard of taste', in *Of the Standard of Taste and Other Essays*, Indianapolis: Library of Liberal Arts (first published 1757).

Hume, D. (1975a) *Enquiries Concerning Human Understanding and Concerning the Principles of Morals*, L. A. Selby-Bigge (ed.), Oxford: Oxford University Press (reprinted from 1777 edition).

Hume, D. (1975b) *A Treatise of Human Nature*, L. A. Selby-Bigge and P. H. Nidditch (eds), Oxford: Oxford University Press (first published 1739).

Hume, D. (1977) *An Enquiry Concerning Human Understanding*, E. Steinberg (ed.), Indianapolis: Hackett (first published 1748).

Hume, D. (1978a) *Enquiries*, L. A. Selby-Bigge and P. H. Nidditch (eds), Oxford: Oxford University Press (first published 1748, 1751).

Hume, D. (1978) *A Treatise of Human Nature* (2nd edn), L. A. Selby-Bigge and P. H. Nidditch (eds), Oxford: Oxford University Press (first published 1739).

Hume, D. (1983) *An Enquiry Concerning the Principles of Morals*, J. Schneewind (ed.), Indianapolis: Hackett (first published 1751).

Irwin, T. H. (1977) *Plato's Moral Theory*, Oxford: Oxford University Press.

Irwin, T. H. (1988) *Aristotle's First Principles*, Oxford: Oxford University Press.

Jackson, F. (1984) 'Weakness of will', *Mind* 93: 1–18.

James, H. (1973) *The Ambassadors*, Harmondsworth: Penguin Books (first published 1903).

James, W. (1950) *The Principles of Psychology*, New York: Dover Publications (first published 1890).

James, W. (1978) *Pragmatism: A New Name for Some Old Ways of Thinking, and The Meaning of Truth: A Sequel to 'Pragmatism'*, Cambridge, Massachusetts: Harvard University Press (first published 1907 and 1909).

James, W. (1979a) *The Will to Believe and Other Essays in Popular Philosophy*, Cambridge, Massachusetts: Harvard University Press (first published, 1897).

James, W. (1979b) 'The dilemma of determinism', in *The Will to Believe and Other Essays in Popular Philosophy*, Cambridge, Massachusetts: Harvard University Press (first published in 1897).

James, W. (1979c) 'The moral philosopher and the moral life', in James 1979a (first published in 1891).

James, W. (1983) *Talks to Teachers on Psychology and to Students on Some of Life's Ideals*, Cambridge, Massachusetts: Harvard University Press (first published 1899).

James, W. (1988) *Manuscript Essays and Notes*, Cambridge, Massachusetts: Harvard University Press.

Jeffrey, R. C. (1974) 'Preference among preferences', *Journal of Philosophy* 71: 377–91.

Kagan, J. (1984) *The Nature of the Child*, New York: Basic Books.

Kagan, J., Reznick, J. S. and Snidman, N. S. (1988) 'Biological bases of childhood shyness', *Science* 240: 167–71.

Kahneman, D., Slovic, P. and Tversky, A. (eds) (1982) *Judgment under Uncertainty*, Cambridge: Cambridge University Press.

Kamm, F. M. (1985) 'Supererogation and obligation', *Journal of Philosophy* 82: 118–38.

Kant, I. (1933) *Critique of Pure Reason*, translated by N. Kemp Smith, London: Macmillan.

Kant, I. (1934) *Religion within the Limits of Reason Alone*, New York: Harper & Row (first published 1795).

Kant, I. (1948) *The Moral Law: Kant's Groundwork of 'The Metaphysic of Morals'*, translated by H. J. Paton, London: Hutchinson (first published 1785).

Kant, I. (1956) *Critique of Practical Reason*, Indianapolis: Bobbs-Merrill (first published 1788).

Kant, I. (1960a) *Religion within the Limits of Reason Alone*, translated by T. M. Greene and H. H. Hudson, New York: Harper & Row (first published 1795).

Kant, I. (1960b) *Observations on the Feeling of the Beautiful and Sublime*, translated by J. T. Goldthwait, Berkeley: University of California Press (first published 1764).

Kant, I. (1962) *The Moral Law: Kant's Groundwork of 'The Metaphysics of Morals'*, London: Hutchinson University Library (first published 1785).

Kant, I. (1963a) *Lecture on Ethics*, Indianapolis: Hackett.

Kant, I. (1963b) *Lectures on Ethics*, translated by L. Infield, New York: Harper & Row.
Kant, I. (1964a) *Groundwork of 'The Metaphysics of Morals'*, translated by H. J. Paton, New York: Harper & Row (first published 1785).
Kant, I. (1964b) *The Doctrine of Virtue: Part II of 'The Metaphysic of Morals'*, translated by M. J. Gregor, New York: Harper & Row (first published 1797).
Kant, I. (1969) 'On a supposed right to lie from benevolent motives', translated by L. W. Beck, in L. W. Beck (ed.), *Kant's Critique of Practical Reason and Other Writings in Moral Philosophy*, Chicago: University of Chicago Press (first published 1797).
Kant, I. (1971) *The Doctrine of Virtue: Part II of 'The Metaphysics of Morals'*, Philadelphia: University of Pennsylvania Press (first published 1797).
Kant, I. (1974) *Anthropology from a Pragmatic Point of View*, translated by M. J. Gregor, The Hague: Nijhoff (first published 1797).
Kant, I. (1981) *Grounding for 'The Metaphysics of Morals'*, translated by J. Ellington, Indianapolis: Hackett. (Prussian Academy pagination. First published 1785.)
Kemp Smith, N. (1941) *The Philosophy of David Hume*, London: Macmillan.
Kenny, A. (1963) *Action, Emotion, and Will*, New York: Humanities Press.
Kohl, H. (1984) *Growing Minds: On Becoming a Teacher*, New York: Harper & Row.
Kohlberg, L. (1981) *The Philosophy of Moral Development*, San Francisco: Harper & Row.
Korsgaard, C. (1983) 'Two distinctions in goodness', *Philosophical Review* 91: 169–95.
Kydd, R. (1964) *Reason and Conduct in Hume's Treatise*, New York, Russell & Russell.
La Bruyere, J. D. (1891) 'Les caractères', in H. Morley (ed.), *Character Writings of the Seventeenth Century*, London: G. Routledge.
Lange, C. G. (1922) *The Emotions*, Baltimore: Williams and Wilkins Company.
Larmore, C. (1987) *Patterns of Moral Complexity*, Cambridge: Cambridge University Press.
LePore, E. and McLaughlin, B. (eds) (1985) *Actions and Events: Perspectives on the Philosophy of Donald Davidson*, Oxford: Basil Blackwell.
Lewis, D. (1976) 'Survival and identity', in A. Rorty (ed.), *The Identities of Persons*, Los Angeles: University of California Press.
Lind, M. (1987) *Emotions and Hume's Moral Theory*, unpublished doctoral dissertation, MIT.
Lind, M. (Unpublished) 'Hume and neo-classicist moral theory'; paper read at the Fourteenth World Congress in Philosophy of Law and Social Philosophy, Edinburgh, 1989.
Lobel, K. (ed.) (1986) *Naming the Violence: Speaking Out about Lesbian Battering*, Seattle: Seal.
Louden, R. (1988) 'Can we be too moral?' *Ethics* 98: 361–78.
McConnell, T. C. (1978) 'Moral dilemmas and consistency in ethics', *Canadian Journal of Philosophy* 8: 269–87 (reprinted in Gowans 1987).
McDowell, J. (1979) 'Virtue and Reason', *Monist* 62: 331–50.
MacIntyre, A. (1981) *After Virtue: A Study in Moral Theory* (1st edn), Notre Dame: University of Notre Dame Press.
MacIntyre, A. (1984) *After Virtue: A Study in Moral Theory* (2nd edn), Notre Dame: University of Notre Dame Press.
MacIntyre, A. (1988) *Whose Justice? Which Rationality?* Notre Dame: University of Notre Dame Press.
Mackie, J. L. (1977) *Ethics: Inventing Right and Wrong*, New York: Penguin.
McLaughlin, B. and Rorty, A. (1988) *Perspectives on Self-Deception*, Berkeley: University of California Press.
Marcus, R. B. (1980) 'Moral dilemmas and consistency', *Journal of Philosophy* 77: 121–36 (reprinted in Gowans 1987).
Mendus, S. (1984) 'The practical and the pathological', *Journal of Value Inquiry* 19: 235–43.
Menninger, K. (1968) *The Crime of Punishment*, New York: Viking Press.
Merleau-Ponty, M. (1963) *The Structure of Behavior*, Boston: Beacon Press.
Mill, J. S. (1957) *Utilitarianism*, New York: Bobbs-Merrill (first published 1861).
Mill, J. S. (1978) *On Liberty*, Indianapolis: Hackett (first published 1859).
Miller, D. (1981) *Philosophy and Ideology in Hume's Political Thought*, Oxford: Oxford University Press.
Milne, A. A. (1974) *Winnie-the-Pooh*, New York: Dell Publishing Company.
Mitsis, P. (1988) *Epicurus' Ethical Theory: The Pleasures of Invulnerability*, Ithaca: Cornell University Press.
Molière, J. B. (1869) *L'Avare, Le Malade Imaginaire, Le Misanthrope*, in *Œuvres Complètes*, Paris: Charpentier.
Mossner, E. C. (1980) *Life of David Hume* (2nd edn), Oxford: Oxford University Press.

Murdoch, I. (1970) *The Sovereignty of Good*, London: Routledge & Kegan Paul.
Murdoch, I. (1971) *The Sovereignty of Good*, New York: Schocken Books.
Murphy, J. G. (1972) 'Moral death: A Kantian essay on psychopathy', *Ethics* 82: 284–98.
Nagel, E. (1961) *The Structure of Science: Problems in the Logic of Scientific Explanation*, New York: Harcourt, Brace & World.
Nagel, T. (1970) *The Possibility of Altruism*, Princeton: Princeton University Press.
Nagel, T. (1979a) 'Moral luck', in *Mortal Questions*, Cambridge: Cambridge University Press.
Nagel, T. (1979b) 'What is it like to be a bat?' in *Mortal Questions*, Cambridge: Cambridge University Press.
Nagel, T. (1979c) 'The fragmentation of value', in *Mortal Questions*, Cambridge: Cambridge University Press.
Nagel, T. (1986) *The View from Nowhere*, New York: Oxford University Press.
Nietzsche, F. (1966) *Beyond Good and Evil*, translated by W. Kaufmann, New York: Vintage Books (first published 1886).
Nietzsche, F. (1967) *Will to Power*, translated by W. Kaufmann and R. J. Hollingdale, New York: Random House (first published 1901).
Nietzsche, F. (1982) *Daybreak: Thoughts on the Prejudices of Morality*, translated by R. J. Hollingdale, Cambridge: Cambridge University Press (first published 1881).
Nisbett, R. E. and Wilson, T. D. (1977) 'Telling more than we can know: Verbal reports on mental processes', *Psychological Review* 84: 231–59.
Noddings, N. (1984) *Caring: A Feminine Approach to Ethics and Moral Education*, Berkeley: University of California Press.
Norton, D. F. (1982) *David Hume*, Princeton: Princeton University Press.
Nozick, R. (1974) *Anarchy, State, and Utopia*, New York: Basic Books.
Nussbaum, M. (1985) 'The discernment of perception: An Aristotelian conception of private and public morality', in J. Cleary (ed.), *Proceedings of the Boston Area Colloquium on Ancient Philosophy*, 151–201, New York: University Press of America.
Nussbaum, M. (1988) 'Comment on Paul Seabright', *Ethics* 98: 332–40.
Oakley, J. (1988) 'Morality and the emotions'; unpublished doctoral dissertation, La Trobe University, Bundoora, Victoria, Australia.
O'Flaherty, W. D. (1978) 'The clash between relative and absolute duty: The dharma of demons', in W. D. O'Flaherty, J. Duncan and M. Derrett (eds), *The Concept of Duty in South Asia*, New Delhi: Vikas Publishing House.
Olson, M. (1965) *The Logic of Collective Action*, Cambridge, Massachusetts: Harvard University Press.
O'Neill, O. (1975) *Acting on Principle*, New York: Columbia University Press.
O'Neill, O. (1985) 'Consistency in action', in N. Potter and M. Timmons (eds), *Morality and Universality*, Reidel Publishing Company.
Parfit, D. (1984) *Reasons and Persons*, Oxford: Oxford University Press.
Peacocke, C. (1985) 'Intention and akrasia', in B. Vermazen and M. Hintikka (eds), *Essays on Davidson: Actions and Events*, Oxford: Oxford University Press.
Pears, D. (1980) 'Courage as mean', in Rorty 1980b.
Pears, D. (1984) *Motivated Irrationality*, Oxford: Oxford University Press.
Perry, J. (1976) 'The importance of being identical', in A. Rorty (ed.), *The Identities of Persons*, Los Angeles: University of California Press.
Peters, R. S. (1966) 'Moral education and the psychology of character', in I. Scheffler (ed.), *Philosophy and Education: Modern Readings* (2nd edn), Boston: Allyn and Bacon.
Piaget, J. (1932) *The Moral Judgment of the Child*, New York: Free Press.
Piper, A. M. S. (1985) 'Two conceptions of the self', *Philosophical Studies* 48, no. 2: 173–97.
Piper, A. M. S. (1987) 'Moral theory and moral alienation', *Journal of Philosophy* 84: 102–18.
Piper, A. M. S. (1988) 'Pseudorationality', in A. Rorty and B. McLaughlin (eds), *Perspectives on Self-Deception*, Berkeley: University of California Press.
Piper, A. M. S. (1989) (Unpublished) 'The meaning of "ought" and the loss of innocence'.
Plato (1963a) *Phaedrus*, translated by R. Hackforth, in E. Hamilton and H. Cairns (eds), *Collected Dialogues of Plato*, Princeton: Princeton University Press.
Plato (1963b) *Symposium*, translated by M. Joyce, in E. Hamilton and H. Cairns (eds), *Collected Dialogues of Plato*, Princeton: Princeton University Press.
Plato (1974) *Republic*, translated by G. Grube, Indianapolis: Hackett.

Plato (1979) *Gorgias*, translated by T. Irwin, Oxford: Oxford University Press.

Prichard, H. (1912) 'Does moral philosophy rest on a mistake?' *Mind* 21:21–37 (reprinted in *Moral Obligation*, Oxford: Oxford University Press, 1949).

Railton, P. (1984) 'Alienation, consequentialism, and the demands of morality', *Philosophy and Public Affairs* 13: 134–71.

Railton, P. (1986) 'Moral realism', *Philosophical Review* 95: 163–207.

Rawls, J. (1971) *A Theory of Justice*, Cambridge, Massachusetts: Harvard University Press.

Rawls, J. (1975) 'The independence of moral theory', *Proceedings and Addresses of the American Philosophical Association* 48: 5–22.

Rawls, J. (1989) 'Themes in Kant's moral philosophy', in E. Forster (ed.), *Kant's Transcendental Deductions*, Stanford: Standford University Press.

Rawls, J. (Unpublished) Lectures on the ethics of Butler, Hume, and Kant and handouts from a course on social and political philosophy, Harvard University, Cambridge, 1979, 1980.

Raymond, J. (1986) *A Passion for Friends: Toward a Philosophy of Female Affection*, Boston: Beacon.

Read, K. E. (1955) 'Morality and the concept of the person among the Gahuku-Gama', *Oceana* 25: 185–230 (reprinted in J. Middleton, ed., *Myth and Cosmos*, Doubleday, New York, 1967).

Reed, T. E. (1969) 'Caucasian genes in American negroes', *Science* 165: 762–8.

Rich, A. (1979a) *On Lies, Secrets, and Silence: Selected Prose, 1966–1978*, New York: Norton.

Rich, A. (1979b) 'Women and Honor: Some notes on lying', in *On Lies, Secrets, and Silence: Selected Prose, 1966–1978*, New York: Norton.

Rich, A. (1980) 'Compulsory heterosexuality and lesbian existence', *Signs* 5: 631–60.

Ringelheim, J. (1985) 'Women and the holocaust: A reconsideration of research', *Signs* 10: 741–61.

Roberts, R. (1988) 'What an emotion is: A sketch', *Philosophical Review* 97: 183–209.

Rorty, A. (1976a) 'Character, Persons, selves, individuals', in A. Rorty 1976b (reprinted in A. Rorty, *Mind in Action: Essays in the Philosophy of Mind*, Boston: Beacon Press 1988).

Rorty, A. (ed.) (1976b) *The Identities of Persons*, Los Angeles: University of California Press.

Rorty, A. (ed.) (1980a) *Explaining Emotions*, Berkeley: University of California Press.

Rorty, A. (ed.) (1980b) *Essays on Aristotle's Ethics*, Berkeley: University of California Press.

Rorty, A. (1990) 'Pride produces the idea of self: Hume on moral agency', *Australian Journal of Philosophy*.

Rorty, R. (1989) *Contingency, Irony, and Solidarity*, Cambridge: Cambridge University Press.

Ross, L. and Anderson, C. A. (1982) 'Shortcomings in the attribution process: On the origins and maintenance of erroneous social assessments', in Kahneman, Slovic and Tversky 1982.

Ross, W. D. (1930) *The Right and the Good*, Oxford: Oxford University Press.

Ross, W. D. (1939) *The Foundations of Ethics*, Oxford: Oxford University Press.

Rotter, J. B. (1980) 'Interpersonal trust, trustworthiness, and gullibility', *American Psychologist* 35: 1–7.

Rousseau, J.-J. (1961) *Émile*, Paris: Garnier-Flammarian (first published 1762).

Rousseau, J.-J. (1985) *A Discourse on Inequality*, translated by M. Cranston, Harmondsworth: Penguin (first published 1755).

Ruddick, S. (1989) *Maternal Thinking*, Boston: Beacon Press.

Ryle, G. (1949) *The Concept of Mind*, London: Hutchinson's University Library.

Sandel, M. (1982) *Liberalism and the Limits of Justice*, New York: Cambridge University Press.

Sartre, J.-P. (1943) *L'Etre et le Néant*, Paris: Gallimard.

Sartre, J.-P. (1964) *L'Existentialisme est un Humanisme*, Paris: Nagel.

Scheffler, S. (1982) *The Rejection of Consequentialism*, Oxford: Oxford University Press.

Schiffer, S. (1976) 'A paradox of desire', *American Philosophical Quarterly* 13: 195–203.

Schoeman, F. (1985) 'Aristotle on the good of friendship', *Australasian Journal of Philosophy* 63: 269–82.

Schopenhauer, A. (1965) *On the Basis of Morality*, translated by E. F. J. Payne, Indianapolis: Bobbs-Merrill (first published 1841).

Schuman, H., Steeh, C. and Bobo, L. (1985) *Racial Attitudes in America: Trends and Interpretations*, Cambridge, Massachusetts: Harvard University Press.

Seabright, P. (1988) 'The pursuit of unhappiness: Paradoxical motivation on the subversion of character in Henry James's *Portrait of a Lady*', *Ethics* 98: 313–31.

Selby-Bigge, L. A. (1964) *The British Moralists*, New York: Library of Liberal Arts.

Sherman, N. (1989) *The Fabric of Character*, Oxford: Oxford University Press.

Shoemaker, S. (1963) *Self-Knowledge and Self-Identity*, Ithaca: Cornell University Press.

Shoemaker, S. (1984) 'Personal identity: A materialist's account', in S. Shoemaker and R. Swinburne, *Personal Identity*, Oxford: Basil Blackwell.

Shweder, R. and Bourne, E. (1984) 'Does the concept of the person vary cross-culturally?' in R. Shweder and R. Levine (eds), *Culture Theory: Essays in Mind, Self, and Emotion*, Cambridge: Cambridge University Press.

Sidgwick, H. (1893) 'Unreasonable action', *Mind* 2: 174–87.

Sidgwick, H. (1981) *The Methods of Ethics* (7th edn.), Indianapolis: Hackett (first published 1907).

Slote, M. (1978) 'Time in counterfactuals', *Philosophical Review* 87: 3–27.

Slote, M. (1983) *Goods and Virtues*, Oxford: Oxford University Press.

Slote, M. (1984) 'Morality and self-other asymmetry', *Journal of Philosophy* 81: 179–92.

Slote, M. (1985) *Common-sense Morality and Consequentialism*, London: Routledge & Kegan Paul.

Slote, M. (1988) Critical notice of C. Taylor in *Human Agency and Language: Philosophical Papers*, Vol. 1, *Canadian Journal of Philosophy* 18: 579–87.

Slote, M. (1989) *Beyond Optimizing*, Cambridge, Massachusetts: Harvard University Press.

Smith, A. (1976) *The Theory of Moral Sentiments*, Indianapolis: Liberty Classics (first published 1759).

Smith, B. H. (1988) *Contingencies of Value*, Cambridge, Massachusetts: Harvard University Press.

Stern, D. (1985) *The Interpersonal World of the Infant*, New York: Basic Books.

Stocker, M. (1966) 'Supererogation'; unpublished doctoral dissertation, Harvard University.

Stocker, M. (1976a) 'The schizophrenia of modern ethical theories', *Journal of Philosophy* 73: 453–66.

Stocker, M. (1976b) 'Agent and other: Against ethical universalism', *Australasian Journal of Philosophy* 74: 206–20.

Stocker, M. (1981) 'Values and purposes: The limits of teleology and the ends of friendship', *Journal of Philosophy* 78: 747–65.

Stocker, M. (1986) 'Friendship and duty: Toward a synthesis of Gilligan's contrastive ethical concepts', in E. Kittay and D. Meyers (eds), *Women and Moral Theory*, Totowa, New Jersey.: Rowman and Allanheld.

Stocker, M. (1989) *Plural and Conflicting Values*, Oxford: Oxford University Press.

Strawson, P. F. (1962) 'Freedom and resentment', *Proceedings of the British Academy* 48: 1–25 (reprinted in Watson 1982).

Stroud, B. (1977) *Hume*, London: Routledge & Kegan Paul.

Sullivan, W. (1988) 'Calling or career: The tensions of modern professional life', in A. Flores (ed.), *Professional Ideals*, Belmont, California: Wadsworth.

Taylor, C. (1971) 'What is involved in a genetic psychology?' in C. Taylor 1985a.

Taylor, C. (1976) 'Responsibility for self', in A. O. Rorty 1976b (reprinted in Watson 1982).

Taylor, C. (1977a) 'What is human agency?' in T. Mischel (ed.), *The Self: Psychological and Philosophical Issues*, Oxford: Basil Blackwell (reprinted in C. Taylor 1985a).

Taylor, C. (1977b) 'Self-interpreting animals', in C. Taylor 1985a.

Taylor, C. (1979) 'Atomism', in C. Taylor 1985b.

Taylor, C. (1981) 'The concept of a person', in C. Taylor 1985a.

Taylor, C. (1982) 'The diversity of good', in C. Taylor 1985b.

Taylor, C. (1985a) *Human Agency and Language: Philosophical Papers*, Vol. 1, Cambridge: Cambridge University Press.

Taylor, C. (1985b) *Philosophy and the Human Sciences: Philosophical Papers*, Vol. 2, Cambridge: Cambridge University Press.

Taylor, C. (1989) *Sources of the Self: The Making of Modern Identity*, Cambridge, Massachusetts: Harvard University Press.

Taylor, G. (1985) *Pride, Shame, and Guilt*, Oxford: Oxford University Press.

Taylor, M. (1987) *The Possibility of Cooperation*, Cambridge: Cambridge University Press.

Taylor, R. (1985) *Ethics, Faith, and Reason*, Englewood Cliffs, New Jersey: Prentice-Hall.

Telfer (1970/71) 'Friendship', *Proceedings of the Aristotelian Society* 71: 223–41.

Theophrastus (1967) *Characters*, Baltimore: Penguin.

Thomas, L. (1988) 'Rationality and affectivity: The metaphysics of the moral self', *Social Philosophy and Policy* 5: 154–72.

Thomas, L. (1989a) 'Trust and survival: Securing a vision of the good society', *Journal of Social Philosophy* 20: 34–41.

Thomas, L. (1989b) *Living Morally: A Psychology of Moral Character*, Philadelphia: Temple University Press.

Thompson, J. (1983) 'Parenthood and identity across time', *Journal of Philosophy* 80: 201–20.

Trianosky, G. (1988) 'Rightly ordered appetites: How to live morally and live well', *American Philosophical Quarterly* 25: 1–12.

Urmson, J. O., 'Aristotle's doctrine of the mean', in Rorty 1980b.

Van Gulick, R. (1988) 'A functionalist plea for self-consciousness', *Philosophical Review* 92: 149–81.

Walker, M. U. (1987) 'Moral particularity', *Metaphilosophy* 18: 171–85.

Wallace, J. (1978) *Virtues and Vices*, Ithaca: Cornell University Press.

Wallace, J. (1988) *Moral Relevance and Moral Conflict*, Ithaca: Cornell University Press.

Watson, G. (1975) 'Free agency', *Journal of Philosophy* 72: 205–20 (reprinted in Watson 1982).

Watson, G. (1977) 'Scepticism about weakness of will', *Philosophical Review* 86: 316–39.

Watson G. (ed.) (1982) *Free Will*, Oxford: Oxford University Press.

Watson, G. (1987a) 'Responsibility and the limits of evil: Variations on a Strawsonian theme', in F. Schoeman (ed.), *Responsibility, Character, and the Emotions*, Cambridge: Cambridge University Press.

Watson, G. (1987b) 'Free action and free will', *Mind* 96: 145–72.

Wescott, M. (1986) *The Feminist Legacy of Karen Horney*, New Haven: Yale University Press.

White, S. L. (1988) 'Self-deception and responsibility for the self', in B. P. McLaughlin and A. O. Rorty (eds), *Perspectives on Self-Deception*, Berkeley: University of California Press.

Whiting, J. (1986) 'Friends and future selves' *Philosophical Review* 94: 547–80.

Wiggins, D. (1980) 'Weakness of will, commensurability, and the objects of deliberation and desire', in Rorty 1980b.

Williams, B. (1973) 'Ethical consistency', in *Problems of the Self*, Cambridge: Cambridge University Press (reprinted in Gowans 1987).

Williams, B. (1976a) 'Morality and the emotions', in *Problems of the Self*, Cambridge: Cambridge University Press.

Williams, B. (1976b) 'Persons, character, and morality', in A. Rorty (ed.), *The Identities of Persons* (reprinted in Williams 1981a).

Williams, B. (1981a) *Moral Luck*, Cambridge: Cambridge University Press.

Williams, B. (1981b) 'Moral luck', in Williams 1981a.

Williams, B. (1981c) 'Internal and external reasons', in Williams 1981a.

Williams, B. (1985) *Ethics and the Limits of Philosophy*, Cambridge, Massachusetts: Harvard University Press.

Williamson, J. (1974) *A New People*, New York: Free Press.

Winters, B. (1981) 'Hume's argument for the superiority of natural instinct', *Dialogue* 20: 635–43.

Wolf, S. (1980) 'Asymmetrical freedom', *Journal of Philosophy* 77: 151–66.

Wolf, S. (1982) 'Moral saints', *Journal of Philosophy* 79: 410–39.

Wolf, S. (1986) 'Above and below the line of duty', *Philosophical Topics* 14: 131–48.

Wolf, S. (1987) 'Sanity and the metaphysics of responsibility', in F. Schoeman (ed.), *Responsibility, Character, and the Emotions*, Cambridge: Cambridge University Press.

Wollstonecraft, M. (1982) *A Vindication of the Rights of Woman*, Harmondsworth: Penguin (first published 1792).

Wong, D. (1988) 'On flourishing and finding one's identity in community', in P. A. French, T. E. Uehling and H. K. Wettstein (eds), *Ethical Theory: Character and Virtue*, Vol. 13 of Midwest Studies in Philosophy, Notre Dame: Notre Dame University Press.

Wootton, B. (1959) *Social Science and Social Pathology*, London: Allen and Unwin.

Wootton, B. (1963) *Crime and the Criminal Law*, London: Stevens and Sons.

Workman, P. L., Blumberg, B. S. and Cooper, A. J. (1963) 'Selection, gene migration, and polymorphic stability in a U.S. white and negro population', *American Journal of Human Genetics* 15, no. 4: 429–37.

Zipursky, B. (1987) 'Objectivity and linguistic practice'; unpublished doctoral dissertation, University of Pittsburgh.

# 4

# VIRTUE ETHICS AND SATISFICING RATIONALITY

## *Christine Swanton*

Virtue ethics is praised for its ability to provide greater depth and richness to moral and related theory concerning the practical life. In this chapter, I shall show what virtue ethics can offer the debate concerning optimising versus satisficing rationality. What Gary Watson calls the 'primacy of character'[1] can motivate an agent-oriented conception of rationality where expressing one's virtuous character provides reason for a radical kind of satisficing.

The argument for this has two basic steps. First, manifesting one's virtuous character can be a rational response to a situation. Second, virtue is not necessarily displayed in optimising behaviour, let alone behaviour that promotes or produces maximal value. Rather there are a variety of types of response to value or valuable things which display virtue. In particular, virtue may be displayed in *expressing* the feelings, desires, attitudes, emotions characteristic of virtuous response to those values or valuable things.[2] For example, friendship is characteristically manifested in behaviour which is an expression of intimacy or friendly feelings, and which may on occasion be inimical to optimising rationality. Moderation is characteristically displayed in expressions of attitudes of being content with an adequate rather than maximal amount of a personal good. Anti-perfectionism is characteristically manifested in an expression of a desire not to be too hard on oneself or on others. All these responses, I shall argue, may underpin satisficing behaviour.

I do not propose to develop here a full account of agent-oriented rationality. For example, I do not explore the issue of whether the expression of mere moods, inclinations, feelings and states of character falling short of virtue can also, at times, be rational though suboptimal in the way described by Philip Pettit as 'unmotivated' and 'profoundly irrational'.[3] My aim in this chapter is more limited. I appeal to virtue-ethical insights to show that Pettit's attack on satisficing can be questioned.

Though virtue ethics provides a basis for defending satisficing rationality I shall assume an act-based conception of 'best' action, a conception which is standardly presupposed by those who attack satisficing. It is still unclear what a fully virtue-ethical, agent-oriented notion of best action would look like[4] and I shall not approach these murky and highly troubled waters here.

## 1.

There is a kind of satisficing which has been called satisising[5] and which Philip Pettit[6] calls 'unmotivated submaximization'. My aim is to rebut this suggestion within a virtue-oriented conception of rationality. In 'unmotivated submaximization', a good enough option may be preferred to a better. It is assumed that a better option is included in a set of options that have been enumerated and evaluated. I shall follow Michael Slote in calling this satisficing, a view which he has defended in 'Satisficing Consequentialism',[7] 'Moderation Rationality and Virtue', and *Beyond Optimizing: A Study of Rational Choice*.[9]

Radical satisficing as defined above is contrasted with a kind of satisficing Pettit favours. His satisficer may intentionally not maximise, provided that an intention not to maximise is an indirect way of achieving the desired result – value maximisation. You attain the target by aiming at another.[10] According to Pettit and Geoffrey Brennan,[11] intentionally not to maximise is rational under a variety of circumstances that satisfy the conditions labelled calculative elusiveness and calculative vulnerability.

A benefit such as spontaneity is calculatively elusive if it is one that 'evaporates under a regime of sustained action calculation'.[12] Such benefits are to be attained by the cultivation and maintenance of relevant 'predispositions' defined by Pettit and Brennan as 'states whose manifestation in action means that the action is not chosen on a fully calculative or deliberative basis'.[13] A benefit is calculatively vulnerable if it cannot be secured by action on a relevant predisposition which is monitored in order to ensure that such action is indeed for the best. Such benefits are 'vulnerable to the presence of calculation, even in a supervisory role'.[14]

Pettit-type satisficing is rational, for Pettit, because it is a rational strategy within restrictive consequentialism, which is a maximising consequentialist position because the goal is maximisation, and which is 'restrictive' because maximisation is not necessarily applied in decision making. The restrictive consequentialist employs 'restrictive' or 'pre-emptive' maxims telling an agent 'to do A under condition C given at least that there is no (loosely specified sort of) emergency'.[15] Emergencies comprise situations that are 'out of the ordinary run'[16] or ones where the agent knows that following the maxim is suboptimal.

In arguing against Slote, Pettit claims that inasmuch as satisficing is shorn from a connection with restrictive maximising consequentialism, satisficing is irrational. The failure directly to pursue the best by operating various satisficing strategies is fine, but the choice of less than the best from a set of enumerated and evaluated options has nothing to commend it.

In this chapter, I shall justify the rationality of Slote's satisficing in terms of a virtue-oriented nonconsequentialist framework. The precise position to be defended has to be formulated with care, for there is scope for many areas of ambiguity. The first crucial area is one to which Slote draws attention, namely, an ambiguity in the word 'option': an option may be understood as the results of an action, or as the action itself.[17] This distinction results in two notions of satisficing:

(A) An action that has good enough results may rationally be preferred to one judged to have better results.
(B) An action that is good enough may rationally be preferred to one judged to be better.

However, defending (A) within a virtue-oriented nonconsequentialist framework may simply look like a preference for non-consequentialism over consequentialism. My defence of satisficing will be a defence of version (B) which is more encompassing than (A). For, according to (B), an action could be judged better than an alternative on either consequentialist or non-consequentialist grounds, and yet be rejected. (B) is compatible not only with satisficing consequentialism, but also with satisficing non-consequentialism.

A second area of ambiguity lies in the notion of rational rightness or correctness. There are four possible interpretations:

(a) It is always rationally preferable, perhaps even required, to satisfice.
(b) It is always rationally permitted to satisfice.
(c) It is sometimes rationally required to satisfice.
(d) It is sometimes rationally permitted but not required to satisfice.

I shall reject both (a) and (b). My defence of (b) will allow for the possibility both of (c) and (d).

It would be tempting to ignore (a) altogether, were it not for the fact that Pettit interprets the 'unmotivated satisficer' – in particular Slote – as committed to (a). It is therefore useful to get this false target out of the way. According to Pettit:

> The unmotivated satisficer prefers a strategy guaranteeing only a good enough result to one ensuring the best . . . This means that such a satisficer will have to support a policy of submaximization in any situation where all the options have been enumerated and evaluated.[18]

In addition, as Pettit makes clear in his critical review of Slote's *Common Sense Morality and Consequentialism*,[19] he believes Slote does not recommend the above strategy simply in cases 'where it happens that all the options available have been already examined'.[20] He claims further that:

> Faced with the necessity to choose, Slote's submaximizing procedure then would have us each go through the full gamut of alternative options, establishing their comparative value. And it would have us do this with a view to selecting something less than the best: an option which is good enough.[21]

The problem with Pettit's interpretation is that the view is so implausible: one can only sympathise with Pettit's claim that satisficing, so understood, is 'profoundly irrational'. I think, however, that Slote is not to be interpreted in the way Pettit suggests. The textual evidence Pettit provides for his interpretation is the following: 'The procedure requires that the agent "explicitly reject the better for the good enough"'.[22] This quote has been taken out of context however. What Slote actually says is this:

> However, the example of not taking the afternoon snack challenges the idea that the satisficing individual will never explicitly reject the better for the good enough.[23]

There is no claim that the satisficer must reject the best: rather, it is not the case that he must never reject the best. Slote's strategy is to show by way of examples that there are contexts in which satisficing is rationally (and indeed morally) permissible. By 'rationally permissible' is meant rational in the sense of not irrational – the action at issue is not rationally required, but nor is it irrational.

## 2.

The general strategy of my defence of (B)-type satisficing can now be stated. First, I accept what has been an implicit assumption made by those who charge that satisficing is unmotivated: viz. assumption (P):

> (P) The best action in circumstances C is the one that best fits C, and what makes an action fit C has to do with either or both the intrinsic features of the action (e.g. it being the keeping of a promise, or an act of truth telling) or the consequences of the action.

Call the features which make an action 'fit' C its good-making features (or if preferred, its right-making features). W. D. Ross can be understood as a non-consequentialist maximiser, for he believed that an action was all things considered right if and only if, of all the actions available to the agent, it was the one which maximised the net balance of right-making features over wrong-making features.[24] For Ross, the fittingness of an action was a function of a variety of right-making features of the action (e.g. it being the keeping of a promise), including ones pertaining to its consequences. Satisficing nonconsequentialism is opposed not only to maximising restrictive consequentialism, but also to maximising nonconsequentialism.

Given the above assumption about what makes an action best, I argue for the rationality of satisficing by arguing for assumption (Q):

> (Q) Even though an agent knows that A is the best action, she may have an undefeated reason for choosing another action.

More specifically, such a reason may be agent-centred. My point will be that though (P) is conceded, the rationality of an agent's choosing an action can be a function of quite agent-oriented considerations – e.g. the rationality of expressing his virtuous character: of acting from desirable or at least not undesirable traits. As a consequence of this strategy, I will not violate Schmidtz's necessary condition of rationality:

(R) 'One's choice is rational only if one did not recognize clearly better *reasons* for choosing any of one's foregone alternatives'.[25]

One may have an undefeated reason for foregoing a better alternative, when one acts out of friendship, love, courage, and so on, even where such action does not directly or indirectly optimise results. This rationality stems from the rationality of a desire to be the sort of person who is a friend and acts as one, who expresses his love for someone and, in general, who expresses the attitudes, desires, emotions and feelings which are the mark of, and characteristic of, virtuous response to valuable objects.

In more general terms, the rationality of satisficing is based on the rationality of an agent sometimes acting from agent-oriented as opposed to act-oriented rationality. It is assumed that knowing submaximisation may be rational if displaying a virtue whose non-manifestation on a given occasion may signal corruption or betrayal of an important and valuable character trait. Knowing submaximisation appears unmotivated because given that one knows what action is best it seems impossible to have an undefeated reason for choosing an action known to be inferior. However if (Q) can be motivated by an appeal to agent-centred considerations of the sort described, then knowing submaximisation can be seen not to be unmotivated, and not to be 'profoundly irrational'.

## 3.

My defence of satisficing has two parts. First, the rationality of satisficing with respect to personal goods; and then those cases with a moral dimension. My strategy in both cases is to motivate belief in (Q) by appealing to certain virtues: in the present case, moderation and anti-perfectionism.

Consider first moderation. Work has been done in this area by Slote, who argues that the habit of cultivating moderate needs, and being content to satisfy those needs and no more, rationalises satisficing over personal goods, such as the case of the afternoon snack described above. The issue then is: how can it be rational to choose a lesser degree of wellbeing when a greater level is known to be at hand in the purely self-regarding contexts described by Slote? We are assuming then, as Slote appears to, that *from the point of view of personal goods*, choosing the snack is the best action. Speaking of a similar example, Slote says:

> Someone who makes such a wish clearly acknowledges the possibility of being better off and yet chooses – knowingly and deliberately – a lesser but personally satisfying degree of well being.[26]

I shall now argue that the agent nonetheless could be seen as having an undefeated reason to forego the best action.

On my view, the rationality of the satisficer's choice is to be understood in terms of the rationality of *expressing* the attitudes characteristic of the virtue of moderation. Rather than being 'unmotivated', as Pettit would have it, her satisficing is motivated in a way not often recognised. It is a common mistake, as Michael Stocker points out,[27] to believe that action done for a reason, i.e. motivated action, is always action done *for the sake of* some end. The idea that the end must be future-directed, as in consequentialist models of rationality, is a relatively extreme species of this mistake. But some motivations are not goal-directed at all, but are 'expressive', as in 'I did it *out of* friendship'. (See below.) In the present case, 'I did it *from* moderation' expresses the satisficer's motivation better than 'I did it for the sake of promoting *x* (a personal good)'. If the latter kind of motivation is at issue, then it becomes puzzling why one does not go for more rather than less of an acknowledged good. (It is assumed, with Slote, that the agent recognises she would be better off if she chose more.)

The rationality of non-teleological motivation – and specifically manifestation of a trait in expressive behaviour – can be captured in the following thought. To have a 'habit' of moderation which one 'switches off' the moment one perceives that being 'immoderate' secures greater personal good is to fail to be true to oneself – to the character and dispositions one has developed and cultivated over time. Indeed, one might say, to be ready to switch off in this way is to fail to have the *virtue* of moderation. It is questionable whether one has the virtue of moderation when one is prepared to maximise, albeit in the restrictive consequentialist's way. For, as Slote points out, the virtue is one in which it is not the case that, in all contexts, one *cares* about opportunities to maximise. It is precisely the virtue of being content with adequate rather than maximal personal good. It is not merely the virtue of not always being disposed to calculate the maximal quantity.

It is true that these claims acquire greater plausibility to the extent that moderation is indeed a virtue, and one may take issue with that claim. It is beyond the scope of this chapter to discuss moderation as a virtue in detail, but the difficulties of delineating it so that it can plausibly be described as a virtue should be acknowledged. As we have seen, Slote understands this virtue in terms of relative non-neediness and non-greediness: a willingness to be satisfied. However, it is very difficult to assess even within broad parameters of vagueness what moderation amounts to, if we do not delimit the virtue with a recognition of, and preparedness to act on, knowledge of personal vulnerability. For clearly, a willingness to be satisfied may still allow for eating and drinking or smoking to the point of damage; and a non-neediness, if taken too far, could lead to the excesses of Stoicism where pleasure is eschewed as a personal good altogether. It seems that the characterisation offered by Slote leads to excessive vagueness or an arbitrary delimiting of moderation in terms of some perhaps aesthetic or conventional ideal of what is 'proper' or 'seemly' or 'dignified'. When moderation is delimited by an Aristotelian conception of 'the mean is relative to the individual', when that mean is determined by a knowledge of personal vulnerability to damage, then a person with a weak chest will smoke little if at all; a person who puts on weight easily will resist the chocolate eclairs, whereas one who finds it hard to gain weight will eat several if she is in the mood, and so on. Being moderate is not just a matter of being non-greedy and non-needy, it is a matter too of recognising one's weaknesses and behaving appropriately with regard to them. If one is not going to be damaged, and doing something gives pleasure or is fun, then (unless other-regarding considerations or important points of etiquette come into play) there is nothing wrong with acting greedily and needily in a conventional sense. Indeed, if this is not recognised, we are in danger of invoking a merely aesthetic idea of moderation against which Nietzsche railed:

> Moderation sees itself as beautiful; it is unaware that in the eye of the immoderate it appears black and sober, and consequently ugly looking.[28]

Despite the difficulties in offering a more precise account of the virtue of moderation, however, Slote's basic idea that a willingness to be sated is at the core of the virtue is correct, and it is the rationality of an agent's expression of that attitude which underpins satisficing.

Let us now consider another case, in which the virtue of anti-perfectionism comes into play. In the previous example, the agent was assumed to concede that the best action was taking the extra snack, but she could be seen as having an undefeated reason to express attitudes consonant with the virtue of moderation. The level of wellbeing she had already attained was good enough, and agent-oriented rationality held sway.

It would be a mistake to assume, however, that all satisficing is rationalised by manifesting the virtue of moderation. Consider now the case of the immoderate satisficer. Like Slote's moderate satisficer, he too is unfortunate enough to have a fridge in his office provided by the company, which alas, contains candy bars. In this new case, the agent is assumed to concede that the best action is *not* to take the extra snack. He decides, however, that though eating on this occasion is a minor peccadillo, it is a 'not bad enough' option to avoid, given the strength of his desires and other contextual features. In short, he intentionally chooses the inferior option because it is 'good enough' in the sense of not bad enough (he after all will eat just one small fibre-enriched bar while rejecting a large chocolate and caramel bar).

In Chapter 5 of *Beyond Optimizing*, Slote, too, appears to defend this kind of satisficing. My defence, to be outlined below, will be different from and more radical than Slote's. To make the contrast, let me present the structure of his defence, as applied to my example.

1. To refrain from taking the bar is, in the agent's eyes, the best available action. Therefore,
2. To refrain from taking the bar is the most rational available action.

But

3. To perform the best action in this circumstance is rationally supererogatory.
4. Rationality is a notion according to which to be rational simpliciter is equivalent to being adequately rational.
5. Given that refraining from taking the bar is supererogatory, taking the bar is adequately rational, and therefore rational.

To the charge that taking the bar is irrational because weak-willed, Slote makes the sensible claim that weakness and strength of will are themselves matters of degree. He claims (of another case) the following:

> He may feel that although going as far as he did was not the best available action, it was not in the circumstances a bad thing for him to do. What he did was not ideally rational, but neither, he may feel, was what he did simply unacceptable:

although it demonstrated some weakness of will, it demonstrated considerable strength of will as well.[29]

My own defence of (B)-satisficing is more radical than Slote's. I sever the connection between 1 and 2 above: that is, I shall question the assumption that the best action is necessarily the most rational action. The severing of this connection is made possible by my assumptions (P) and (Q) above, and is again mediated by a virtue – anti-perfectionism. There are times, I shall claim, where manifesting the virtue of anti-perfectionism is not a less rational course of action than performing the best action where the latter is rationally supererogatory. Let me elaborate.

The satisficing motivation of our immoderate agent has been expressed in the following terms by Stocker.[30] Although (a) all things considered his life would be better if he were not self-indulgent, it is nonetheless the case that (b) making this effort would be hard on him, and (c) now he wants to lead the kind of life where he is not so hard on himself. I shall build on this account, which leaves much unexplained; in particular, Pettit's charge that *taking* the chocolate bar is unmotivated if the agent judges that it is best here and now *not* to take the bar still has force.

My reply to the charge is this. Action in line with Stocker's judgment (c), taking the bar, is rational qua manifestation of a virtue – anti-perfectionism. I admit that Stocker's judgement (c) does not yield a here-and-now judgment that it is best to take the bar; indeed the agent judges it best to *refrain* from taking the bar. Rather, Stocker's judgment (c) is a 'background' judgment about the kind of agent the 'self-indulgent' satisficer wants to be. Given this, how is action in line with (c), taking the bar, rational? After all, it is judged to be not the *best* available action.

The solution once again is to appeal to virtue-based expressive rationality – in this case the rationality of acting in line with the background judgment of not being hard on yourself. The motive of not being too hard on yourself, which provides the motive for satisficing, is the expression of an attitude or desire manifesting a virtue – anti-perfectionism. Thus, inasmuch as taking the bar is weak, even weak-'willed', it is not inappropriately weak. According to the virtue of anti-perfectionism, it is sometimes appropriate to fail to be rationally supererogatory.

In 'Moderation, Rationality and Virtue', Slote suggests that perfectionism is an 'antivirtue' for several reasons. First, he claims that the person who has a tendency to 'eke out the most of best he can in every situation'[31] strikes someone who 'witnesses or hears about it as lacking in self sufficiency' (ibid.).[32] Such a person is too dependent on external factors for happiness, is insufficiently reliant on his own sense of contentment with life as it is. One thinks of the person who is obsessed with the idea of quality time – no part of the day can be frittered away or ever spent submaximally, each moment is to be crammed with worthwhile or at least necessary pursuits. To use Slote's words, this makes the optimiser seem 'needy and somewhat desperate'.[33]

As a result of the effort required to calculate worthwhileness and priorities among pursuits, the perfectionist is a rather stressed individual who finds it difficult to relax, and who suffers the anxieties and regrets occasioned by failure to act in line with those calculations. Not only are perfectionists stressed, they are also 'cramped and constrained',[34] unable to break out of the shackles of what calculation requires. Such a person cannot take uncalculated risks, act from devilment or mischievousness, creative urges, or, less high-mindedly, for the sake of immediate pleasure or titillation. Finally, the perfectionist is unlikely to be tolerant of satisficing tendencies in others. Such tendencies will be seen as 'slack', even downright irresponsible. The perfectionist is likely to be carping and critical, exhausting and undermining the egos of his partners by constant exhortation to improvement. In short, a perfectionist could be impossible to live with.

The restrictive maximiser may well reply to Slote's account of the virtue of anti-perfectionism that the 'virtue' of anti-perfectionism licenses non-calculation in the interests of maximisation, but does not license knowing submaximisation. Again, however, I wish to claim that once the virtue is acquired it may be appropriate to *express* the attitudes and desires which one possesses by virtue of being the sort of individual who is not a perfectionist.

Now, of course, it is not always the case that immoderate or self-indulgent satisficing is a manifestation of an anti-perfectionist virtue. Much satisficing may well be *inappropriately* weak. Our candy-bar eater would not be acting according to the virtue if his indulgence were excessive or otherwise inappropriate: if, for example, given certain contexts, he took two bars, or an enormous caramel bar, if he was in danger of spoiling his appetite for a healthy meal, or a meal to which he had been invited by a friend, if he was prone to start on chocolate binges once he indulged his desire to take the bar, and so on.

To conclude: the rationality of satisficing is again premised on the rationality of manifesting a virtue by expressing desires, attitudes, emotions characteristic of it. The manifestation of this virtue in the case discussed does not translate into a judgment that it is *best* to eat the bar here and now: hence I have severed Slote's connection between doing what is best – the supererogatory action – and doing what is most rational. It is the idea of expressive rationality which severs this connection.

## 4.

Let us turn finally to moral, or more clearly moral contexts, which are other-regarding. Pettit and Brennan name some moral virtues which they claim rationalise restrictive maximising consequentialism, but not satisficing. Let us consider the rationality of expressing a virtuous disposition such as friendship in knowingly suboptimal behaviour. They claim that the value of friendship provides a reason against calculation or calculative monitoring. For these are antipathetic to the virtue of friendship if standardly practised. There are two issues here. First, as Pettit and Brennan emphasise, there is the damage done by the inevitable perception by our friends of calculative behaviour unbecoming to a friend.[35] Second, such behaviour is inimical to the integrity of the friend's indulging in it, assuming he values the virtue of friendship.

These claims also tell against restrictive maximisation, however. It is not just that the maximising goal should be kept out of 'deliberative play'.[36] The maximising goal should be kept out of play altogether, because acting on it, whether or not such action is the result of deliberation, may be inimical to the value of friendship. If a friend is going to suspect you because you are *calculative* in the service of a maximising goal, that friend will also suspect you if you are prepared to act in the service of that goal *whenever* you know that betraying the friendship will serve that goal. Similarly, if you value your integrity in the following respect – you do not want to be the sort of person who betrays friendships in the interest of maximisation – you will value (in appropriate situations) not merely *non-calculative* maximising behaviour but also *not acting* on maximising considerations.

Pettit and Brennan may make the following kind of reply. If optimific action on given occasions is in the long run going to destroy the friendship, then friendship is what they call a 'vaguely defined Gestalt',[37] i.e. a good whose utility is not a linear function of the individual utilities of the acts contributing to those goods. An example given is sound teeth: it may be that each individual act of brushing is suboptimal, given the costs. Nonetheless, the combined effects of never brushing is suboptimal: the good of sound teeth is lost. The response to this phenomenon, according to the restrictive maximising consequentialist, is to fail to act optimifically on sufficiently many occasions – as many occasions as are necessary to secure (or to avoid losing) the good.

To avoid this complication, let us assume that long-run optimality, too, is secured by friendship betrayal even if the friendship is destroyed, and that this is known without calculation. How then can satisficing be rational? My reply is again based on a conception of virtue-based rationality. The person who has the *virtue* of friendship will set store on a holistic pattern of responses expressive of being a friend, even where, on given occasions, such responses are contrary to restrictive maximising rationality. Such a person will have a conception of 'emergency' different from that of the restrictive maximiser. Given the heavy presumption in favour of expressive rationality, a *sufficiently* great amount of good must be secured by a departure from a non-absolutist virtue-based maxim in order for a violation to be either permitted, or even required.

Pettit and Brennan might well reply that I have not defended (B)-type *satisficing*, for have I not simply just rejected consequentialism? Has it not just been conceded that the 'satisficer' believes that not betraying the friend is simply the best action?

This has not been conceded. Our non-consequentialist satisficer is assumed to believe that on this occasion, friendship betrayal is the best action: it best fits the circumstances, precisely because of its consequences in this case. But she also believes that someone possessing the *virtue* of friendship may yet have an undefeated *reason* not to betray her friend: expression of virtuous character takes rational precedence over performing the best action, assuming the action performed is good enough. And *ex hypothesi* it is good enough: the satisficer's conception of 'emergency' is such that an emergency has not obtained. For example, the friend, suffering from stresses of overwork has performed an administrative blunder which, if revealed, would avoid certain inconveniences to a large number of clients, but would cause her embarrassment. Now, one might think that if the agent does not reveal the error, she believes either that non-revelation is the best thing to do, or that she is in the grip of an unresolvable dilemma. My assumption however is that she believes on the contrary that revelation is the best thing to do – it is the thing that best fits the circumstances – but that she does not (rationally) have to do it. Given her character as a friend why should she put herself on the line, doing violence to what is expressive of her feelings as a friend, and what is worthy of her given her status as a friend? Certainly, 'being an unfriendly act' is an intrinsic feature of an action which constitutes, as Ross would put it, a 'wrong-making' feature. But, it is conceded, the consequences of performing the unfriendly act are sufficiently good that being unfriendly is the best thing to do. From the perspective of agent-oriented rationality, therefore, it is not the mere fact of the wrongness of being unfriendly that makes it rational for her not to betray her friend: rather, it is her *expression* of unfriendliness and the violence done to her friendly feelings which suggest the rationality of non-betrayal.

Let us now consider a clearer case where a wedge can be driven between an agent's recognition that a rejected action is best, and her being rationally justified in rejecting that action. An example is provided by Slote:

> Consider a doctor who wants to help mankind but is for personal reasons particularly affected by the plight of people in India – perhaps he is attracted to Indian art or religion or is very knowledgeable about the history of India.[38]

Imagine that this doctor could save more lives in Africa, and knows this; yet he goes to India. In this case, it is tempting to think that the doctor is really a maximiser: he puts really high value on indulging his passions for India. But this is surely implausible. Anyone who valued in this way would be intolerably egocentric. I want to suggest that Slote's doctor is really a satisficer, for he does not accept that a state of affairs in which he saves 500 lives and gratifies his passion for Indian art has a higher value than a state of affairs in which he saves 600 lives and does not indulge his passion. Rather, Slote's satisficer has allowed an agent-centred reason to trump reasons for performing the best action. Such a satisficer does not perceive himself as an instrument for the production of good, but as an agent with his own projects and needs that may legitimately take precedence over *optimisation* of value. His preferences for India are based not on an overall judgment of superior value, but on an 'agent-centred prerogative'[39] – a prerogative which can allow one to fail to maximise value in the interest of recognising and indulging one's needs, preferences or integrity. Certainly, our agent *prefers* to go to India, but preference rankings are not necessarily value rankings, even where personal values are involved.[40] Slote's doctor, then, may judge that the best action – the supererogatory action – is to go to Africa. Yet, on the view canvassed, the supererogatory action is not necessarily the most rational. Again, the link between the best action and the most rational action is severed by the notion of expressive rationality: in many circumstances the preference for expressing a virtuous (or at least non-vicious) commitment is not less rational than being supererogatory.

A number of virtues could be seen as underlying the doctor's satisficing behaviour. One might for example imagine that he has been a very hard-working doctor, easily prey to guilt, and to pressure from others to perform. Indulging his passion for art may be an expression of new-found self-assertiveness or self-protection. It is natural too to think that anti-perfectionism underlies his behaviour. Manifesting the trait of anti-perfectionism may justify suboptimal behaviour not only in the domain of personal goods, but also in many moral contexts. In general, the virtue of anti-perfectionism is the virtue of not being overly hard on oneself by always striving for and wanting perfection, whether with respect to personal or moral goods. One can be hard on oneself in a variety of ways, not just in 'eking out the most or best in every situation' by being obsessed with quality time or maintaining a perfect garden, house or career. One can also be a perfectionist in the moral domain: the perfectionist optimiser will ruthlessly put aside her squeamishness, projects and so forth when optimising rationality demands it. What is suggested is that, in the name of not being hard on oneself, the agent will preserve her own peace of mind, her own happiness, and will without guilt avoid falling prey to the fragmentation of character that optimizing demands. Such tendencies are not selfish – concern for one's own projects, commitments and loved ones is not to be consigned to the realm of the merely prudential. What the virtue of anti-perfectionism preserves is the guiltlessness and harmony of a person who is not at the beck and call of the exigencies imposed by the world – when those exigencies are detected without deliberation, and demand response in a manner which thwarts her own purposes, and does violence to her virtue. Expressive rationality crucially allows that the detection, without deliberation, of an optimal action, does not necessarily have to count as an emergency demanding response.

It is important to note that an appeal to anti-perfectionism is not necessarily tied to an attack on maximising *consequentialist* accounts of rationality. Consider someone who has a nonconsequentialist view of rightness, and believes that the best action is one in which she keeps a promise. However, temperamentally, she likes to produce good, and can hardly bear to see opportunities for producing good lost. She thinks that most good would be produced in this case by breaking the promise; furthermore, since the promise is not very important or solemn, she thinks that breaking the promise in this case is 'good enough'. Disturbed by squeamishness at failing to promote good, she breaks the promise – expressing the trait of anti-perfectionism, she goes with her emotions and is not hard on herself.

It is important to note too, that anti-perfectionism as a virtue permitting satisficing in certain circumstances will not license any appeal to temperament or emotion as a way of avoiding the demands of optimisation. In particular, I can agree with Marcia Baron's claim that the following kinds of appeal do not express the virtue:

> Fairness is not my forte. It is unreasonable to expect it of me when it is hard for me, so contrary to my nature. Give me something easier to do.[41] . . . Ah, I have met my weekly quota; now I can relax.[42]

Such a way of delineating anti-perfectionism is in most contexts at least insufficiently demanding and insufficiently situation-specific. My point is merely that 'not being too hard on oneself' sometimes rationally legitimises suboptimal behaviour insofar as it constitutes action expressing a virtue.

In this chapter, I have defended the possibility of nonconsequentialist satisficing within a virtue-ethical framework. Nonconsequentialist satisficing is to be distinguished not only from restrictive maximising consequentialism which permits nonconsequentialist strategies, but also from restrictive satisficing consequentialism,[43] because it is possible for 1. the agent to know (without calculation) that a preferred action has *consequences* which are not satisfactory; 2. the rejected action to be better than the one preferred precisely because of its superior consequences; 3. the preferred action to be good enough (because of features other than consequences; and 4. the agent to be rationally justified in his preference because of agent-centred features.

In essence, an agent-oriented ethics of virtue allows for the possibility that the rational authority of character, manifested in action expressing one's character, will at times override the rational authority of optimality, within satisficing limits. Clearly character is not always to have rational authority: that would be to permit a range of vices, such as self-indulgence, excessive squeamishness, laziness. This fact opens up issues which need to be explored: just how and when can expressing character have rational authority over optimality? How limited or wide-ranging, within what parameters of vagueness, is agent-oriented rationality, as opposed to act-oriented rationality? And to what extent can inner states of the agent, other than character, underpin the legitimacy of satisficing – e.g. moods, feelings, emotions?

A further and even deeper issue also needs to be more thoroughly explored. Though the idea that the rationality of not 'betraying' virtuous traits in the kinds of circumstances portrayed is attractive to many, it would be good to have a deeper justification for such a general view of rationality. To answer this question satisfactorily would take us well beyond the confines of this chapter, but I shall conclude by touching on this question, outlining some possible lines of enquiry.

The thesis of this chapter is of a piece with a fact that the rise of virtue ethics has done much to emphasise in recent times – the importance of good character for personal flourishing, the social fabric, the flourishing of one's children, and indeed, the wellbeing of the wider ecological community. If good character is so important, is it not natural that it should have some rational authority? Indeed, is it consistent with the idea that one has *character* that it does not have such authority on suitable occasions? Certainly it appears to, *de facto*: were Jim in Bernard Williams' famous example[44] to say that to kill an innocent would not be worthy of him, that he could not bring himself to do it, even though he were to admit that such an act is optimific and could immediately see that, the force of character would be seen as very powerful. And it would be exerting an authority over his individual acts. He would not be picturing himself as a characterless agent, weighing all reasons as if conforming to the pattern of his character was not a framework or background for his conception of himself as a rational agent.

However, how can one justify such deference to character? Why should appeal to character let one off the optimising hook? One approach might appeal to the autonomy of the agent. The idea is that a properly autonomous self-governing agent can properly reject options which on some conceptions of rationality would be optimific but which do not express the feelings, inclinations, emotions and attitudes which are 'innocent' in the sense of being characteristic of virtuous or at least non-vicious response to a value or valuable thing. However, if autonomy is to provide an underpinning for the legitimate expression of one's character at the cost of acting suboptimally, the idea of autonomy must be specified in a way that makes it attractive as a rational ideal. For on a bare notion of autonomy, even morally permitted actions expressing one's autonomy may be irrational. The fact that you are morally permitted to stand for three days in the university quad clad in silk pyjamas in the pouring rain and cold, does not make this action a rational exercise of one's autonomy.[45] This observation does not however vitiate a claim that autonomy is the underlying basis for a character-based conception of rationality. One would need, however, to employ a rich notion of autonomy – a virtue-ethical one – which might be developed along the following lines.

Though the independence which is at the heart of autonomy is a feature which cannot license all actions exhibiting independence as rational, it is the core of the virtue. An enriched account of autonomy must qualify the core of independence, but first let me observe its importance. The basic idea is that autonomy reflects or sanctions not so much the need for an agent to preserve her own integrity, or a non-striving for perfection, both of which are neglected or ignored by highly directive and external theories of rightness and rationality, but rather the importance of exhibiting, maintaining, fostering and so forth her independence. This independence means that she can take seriously her own inclinations where these are sufficiently innocent or harmless. It means that they do not lose their innocence the moment that the agent knows (without deliberation) that acting on them would be suboptimal. For their suboptimality may have nothing to do with her, and to be always taking into account the ways others have shaped the world would be to pay insufficient regard to her independence from the wants and indeed capricious actions of others. Now of course there will be considerable room for debate concerning the scope of the excellence of autonomy: when is acting on one's innocent enough inclinations selfish, self-centred, insouciant of the interests of others, 'unclubbable', uncaring of communitarian values or interests? And it may be thought puzzling that autonomy should be thought of as an excellence or a laudable state. It is such because the tendency to conform, to succumb to the pressures of others, paying insufficient regard to the worthwhileness of acting on one's own inclinations, is a common human failing.

The virtue of autonomy is best understood through an account of the enormous range of opposed vices, which can be clustered under the notion of vices of excessive and insufficient independence. As the standing in the quad example shows, and countless other examples would also show, the excessive displaying of independence can be absurdly eccentric or self-indulgent, or it may display obstinacy, rigidity or self-destructiveness. Again, a person's independence may demonstrate a complete lack of caring or ruthlessness as opposed to a desirable self-sufficiency. Alternatively, a person's independence may disguise an authority problem where resisting authority, far from being a virtue, is a manifestation of hostility which therapy would reveal to be a defect which causes a failure to live well in a situation where there are, of necessity, authority relations. His hostility to authority not only affects deleteriously his relations with colleagues, and the effectiveness of his contribution, it also makes him unhappy in his job. At the other end of the scale, there are a great variety of vices of 'insufficient' independence – non-self-assertiveness, tendency to live one's life through others, diffidence or fear in experimentation, excessive self-sacrifice, servility.

An alternative deep justification for character-based rationality may rely on the desideratum of integration in the agent. Being at the beck and call of the exigencies imposed by the world is not just destructive of the agent's integrity, nor just interferes excessively with her projects. The problem is not just that what turns out to be best on any given occasion may rarely intersect with an agent's rational life plans. Optimisation may simply be at odds with innocent inclinations, which flow from the kind of person she is. The problem of fragmentation is not the same problem as that of loss of integrity. Nor are the dangers of fragmentation the same as the dangers of lack of independence and autonomy. A highly independent agent who is perfectionist in his zeal to optimise may in consequence lead an excessively fragmented and exhausting life, with attendant psychological ills. Rather, the problem is a continuing sense that one cannot act in line with one's settled dispositions, e.g. to act on spontaneous (innocent) inclinations, to socialise with one's friends, to rest or indulge in favoured leisure pursuits, to spend time thinking, without seeing oneself as irrational.

A third, and again quite different ground, for character-based rationality relies on a scepticism about the desirability of agents' relying on case-by-case assessments of optimality. Though agents may often be confident in their assessments of what is the best action, there is a functional explanation, it may be argued, for tendencies to feel constrained by the 'authority' of their characters despite such confidence. We are beings of limited rationality liable to be swayed by self-interest, passing moods, passing enthusiasms and beset by limited information, much of which is suppressed, distorted or not used anyway. Philosophers, no doubt because of their professional faith in the power of rational argument, seem to have an over-optimistic faith in the ability of human beings to be rational autonomous authorities *on each opportunity of action*. Just as human beings need social codes to keep them in line, to prevent them from always carrying out and acting on full weighing of reasons, as Conrad Johnson recognises,[46] so they need character to provide a backdrop of habit and authority. Living well involves having good character, because only if one has good character does it become effortless and natural to act rightly. But this effortlessness and naturalness comes from being happy to conform one's behaviour to the patterns laid down by one's character. Now, as Dewey emphasises, these habits cannot be rigid or inflexible – there must be creative adjustment to novel situations. This creative adjustment is not tantamount, however, to ignoring the dictates of character whenever a novel situation arises. Just as a judge cannot exercise total discretion in hard cases, pretending that legislation does not exist or has no authority at all, so the agent will feel the pull of her character in her claims that she feels very uncomfortable doing thus, even though option rationality enjoins it.

In this chapter I have defended the view that an action which is good enough may rationally be preferred to one judged to be better. The goodness of an action is understood as a function of good- or bad-making features (or, if preferred, right- and wrong-making), features which can include factors other than results or consequences. The features which make an agent best or better are not understood in an agent-centred way, but what makes it rational for an agent to choose an action can include agent-centred features. Though a full agent-oriented account of rationality is not given,

I have appealed to some virtue-ethical insights to question Pettit's claims that the kind of satisficing defended is 'unmotivated' and 'profoundly irrational'.[47]

## ENDNOTES

1. See Chapter 3 of this volume, Gary Watson's 'On the Primacy of Character'.
2. For more on types of virtuous response see my 'Profiles of the Virtues', *Pacific Philosophical Quarterly* 76 (1995), 47–72.
3. See 'On the Primacy of Character'.
4. See Chapter 5 of this volume, Rosalind Hursthouse, 'Virtue Theory and Abortion', and Daniel Statman, 'Introduction'.
5. By Richard Routley (Sylvan), in 'Maximising Satisficing, Satisizing: The Difference in Real and Rational Behaviour under Rival Paradigms', Discussion Papers in Environmental Philosophy #10, Research School of Social Sciences, Australian National University, 1984.
6. 'Satisficing Consequentialism', *Proceedings of the Aristotelian Society*, Supp. LVIII (1984), 165–76, esp. 172.
7. Ibid., 139–63.
8. In Sterling M. McMurrin (ed.), *The Tanner Lectures on Human Values VII*, Salt Lake City: Utah University Press (1986), 56–99.
9. Cambridge: Harvard University Press (1989).
10. See Pettit's distinction between wide-scope and narrow-scope consequentialism in op. cit., 165.
11. 'Restrictive Consequentialism', *Australasian Journal of Philosophy*, LXIV (1986), 438–55.
12. Ibid., 442.
13. Ibid., 440.
14. Ibid., 440.
15. Ibid., 453.
16. Ibid., 445.
17. *Beyond Optimizing*, 24–5.
18. Pettit, op. cit., 172.
19. 'Slote on Consequentialism', *The Philosophical Quarterly*, XXXVI (1985), 399–412.
20. Ibid., 402.
21. Ibid., 403.
22. Ibid., 402.
23. *Common Sense Morality and Consequentialism*, New York: Routledge & Kegan Paul (1985), 41–2; 'Satisficing Consequentialism', 146.
24. See *The Right and the Good*, Oxford: Clarendon Press (1930), 41.
25. D. Schmidtz, *Rational Choice and Moral Agency*, Princeton: Princeton University Press (1995), 38.
26. *Beyond Optimizing*, 15.
27. 'Values and Purposes: The Limits of Teleology and the Ends of Friendship', *The Journal of Philosophy*, LXXVIII, 12 (December 1981) 747–65.
28. *Daybreak*, section 361.
29. Slote, op. cit., 119.
30. *Plural and Conflicting Values*, New York: Oxford University Press (1990), 320.
31. Slote, op. cit., 87.
32. Ibid.
33. Ibid.
34. Ibid., 93.
35. Pettit and Brennan, op. cit., 450.
36. Op. cit., 455.
37. Op. cit., 452.
38. 'Satisficing Consequentialism', 155.
39. For a discussion and defence of agent-centred prerogatives, see Samuel Scheffler, *The Rejection of Consequentialism*, New York: Oxford University Press (1982).
40. David Lewis claims that to judge valuable is to desire to desire but even this controversial view does not identity judgments of value with first-order preferences. See 'Dispositional Theories of Value', *Proceedings of the Aristotelian Society Supp. Vol.* (1989), 113–37.

41. 'Kantian Ethics and Supererogation', *Journal of Philosophy* (1987), 252.

42. Op. cit., 250.

43. I am grateful to Philip Pettit for pointing out this possible position to me.

44. J. J. C. Smart and B. Williams, *Utilitarianism For and Against*, New York: Cambridge University Press (1973), 98–9.

45. The notion of autonomy required to underpin the kind of satisficing permitted by character-based rationality must therefore be richer than the bare notion of autonomy employed by Michael Slote to justify moral permissions to pursue suboptimal innocent projects. See *Common Sense Morality and Consequentialism*.

46. See his 'The Authority of the Moral Agent', in Samuel Scheffler (ed.), *Consequentialism and its Critics*, New York: Oxford University Press (1988), 261–87.

47. I wish to express my gratitude to Philip Pettit and Michael Slote for their writings, conversations and comments on 'Satisficing and Virtue' from which much of this chapter is derived. I would also like to thank Fred Kroon for helpful comments on an earlier draft, and Michael Byron for fruitful conversation, and allowing me to read work in progress 'Satisficing and Optimality'.

# 5

# VIRTUE ETHICS AND THE EMOTIONS

## *Rosalind Hursthouse*

Does virtue ethics give a better account of the moral significance of the emotions than deontology and utilitarianism? And if so, is this just an historical accident, which may well cease to be so when proponents of the latter two theories turn their attention to the matter, or is it somehow intrinsic to the three different approaches that virtue ethics is superior in this regard and that deontology and utilitarianism must inevitably fail? I have always thought that virtue ethics does give a better account than the other two approaches – that was, indeed, one of the things that attracted me to it in the first place – but I am no longer sure, as I used to be, that this is much more than an historical accident.

Consider, for a start, the emotion of regret, often described as the appropriate reaction to being compelled by circumstances to do the sort of thing that, in more ordinary circumstances, one would regard as morally objectionable. Now it is true that standard utilitarianism and deontology, in being 'act-centred' rather than 'agent-centred' as virtue ethics is, do not encourage their proponents, immediately, to think about agents' emotions. So it is not very surprising that when their proponents consider quandaries, they concentrate exclusively on the question, 'Which is the right decision or act in this case, x or y?' And since one cannot decide to feel regret, and feeling regret is not an *act* in the required sense, they thereby cut themselves off from thoughts about bringing in that sort of emotional reaction, and answer merely 'x' (or 'y', as the case may be). In contrast, a proponent of virtue ethics, concentrating on the different question, 'What would a virtuous agent do in these circumstances?' is, given the concentration on the agent, and the wider scope of 'do', all set up to answer (for example) 'x, after much hesitation and searching for possible alternatives, feeling deep regret'.[1]

But once the possibility of giving the virtue ethicist's answer has been noticed, nothing in their 'act-centredness' seems to debar utilitarians and deontologists from talking about agents too and consistently adding remarks about regret to their previous answers. That, so far, they have tended not to, just seems an accident.

The central issue people seem to have in mind when they think of virtue ethics as giving the superior account of the moral significance of the emotions is, I think, the issue of 'moral motivation'. The debate concerns a famous passage in the first section of Kant's *Grundlegung*, and an apparent conflict between what this passage says and a central thesis of Aristotelian ethics. If I am right in thinking that this is the central issue people have in mind, we should pause to note a few oddities about it. 1. It can hardly aspire to showing that virtue ethics is superior to both deontology *and* utilitarianism on the emotions since the latter is uncommitted on moral motivation. 2. It fails to engage with non-Kantian deontology – and surely a deontologist might still be recognisably Kantian while still repudiating some of Kant. 3. It does not look as though it will suffice to ground a general claim about the moral significance of *the* emotions. Even if it shows that sympathy, compassion and love are morally significant, what about fear, anger, joy, sorrow, hope, pride, shame, despair, admiration, gratitude, embarrassment and so on? Nevertheless this issue is worth considering in some detail, to deepen the understanding of neo-Aristotelian virtue ethics and to explore the extent to which it is at loggerheads with Kant in the *Grundlegung*.

At the end of Book I of the *Nicomachean Ethics*, Aristotle introduces a distinction between the 'continent' or 'self-controlled' type of human being (who has *enkrateia*), and the one who has full virtue (*aretē*). Simply, the continent character is the one who, typically, knowing what she should do, does it, *contrary* to her desires. The fully virtuous character is the one who, typically, knowing what she should do, does it, desiring to do it. Her desires are in 'complete harmony' with her reason; hence, when she does what she should, she does what she desires to do, and reaps the reward of satisfied desire. Hence, 'virtuous conduct gives pleasure to the lover of virtue';[2] the fully virtuous do what they (characteristically) do, *gladly*.

So Aristotle draws a distinction between two sorts of people – the 'continent' or self-controlled and the 'fully virtuous' – and he *weights* that distinction, as the phrases show, a particular way; the fully virtuous agent is morally superior to the merely self-controlled one.

Now, on the standard reading of the *Grundlegung* passage, Kant draws the same distinction as Aristotle, but weights it the other way – the self-controlled agent is claimed to be morally superior to the agent who would, in Aristotle's terms, have full virtue, because she desires to do what she does. He describes the benevolent actions of people 'of so sympathetic a temper that . . . they find an inner pleasure in spreading happiness around them and can take delight in the contentment of others as their own work' as having 'no genuinely moral worth' and contrasts them unfavourably with the benevolent actions of two other people who, unmoved by any feelings of sympathy, act 'without any inclination for the sake of duty alone'; their actions have 'genuine moral worth'. This looks like bad news for Kant, for it seems to be (and has been claimed to be) tantamount to the wildly implausible claim that the person who visits her friend in hospital 'because she *is* her friend' is morally inferior to the one who visits her 'out of a sense of duty'.[3]

I used to read the *Grundlegung* passage in this way, but have now come to believe that Aristotle and Kant are much closer than is usually supposed.[4]

## PHILIPPA FOOT IN *VIRTUES AND VICES*

I was initially led to change my mind by Philippa Foot's penetrating discussion of Kant's passage in *Virtues and Vices*.[5] Foot introduces her discussion by pointing to an apparent contradiction in our everyday thoughts about morality. 'We both are and are not', she says, 'inclined to think that the harder a man finds it to act virtuously the more virtue he shows if he does act well. For on the one hand great virtue is needed where it is particularly hard to act virtuously; yet on the other it could be argued that difficulty in acting virtuously shows that the agent is imperfect in virtue: according to Aristotle, to take pleasure in virtuous action is the mark of true virtue, with the self-mastery of one who finds virtue difficult only a second best. How then is this conflict to be decided?'[6]

One rather weak response to the difficulty, which she does not consider, might be to say that 'commonsense' morality just *does* contain contradictions, that different approaches (Kantian, Aristotelian) pick up on different sides, and that the only thing for moral philosophers to do is go for one approach rather than the other and give up, or remake, commonsense morality. So, one might say, it is just a brute fact that the Kantian approach captures the commonsense view on courageous actions, whereby the one who shows most courage is 'the one who wants to run away but does not', and the Aristotelian approach captures the commonsense view on benevolent or charitable actions, whereby the one who shows most benevolence or charity is the one 'who finds it easy to make the good of others his object' (ibid.). Enlightened by the correct moral theory, we must revise our pre-theoretic ideas about courage or charity, comforting ourselves with the thought that we have, at least, managed to remove contradiction.

But Foot finds a better response; she finds some points in Kant with which Aristotelians may, and indeed, should agreed. Her discussion forces us to note that the *enkrateia/arete* distinction needs to be applied with some discretion and that the claim 'virtuous conduct gives pleasure to the lover of virtue' needs careful qualification. Moreover, as I shall go on to argue, there are points of agreement beyond those that she mentions.

So, how are we to resolve the conflict between the thoughts 'the harder it is for a man to act virtuously, the *more* virtue he shows if he acts well' and 'the harder it is, the *less* virtue he shows'? Foot's answer is that each may be true with respect to different cases, depending on what it is that 'makes it hard' to act well. Some things that 'make it hard' for someone to act well 'show that virtue (in him) is incomplete',[7] less than full virtue, for what 'makes it hard' pertains to his character. These are the cases of which it is true that 'the harder it is for him, the less virtue he shows', and the ones that the *enkrateia/arete* distinction – which is a distinction between different *characters* – applies to. But other things that 'make it hard' for someone to act well do not pertain to their character; rather, they are circumstances in which the virtuous character is 'severely tested' and comes through. These are the cases of which it is true that 'the harder it is for him, the more virtue he shows', and here the *enkrateia/arete* distinction does not apply.

Consider courage. This has always looked like a somewhat awkward virtue for the *enkrateia/arete* distinction and it is significant that Aristotle himself regards it as necessary to qualify his claim that the exercise of every virtue is pleasurable with respect to it.[8] Although his remarks in this passage are open to different interpretations,[9] what seems beyond dispute is that someone who wants to risk and endure frightful pain or death, and enjoys doing so, is not courageous but a masochist, or a dare-devil maniac. Even when the courageous are not acting contrary to an inclination to run away or preserve themselves, they are not, in any ordinary sense, 'doing what they want to do' and thereby reaping the pleasure of satisfied desire.

Nevertheless, there still seem to be neo-Aristotelian cases (off the battlefield) where the distinction applies; parents who have to conquer their fear in order to go to the rescue of their children do not compare favourably with those parents who fly to the rescue with no thought of their own safety; Hume's friends marvelled at the way in which he conducted himself towards the end of his life, in such a way that 'Death for the time did not seem dismal' as Boswell reported, let alone fearful. In such cases, fearlessness, rather than the conquering of fear, merits the highest esteem, since it reflects the agent's values and, thus, character. But if the fear that has to be conquered does not connect with one's values, but is, as we say, pathological, the judgment goes the other way; as Foot points out, 'if someone suffers from claustrophobia or a dread of heights he may require courage to do that which would not be a courageous action in others'.[10] Being subject to some phobia is being in circumstances that *call* on one's courage; if one comes through, one merits esteem.[11]

Consider honesty. If it is 'hard for me' to restore the full purse I saw someone drop because I am strongly tempted to keep it and have to conquer the temptation, I am less than thoroughly honest and morally inferior to the person who hastens to restore it with no thought of keeping what is not hers. But there are two different examples of the agent who thus hastens to restore the purse. There is the one who has a nicely full purse of her own, and the one who is poor. The former *may* be as thoroughly honest as the latter (a point Kant seems to overlook when discussing the shopkeeper who deals honestly with his customers) but, if she is, her honesty has not been, on this occasion, severely tested, because it is easy for her to restore it – what is a full purse to her? For the poor agent, 'it is hard' to restore it, hard insofar as she is hardily circumstanced, and the poorer she is – the harder it is for her to restore the purse – the more honesty she shows in unhesitatingly and readily restoring it. Here again, we should note qualifications that must be put on the statement that 'virtuous activity gives pleasure to the lover of virtue'. If the purse that the poor agent restores goes to someone who is manifestly a 'profligate debauchee' then Hume is quite right to say that there cannot be any ordinary motive involved, only the motive of restoring to someone that which is theirs, and I see no reason why any Aristotelian should deny to the fully honest the thought that it is a damned shame that this had to be done. The 'pleasure' the fully honest agent derives from this particular act is of an attenuated, not a characteristic, sort.

Consider now the (non-Aristotelian) virtue of charity or benevolence. It might seem that the (successful) exercise of this could not fail to give straightforward pleasure to one who genuinely possesses the virtue, for should not a genuine attachment to the good of others guarantee joy in their joy, pleasure in their pleasure? Must it not quite generally be the case that anyone who 'finds it hard' to help another possesses only the inferior, 'enkratic' form of this virtue? No, for here we come to one of Kant's philanthropists, the one whose mind is 'overclouded by sorrows of his own'. To say of him, when he does what is charitable, with difficulty and without pleasure, that he thereby acts less well, or shows himself to be less perfect in the virtue of charity, than someone else who does the same gladly, would be a mistake, for what 'makes it hard' for him to act well here does not show that his virtue is incomplete.

There is no reason why an Aristotelian should not agree with Kant that there is something particularly estimable about the action of the sorrowing philanthropist. For here, the 'difficulty that stands in the way' of his virtuous action is of the sort that 'provides an occasion'[12] for much virtue. It is his sorrow which makes noticing and attending to the needs of others particularly difficult, and as Foot rightly remarks, if he still manages to act with charity this 'most shows virtue', because 'this is the kind of circumstance that increases the virtue that is needed if a man is to act well'.[13] The fact is that it is difficult to do anything much when one's mind is overclouded by sorrow, and impossible to take pleasure in anything; the difficulty and lack of pleasure in acting this man finds spring from the nature of sorrow, not from his character, and it is only difficulties that spring from one's own character that show the virtue to be incomplete. So if the answer to 'Why does this person find it hard to make the good of others her object?' is 'Her mind is overclouded by sorrow' then the fact that she finds it hard is no reflection on her virtue; she may still count as being fully virtuous rather than merely 'continent'.

So, following Foot, we may conclude that Kant's estimation of the sorrowing philanthropist should not be read as a straightforward denial of Aristotle's weighting of the *enkrateia/arete* distinction. Instead, that distinction, and the concomitant Aristotelian claim that 'virtuous conduct gives pleasure to the lover of virtue' should be given qualified and particularised interpretations in a way that does justice to Kant's example.

But what about his other examples? Surely we can discern the denial in what he says about the happy philanthropists who 'find an inner pleasure in spreading happiness around them'. Foot does indeed imply that, in denying that their charitable actions have 'genuine moral worth' Kant has simply made a mistake about the virtue of charity. 'For charity is', she says, 'a virtue of attachment as well as action, and the sympathy that makes it easier to act with charity is part of the virtue.' She is right that he has made a mistake about the virtue of charity but I suspect too that Kant may have a picture of the happy philanthropists in mind which would justify his dismissal of their actions as 'lacking moral worth'. This is the point at which I leave Foot's discussion and seek to show that there is even more agreement between Kant and the Aristotelian approach than she identifies.

## ACTING 'FROM INCLINATION'

What does Kant imagine his happy philanthropists to be like? What *is* it to be the sort of agent who acts 'from inclination not from duty'? At the end of this section I shall suggest that these questions are much harder to answer than it might at first appear. But, for the moment, let us construct a picture as follows.

Suppose we began by thinking of certain emotions, say sympathy, compassion and love, as good or nice ones. Without committing ourselves to tendentious details about what an emotion is, or what it is to feel one, we can say safely that each characteristically involves such desires as the desire to help others, to comfort them in their affliction, to give them what they want and need, i.e. that they motivate one to do such things, and also that they characteristically involve emotional *reactions* – felt pain or sorrow at another's pain or grief, felt pleasure or joy at another's pleasure or joy.

Now we note an important difference between people; some are very prone to feel these emotions, others very little or not at all. (Some are in between, but let us leave them out of it.) This seems to be a difference in their characters; the former are charitable (or, as people tend to say nowadays, benevolent); the latter callous and selfish. So we might regard possessing the virtue of charity (or benevolence) as being very prone to feel these emotions on suitable occasions. Can we note a further difference between people – that some are very prone to feeling these emotions without being prompted to many actions by them, whereas others are thus prompted? Given that we said that the emotions in question characteristically involve desires to act, this seems unlikely, but, just in case, we could make it explicit and say: possessing the virtue of charity is being very prone not only to feel but to act from the emotions of sympathy, compassion and love, prompted by the desires associated with them.

Is this an adequate conception of the virtue of charity or benevolence? Well, it passes two tests. It certainly grounds the *enkrateia/arete* distinction; someone who tends to help others and to spread happiness around but feels no joy over their joy or sorrow when she cannot help, lacks the virtue in question, though clearly coming closer to it than someone who does not tend to do such things. It also makes the virtue of charity out to be, as Foot requires, 'a virtue of attachment' which corrects 'a deficiency of motivation' common to human nature. And it is not, I think, an uncommon conception.[7] If not Hume's,[8] it is at least recognisably Humean and it is plausible to suppose that Kant's target in this passage is Hume.

It is Hume who has said that 'If any man from a cold insensibility, or narrow selfishness of temper, is unaffected with the images of human happiness or misery, he must be equally indifferent to the images of vice and virtue'[16] – which is to say that he will never do what is benevolent or refrain from doing what is callous or cruel, because inclination or 'passion' will never move him to do so. To which Kant, we may suppose, replies, echoing his words, suppose a man were 'cold in temperament and indifferent to the sufferings of others'; assuredly he *would* still find in himself a source that would enable him to do what is benevolent; he will do it, not from inclination but from duty. So perhaps Kant's happy philanthropists have this sort of Humean benevolence.

It will indeed be true of them that, as described by Kant, they are 'of so sympathetic a temper that, without any further motive of vanity or self-interest, they find an inner pleasure in spreading happiness around and can take delight in the content of others as their own work'; that is just what makes them, at first sight, so attractive – just the sort of character, one might think, that one wants to visit one in hospital. And *when*, in action, they hit on 'what is beneficial and right' their actions deserve praise and encouragement, as he says. But there is the rub, for, as described, they are liable to go wrong in a number of ways. How come?

In Kantian terms, they are liable to go wrong because the emotions are *unreliable* as sources of acting well. But this is not something with which any Aristotelian need disagree. In Aristotelian terms, we reach the same conclusion at greater length and on different grounds.

We may say that sympathy, compassion and love attach one to 'the good' of others, involving desires to benefit and not harm them. But, more cautiously, we should say that they attach one to 'the apparent good' of others (and, correspondingly to 'apparent benefit' and 'apparent harm'), their 'good' as conceived by the one who feels the emotions. And a misconception of what is 'good' for others and of what benefits and harms them, may result in someone's being prompted to act wrongly by the emotions in question. (For example, compassion misguided by a misconception of 'good' may prompt someone to lie rather than tell the hurtful truth that the other needs to know.) Moreover, even when guided by a correct conception, the emotions may prompt one to actions that other considerations should tell against; perhaps this person does not merit sympathy and charitable action but others, unnoticed, do; perhaps, not having paused to think, one will wind up doing more harm than good; perhaps others would make a much better job of it (there is sometimes a sort of greediness and vanity in wanting to be the one who helps); perhaps one *can't* help, not because it is physically impossible, but because it is morally impossible in that it involves breaking a certain promise, or violating the other's, or another's, rights. And finally, one may fail to feel the emotions (and hence to be prompted to action by them) when other emotions get in the way – hatred or embarrassment or self-pity or, indeed, personal sorrow – and thereby fail to act as one should. In short, the emotions of sympathy, compassion and love, viewed simply as psychological phenomena, are no guarantee of right action, or acting well. There is nothing about them, *qua* natural inclinations, which guarantees that they occur 'in complete harmony with reason', that is, that they occur when, and only when, they should, towards the people whose circumstances should occasion them, consistently, on reasonable grounds and to an appropriate degree, as Aristotelian virtue requires. Moreover, even if, *per impossibile*, they should become so correctly tuned as to be 'in complete harmony with reason' without reason's influence, their promptings would still need to be regulated by *phronesis* or practical wisdom. They may prompt one to a good end, but the agent still has to be good at deliberation to be (reasonably) sure of attaining it, and the good of others, though a good end, is not the only good to be pursued in acting well.

So if Kant's happy philanthropists, who act 'from inclination, not from duty' are as described, they cannot be regarded as having an Aristotelian version of the non-Aristotelian virtue of charity or benevolence. Kantians and Aristotelians agree on the fact that this sort of agent cannot be relied upon to act well. And now for the further question: can Aristotelians agree with Kant that, when their actions do hit on 'what is beneficial and right', those actions 'lack genuine moral worth, *because* they are done from inclination not from duty'? Well, not in those terms, of course, since 'duty' and 'moral worth' are terms of art in Kant and nothing straightforwardly corresponding to them can be found in Aristotle nor even reconstructed in neo-Aristotelianism. But, in other terms, there is a significant measure of agreement to be found.

We should not forget that Kant and Aristotle significantly share a strongly anti-Humean premise about the principles or springs of movement (or 'action' in the broad sense of the term). According to Hume, there is only one principle of action, the one we share with animals, namely passion or desire; according to both Aristotle and Kant there are two, one which we share with the other animals, and one which we have in virtue of being rational. Of course we all know that the ideal Kantian agent acts from a sense of duty, not from inclination, but if 'inclination' is *that-principle-of-movement-we-share-with-the-other-animals*, then the virtuous Aristotelian agent doesn't act from inclination either, but from reason (*logos*) in the form of 'choice' (*prohairesis*).

In the *Eudemian Ethics* Aristotle says 'with the other animals the action on compulsion is simple (just as in the inanimate), for they have not inclination and reason (*logos*) opposing one another, but live by inclination; but man has both, that is at a certain age, to which we attribute also the power of action; for we do not say that a child acts, or a brute either, but only a man who does things from reasoning'.[17] So, in Aristotelian terms, we could say that the happy philanthropists, supposing them to have 'Humean' benevolence as described, do not *act* in the strict sense of the term at all; they live *katapathos*, like an animal or a child; their 'doings' issue from passion or emotion (*pathe*) not 'choice' (*prohairesis*). And here is the sense an Aristotelian may attach to the Kantian claim 'their "actions" (in the broad sense) lack genuine moral worth because they act from inclination not from duty'. It is *actions* proper, which issue from reason, that are to be assessed as virtuous (or vicious), but their 'doings' are not actions, and therefore cannot be said to be, and esteemed as, virtuous ones.

So, in contrast to the standard reading of this passage, I maintain that neither the esteem Kant gives to the sorrowing philanthropist nor his (relative) denigration of the happy philanthropists should be regarded as drawing Aristotle's *enkrateia/arete* distinction and, implausibly, reversing the weighting he gives to it. The esteemed sorrowing philanthropist need not be regarded as having mere *enkrateia* (because of Foot's points) and the denigrated happy ones should not be regarded as having *arete* (because they do not act 'from reason').

However, those who have detected something deeply wrong about Kant in this passage, who wanted to sum it up by saying 'Kant cannot give a proper account of the moral significance of the emotions', and thought that, somehow, virtue ethics gives a better account, have not been quite astray. The key example in this passage is the third philanthropist, whom nature has 'not exactly fashioned' to be one, whose character

Kant describes as having 'a moral worth *and beyond all comparison the highest*' (my italics). But, in the terms of the Aristotelian distinction, the third philanthropist clearly has, at best, *enkrateia* rather than *arete* and, in reserving for his character the highest moral worth, Kant displays in this passage, not a reversal of Aristotle's weighting of the *enkrateia/arete* distinction but a total lack of recognition of its existence. Moreover, the explanation of this failure of recognition is Kant's picture of the emotions; he does not have the understanding of them that generates that distinction. The issue is not so much over 'moral motivation', nor Kantian problems with impartiality *v* friendship or love, but over the nature of full virtue and the role emotion plays in it.

The fact is that the agent with, in Aristotelian terms, the full virtue of charity, does not appear in this passage. I pretended he did when following Foot on the sorrowing philanthropist, in order to make clear that Aristotelians can accommodate the point that it is sometimes hard for the agent with full virtue to act well. But, sticking to the text, the sorrowing philanthropist is someone with Humean benevolence, liable to go wrong in a variety of ways, who hitherto has acted only from inclination and now, 'for the first time' acts 'for the sake of duty alone'; not a new sort of philanthropist who has been introduced in contrast to the happy ones. And, in Aristotelian terms, this is hardly a coherent picture.

Let us ask again, what is it to be the *sort* of agent who acts 'only from inclination', not from 'a sense of duty' or reason or whatever: that is, someone who acts 'only from inclination', not just on a particular occasion but as a general way of going on? In Aristotelian terms, as we just said, it is to be the sort of agent who lives *katapathos*, like an animal or child – that is the way children and animals go on. But what fairly ordinary adult lives like an animal or child?

It might be thought that, for Aristotelians, the answer to that question is 'the adult with natural virtue', but Aristotle's tantalisingly brief remarks on natural virtue near the end of Book 6 of the *Nicomachean Ethics*[18] (1144b1–17) do not clearly bear this out. He says that the natural dispositions (towards, say, temperance or courage) are found in (some) children and animals, notes that without 'intelligence' (*nous*)[19] they are apt to be harmful, and says that if the subject with the natural disposition(s) acquires 'intelligence', his disposition, while still resembling the natural one, will now *be* virtue in the full sense. But he does not say explicitly that natural virtue can be found in adults[20] and, when we look at what he says about prodigality in Book 4, we may see the omission as deliberate. The prodigal man is said to be open-handed and eager to give, much closer to having the virtue of liberality than the illiberal or mean one; if he could be trained or otherwise changed (to give and receive 'in the right degree or manner') he would have the virtue. But there is no suggestion that he has the 'natural virtue' of liberality; on the contrary, prodigality is said to be a vice.

Now a child who was 'open-handed and eager to give' would surely have the natural virtue of liberality; since she has not yet reached 'the age of reason', her mistakes in giving and receiving do not manifest culpable ignorance. But once one is an adult, such mistakes *do* betray culpable ignorance and one is blameworthy. An adult can't just say to herself 'I am preserving my childish innocence, acting only from inclination with no thought of whether I am thereby acting well' and make that true by saying it. On the contrary, this would count as, culpably, being inconsiderate, feckless and self-indulgent, as acting that way *not* 'from inclination' but from choice (*prohairesis*), having decided (for some reason) that acting in accordance with one's inclinations *was*, in general, acting well.[21] Once one has become an adult and acquired reason, the only thing that would clearly count as being the sort of agent who acts 'only from inclination' not from reason, is being the sort of agent who is akratic or 'weak-willed' in character.[22]

So full virtue, which can be possessed only by adults, cannot be a child's natural virtue with reason, in the form of practical wisdom simply added on.[23] It is only with respect to the doings of children and brutes (and perhaps occasional impulsive doings of adults) that it makes sense to say that they act (in the broad sense) 'from inclination'.[24]

What, now, is to be said about the simple contrast between the two agents who visit a friend, one 'because she *is* her friend', the other 'out of a sense of duty'? With hindsight, it is revealed to be far less simple as a criticism of Kant on 'moral motivation'. If we take it as the contrast between a child moved by inclination, by the emotion of love (or friendship or sympathy – it doesn't matter which) and an adult moved by reason (either with full virtue or enkratic) then it is far from implausible to say the first is morally inferior to the second. But if we try to take it as embodying the Aristotelian contrast between *enkrateia* and *arete*, it has been set up in the wrong way. Insofar as it makes sense to talk of Aristotle's view on 'motivation', the self-controlled and the fully virtuous have the same 'motivation': they each act from 'choice' (*prohairesis*). The difference between them lies not in their 'motivation' or reasons for action, but in their condition; the fully virtuous are better disposed in relation to their emotions than the self-controlled,

## ARISTOTELIAN VIRTUE AND THE EMOTIONS

So now let us turn to the role emotions play in full virtue. I begin by stating, without argument, what I think an Aristotelian ought to mean, minimally, by 'the emotions are morally significant'. This is basically made up of three claims.

1. The virtues (and vices) are morally significant.
2. The virtues (and vices) are all dispositions not only to act, but to feel emotions, as *reactions* as well as impulses to action. (Aristotle says again and again that the virtues are concerned with actions and feelings.)
3. In the person with the virtues, these emotions will be felt on the *right* occasions, towards the *right* people or objects, for the *right* reasons, where 'right' means 'correct' as in 'The right answer to "What is the capital of New Zealand?" is "Wellington"'.

We should note immediately that the second claim really does give something like a logically proper ground for the *general* claim '*the* emotions are morally significant'. It thereby stands in marked contrast to some rather weak literature which seeks to support that general claim by a piecemeal approach which at best considers that no more than 'a few emotions (love and sympathy, or regret and pride) are morally significant'.

We should note too that the claims in combination give some value to the view that the feeling of certain emotions on certain occasions has intrinsic *moral* value, rather than merely instrumental value or some other sort of intrinsic value. Feeling *this* emotion *then* could be said to have 'intrinsic moral value' simply insofar as it is the manifestation of virtue. It is here, I think, that the (initially, apparently rather minor) issue about regret should figure as significant. Cases of emerging, with regret, from distressing or tragic dilemmas are, in the context of 'the moral significance of the emotions', to be thought of as but some amongst a great range of situations in which we want to say 'The way to feel here/ what one should feel about this/ what anyone decent would feel about this/ is . . .'. Another way to describe the very same fact would be that it has intrinsic moral value insofar as the emotional response had right, i.e. correct, rational content.

Finally and most importantly, we should note that the third claim introduces the crucial notion of feeling emotions *rightly* or *correctly*, where that is a cognitive notion. When we recall that the agent with Humean benevolence, and children with natural virtue, notably fail to do this, we are in a position to see that virtue is not merely a matter of being disposed to act well with a few dispositions to feel 'nice', sympathetic (or perhaps empathetic) reactions thrown in to make up the full weight. Just as Augustine's famous instruction 'Love, and do what you will' turns out not to be a licence to 'follow one's heart', but to embody extremely stern directions concerning what really counts as love, so the claim that full virtue involves feeling emotions correctly makes it clear that this would not be possible (in general) without the influence of reason.

What account of the emotions allows this claim to be true? One account that will *not* allow for it is one that makes the emotions no part of our rational nature. And there is indeed much in Kant to suggest that, although he shares with Aristotle the view that we have not just one, but two principles of movement, in other respects his philosophical psychology is Humean. He seems committed to the view that our emotions or inclinations are no part of our rationality. They come from the non-rational, animal side of our nature; if they happen to prompt us to act in accordance with the judgments of reason about what ought to be done we are lucky; if they incline us against them we find life difficult, but their prompting us in the right direction is no mark or indication of their rationality. The emotions are not rational in any way.

A different account, with a tradition that dates back to the Stoics, has it that the emotions are indeed part of our rational nature, for they are, or are partially constituted by, judgments, at least some of which are evaluative. On the face of it, this account marries well with the claim that emotions may be had rightly or correctly; roughly, an emotion is had correctly when the judgment (or set of judgments) which (partially) constitutes it is true (or, perhaps, reasonable given the evidence available). As an enormous literature on this topic has made clear, this 'cognitive account' faces numerous difficulties; for my present purposes, it suffices to mention just two. One is the difficulty in finding a suitable judgment (or set of judgments) to ascribe to someone who is only too aware of the fact that her emotion is irrational in some way, but is in the grip of it notwithstanding; I know perfectly well that the insect is harmless but am still terrified of it, that the tin-opener is not defying me and did not cut my thumb on purpose but am still furious with it, that my partner is a worthless skunk but I still love him, heaven help me. The second is that, even if we allow that toddlers and the higher animals can have some beliefs, there really is something very odd about maintaining that they make judgments, especially evaluative judgments; but unless they do, then, on the cognitive account, they do not have emotions either. These two objections might be summed up as one more general one; that on the cognitive account, the emotions are *too* rational, too akin to the judgments of theoretical reason.

What seems needed is an account which avoids these two extremes – of animal and non-rational and theoretic and utterly rational. On Hume's, and Kant's, picture of human nature, there *is* no logical space between the two. But Aristotle's division of the parts of the soul into rational and non-rational is not so hard and fast. We may classify the desiderative part of the soul with the nutritive part, as non-rational, he says – but then we must divide the non-rational part of the soul in two, distinguishing the desiderative part by saying that it participates in reason as the nutritive soul does not. Alternatively, we may classify the desiderative with the theoretical part of the soul as rational – but then we must divide the rational part of the soul in two, and say that the desiderative listens to, or obeys, the theoretical part.

So the Aristotelian picture of human nature creates a space for the emotions – in what is called the desiderative part of the soul – which allows them to be, shall we say, Janus-faced; one face is animal and/or non-rational; the other is rational. And this allows us to be struck, as surely we should be, not only by the fact that human beings are subject to some emotions which non-rational animals are also subject to, not only by the fact that human beings are subject to some emotions that non-rational animals notably lack (for instance pride, shame and regret) but, much more significantly, by the way in which reason can radically transform an emotion that human beings certainly share with animals, such as fear. How very unlike the other animals human beings are when they endure agony, and risk their lives, for justice and truth, or are terrified by the prospect of university examinations; when they are ready to die for glory, but tremble at the prospect of humiliation. The emotion that in the other animals is essentially connected to physical self-preservation or preservation of the species, can be transformed in human beings into an emotion connected with the preservation of what is *best*, most worth preserving, in us and our species. And the correctness (or incorrectness) of our view of that is an aspect of our rationality.

What then is an appropriate account of the emotions? The *details* need not concern us here; what will suffice, I believe, is the broad claim that the emotions involve ideas, or images (or thoughts or perceptions) of good and evil, taking 'good' and 'evil' in their most general, generic sense, as the formal objects of pursuit and avoidance. (Readers who find 'good' and 'evil' odd in this context may substitute 'value' and 'disvalue'.)

Many philosophers have noticed the fact that our emotions involve ideas, or thoughts, of good and evil. Some use the phrase 'of pleasure and pain' as (supposedly) interchangeable with 'of good and evil'; others distinguish the phrases. Some empha-sise the fact that (most) emotions are in part constituted by, or at least generate, a desire to do something, construing these desires as themselves involving ideas or thoughts, of good and evil (pleasure and pain). Hence it may be said that fear is in part, or generates, the desire to run away from something, this desire itself involving the idea of staying put as evil or painful; that love is in part, or generates, the desire to be with the loved one, this desire itself involving the idea of being with the loved one as good or pleasant. Some emphasise the way the causes, or objects, of the emotions are, or must be, thought of, or perceived or construed; something we fear or hate must be thought of, perceived, as evil (painful) in some way; something we hope for or love as good (pleasant). Some, noting that the desires characteristic of (some of) the emotions actually involve the objects (or causes), introduce further complexity; hence hatred may be said to involve the idea that evil's coming to someone thought of as evil is (or would be) itself good; anger to involve the idea that evil's coming to someone who has caused evil is (or would be) itself good . . . and so on.

In short, there is much variety and disagreement, but a discernible common ground, namely the vague remark that our emotions involve ideas, or thoughts, or perceptions, of 'good and evil', taking 'good' and 'evil' in their most general, generic, sense.[25]

In his otherwise admirable paper 'Morality and the Emotions', Williams appears to overlook this point. Seeking, in 1965, to explain why 'recent' moral philosophy in Britain had neglected the emotions, Williams found part of the answer to lie in the preceding and prevailing preoccupation with 'the most general features of moral language, or . . . evaluative language' and the consequent concentration on 'such very general terms as "good", "right" and "ought"'. This concentration, he said, 'has helped to push the emotions out of the picture' for '(i)f you aim to state the most general characteristic, and connexions of moral language, you will not find much to say about the emotions; because there are few, if any, *highly general* connexions between the emotions and moral language'.[26]

But Williams was too kind to his predecessors and contemporaries; the highly general connection between the emotions and the very general terms 'good' and 'bad/evil' was sitting there, right under their noses, *manifest* in the accounts of, at least, Plato, Aristotle, the Stoics, Aquinas, Descartes, Locke and Hume. They left the emotions out of the picture not for lack of any general connection between them and the terms they were obsessed with, but because they fed on a very one-sided diet of examples.

Now note that the vague remark stating the general connection falls far short of the much more explicit claim that the emotions involve, or are, evaluative *judgments*. The burnt child fears the fire and is distressed by its mother's anger long before it is of an age where we can talk of its making judgments, evaluative or otherwise. Indeed, even the claim 'the emotions involve thoughts of good and evil', when applied to small children, has to be construed with some care; it signifies the appropriateness of our talking to them in terms of generic good and evil when responding to their manifested emotions rather than the ascription of views.

However, the vague remark is obviously related to the more explicit one and, vague as it is, it is sufficient to ground the claim that no emotion *in us* is just the same as it is in the other animals. For, in virtue of our reason, we are language-users. We, unlike the other animals, can draw the distinction between what appears to us to be so, and what is really so. Unlike the other animals we can express our ideas or thoughts or perceptions about generic good and evil in sentences which figure, in our languages, as expressions of belief, up for assessment as true or false, correct or erroneous, reasonable or unreasonable.

## THE EDUCATION OF THE EMOTIONS

Another fault of Williams' predecessors and contemporaries was that, though concentrating on 'the most general features of . . . evaluative language' they failed to think about the fact that such language has to be taught, and thereby failed to think about moral education and upbringing. We are taught to use sentences which contain the words (equivalent to) 'good' and 'evil' and their cognates and species from a very early age, at the same time as we are taught how to conduct ourselves. And a central aspect of this teaching is the training of the emotions.

The immense complexity of the ways in which the emotions are trained, and values thereby inculcated, can be called to mind by considering a paradigm case of *bad* training, namely, the inculcation of racism.[27]

Recall, firstly, how extreme racism expresses itself in emotion, the way it generates not only hatred and contempt, but fear, anger, reserve, suspicion, grief that one's offspring is going to marry a member of the rejected race, joy when evil befalls them, pity for members of one's own race who are bettered by them, pride when one succeeds in doing them down, amusement at their humiliation, surprise that one of them has shown signs of advanced humanity, horror or self-contempt at the discovery that one has felt fellow-feeling for one – it is hard to think of a single emotion that is immune to its corruption.[28] It can even extend its influence to the appetites, since the rejected race's food and drink can be found disgusting, and sexual relations with its members perversely attractive.

Recall, secondly, that no-one relatively free of racism thinks that *any* of these emotional responses is in any sense natural; they all have to be inculcated, and from a very early age. Children have to be taught to fear, particularly, adults of a different race, to hate and suspect and despise its younger members, to be amused or otherwise pleased when they are hurt; angry or suspicious when they are friendly, to join in rejoicing when it is heard they have been done down, to admire those who have brought about their downfall; to resent, or dismiss their doing well.

And recall, thirdly, what we are beginning to understand about how racism is inculcated and how hard it is to eliminate. The last thirty years or so have seen a growing awareness of the ways in which we are influenced by the representations of racial stereotypes, of the racism implicit in many of our myths and metaphors, our images and archetypes, and a corresponding awareness that the most dedicated and sincere concern for charity and even justice is liable to be perverted and misdirected until we have both recognised, and rooted out, the racism that expresses itself in *emotional responses* we still defend as innocent, or justified, or reasonable – or beyond our control.

When we bear in mind this real example, of the inculcation of racism, it becomes vividly clear that 'the' way in which the training of the emotions shapes one's thoughts of generic good and evil cannot be divided neatly into the rational and the non-rational. It is, on the one hand, rational, insofar as children being inculcated in it are being taught applications of the generic terms 'good' and 'evil' (such people are *dangerous, ignorant, perverted*, he tried to get you to go to his place!/to eat his food? what *cheek*, how *disgusting*; she wouldn't have anything to do with him? quite *right* too, how *brave*, how *sensible* – these are all terms whose application we pick up from those who bring us up). And it is rational, further, insofar as some explanatory or justifying putative facts will be interwoven with the training – such people are dangerous *because* they can't control their passions, *because* they hate us, *because* they are cunning and devious, are not being brave *because* they don't feel pain the way we do, do not deserve pity *because* they always make a fuss – and putative evidence given for such claims. In these two ways it is a training peculiarly appropriate to rational animals.

On the other hand, it is non-rational insofar as it proceeds, one might say, by unconscious imitation, Humean sympathy and conditioning; the children just come to respond emotionally in the same way as those who are bringing them up, in a way that is at least akin to the way in which the young of some other species acquire their emotional responses.

Finally, it is, of course, non-rational, or *ir*rational, in the sense that the whole system of the application of the terms, their putative explanations and justifications, is a tissue of falsehoods and inconsistencies. But, as we know to our cost, the recognition of this fact does not suffice to undo the training. Coming to realise that some of one's emotional reactions have been not only entirely stupid but wicked is no guarantee that one won't go on having them.

Is it possible to extirpate them, to undo a childhood training in racism and re-train emotional reactions, in this area, into 'complete harmony' with reason: given, that is, the presence of a dedicated concern for charity and justice? The answer to this, I think it must be said, is that we still do not know.

We do know that reason can, directly, achieve a certain amount; one can catch oneself having the emotional reactions, drag the relevant stupid thoughts about good and evil to the surface of consciousness and hammer them with rational beliefs – I have *nothing* to fear from this person, she did *not* insult or patronise me, but asked a reasonable question, I have every *possible* reason to trust this person, and none not to; it is not at all surprising that she should be a mathematician. And we know that familiarity, in the sense of habitual acquaintance and intimacy (once again, given the dedicated concern), far from breeding contempt, breeds fellow-feeling, and can achieve much by way of casting out fear, hatred, suspicion and misplaced surprise.

But total re-training may nevertheless be impossible. Aristotle, acknowledging his debt to Plato, emphasises 'the importance of having been trained in some way *from infancy* to feel joy or grief at the right things' (my italics[29]); given the emotions' non-rational face, it may be that reason cannot unseat entirely bad training in childhood, and that relationships of love and trust formed in adulthood cannot entirely undo a kind of unconscious expectancy of evil which still manifests itself in racist emotional reactions.

If, sadly, that is so, what follows? It certainly does not follow that anyone subject to such reactions can shrug them off and say 'Oh well; they are beyond my control; I just can't help reacting that way'. For since we know that some re-training is possible, and do not know when, if ever, it ceases to be effective, anyone decent must be anxiously seeking ways to control these reactions, refusing to give up hope. But what does seem to be entailed is that those of us who had racism inculcated in us early are unlucky; through no fault of our own, and despite our greatest efforts, we may remain morally inferior to those who, in virtue of good training in childhood and rational principle, achieve complete harmony between their emotions and reason and thereby full virtue.

What would be involved in denying this entailment? We would have to insist that we can be as perfect in charity and justice as any human being can be, despite being subject to racist emotional reactions, as long as we keep them from manifesting themselves in action or omission (and, perhaps, as long as we continue to try to extirpate them). Well, someone might insist on saying that, but it sounds astonishingly arrogant, and one doubts that members of the rejected race will agree.[30] And perhaps it is examples such as racism that are needed to unseat the distaste that many people feel for what Williams has christened 'constitutive moral luck'.

If we try to think of Kant's third philanthropist as 'indifferent to the sufferings' of a particular oppressed race, because of his racist upbringing (which is a great deal easier than trying to imagine someone who is genuinely indifferent to the sufferings – *any* sufferings? – of other human beings – *any* other human beings?), we would surely not think of him as a moral exemplar just because he acts to benefit a member of the oppressed race 'out of duty', notwithstanding the indubitable fact that he had no control over his upbringing. If he has not devoted any effort to trying to undo the effects of his upbringing but is resting content with the claim that it was not his fault and his emotions are beyond his control then he is corrupt. If he has tried but not succeeded at all then he has not tried hard enough (for we know that some retraining is possible) and is at the very least suspect. What if he is still fairly young, has only recently started trying and hence has not succeeded much? Then, naturally, he will find it harder to do what is charitable and just than someone who, with the same bad upbringing, has been trying to undo it for longer, but his finding it harder does not make him morally superior to the one who now finds it easier than it used to be, quite the contrary.

Why do those of us who had racism inculcated in us think that we must strive, and continue to strive, to undo the effects of that upbringing? Not because we think it will make it easier for us to do what is charitable and just (though it will) but because we think it will make us better people, more charitable and just than we are at present. Why do we try to bring up our children differently? Not in the hope that it will make their moral lives less a matter of striving than ours have been (though, with respect to racism, it should) but in the hope that they will turn out better than we have, more charitable and just. How could we think that we ought to give our children a good upbringing, that we owed it to them, if we thought that it had no effect on whether they turned out better or worse? But whether or not we ourselves had a good upbringing is just a matter of luck.[31]

## CONCLUSION

It is, I think, true, that where Aristotle, and thereby the Aristotelians, have an edge over Kant (and, indeed, Hume) with respect to the moral significance of the emotions, is in the account Aristotle gives us of human rationality, an account that allows the emotions to participate in reason and thereby play their proper role in the specification of full virtue. Much modern moral philosophy, deontological and utilitarian, has followed Kant, or Hume, rather than Aristotle, on human rationality, and thereby still suffers from the fault to which Anscombe drew attention back in 1958 – it lacks 'an adequate philosophy of psychology'.[32] But although this may give the Aristotelians an edge over Kant, I do not see, off hand, any deep reason why it should give them an intrinsic edge over Kantian deontologists. As the recent revived interest in *The Doctrine of Virtue* reveals, there are, in fact, hints in Kant's later writings[33] that he did recognise some rational emotions; but even if there were not, deontological moral philosophers might still, it seems to me, be recognisably Kantian (insofar as they start with the Categorical Imperative) and add on an Aristotelian account of the emotions, just as virtue ethicists are still recognisably Aristotelian (insofar as they start with the Aristotelian account of the virtues) when they add on non-Aristotelian virtues such as charity and repudiate Aristotle's sexism. Nor do I see any immediate inconsistency in utilitarians' adding it on; once they have noticed how optimific it would be if everyone were brought up, or trained themselves, to have the right emotions, on the right occasions, to the right extent, towards the right people or objects, should they not welcome the idea?

It might turn out that thoroughly worked-out attempts to 'add on' the older account of the emotions changed the deontology and utilitarianism into virtue ethics in all but name; then indeed we might claim that virtue ethics is intrinsically superior in this regard. But until we see what such attempts look like, that should remain an open question; perhaps its current pre-eminence in this area will turn out to have been an historical accident.

* I am grateful to Philippa Foot and Christine Swanton for detailed criticisms of earlier versions of this chapter.

## ENDNOTES

1. I discuss the issue of how utilitarianism, deontology and virtue ethics can respond to dilemmas in 'Fallacies and Moral Dilemmas', *Argumentation*, 9, 1995, 1–16.
2. Aristotle, *Nicomachean Ethics* (1099a12).
3. The example is now standardly used in this abbreviated form; in its original form it was much richer in details, which, importantly, made the *characters* of the agents clear. See Michael Stocker, 'The Schizophrenia of Modern Ethical Theories', *Journal of Philosophy* LXII (1976), 453–66.
4. Robert Louden, in 'Kant's Virtue Ethics' (this volume, Chapter 16) and Christine Korsgaard, in 'From Duty and for the Sake of the Noble', in Stephen Engstrom and Jennifer Whiting (eds), *Rethinking Happiness and Duty*, New York, Cambridge University Press (1995) also find more agreement between them than is allowed by the standard reading.
5. In Philippa Foot, *Virtues and Vices*, Oxford: Basil Blackwell (1978), 1–18.
6. Op. cit., 10.
7. Op. cit., 11.

8. *Nicomachean Ethics* (1117b10).

9. John McDowell, for example, maintains that the virtuous understand the notions of 'benefit, advantage, harm, loss and so forth' in such a way that no 'sacrifice' necessitated by virtue counts as a loss. ('The Role of Eudaimonia in Aristotle's Ethics', reprinted in *Essays on Aristotle's Ethics*, Amelie Rorty (ed.), California: University of California Press (1980), 369–70. He cites D. Z. Phillips, in 'Does it Pay to be Good?' *Proc. Arist. Soc.* n.s. 65 (1964–5), who insists that when virtue requires me to lay down my life, the virtuous 'see death as a good'.

10. Foot, op. cit., 12.

11. This is a 'neo-' Aristotelian point; had Aristotle recognised claustrophobia, it seems likely that he would have regarded it as a defect that made the virtue of courage unattainable.

12. Foot, op. cit., 11.

13. Op. cit., 13.

14. It is, I think, Lawrence Blum's. Near the end of *Friendship, Altruism and Morality*, London: Routledge & Kegan Paul (1980), he says 'it is possible to cast much of the argument of this book in the language of character and of virtues. For I have regarded compassion, sympathy and concern (or concernedness) as virtuous traits of character, associated with the emotions denoted by the same terms'. He assumes that I have the virtue of compassion if I have a compassionate character, and that I have a compassionate character if, simply, I am prone to feel, and act out of, the emotion of compassion on suitable occasions. It is also, I suspect, the conception that leads Frankena to coin the phrase 'principles without traits (virtues) are impotent and traits without principles are blind' (*Ethics*, 2nd edn, New Jersey: Prentice-Hall (1973), 65).

15. I do not claim that it is Hume's. Oddly enough, Hume never says explicitly what he thinks possession of a virtue consists in, and how Humean passions might figure in a virtue when rendered suitably 'calm' is a large topic. See Annette Baier, *A Progress of Sentiments*, Cambridge, Massachusetts: Harvard University Press (1991).

16. David Hume, *An Enquiry Concerning Human Understanding*, ed. L. A. Selby-Bigge, revised by P. Nidditch, Oxford: Clarendon Press (1975).

17. Aristotle, *Eudemian Ethics* (1224a25–30).

18. *Nicomachean Ethics* (1144b1–17).

19. It is not clear whether Aristotle is using *nous* here in the casual, popular sense – as we use it – or in the technical sense he has been discussing earlier. But either way, it is not something that children and brutes have.

20. I do not deny that one can interpret Aristotle here as implying that adults can have natural virtue; I do deny that this is the most plausible interpretation.

21. Perhaps someone (rather silly) might become convinced that they should try to become a sort of Noble Savage.

22. For an excellent discussion of weakness of will and weakness of character, see Christine Swanton, *Freedom: A Coherence Theory*, Indianapolis: Hackett Publishing Company (1992).

23. As, perhaps, Louden is inclined to suppose. ('Kant's Virtue Ethics', this volume, Chapter 16.)

24. I take Marcia Baron's first 'variety' (in 'Varieties of Ethics of Virtue', *American Philosophical Quarterly*, No. 22, 47–53) which she thinks Lawrence Blum would be drawn to, to be an instructive failure to attach sense to there being a sort of adult who acts only 'from inclination'. The agent 'desires to help others' etc., but has 'no moral concepts in the abstract: no concept of . . . goodness'. When children act from their inclination to help others, and get it wrong, and say, for example, 'She wanted to take the bandage off', we don't ascribe a mistaken conception of goodness to them; they are too young to have such conceptions. But an adult who has acted similarly can't excuse themselves by saying 'I was trying to help, but have no views about whether what I did benefited or harmed her, no concept of what is good, or bad, for human beings'.

25. For the kind of discriminating detail that makes the 'vague remark' into a plausible and illuminating thesis, the best source is still Aquinas, not just in *Summa Theologiae*, Ia2ae, (QQ.22–30) on 'The Emotions' but all through IIa2ae (QQ.1–189) on hope, fear, despair, charity, joy, hatred, *acedia*, envy, anger, curiosity. . . . Descartes, in *The Passions of the Soul*, gives a rather watered down, but still instructive version.

26. B. Williams, *Problems of the Self*, Cambridge: Cambridge University Press (1973), 208.

27. It is a tricky question whether 'racism' connotes rejection of another race, or, more particularly, rejection in the context of oppression. My first two sets of remarks about the ways in which

a racist upbringing affects our emotions are, I think, fairly uncommitted on this; blacks and whites, Gentiles and Jews may be affected in the same way. But the third set tends towards the concept of racism that necessarily involves oppression. It is the oppressing race, the one that imposes the myths and metaphors, whose charity and justice is liable to be perverted by that imposition.

28. In discussion, someone optimistically suggested love. But although there are heart-warming examples of love's triumph over racial prejudice, there are also examples of its failure to survive the discovery that the loved one has 'tainted' blood.

29. *Nicomachean Ethics* (110b11–12).

30. Justice is said, even by virtue ethicists, not to involve the emotions, but the example of racism seems to me to show that this is a mistake.

31. Space prohibits my considering the question of whether one can fail in full virtue because of one's 'natural temperament'. But my animadversions against natural virtue in adults clearly extend to 'natural vice'. No-one who is thoroughly cold-hearted as an adult is so through no fault of his own. See Gregory Trianosky, 'Natural Affection and Responsibility for Character: A Critique of Kantian Views of the Virtues', *Identity, Character, and Morality*, Owen Flanagan and Amélie Oksenberg-Rorty (eds), Cambridge, Massachusetts: M.I.T. (1990), an article from which I have greatly benefited.

32. G. E. M. Anscombe, 'Modern Moral Philosophy', *Ethics, Religion and Politics*, Minneapolis: University of Minnesota Press (1981).

33. See Louden 'Kant's Virtue Ethics', this volume, Chapter 16. Note, further, 'Sympathetic Feeling is Generally a Duty' (in *The Doctrine of Virtue*, 456–7), where Kant commends 'the capacity and the will to share in others' feelings' as an appropriate feeling for 'man . . . regarded . . . as an animal endowed with reason'.

# 6

# EMOTIONAL IDENTIFICATION, CLOSENESS AND SIZE: SOME CONTRIBUTIONS TO VIRTUE ETHICS

## *Michael Stocker*

For a considerable part of my professional life, I have been disturbed and fascinated by the way people, our subjectivity and the various sorts of relations we have with each other, are absent from our work in ethics. We need to investigate why so many ethicists have been so comfortable not dealing with these. We also need to correct – or continue to correct – this lack. This is what I propose to do, in a very limited way, in this chapter.

It may be useful to review some personal history. My early paper, 'Agent and Other', argued that ethics should recognise foundational moral differences between agent and other – how, for example, act and agent evaluations can depend on whose value, the agent's or another's, is involved, not (or not just) the amount of value.[1] In other early works I argued that many of our most important values and evaluative concerns depend on structures of care, concern, emotion and character: for example, that there are deep and pervasive connections between act and agent evaluations, and that many of our most important goods, such as friendship, depend constitutively on structures of motivation.[2] They further argued that these structures are importantly different in many people; and that we make serious errors – such as holding that the good must always attract – if we focus all our attention on, say, ambitious, successful men who, perhaps correctly, see the world as their oyster.[3] I have found Aristotle's ethics – one of our preeminent virtue ethics – and, more recently, psychoanalysis, congenial areas and styles to work in and from in developing these themes.

Am I, therefore, an adherent of virtue ethics? If virtue ethics is a *theory* of ethics, with all the weight we now attached to 'theory', I would prefer to say no. If virtue ethics is the view that all, or nearly all, important ethical issues are to be settled by recourse to virtues and virtuous people, then again I would prefer to say no. In this last, if not also the first, I think I join with Aristotle. As I read him, he thought politics a higher and more inclusive discipline than ethics. As I also read him, he thought 'external' goods, such as peace, prosperity, good health and good laws, essential for a good life. One way we can see some reason to join him is by noting the difficulties we have when trying just to list, without even going into detail, the virtues of good people in bad societies. To put the point briefly, it is easy enough to see that the moral virtues of bad and hard societies and times are not those of good and easier ones. But it is very hard to see how, either in particular or in general, to tailor virtues to the particularities of bad societies: for example, to know when discretion is the better part of valour, when compliance is morally compromising, when resistance is all right or required, when one should work from within or from without, and so on. The debates of serious political parties and revolutionaries show us the importance and also the difficulties of these issues.

Perhaps virtue theory can deal with these issues. Perhaps what is bad about bad social and societal arrangements can be diagnosed and described in terms of the ways they deform, hinder, or preclude virtue or virtuous life or in terms of what would be done or approved of by virtuous people. And perhaps remedies that will effect the needed evolution, rectification or revolution could be suggested by virtue theory. I do not know if virtue ethics can do this. But I do know that if virtue theory can do this, it would be far in advance of our other theories, which give little real guidance here.

Another way to join Aristotle is by noting just how important rules, laws, and procedures – whether legislative, or more likely for us, administrative – are for us and our lives. I doubt if most contemporary academic philosophers have it made clear to us just how important rules and procedures are, and how many of these are formulated or created, and certainly enforced, by bureaucratic, administrative agencies.[4] This may be a stroke of good luck for us in the way we live our lives.

But it serves us poorly by allowing, perhaps encouraging, us to give misleading and sometimes fanciful accounts of political philosophy: for example, in terms of legislators who are to be judged by the criteria of virtue theory. It allows or encourages us to offer a virtue-theory account of the law, in terms of legislators deliberating, ideally in the manner of virtuous people. In saying this, I do not in any way mean to suggest that administrators are, perhaps must be, lacking in virtue, or that legislators must or even do enjoy a sufficiency of it. I mean only that the ideal of virtuous people being, in themselves, the touchstone of good law-making fits poorly, if it fits at all, with administrative practice. Once again, the reason is not that administrators are not virtuous or that there is no room for virtue in administration. It is, rather, that an important part of administrative virtue has to do with dealing well with laws, procedures, precedents, limitations, and so on – where these are not, in turn, developed or judged just in ways proper to virtue theory: that is, in terms of what virtuous people would determine.

To be sure, there are formulae that may make it look as if this can be easily handled by virtue theory. For example, a proposed test might be whether a given administrative rule is the sort of rule that a virtuous administrator, paying virtuous attention to the purposes, precedents, and so on of that administrative agency would approve of.

But how are we to think of the claim that what satisfies this formula really is a part of, or is even consistent with, virtue theory? There seems strong reason to hold that an ethical theory of type $T_1$ cannot make use of any favoured element of another theory $T_2$. In fact, many of us use some such metatheoretical principle to argue that other theorists, especially consequentialists, prefer theft to honest toil by simply incorporating aspects of other theories into their own theories and then saying that this is what one meant, or should have said, all along. As we know all too well, this is a near irresistible danger of working in, and developing and defending, an ethical theory.

But perhaps that principle is too stringent. Perhaps we should hold that a theory of one sort can use favoured elements of another theory, so long as it does this in its own particular ways, or at least ways that cohere well with its spirit. So, it may be that virtue theory can make recourse to rules, laws, and the like. I will leave these issues to those with interests in theories of theories.

In short, then, I do see considerable problems for virtue theory. But I also continue to see it, or its close relations, as the most congenial areas in which to continue explorations of the importance of people, and of their differences, as well as of character, subjectivity, and intrapersonal and interpersonal relations. What follows is presented as a contribution to this, put in terms of emotional closeness, identification and emotional size. In earlier work, I argued for the importance of such categories and phenomena; for example, 'Schizophrenia' and 'Values and Purposes' argued for their importance for friendship. This work continues with those themes, showing how important they are still more generally if we are to appreciate, evaluate and understand ourselves.

Righteous indignation is a sort of anger; and as befits a sort, it is different from some other sorts of anger. I may be righteously indignant about and aggrieved by the misdeeds of my country or its leaders, such as the contemptuous, spiteful or insolent way they are treating another country or a local minority. This anger is grounded on, among other things, two features: *what* my country or its leaders did, and that *they* did it. Although I can get angry in any number of different ways, I do not think I could get indignant about similarly bad acts done by countries with which I do not identify, which are harming others with whom I do not identify.

The identification required for indignation, or a closely related sort of identification, can be heightened by feeling, correctly or not, that you are seen and identified as joined with those others; and by your feeling, correctly or not, that you are called upon to answer for those others. So, as discussed in Sartre's *Anti-Semite and Jew*,[5] just as anti-Semites may use the misdeeds of any Jew to downgrade any other Jew, anti-Semites may also think that any Jew can be called upon to answer for the misdeeds of any other Jew. But neither a French Jew nor a French Catholic is likely to think that just any French Catholic can be called upon to answer for just any French Catholic. Similarly, many Whites in contemporary USA call on Black leaders to answer for – to denounce and disavow – objectionable statements made by other Blacks, especially other Black leaders. This is so even though the Whites know that the Blacks they call upon to answer for those others have no control over those others, and indeed have no connection with them except that they all are Black or Black leaders; and even though, typically, Whites do not see the need for them or their White leaders (often they are, themselves, those leaders) to condemn objectionable statements made by Whites about Blacks.

Just as those who are targets of prejudice may be called upon to answer for the misdeeds of others 'like them', they may, in various ways, accept this role. Some accept it explicitly and publicly – defending, explaining, disavowing, attacking their fellows. Some others, while denying any responsibility for those others, and any responsibility to answer for them, nonetheless do at least give the appearance of accepting one or both of these sorts of responsibility, as shown by their embarrassment and shame over the misdeeds of those others.

Some other people – not all of whom are victims of prejudice, although being a victim does help – identify negatively and hostilely with those they think of as just like them, precisely to differentiate themselves from these others. As Vladimir Jankélévitch says, speaking of those who are at once the other and the almost the same,

> My identity, in relation to you, consists precisely of the ways in which I am different from you . . . the more you resemble me the harder it is for anyone to see these crucial differences. Our resemblance threatens to obliterate everything that is special about me . . . I have no alternative but to hate you, because by working up a rage against you I am defending everything that is unique about me.[6]

This helps us understand the strangely virulent animosity between those who share almost the same positions and ideologies, which leads some to spend more time fighting with those close to them, rather than those who are their real, and common, enemies.

As these sorts of people show, we must reject a frequently made, and basically hopeful and ameliorative, claim that with full empathetic understanding of others, we will almost necessarily come to sympathise with them, to like and accept them, or at least to soften any negative views about them. This is Seneca's 'bet' as Martha Nussbaum puts it in 'Equity and Mercy'.[7] But as just noted, to know people better need not lead to liking them more. Sometimes because of what is learned and sometimes because of what this means, some people find that to know someone is to hate that person, and that to know that person better is to hate that person more.

One important conclusion to draw here is that there is no *one* form of identification, not even with people just like you. We must thus give up hope of finding an important, common and unifying, feature of identification. Nonetheless, there is a lot to learn by looking at particular forms of identification.

Following Sartre, I suggest that the sort (or sorts) of identification found in feeling called upon to answer for others 'like you' is a characteristic of victims of, say, anti-Semitism and racism, but not of those who are and feel themselves full and powerful members of society. So, French Jews have this sort of identification with other French Jews, but French Catholics do not have it with other French Catholics. This may well be right, so far as it goes. But more should be said about its assumptions involving interpersonal, social and political relations.

First, let us consider some of these assumptions. Sartre claims that French anti-Semitism of his time is intelligible only as, on the one hand, an interplay of post-enlightenment individualism, and on the other, atavistic, essentially magical, noncausal, forms of thinking of people as members of communities, races, and the like. He claims that French anti-Semites think of themselves as belonging to a mystical union of the real French, and that they also think of all Jews as belonging to a mystical union of the whole body of Jews. On the other hand, those who embrace post-enlightenment individualism – according to Sartre, this includes most French Jews and many other French people – think of themselves as individuals who, as it happens, are French or Jewish or both.

Identification of people, others or oneself, in terms of a group can give expression to prejudice, such as anti-Semitism or racism. And perhaps such prejudice requires thinking of people that way. Nonetheless, such identification need not have anything to do with prejudice. It may bespeak some other sort of group solidarity, having nothing to do, as victim or victimiser, with prejudice. Indeed, if Sartre is right in holding that group identification was typical of pre-enlightenment thought, we can see that, at least then, such identification need not involve, much less bespeak, prejudice. (It is another issue that, even then, it may well have been fertile ground for prejudice.)

Further, being or feeling called upon to answer for strangers who are 'like you' involves a very particular sort of power relation. Not just anyone can make me, or make me feel, answerable for others, especially for strangers; and I can show what power I have by refusing to be or feel answerable for them or others. So, prejudice, with its demands of being answerable for others, including strangers, involves a very significant power relation of correlative superiority and inferiority.

Let us consider some other sorts of determinants of being or feeling called upon to answer for strangers who are 'like you'. Many people think that the Germans, even those born after the end of World War Two, should identify with and feel shame over what their country and fellow Germans did in that war. And many Germans did feel such shame. Perhaps what is operative here is the severe gravity of what Germany and the Germans did. I offer this as a psychological account, not a moral account: we can see how the gravity can 'force' such identification without thinking that the justifiability of such identification depends on such gravity.

In addition, context can be important for identification for some people. For example, some Americans are embarrassed if, while in a foreign country, they see another American acting boorishly. Other Americans may see that American act boorishly and simply shrug, or feel sorry for the person on the receiving end of the American's behaviour. Yet many, perhaps most, of the first Americans would not feel anything about the same sort of rudeness back home in the USA. They may experience it simply as a bit of unpleasantness that in no way bears on them at all as individuals, much less as Americans.

Another example showing the importance of context might be useful. Some people are embarrassed by, even ashamed over, a family member doing in public what, when done at home, is accepted without any adverse feeling, for example, telling dialect jokes or burping. Other people are 'more consistent', expecting and accepting the same behaviour in both places, or finding it embarrassing in both.

There is, then, no one account of such identification. Indeed, there are any number of different social, psychological and contextual factors important for it. For our purposes, we have looked at enough of them.

Let us now turn to some ways in which closeness is important in some other, and more everyday, non-theoretical ways. I will start with minor, but common enough, emotions about cars and driving. Those who would query my use of such cases and emotions – thinking perhaps that they are trivial or are too involved with day-to-day life – should remember that Oedipus slew his father in a fight over who should give way to whom at a road junction.

It is hardly noteworthy if I am annoyed by your delaying me by driving too slowly. But, special considerations apart, I will probably not be annoyed by your delaying others by driving too slowly. Some of those special considerations change the case so that, once again, you cause me bother. I might be waiting for the other people you delay. Another sort of similar consideration is far more important for present purposes. Here, because of the ways I care for those others, even identify with them, I am annoyed by your delaying them. Or consider another driving case: parking a car well out from the side of the road, rather than pulling close to the curb. I know many people who react with amused contempt to any driver who parks this way, thus delaying others. But, when they, themselves, suffer such delays, they typically react with annoyance, even anger, but rarely with contempt. And still more rarely – and then only in somewhat special frames of mind, such as some forms of detachment and ruefulness – do they react with amused contempt.

In these cases, differences in emotional distance engender different emotions: annoyance if I or someone close to me is delayed, and perhaps no feeling at all or amused contempt if a stranger is delayed. As this shows, closeness and distance cannot be seen simply as bearing on the strength of an emotion, as if a change in distance only changes the strength of what is otherwise the same emotional response.

Fear and pity, *phobos* and *eleos*, as understood by Aristotle, are also good examples of how emotional distance and difference of emotions are interrelated. He holds that, in general and with an important proviso about closeness, whatever causes me to feel fear when it threatens or happens to me, causes me to feel pity when it threatens or happens to others.[8] Fear and pity, then, are about the same harms and dangers. The difference is that in the case of fear, I am the harmed or threatened person, whereas for pity, someone else is. More exactly, although fear for oneself receives almost all his attention, he allows that one can fear also for those who are very close to one. So, a parent can fear for a child.[9] Pity, too, requires closeness. The person who pities must feel close enough to the pitied person,[10] – but far enough away not to fall within the range of fear.

Thus, according to Aristotle, whether danger to a person arouses in me fear, pity, or neither – and perhaps no feeling at all or only sadness and regret – depends on the closeness of the endangered person to me. And this closeness is shown by whether danger arouses fear, pity, or neither. Similarly, whether a slight to someone angers me depends on and shows that person's closeness to me.

For some of us, however, pity can range far more widely.[11] It can extend to those who are quite distant. We may even pity animals, such as a wounded sparrow seen along the roadside. We think that this shows that our experiences of closeness – of feeling close, and thus being close – go beyond his.

This may suggest that our evaluative-emotional world is less concerned with relations than Aristotle's. Perhaps this is right, or perhaps, just as we are indifferent to some relations Aristotle's people were concerned with, they are indifferent to some areas that are of concern to us. Such comparisons, especially when they go into issues of amount – who cares more about relations – are difficult and, too often, unrewarding. Rather than pursue them, I want to turn to what might be thought to be a principled reason for rejecting the importance of relations for emotions. This reason is made up of two parts. The first asserts universality, holding that emotions should be mediated only by value, no matter whose. The second asserts proportionality, holding that emotions should be proportional in strength to the amount of value involved.

There is a familiar analogue about acts to this view about emotions. This is the claim that only value, taken quite generally, and its amount, not whose it is or its kind, are relevant for act evaluations. Such a view holds, among other things, that the distinction between self and other should make no difference to act evaluations, and that the 'strength' of act evaluations is proportional to the amount of value involved. Straightforward consequentialist maximisation is one such theory.

As noted at the outset, I think that much that is absolutely basic and central to our life and to our values is sensitive to identification, distance, and closeness, not just to value and amount of value. Thus, I reject universalistic proportionality and both of its parts, its universalism and its proportionality. I think it is quite generally true, for us as well as for Aristotle's people, that emotions that are appropriate and that show one to be a good person need not vary just with the amount of value of what the emotion is about.

To see this let us start by noting that in terms of value taken generally, atrocities and massacres are hugely worse than the death of a parent, say. The view that emotions should be proportional to value would, thus, hold that the proper emotional reaction to the massacres and atrocities should be hugely greater than the appropriate bereavement and mourning. Even if we can imagine what such hugely stronger or hugely greater emotions would be – perhaps they would involve suicide or lifelong service or devotion to the memory of the victims – they are not required.[12] And in many cases, they are inappropriate – an inappropriate giving up on life or a lack of moral and emotional proportion.

I would add that these last claims are about people who merely know about these happenings, and perhaps have suffered from them. They are not about people who bear responsibility for these losses and terrible events. The emotional demands on those who bear responsibility for the happenings may well be different. For some of these people, it might be that nothing in a human life would be adequate, not even a painful suicide preceded by many years of self-torment or a life of service and devotion to memory of their victims or to helping survivors or some other appropriate people.

Were our emotional responses, or our proper and appropriate emotional responses, proportional to value, it would be near enough impossible to explain how we could, or should be able to, read in a calm and unbothered way about past atrocities, such as those perpetrated by Ghengis Khan. Unless for some special reason we get caught up in the story, few of us feel fear for his victims. I doubt if most of us even feel pity for them. It is not that we think they do not deserve our pity. Rather, we feel little more than a small shudder of sadness on their behalf – so little that it is too much to say that we feel even a slight amount of pity for them. They are simply too distant from us to affect us even that much.

Matters are different if one identifies with those victims – as, say, present-day Jews do with the victims of the Holocaust, as present-day Armenians do with those killed in their dispersal and massacres following World War One, and present-day Afro-Americans do with those who died while being transported to be slaves or while they were slaves. Our point here is not that only those who already identify with these and other victims can feel for them. Rather, it is to suggest that at least part of what it means to identify in these cases is to feel with and for these victims.

I want now to turn to a related criticism of universalism and proportionality in regard to emotions. Aristotle claims that 'On some actions . . . forgiveness is [bestowed], when one does what he ought not under pressure which overstrains human nature and which no one could withstand'.[13] This may be talking only about second-person or third-person evaluations and emotions: those concerning other people and their acts. If so, a close analogue also holds for first-person evaluations of acts and agents, and emotions about these. In first-, second- and third-person cases, even if an act that merits forgiveness involves far more disvalue than an act that merits blame, the act that merits forgiveness can also merit a far 'gentler' emotion than the act that involves less disvalue. So too, in regard to the agent: the agent who is overstrained may deserve no blame at all, but only pity or forgiveness, while the other may deserve no pity or forgiveness, but only blame – again, even though the former may have done what involves far more disvalue.

Much the same holds for events that 'merely' befall people. Some losses, such as the death of a young child by murder, an accident or illness, may so overstrain a person that no accurate correlation can be made between the value of what happened and the strength of the 'proper' emotion. At least as clearly, no such correlation can be made between the value of what happened and an evaluation of a person for having or not having emotions of the 'right' strength.

Consider, for example, a person whose child has just been murdered. We can easily imagine this person in quiet, dissociated shock, or wild with grief, or filled with vengeful rage, or stunned over what society has become, or saddened to the core. In no way do I find any of these emotions even questionable, much less untoward or indicative of a poor character. And indeed, I do not have much, if any, sense of what would be the right amount of emotion – right, either in regard to what was suffered or the emotions a good person would have. In contrast, however, it is easy to see how we might think poorly of, or at least have serious questions about, a parent who felt no more concern about a child being in danger of losing an arm to an infection than about the child's suffering a minor burn. This holds both for a parent who 'downgrades' the former to the level of the latter, or who magnifies the latter to the level of the former.

I must add that my claims concerning emotions about terrible events are consistent with also holding that some emotions and emotional reactions to these terrible events are, at best, questionable, if not deplorable. Here we might consider parents who – not as a manifestation of shock, but quite sincerely and as an accurate and straightforward expression of their feelings about the death of their infant – say, 'Well, you win some, you lose some'.

To this, too, I must add something: these comments are about people like most of us, that is, people with adequate medical care, living in adequately safe environments. But there are many other people, who see only a small proportion of their children live to the age of five. For these people, a lack of emotional investment in infants and young children might be precisely what is called for and what even the best people in those situations would feel.[14]

A general point about the cases just considered should be made. Especially in those cases where people are overstrained, the criteria and measure for evaluating acts and agents are not, or not largely, the value or disvalue of what is done or of what happens. Similarly, the criteria and measure for the appropriateness of emotions about such doings and those who do them are not just the value or disvalue of those doings. Rather, at least to some large degree, it has to do with the person and how the person came to be in such a situation, how the person bears it, and so on.

For example, I might be overstrained, driven to distraction and crazed, by the thought of continuing down a path on which I see a snake. I might be as overstrained here as Agamemnon was by having to choose between Iphigeneia and the progress of the fleet against Troy. But my being overwhelmed and crazed by the snake tells against me. It shows me weak, or soft, or phobic, or possessed of or by some other defect. Further, that poor evaluation of me carries over, in complex and circuitous ways, to evaluations of my terror and other resulting emotions. The matter is quite different for those who are overwhelmed by what is truly overwhelming – such as, on some accounts anyway, Agamemnon. Such people may deserve pity and forgiveness, not blame. Correlatively, their terror or madness may deserve acceptance or, at the least, no adverse word or thought, and perhaps even a compassionate lack of scrutiny and attention.[15]

Much of what I have claimed is familiar, or would be familiar to anyone who pays attention to what our lives are like and what we find important in our lives. I think that too many ethicists have not paid nearly enough attention to this. I hope that they will start doing so; and I think that virtue ethics can aid them in this. They will have to give up simple and elegant theories, and perhaps theories quite generally. My reminders about identification, closeness and size are intended to help show the problems, approaching if not reaching the impossibility, of doing ethics without taking account of these in ways that are true to their great variability and complexity. I hope that the reminders have, thus, furthered a better appreciation of people, character and virtue – and the value of giving these importance, if not pride of place, in thinking about ethics.

* The material in this chapter is developed further in *Valuing Emotions* written with Elizabeth Hegeman, New York: Cambridge University Press (1996). My thanks are owed Hegeman for material in this chapter.

## ENDNOTES

1. In this, I was joined for a while by Michael Slote. But in his latest works, he seems to have gone back to the philosophical fold, holding that, because of its theoretical simplicity, an ethics which sees no distinctions, in principle, between self and other is to be preferred. See Michael Stocker, 'Agent and Other: Against Ethical Universalism', *The Australasian Journal of Philosophy*, 54 (1976), 206–20; Michael Slote, 'Morality and Self-Other Asymmetry', *The Journal of Philosophy* 81 (1984), 179–92, and *From Morality to Virtue*, New York City: Oxford University Press (1992). See also my commentary on *From Morality to Virtue*, 'Self-Other Asymmetries and Virtue Theory', *Philosophy and Phenomenological Research*, 54 (1994), 689–94, and Slote's reply, 'Reply to Commentators', *Philosophy and Phenomenological Research*, 54 (1994), 709–19.
2. M. Stocker: 'Act and Agent Evaluations', *The Review of Metaphysics*, 27 (1973), 42–61; 'The Schizophrenia of Modern Ethical Theories', *The Journal of Philosophy*, 73 (1976), 453–66; 'Values and Purposes: The Limits of Teleology and the Ends of Friendship', *The Journal of Philosophy*, 78 (1981), 747–65.
3. 'Desiring the Bad', *The Journal of Philosophy*, 76 (1979), 738–53.
4. Thanks are owed to David Slawson here.
5. New York City: Schocken Books, 1976.
6. As presented by Paul Berman in 'The Other and the Almost the Same', *The New Yorker*, 70, No. 2 (February 28, 1994), 61–71, p. 62.
7. *Philosophy and Public Affairs*, 22 (1993), 83–125.
8. Aristotle, *Rhetoric*, II.5, 1382b26 ff. and II.8, 1185b27 ff.
9. Aristotle, *Nicomachean Ethics*, III.6, 1115a22 ff. and *Rhetoric*, II.8, 1386a19 ff.
10. *Rhetoric*, II.8, 1386a17 ff.
11. Thanks are owed to Jonathan Bennett for discussion here.
12. Thanks are owed to Frances Kamm for this example. On mourning and its excesses, see Sigmund Freud, 'Mourning and Melancholia', in Volume 14 of James Strachey (ed.), *The Standard Edition of the Complete Psychological Works of Sigmund Freud*, London: The Hogarth Press (1986).
13. *Nicomachean Ethics*, III.1, 1110a23 ff.
14. On this see Nancy Scheper-Hughes, *Death Without Weeping: The Violence of Everyday Life in Brazil*, Berkeley: University of California Press (1992).
15. In developing these views about what overstrains us, I think I join, and I know I have been helped by, Bernard Williams, *Shame And Necessity*, Berkeley: University of California Press (1993), 134–5.

# 7

# FROM MORALITY TO VIRTUE

## *Michael Slote*

Philosophical interest in virtue and the (particular) virtues has had a long and – though the term is inadequate – distinguished history. Although, in modern times, the interests of ethicists have largely shifted towards questions of right and wrong and towards the formulation of principles of duty and/or obligation, the predominant virtue ethics of the ancient world has exerted a significant influence across the centuries. In recent years, and for reasons it is difficult to be entirely sure of, there has in fact been a considerable revival of interest in virtue ethics. There have been a number of notable efforts to characterise both particular virtues and some interrelations among particular virtues, and attempts have also been made to offer more or less general accounts of what virtue, or a virtue, is. In addition, several philosophers have urged us to start approaching ethics as a whole through a primary or initial focus on virtue-related concepts, and these calls for change have often been defended by attributing major flaws to currently more prominent forms of ethical theory or by reference to a more pervasive sense of the futility or sterility of recent ethical debate. Yet despite – or because of – all the calls for a new approach, I believe no one has actually set about constructing ethical theory, from the ground upward, on a virtue-theoretic basis – no attempts, as far as I know, have been made to bring the foundational issues and conceptual distinctions that have animated recent discussions, say, among utilitarians, Kantians, and common-sensists into specific relation to the structures and content that characterise, or are likely to characterise, a fundamentally virtue-theoretic approach to the problems and phenomena of ethics. In the first part of this chapter, I point to some crucial problems in Kantianism and commonsense approaches to ethics. In the second part, I begin the positive development of a virtue ethics approach.

## 1. THE IMPLICATIONS OF ASYMMETRY

In this part, I am going to argue that the commonsense and Kantian conceptions of morality are not only problematic but internally incoherent. In recent years, it has been pointed out that contrary to consequentialism, commonsense morality grants agents a moral permission to pursue innocent projects and concerns in ways that are not optimific, not productive of the greatest overall balance of good.[1] These moral permissions allow the agent to favour herself, to some extent, over other people: to seek her own good on some occasions when she could do more good by trying to help others, and this, of course, is precisely what standard utilitarianism does not allow one to do. In the present context I shall also refer to such permissions as *agent-favouring* permissions, because I would like to draw a contrast between this familiar category of commonsense moral permission and a less familiar form of moral permission that treats it as morally permissible for agents to neglect their own projects and concerns and even, in fact, to thwart them.

Our intuitive moral thinking seems to regard it as entirely permissible, though of course hardly advisable or rational, for an individual to deny herself the very things she most wants or to cause herself unnecessary pain or damage. (Here common sense diverges from Kantian ethics – criticism of the latter will come in later in our discussion.) Even if no one else stands to benefit from such self-sacrifice, even if there is no reason of moral deontology for it, such an act of self-sacrifice does not seem morally wrong,[2] and it is appropriate to refer this new class of permissions as *agent sacrificing* in order to mark the contrast with the agent-favouring permissions that are already so well-known in the ethics literature. Both sorts of permission allow for non-optimific action, but in addition the agent-sacrificing permissions allow for (non-optimific) behaviour that doesn't even serve the interests or concerns of the moral agent. So if, as we might put it, agent-favouring permissions allow the substitution of the agent's good for the larger overall good that consequentialism uses as the standard of right action, then agent-sacrificing permissions morally allow for action that cannot be justified by any appeal to what is good or best, allow, indeed, for action that must inevitably seem stupid, absurd, or irrational by comparison with agent-favouring behaviour. However, we should not immediately assume that commonsense morality itself cannot sensibly make moral accommodation to behaviour that itself is not sensible, and for the moment at least we need only focus on the fact that commonsense morality does seem to permit such senseless or stupid behaviour.

Consider, then, what our ordinary moral thinking seems to allow and to forbid with regard to our treatment of *other people*. Negligently to hurt another person seems, intuitively, to be morally wrong in a way or to a degree that it does not seem wrong through negligence to hurt oneself. (It can be wrong to hurt oneself if one thereby makes it impossible for one to fulfil certain obligations, but I am speaking of less complex situations.) Similarly, if one could easily *prevent* pain to another person, it is typically thought wrong not to do so, but not to avoid similar pain to oneself seems crazy or irrational, not morally wrong. And so given the agent-sacrificing commonsense permissions we have described, we may now also speak of an *agent-sacrificing* (or *other-favouring*) *self-other asymmetry* that attaches to what is commonsensically permissible. Various ways one may permissibly act against one's own interests or wellbeing are ways one is commonsensically not allowed to act against the interests or wellbeing of others.[3]

But isn't there another side to this coin in virtue of the familiar agent-favouring permissions that we have also attributed to our commonsense moral thinking? We ordinarily think people have a right to neglect their own interests, but don't we also believe that one may to a certain extent permissibly favour one's own interests over those of other individuals and doesn't this latter give rise to some sort of agent-favouring self-other asymmetry? If so, don't we then also face the considerable problem of explaining how our commonsense permissions can simultaneously yield agent-favouring *and* agent-sacrificing asymmetries?

These difficulties can be avoided, however, if one recognises that our agent-favouring permissions provide no obvious footing for asymmetry. I may be permitted to act against overall optimality in the pursuit of my own concerns, but this yields an agent-favouring asymmetry only if the analogous claim with respect to *other* people seems commonsensically suspect, and in fact it isn't. Just as one may favour *one's own* interests or special concerns, there seems to be nothing intuitively wrong with helping *another person* in an overall non-optimific fashion.

However, there is a great deal more to be said about the agent-sacrificing self-other asymmetry we have located in commonsense morality. We have thus far largely concentrated on the asymmetry of our commonsense moral permissions, but we have also just briefly indicated that such symmetry is also to be found in our views of (positive or comparative) moral merit, and it is time now to focus our attention on the way self-other asymmetry of an agent-sacrificing kind applies outside the area of permissions. Moral theorists tend to assume that moral evaluation is our most fundamental and/or important form of ethical evaluation. But the aspects of self-other asymmetry we shall now focus on force us to question whether either commonsense or Kantian morality can properly fulfil such a role.

The point I wish to make about both these forms of morality is perhaps best approached by means of a contrast with a well-known aspect of (utilitarian) consequentialism. The latter allows neither for agent-sacrificing nor for agent-favouring permissions of the sort we have described, because it is entirely agent-neutral: no one person may be treated in any fundamentally different way from any other, and this uniformity of treatment crosses the boundary between self and other as well as that between different others. In consequentialism, if something is permitted with respect to one individual, it is acceptable with respect to any other individual as long as the causal-evaluative facts on which moral judgments are based remain otherwise the same. And if, for example, it is wrong for me to hurt another person when, by not doing so, I can create more overall good, then it is wrong for me to hurt myself in similar circumstances. Even if I hurt myself in order to help others, my act will count as wrong, if I could have done more overall good by favouring myself more and benefiting others less.[4] Furthermore, if the agent's sole choice is between helping herself and helping another person to exactly the same extent, the two possible acts are of equal moral value, are equally good morally, according to any recognisable form of consequentialism. But if the agent has to choose between helping herself more and helping another less, or between helping another person more and helping herself less, the morally better action, in consequentialist terms, will always be the one that does the most good.[5] And this also holds for choices exclusively concerned with the good of the agent or exclusively concerned with the good of others. As a result, I think we may say that consequentialism treats the good of the agent and that of any given other as counting equally towards favourable moral assessment.

Note the contrast with egoism. The latter presumably regards what helps the agent more as automatically morally better than what helps the agent less, but makes no similar comparative judgment about effects on other people. It is only when the agent's good is (contingently) tied to that of other people, that effects on others can make a difference to egoistic moral evaluation, and so in respect to its comparative moral judgments, egoism is asymmetric in a way that consequentialism clearly is not. Where does commonsense morality fit into this picture?

Unlike egoism, our ordinary thinking tends to regard it, other things being equal, as morally better, or more meritorious, to give more, rather than less, to another person. But when we turn to situations in which the agent is in a position to affect himself in some way, a different picture emerges. We earlier saw that commonsense morality allows or permits the agent to hurt or fail to help himself. But when comparative moral judgments are at issue, the agent's own good also appears to be irrelevant. If I have to choose between helping myself a little or a great deal, the latter choice would not normally be regarded as morally better: wiser, more rational, more prudent perhaps, just not *morally* better. Here there is a marked contrast with both consequentialism and ethical egoism, but not just here. Where both the agent's and another person's good are at stake, our ordinary moral thinking seems to assign the former no positive weight whatsoever. It may be more rational to choose a great good for oneself in preference to a lesser good for another person, but in commonsense terms it is not morally preferable to choose one's own greater good, and it even seems morally better to seek the *lesser* good of another in preference to a greater benefit for oneself. Here again, there is a contrast with both egoism and consequentialism.[6]

Of course, what helps the agent would ordinarily be taken to be capable of indirect moral value. It may be morally better for me to be careful about my health than to be indifferent about it, if a family's or a nation's welfare depends on my keeping healthy, but if in order to make a case for the moral value or merit of some agent-beneficial action, we ordinarily have to say something to tie that action and that benefit to the wellbeing of others, that fact only serves to underscore the asymmetry of comparative evaluations I have just been calling attention to. It is now time to see whether our ordinary understanding of virtue and virtues is subject to any similar asymmetry and whether, if such understanding turns out to be relatively free of such asymmetry, we can use this difference to argue in favour of a virtue-theoretic approach to ethics.

In her ground-breaking article 'Moral Beliefs', Philippa Foot assumes that if a trait of character does not benefit or serve the needs of its possessor, the trait cannot properly be regarded as a virtue. She notes that in the *Republic* Plato takes it for granted 'that if justice is not a good to the just man, moralists who recommend it as a virtue are perpetrating a fraud' and she points out that Nietzsche, unlike present-day moral philosophers, seems to accept a similar view.[7]

Foot herself, however, subsequently retracted this assumption. In some of her later work, she has separated the issue of what counts as a virtue from issues concerning what the agent has reason to do and treated it as intuitively unobjectionable to hold that traits that fail to benefit their possessors may properly be regarded as virtues.[8] For present-day commonsense thinking it might be enough, for example, that a trait be one by which *other people* generally benefit. (As Foot herself notes, what counts as a virtue in functional objects like knives doesn't benefit the knives themselves, only those who use them.)

To the extent that Foot's retraction constitutes a concession to our ordinary thought about virtue and virtues, I think Foot was correct to retract her earlier assumption and recognise that virtues may not benefit their possessors. But it would be a mistake to conclude from this that our ordinary thinking about the virtues is subject to self-other asymmetry similar to that which we have found in commonsense morality. Our assessment of whether a given character trait counts as a virtue (and of whether a given act, in exemplifying a certain character trait, also exemplifies a virtue) is favourably affected by the consideration that the trait in question benefits people other than its possessor. But no less positively, or favourably, is it affected by the consideration that a given trait benefits, or is useful to, its possessor(s). In our ordinary thinking it may not be *necessary* to status as a virtue that a given trait be beneficial (more or less generally) to its possessors, but it certainly *helps to qualify* any given trait as a virtue that it is useful or beneficial to those who possess it, and in fact I think it is entirely in keeping with commonsense views to suppose that both helpfulness to its possessors and helpfulness to others are independently, and in fairly equal measure, capable of conferring virtue status. To consider the issue first on a fairly abstract level, if I hear that people generally need a given trait of character and benefit from possessing it, I will normally think I have been given excellent reason to regard that trait as a virtue.[9] But by the same token if I learn that a certain character trait is generally useful to people other than its possessors, I will also naturally or normally think I have been given reason to regard that trait as a virtue.

When, furthermore, we look at the whole range of traits commonly recognised as virtues, we once again see that both self-regarding and other-regarding considerations are capable of underlying the kind of high regard that leads us to regard various traits as virtues. Justice, kindness, probity and generosity are chiefly admired for what they lead those who possess these traits to do in their relations with other people, but prudence, sagacity, circumspection, equanimity and fortitude are esteemed primarily under their self-regarding aspect, and still other traits – notably self-control, courage and (perhaps) wisdom in practical affairs – are in substantial measure admired both for what they do for their possessors and for what they lead their possessors to do with regard to other people.[10]

It is also worth noting that traits admired for other-regarding reasons do not have any sort of general precedence over predominantly self-regarding virtues that might be taken to entail a self-other asymmetry of the sort we have discussed in connection with commonsense morality. (I think the opposite problem of precedence for self-regarding virtues need not concern us.) The other-regarding traits mentioned above lack any (implicitly) recognised status as greater or more important virtues than the self-regarding traits also mentioned above, and neither does a 'mixed' virtue like courage or self-control or wisdom seem inferior to, or less of a virtue than, such predominantly other-regarding virtues as justice and kindness. We greatly admire probity and fair dealing, but we also have enormous admiration for many self-regarding and mixed virtues, so I think our ordinary thinking in this area gives rise to nothing like the marked or extreme self-other asymmetry that characterises commonsense morality.

Yet even if our ordinary thinking about virtue(s) fails to exemplify the agent-sacrificing (or other-favouring) asymmetry we find in commonsense morality, such self-other asymmetry is clearly *possible* in the realm of virtue, and in fact I believe we have a good example of such asymmetry in Kant's views about what counts as an estimable character trait. Kant's doctrine of virtue is fundamentally a doctrine of moral virtue, but, more important, in the light of what we said above, his views about what counts as *a* virtue entail the same agent-sacrificing asymmetry we find in his view of morality. In *Fundamental Principles of the Metaphysics of Morals*, Kant says that character traits like moderation, perseverance, judgment, self-control, courage, and the ability to deliberate calmly have value and are praiseworthy only conditionally. In the absence of a good will, these traits are not estimable and presumable do not count as virtues.

But (roughly speaking) if the status of moderation or perseverance as a virtue depends on its being accompanied by a Kantian good will and such a will is fundamentally directed towards concern with the wellbeing of others rather than towards the wellbeing of the moral agent, then the agent-sacrificing asymmetry of Kantian moral obligation will translate into similar asymmetry in Kantian views about what properly counts as a good trait of character, as a virtue. Our commonsense views of what counts as a virtue escape this asymmetry, despite the self-other asymmetry of commonsense moral obligation, because, unlike Kant, we ordinarily regard some of the character traits mentioned above as admirable or estimable independently of their accompaniment by moral goodness or virtue. We may have an unfavourable moral opinion of a colleague who mistreats his friends and his family, yet have a high regard for that colleague's devotion to some academic subject, or his coolheadedness, or his fortitude in the face of (deserved or undeserved) personal tragedy.[11]

And so in the area of virtue, the same three possibilities exist as exist in morality, but we find commonsense views occupying a different position among these possibilities. With regard to personal happiness or wellbeing, commonsense and Kantian morality are agent-sacrificingly self-other asymmetric by contrast with the agent-favouring (other-sacrificing) asymmetry of egoism and the self-other symmetry of (utilitarian) consequentialism. But in the field of the virtues it is commonsense that occupies the symmetric position (along with utilitarianism, but I am ignoring some complications here); whereas egoism, once again, is agent-favouringly asymmetric, and only the Kantian view, among those we have mentioned, is agent-sacrificingly asymmetric.

Of course, we have not yet explored the significance, the theoretical implications, of these varying symmetries and asymmetries. To the extent that symmetry is a favourable characteristic of an ethical view, we could perhaps on that basis alone argue for the superiority of either consequentialism or a commonsense ethics of the virtues over a commonsense or Kantian ethics of right, wrong and obligation. But in fact the symmetry in consequentialism and in commonsense virtue ethics has a significance that far outstrips the widely assumed theoretical desirability of symmetry as such. However desirable symmetrical consequentialism may be, it still is subject to the complaint of being too demanding, of requiring too much individual sacrifice. And we are now in a position to show that the agent-sacrificing asymmetry of commonsense and Kantian morality subjects them to the rather similar complaint that they downgrade or deprecate the importance of the moral agent, a charge which, as we will also see, the particular symmetry of our ordinary view of virtue allows the latter to escape.

How can commonsense morality be guilty of devaluing or deprecating the importance of the moral agent? After all, it is itself the source of the criticism that consequentialism and utilitarianism ride roughshod over the particular concerns and projects of the individual by demanding that she sacrifice them whenever they interfere with her production of impersonally reckoned best results. Is commonsense, or Kantian, morality perhaps more demanding than its adherents have realised? Is that the basis for the objection I wish to make to such morality?

I do want to claim that these forms of morality downgrade the (actual) importance of moral agents and their individual concerns, projects, even desires. But the argument for this claim will not be that, like consequentialism, the ordinary and/or the Kantian standard of right and wrong make an insufficient concession to the moral agent's welfare. On the contrary, it will involve, rather, the claim that commonsense and Kantian morality *do* make concessions to the wellbeing and happiness of agents, *but make them only as concessions.*[12]

Commonsense and Kantian ethics permit the moral agent to seek and find her own happiness at the expense, at least to some extent, of overall, or impersonally judged, optimality. But this does not mean that they treat such usefulness to the agent as a source of *positive moral value*. Other things being equal, if an agent has to choose between two actions and one of these would (probably) be more helpful to the agent, then the more helpful action would typically be regarded as one that it is more rational for the agent to perform and, in the appropriate, reasons-related sense, as a better option from the standpoint of the agent. But from the ordinary or Kantian point of view such an act would usually not be considered morally better or morally more praiseworthy or meritorious than the act that would do less good for the agent. The point simply recaptures some of what we were saying earlier: for ordinary or Kantian moral thinking, how morally good or meritorious an act is will depend in part (and especially in the absence of deontological factors) on whether it is directed towards the wellbeing of other people, but not on whether it is directed towards that of the agent.

So in cases where someone helps herself at the expense of overall best results and of the potential good of other people, commonsense morality may maintain the moral permissibility of what the (utilitarian) consequentialist would standardly regard as a violation of moral obligation, but will nonetheless share with consequentialism the judgment that such an action is morally less good than one that would have achieved greater overall good and greater good for other people. And in such cases, therefore, commonsense makes moral concessions to the agent's personal good, but attributes positive moral value only on the basis of what the agent does for the wellbeing of others. (Again, I am assuming an absence of deontological considerations.) And if you wish to object that our ordinary thinking here accords positive moral value to what the agent does solely on her own behalf, but simply refuses to assign *greater* moral value to what is *more* self-beneficial, then consider what we think about purely self-regarding cases where someone has to choose between having or not having something nice. Intuitively speaking, if someone on purely prudential grounds decides to have lunch rather than not eating at all, then, other things being equal, what that person does is neither morally better than the alternative nor, intuitively, the sort of action we would praise as morally a good one. And Kant's conception of morality likewise provides no basis for assigning positive moral value to actions to the extent that they are directed merely towards the happiness or wellbeing of their agents.[13]

In summary, it would appear that over a wide range of cases our ordinary thinking about morality assigns no positive value to the wellbeing or happiness of the moral agent of the sort it clearly assigns to the wellbeing or happiness of *everyone other than the agent*. The fact that an act helps or seeks to help its agent cannot for such thinking provide any sort of ground or basis for the favourable – as opposed to the merely non-unfavourable – evaluation of that action. And harm to the agent seems similarly irrelevant to an act's unfavourable evaluation. I believe that this aspect of commonsense morality is and can be shown to be ethically objectionable.

I should point out, however, that it is hardly objectionable that *some* form of act-evaluation should fail to concern itself with the interests of the agent. The existence of such a mode of evaluation is entirely consistent with a proper concern for the interests of agents as such, because it is entirely consistent with the existence of important forms of evaluation that *do* take the agent's interests positively into account. What seems to deprecate and devalue the moral agent, to rob her of her actual importance, is the assumption, rather, that *at the most fundamental level*, or *in its most central concerns*, substantive ethical thinking gives no positive evaluative weight to the interests of agents as such. Of course, viewed as a recipient of the acts of other agents commonsense and Kantian morality regard the wellbeing of every person as having a positive and fundamental valuational significance. But at the same time, they assign no such significance to the effects of an act on the wellbeing of the act's agent, and the latter fact lies behind the charge that I am bringing against commonsense and Kantian morality.[14] If morality is to function as the centrally important part of our ethical thinking that most of us think it is, then both commonsense and Kantian morality are unfitted for such a role because of the way they depreciate the interests of moral agents both from the standpoint of those agents' evaluation of their own actions and more generally. They each require the agent to be valuationally selfless or self-abnegating with respect to her own actions – though not with respect to other people's actions – and, in effect, they alienate the agent from her own self-interest or welfare when she evaluates the ethical significance of her own actions. But even from a more general standpoint of evaluation, both views regard all effects on the agent's wellbeing as fundamentally irrelevant to the favourable or unfavourable evaluation of a given action, whereas that wellbeing is taken into account when anyone else's actions are being evaluated. Clearly, commonsense and Kantian morality, if seen as concerning themselves with the most central or fundamental questions of ethics, can each be criticised for deprecating or devaluing the welfare interests of the moral agent as such.[15]

Of course the *way* in which these two conceptions of morality can be regarded as devaluing the moral agent and her interests is not precisely the way in which utilitarian consequentialism can, and is commonly thought to, devalue agents and their interests. And by the same token, the way ordinary and Kantian moral thinking impose self-abnegation or self-alienation upon moral agents is to some extent different from the way utilitarian consequentialism imposes these constraints. These differences, as I have already mentioned, have something to do with the difference between conditions of permissibility and conditions of (positive or comparative) moral goodness, but even granting that such differences exist – and that more needs to be said about them – it nonetheless seems highly significant that the very same charges may be levelled at consequentialism, Kantianism and commonsense morality, and ironic, in addition, that commonsense morality, at least, has in recent years been directing such charges at consequentialism and using them in an attempt to demonstrate its own superiority over consequentialism.

In addition to all the above, commonsense morality itself has a difficult time coherently making sense of its commitment to a self-other asymmetry of right and wrong because of some of the *other* things it says about right and wrong.

In particular, ordinary non-utilitarian morality treats our obligations to others as dependent on how near they stand to us in relations of affection or special commitment: obligations to our immediate family (other things being equal) being stronger than to our relations generally, obligations to friends and relations being stronger than to compatriots generally, and obligations to the latter, in turn, being stronger than to the people of other countries.[16] To that extent, ordinary morality reflects the normal structure of an adult's concerns. We are naturally more concerned about and have more reason to be concerned about the wellbeing of friends and relations than of more distant others, and commonsense morality seems to build such differences into the varyingly strong duties it assigns us to concern ourselves with others' wellbeing. However, by means of its self-other asymmetry, commonsense morality also superimposes an absolute moral discontinuity on the structure of concern in which each agent is normally situated. On the one hand, it encourages the idea that strength of obligation weakens as one gets further from the agent, but, on the other, it assumes that there is no moral obligation whatever (except indirectly) for the agent to benefit *himself*. Once one leaves the agent behind, the agent's obligations vary in proportion to his reason for concern, but where he has greatest reason for concern in the natural course of things, he has no direct obligation whatever. And this appears odd and unmotivated, even apart from any utilitarian or consequentialist perspective (though the latter provides one way out of the oddness).

In fact there is one very obvious way to attempt to justify the self-other asymmetry (or some aspects of it), but in the light of what has just been said, the attempt actually makes the picture appear even bleaker for commonsense morality by making it appear impossible to make sense of the above-mentioned discontinuity in commonsense thinking. Let me explain.

One can very naturally attempt to justify the (apparent) lack of moral duties to provide for one's own good, in terms of normal human desires and instincts and plausible assumptions about their influence on our actions. We can be expected to take care of ourselves most of the time, and that, according to the justification, is why there is no need for morality to impose obligations or duties to do so. But this readily available rationale – and it is, roughly, the account Kant offers for our having no duty to seek our own happiness – actually leads to incoherence when combined with the facts about our relations to other people that we mentioned above.[17] We can normally be expected to take better care of our spouse and children than of distant others, yet our obligations to the former are stronger than to the latter, and this is just the opposite of what one should expect if the above rationale were correct about duties to seek one's own good. But it is commonsensically very natural to try to justify the self-other moral asymmetry, and more particularly the absence of duties to seek one's own wellbeing in terms of what is normal and expectable in people, and I think this shows that commonsense is at odds with itself in this general area. What seems like the only possible and sensible rationale for the self-other asymmetry makes nonsense out of another aspect of commonsense morality, and this internal difficulty of ordinary thought about right and wrong offers some further reason, I think, to look for something better than commonsense moral thinking.

At this point I think we ought to consider whether Kant's views have anything like the inharmonious character we have attributed to certain (juxtapositions of) commonsense views or entail the sort of inconsistency or incoherence that we find among commonsense intuitions or opinions. The difficulties we have uncovered in commonsense to some extent propel us in the direction of systematic moral or ethical theory, and Kant's ethical philosophy represents a subtle, powerful and complexly articulated example of such theory that we cannot afford to ignore as a potential alternative to commonsense or intuitionist views.

Earlier we saw that Kantian and commonsense morality are in similar ways unsuitable for a foundational role in ethical theory. The fact that neither treats enhancement of the agent's wellbeing as a basis for (comparative or positive) favourable evaluation of an agent's actions constitutes a reason for thinking that neither of these forms of moral theory can constitute *the* foundation or central part of our ethical thought in general.

But, in addition to all these difficulties, Kant's views about morality lead to paradoxes and inconsistencies that resemble, or perhaps I should say partially overlap, those we have mentioned in connection with commonsense morality. For Kant there are no duties or obligations to pursue one's own happiness, and he seeks to account for this fact via the claims that every man 'inevitably and spontaneously' seeks to promote his own happiness and that the concepts of duty and obligation apply only where an end is adopted reluctantly.[18] But this set of claims leads to incoherence and disharmony only if they are conjoined with the assumption that the strength or strictness of our obligations to benefit others (roughly) varies with the closeness of their personal relations to us. And in fact Kant seems to make this very assumption in the same work where he makes the above points about the absence of any obligation to adopt one's own happiness as an end.[19] So the same incoherence that we earlier attributed to commonsense morality in connection with self-other asymmetry and the variable strictness of duties to others also appears to characterise Kant's moral thinking and constitutes, I believe, an equally strong objection to the latter.

Moreover, Kantian moral theory is subject to an additional form of incoherence, an incoherence resulting partly from the well-trodden ways of self-other asymmetry and partly from an absence of such asymmetry in one of Kant's main formulations of the Categorical Imperative.

Kant's End-in-Itself formulation of the Categorical Imperative runs:

> Act in such a way that you always treat humanity, whether in your own person or in the person of any other, never simply as a means but always at the same time as an end.

And I believe that such a view sits badly with what we have seen Kant to be saying about the absence of duties to pursue one's own happiness.

Kant employs the End-in-Itself version of the Categorical Imperative to argue not only for the wrongness or impermissibility of killing others, but for the impermissibility of suicide as well. Although Kant's views about sacrificing one's own life for the lives or the happiness of others are complex and seem to have developed over time,[20] he very clearly holds that committing suicide when one despairs of one's future or is tired of life is morally unacceptable, and such a prohibition clearly fits in with the self-other *symmetry* of the Categorical Imperative as expressed above. Prohibitions against treating people in certain ways (even as a means to producing certain sorts of overall good results) are quintessentially deontological, and it is obvious that Kant's commitment to deontological restrictions is more self-other symmetric (at least in certain of its aspects) than commonsense morality seems to be. But questions about whether one may permissibly fail to benefit certain people in certain ways fall outside the area, so to speak, of deontology. Roughly speaking, deontology tells us we may not *actively treat* people in various more or less specific ways, and it differs from consequentialism through its claim, among other things, that such treatment cannot be morally justified in terms of overall desirable results. But obligations to confer wellbeing/benefits exist if we may not *fail to confer* such benefits and (again, very roughly) they represent a common element or aspect of commonsense, consequentialist, and Kantian moral views. And the relevance of this sketchily drawn distinction to our present purposes is the contrast it allows us to draw between Kant's deontological views and what he says about obligations to confer benefits.

We earlier saw that Kant espouses an agent-sacrificing self-other asymmetric view about the pursuit of mere benefits or happiness. One has an obligation to help others in their pursuit of happiness, but one has no obligation to pursue one's own happiness (except perhaps derivatively as a means, if one's happiness is one, to the happiness of others or to one's own personal or moral development). Yet Kant's deontology – under one of its aspects – requires self-other symmetry in the treatment of human beings: one may use neither oneself nor anyone else merely as a means. And this odd discrepancy, the tension, as I take it to be, between Kant's deontological and his extradeontological moral views is in itself perplexing and even troubling.

Now this discrepancy exists between Kant's views about perfect duty (the duty not to lie, not to kill, not to mutilate, etc.) and his views about the imperfect duty to confer benefits (which one doesn't have to fulfil at every moment); in an attempt to clarify and defend Kant, one might at this point attempt to justify Kant's alternation between self-other asymmetry and self-other symmetry by means of the distinction between perfect and imperfect duty. But that simply won't work. At a critical juncture Kant clearly refuses to put weight on the distinction between the two kinds of duty, and his failure to do so leads to what can, I think, be called an incoherence in his total ethical view.

Kant's claim that we have no obligation or duty to pursue our own happiness is based partly on the assumption that what we inevitably and spontaneously do cannot be obligatory or a duty. Kant makes no distinction here between imperfect and perfect duty, and so he is committed to holding that what we inevitably, etc., do cannot constitute one of our *perfect* duties.

Kant attempts to derive the wrongness of despondent suicide and killing others from the prohibition against using people merely as means, but he draws out a number of other implications as well: among them, the (notorious) prohibition on masturbation ('self-abuse') and, more relevantly to present purposes, a prohibition on mutilating either oneself or another person. But do we really need a prohibition against wilful *self*-mutilation? If Kant is allowed to have been justified in claiming that we inevitably and spontaneously aim for our own good or happiness, surely there is similar reason to hold that we inevitably and spontaneously (or typically and naturally) refrain from mutilating our own bodies, and so it would appear that the argument Kant uses to justify the absence of a duty to seek one's own happiness can also be used to argue against the existence of any obligation to refrain from wilful self-mutilation. And since the self-other symmetry of Kant's End-in-Itself formulation of the Categorical Imperative entails that there is such an obligation (Kant at least argues that it does), we really do end up with an incoherence or inconsistency in Kant's theory as a whole.

However, precisely because commonsense morality is relatively tolerant of self-mutilation, the problems here uncovered do not infect commonsense thinking about morality. Kant's End-in-Itself formulation of the Categorical Imperative is an important, a central, element in Kant's total moral conception, and so there seems to be at least one important form of incoherence that infects Kantian theory, but is not ascribable to commonsense. However, we have found internal conflicts both within ethical Kantianism and within commonsense morality and we cannot remain contented with either of these views.

## 2. MODES OF SYMMETRY

In section 1, we saw how an agent-sacrificing (self-other asymmetric) approach to morality gives rise, in Kant's ethics, to an agent-sacrificing notion of (what counts as a) virtue; but it was also pointed out that commonsense thinking about (what counts as a) virtue lacks the agent-sacrificing asymmetric character of our ordinary views about morality. It is an advantage of our ordinary thinking about the virtues that it allows both facts about the wellbeing of others and facts about the wellbeing of the agent to support claims about the goodness of some trait possessed by the agent, claims, that is, about the trait's status as a virtue. Thus, I make use of an appropriately self-other symmetric commonsense notion of what it is to be or to exemplify a virtue, as the foundational notion of a larger approach to the problems of ethics that can be shown to be free of the difficulties that undermined commonsense morality and Kantianism in Part 1. To proceed with this approach, we need to consider the forms of symmetry involved in commonsense virtue ethics and in utilitarianism.

Both utilitarianism and commonsense virtue ethics avoid the asymmetry of commonsense morality and Kantianism as just (roughly) characterised and thus avoid the problems and paradoxes of such morality. However, there is another natural sense for the expression 'self-other symmetry' according to which utilitarianism is symmetrical, but (non-moral) virtue ethics is not. It is time we took note of this distinction.

Under utilitarianism, the welfare or preferences of every individual are given equal weight in the reckoning of the goodness of results that constitutes the basis for its claims about moral rightness or betterness. So utilitarianism in that sense expresses or embodies an ideal of equal concern for all persons (or sentient beings): though it doesn't insist that moral agents themselves be equally concerned with every person's good, the calculations that determine the obligations of each agent (or what it is better or worse for the agent to do) are based on a reckoning of good consequences that treats the welfare of each and every person other than the agent as no more or less important than that of the agent. In thus making the standpoint of impersonal or impartial benevolence the fulcrum of all its evaluations, utilitarianism embodies an ideal of uniform or symmetrical concern towards *every* individual that is clearly, as a result, also *self-other* symmetric. (From such an ideal standpoint, however, concern for the agent of a given action may be a small fraction of the total concern that is, as it were, expressed in the utilitarian evaluation of that action. The more people affected by a given action, the less important are the welfare or interests of the agent in determining how that action is to be evaluated.)

There is no reason in advance to suppose that commonsense virtue ethics embodies the particular form of symmetry just described, and one may therefore wonder whether, through a lack of such symmetry, our proposed virtue ethics is at a relative disadvantage vis-à-vis utilitarianism. In fact, commonsense virtue ethics is not self-other symmetrical in the sense just introduced. But I don't believe this will cause problems for virtue ethics, because the latter can be shown to embody its own distinctive ideal of self-other symmetry, one that utilitarianism fails to embody; and so as far as the issue of desirable symmetry is concerned, there will turn out to be little to choose between utilitarianism and commonsense virtue ethics. Nonetheless, the distinction between the two kinds of symmetry we are now discussing may be the key to understanding the main differences between utilitarianism and virtue ethics as ethical norms or ideals, and although the literature of utilitarianism has already made us somewhat familiar with symmetry understood as uniform concern for self and any other person, the form of symmetry that characterises our ordinary thinking about the virtues has been pretty well ignored. Yet it is well worth discussing both in its own right and for the understanding it can give us of the virtue-theoretical approach to ethics.

The form of symmetry we have just attributed to (direct) utilitarianism is clearly absent from commonsense morality. The judgments made by the latter are not predicated on any ideal of equal concern for everyone; on the contrary, the agent counts for *less* than others and *greater* concern for those near and dear as opposed to distant others is morally incumbent upon her. And, as it turns out, the virtue ethics of commonsense also fails to embody the symmetry we have just attributed to utilitarianism. To be sure – and this is a point I will return to shortly – our ordinary thinking about the virtues treats benefit to the possessor of a trait as relevant to its status as a good trait of character. But nothing in our ordinary understanding of the virtues precludes the admirability of traits or acts that involve one in giving preference to certain people over others, and in fact it seems contrary to our usual understanding of the virtues, seems out and out deplorable, for one's actions and character not to give expression to greater concern, for example, for one's spouse and children than for random others. So there is some reason to believe that commonsense virtue ethics is incompatible with the sort of self-other symmetry exemplified by utilitarianism's equal concern for every individual.

Yet that ethics embodies another sort of self-other symmetry we have not yet considered. Traits admired for other-regarding reasons are not normally considered to have any sort of general precedence over predominantly self-regarding virtues. Kindness, justice and generosity are not usually viewed as greater or more important virtues than self-regarding virtues such as prudence, fortitude, sagacity and equanimity or 'mixed' virtues like courage, self-control and practical wisdom; indeed the language of commonsense ethics includes as many terms for self-regarding or 'mixed' virtues as for other-regarding virtues. To that degree, our ordinary thinking about the virtues gives equal emphasis to, is equally concerned with, virtues helping others and virtues helping their possessors, and this latter fact, assuming it is a fact, expresses or embodies a kind of equality or symmetry of concern for self and others.

But note the important difference from the symmetry we have just discussed in connection with utilitarianism. (The symmetries that utilitarianism and commonsense virtue ethics share and which we discussed in Part 1 are not at issue here.) In describing a virtue as (basically) other-regarding, I am treating others as a class or category specified relative to some given choice of possessor, and in saying, therefore, that our ordinary thinking about the virtues seems to place equal weight or importance on virtues helping their possessors and virtues helping people other than their possessors, I am not saying that virtue ethics allows or requires us to have or act on dispositions that embody an equal concern for every single individual. Rather, I am saying that our ordinary thinking about the virtues treats the category of trait-possessor and the category of 'other people' (i.e. people other than the trait-possessor) as of roughly equal importance, and this latter suggests (perhaps it does more than suggest, but

I don't at this point want to claim any more than it suggests) an ideal of character and action that, for any given choice of agent/possessor, exemplifies roughly equal concern for the agent/possessor and for others treated as a class or category to which everyone other than the agent/possessor belongs. In that case, we can say that our ordinary understanding of what is admirable and what counts as a virtue embodies equal concern for self and others, where 'others' is to be understood *in sensu composito*, that is, applying to other people as a class; whereas, by contrast, utilitarianism's ethical ideal expresses equality or symmetry of concern for self and others in a sense that understands 'others' *in sensu diviso*, as applying to each and every other individual as compared to the concern shown for the self (the agent/possessor herself). And this means that utilitarianism and commonsense virtue ethics differ as regards the importance and evaluation of purely self-regarding traits and actions.

Utilitarian evaluation reflects an equality of concern for the self and for every single other individual, and where enough other people can be affected by a trait or activity, concern for the given self/agent/trait-possessor may be practically insignificant by comparison with the sum of concern for other people that is mandated by the situation. Since over a (large part of a) lifetime, most of us can affect thousands, even millions, of other people, the self is likely to be submerged in the sea of concern for others that gives rise to utilitarian ethical judgments. But our ordinary thinking about the virtues – though it may not rule out the possibility of self-sacrifice, even enormous self-sacrifice, as a condition of human admirability or non-deplorability – seems less committed to evaluations that take such little account of the agent/possessor's self-regarding concerns. If its ideal of character and of action involves an equality between the self as a category, on the one hand, and other people taken as a category, rather than individually, on the other, then an evaluative balance is established between self-concern and concern for all others put together, and it is such a (two-way) balance that in my view constitutes the backbone of our ordinary thinking about what is and is not admirable in character, action, desire, etc. Utilitarianism, by contrast, sets up and commends separate balances, as it were, between the self and every single other person (sentient being), and although this in one sense represents an ideal of symmetrical treatment, it should by now be clear that the idea of a merely two-way balance between any given self and the totality or class of others also expresses an ethical ideal of symmetry, one that utilitarianism clearly and necessarily fails to embody

## ENDNOTES

1. On these points see, e.g., S. Scheffler, *The Rejection of Consequentialism*, Oxford: Oxford University Press (1982), passim.
2. I am not talking about masochism, where what seems like self-sacrifice may in some way or degree not be, but of cases where a person could, but won't actually, sacrifice her own dearest projects, etc. In such cases self-sacrifice is permitted, but would be irrational. (It would be a mistake to say of such a person: if she sacrificed the projects, she wouldn't have them as projects and so wouldn't be acting irrationally. This counterfactual claim cannot be defended. Cf. my 'Time in Counterfactuals', *Philosophical Review* 87 (1978), 3–27.)
3. It has been suggested to me that the reason why we are allowed to harm ourselves or avoid some benefit, where we would not be permitted to harm another person or prevent her from receiving similar benefit, lies in the consent implicit in actions we do to ourselves. If I harm

myself or avoid a benefit, I presumably do this willingly, whereas the agent whom I refuse to benefit does not consent to this neglect (and when she does there is nothing wrong with what I do). It might then be thought that agent-sacrificing asymmetry is not a deep feature of commonsense morality, but rather derivative from and justifiable in terms of the moral importance of consent.

But such an explanation will not do. It makes a significant difference, commonsensically, whether I negligently cause another person unwanted harm or negligently do so to myself. Yet consent seems *equally absent* in these two cases. More persuasively, perhaps, if I can either avoid an enduring pain to myself or a short-lived one to you, you and I might both agree that it would be foolish of me to prevent the shorter one to you; so you might not consent to my taking the longer pain upon myself to save you from the shorter pain. Yet there would be nothing morally wrong, commonsensically, in such a sacrifice. But when positions are reversed and I can avoid a short-lived pain to myself or a longer one to you and it is morally right that I should do the latter, you will presumably not consent to my doing the former, and it will be wrong if I do so. Again, consent/lack-of-consent seems not to make the relevant commonsense moral difference. The agent-sacrificing moral asymmetry eludes the distinction between consent and non-consent, and is not thus easily accounted for.

4. On 'agent-neutrality' see Derek Parfit, *Reasons and Persons*, Oxford: Oxford University Press (1984), 27. Note that non-optimising forms of utilitarianism and consequentialism are also strictly agent-neutral. If, for example, one accepts some form of 'satisficing consequentialism', one's criterion of right action will be whether a given act has *good enough* consequences (relative, perhaps, to its alternatives); but such a form of consequentialism will in no way distinguish among agents in its ultimate determinations of what counts as good enough consequences. On this point see my *Common-sense Morality and Consequentialism*, London: Routledge & Kegan Paul (1985), Chapter 3.

5. Even non-optimising forms of consequentialism have the feature just mentioned. And because of this feature, such views allow for moral supererogation in a way that more standard utilitarianism and consequentialism do not.

6. See W. D. Ross, *The Right and the Good*, Oxford: Oxford University Press (1955), 168; and also his *The Foundations of Ethics*, Oxford: Oxford University Press (1939), 72ff., 272ff.

7. See Foot's *Virtues and Vices*, California: Berkeley, University of California Press (1978), 125f.

8. See Foot's 'Morality as a System of Hypothetical Imperatives', in *Virtues and Vices*, 159f., 168. In more recent and as yet unpublished work, Foot seems to be moving back towards her earlier ideas.

9. I am leaving it open whether we want to emphasise the distinction between character traits and personality traits and so argue, for example, that charmingness, however desirable or admirable, is not a virtue.

It has been suggested to me that self-regarding virtues may count as such because they involve admirable self-control, rather than because they benefit their possessors. But one could press a similar argument with respect to other-regarding virtues; and if we intuitively feel that other-regarding virtue has to do with benefiting others and not just with the agent's demonstration of self-control, isn't there reason to say something similar about self-regarding virtue? I might also mention that some self-regarding virtues seem not at all, or at least predominantly, to be a matter of self-control. Farsightedness, for example, is not readily viewed as a matter of self-control, and even self-assurance is a matter not so much of controlling self-doubt (so as to be able to act effectively despite it) as of not having doubts in the first place. Cf. Foot's remarks on honesty in the title essay of *Virtues and Vices*.

10. On this point, see Foot, op. cit., 119 and H. Sidgwick, *Methods of Ethics*, 7th edn, London (1907), 327f., 332, 356.

11. See *Goods and Virtues*, Chapter 3.

12. In speaking here of the concerns and wellbeing of moral agents, I am leaving *simple desires* out of account. But commonsense morality arguably makes concessions to less-than-deep, less-than-serious desires (or intentions) – it is not entirely clear how far commonsense agent-favouring permissions extend in this direction. See my *Common-sense Morality and Consequentialism*, 141f.

13. See, e.g., Kant's *Fundamental Principles of the Metaphysics of Morals*, London (1909), 13f., 16n.

14. Even if Kantianism can treat prudence and prudential action as (non-morally) valuable and admirable, such evaluations will presuppose the moral goodness of the agent or trait-

possessor's will and will thus be conditional, e.g., on whether the individual in question is doing what he should in regard to other people's happiness. To that extent, prudential action will lack the *fundamental* value of moral action (although this doesn't mean that the agent is a mere means to other people's happiness). Clearly this view devalues the moral agent and makes him play second fiddle in relation to other people. Of course, for Kant even the value of seeking others' happiness is conditional on the simultaneous honouring of perfect duties, but then the value of prudence will be doubly conditional, whereas, for Kant, the virtue of promoting others' happiness is not conditional on whether one seeks one's own happiness. It may be conditional on proper self-respect, or non-servility, but in Kant's ethics the latter doesn't require the pursuit of one's own happiness. (On this point, see T. Hill, 'Servility and Self-Respect', *The Monist* 57 (1973), 87–104.) I am indebted here to discussion with Nancy Sherman.

15. However, as Louis Pojman has pointed out to me, Kant's employment in the *Critique of Practical Reason* of the notion of the complete good – of the postulate of proportionality between happiness and moral desert – may be said to undercut the claim that he depreciates the wellbeing of the moral agent, but to do so in religious/metaphysical terms that are philosophically unacceptable nowadays. Most precisely, then, the charge to be brought against Kant or ordinary moral thinking is that it either unacceptably devalues the moral agent or is forced to make unacceptable religious/metaphysical assumptions.

16. Cf. Sidgwick, op. cit., 246.

17. See Kant's *The Doctrine of Virtue*, New York: Harper & Row (1964), 44. Contrast, however, Kant's *Fundamental Principles of the Metaphysic of Morals*, 15, where Kant seems to allow for empirical distractions from the pursuit of one's own happiness.

18. See *The Doctrine of Virtue*, 44.

19. Op. cit., 119. Also 49.

20. See Kant's *Lectures on Ethics*, New York, Harper & Row (1963), 150–4, and compare with *Critique of Practical Reason*, Indianapolis, Bobbs-Merrill (1956), 162; *The Doctrine of Virtue*, 84ff.; and *Fundamental Principles of the Metaphysic of Morals*, 47. Also see M. Gregor, *Laws of Freedom*, Oxford: Basil Blackwell (1963), 135ff.

# 8

# BY VIRTUE OF A VIRTUE

## Harold Alderman

### 1.

Beginning with G. E. M. Anscombe's 'Modern Moral Philosophy' in 1958, various critics – e.g. Frankena, Foot, MacIntyre and Murdock – have, to one extent or another, expressed dissatisfaction with the condition of modern moral philosophy.[1] Prior to this round of critiques, H. A. Prichard in 1912 asked the question 'Is Moral Philosophy Based on a Mistake?' in an essay of that title in *Mind*.[2] One finds precedent for these expressions of discontent with the ground-rules of moral philosophy in both Aristotle and Kant, two thinkers whose reformulations of the questions and procedures of ethics proved seminal for the discipline. Even neglecting other important developments in contemporary moral philosophy (such as those in rights theory), the diversity and rigour of these critiques alone suggest that the prognosis for the discipline of ethics is quite favourable. Philosophy in at least one of its dimensions has recovered that self-reflective attentiveness that marks its most productive phases.

So it is that several of these contemporary critiques raise the suspicion that what is wrong with moral philosophy is that it operates outside a context in terms of which talk about moral laws or moral goods would be intelligible. Our contemporary situation can thus be contrasted with, for example, that of Aristotle for whom a discussion of 'magnificence' was firmly rooted in an Athenian context in terms of which an argument over the merits of that particular virtue might be resolved. Alasdair MacIntyre's *After Virtue* brings this line of reflection into sharp new focus with a series of illuminating discussions concerning the role of the virtues both in the history of moral practices and in the logic of moral argument. In general, MacIntyre tries to show that 'contemporary moral debate is interminable';[3] that is, he tries to show why, given the nature of contemporary moral philosophy, there is 'no rational way of securing moral agreement'.[4] Because I believe MacIntyre is successful in his demonstration, in this chapter I shall take that demonstration for granted and try to construct a set of arguments designed to show how, in terms of a universally accessible paradigmatic character, we have at hand a way of avoiding the 'interminable' regress of moral debate. Thus although my argument is derivative of MacIntyre's diagnosis and dependent, in part, upon his treatment of the concept of virtue, the proposal I develop here for the resolution of moral arguments is, sad to say, somewhat at odds with his own.

I shall be arguing that no rules or goodness theories can provide an adequate foundation for the important theoretical needs the discipline of ethics is expected to meet. In elaborating this argument, in addition to MacIntyre I shall be indebted primarily to the work of Lawrence Becker, A. S. Cua and Stanley Hauerwas, each of whom, in very different ways that will not often be directly addressed here, has made it easier once again to begin taking seriously the idea of virtue and its related family of concepts.[5]

Before going on with my argument, I want to call attention to what I take to be the conceptual power of goodness or law theories, a power I see as lying in their ability to give unity to the phenomena of moral experience. In saying things like 'all persons ought to pursue good X' or 'all persons ought to do their duty Y', both axiological and deontological moral theorists take for granted that we share a common human situation, a situation demanding kindred moral responses. Further, in defending such notions as universal goods and obligations, axiological and deontological moral philosophies argue for an objectivity of goods and rules which yields a presumption against subjectivism or relativism. It is in these two regards that such theories primarily are to be commended. However, in their preoccupation with the objectivity of rules or goods, such theories conceal a crucial feature of morality: the efforts of disparate moral agents to make moral sense of their common experience. Such theories also fail to notice important features of the decision procedures actually employed by moral agents in those times of moral quandary when clarity about moral matters is most desperately needed. Their very preoccupation with the objectivity of goods or rules thus obscures for both axiological and deontological theories the context of moral agency, a context in which rules and notions of the good have – as I shall argue – only a secondary role.

With these reflections in mind, in Section 2 I want to show why *character* is the appropriate, most adequate and necessary terminus of moral argument. There is, as I shall argue, a transcultural dimension of character, one most clearly manifest in the paradigmatic individuals, which constitutes its moral dimension. In Section 3, I continue my defence of the central role of paradigmatic character in moral philosophy by considering the following things: the relation between character and goods, the relation between character and rules, the concept of narrative argument, and the notion of a decision procedure based on the logic of emulation. The task of re-thinking moral philosophy as I see it, then, requires retrieving the concept of paradigmatic character, the concept whose elucidation points directly to the universally human context of moral practices. It is only in this context that it is possible to have something like a rational and non-relative resolution of moral arguments.

**2.**

If one is to avoid infinite regress in any sort of argument it must be possible at some point simply to say something like, 'Look, that's just the way things are' or something like, 'Now, do you see?' When a philosopher reaches such a point in argument all he can do – since he does not have recourse to rhetoric or intimidation – is go through the argument again, perhaps emphasising certain key points, perhaps inventing analogies, or perhaps paraphrasing what he has already said. But he must always get back to some such terminal point, some such grounding appeal, and he must also be able to make clear that he has reached such a point and that – argument exhausted – there is nothing else he can do.

As a class, moral claims are traditionally grounded in metaphysical claims; that is, it is recognised that it makes sense to say 'one ought to do so and so' only because the injunction presupposes that 'some decisive aspect of reality is of such and such a nature'. Thus one sort of ultimate appeal for the resolution of disagreement in moral argument involves showing that someone has got his reality descriptions wrong. Much contemporary debate over the morality of abortion, for example, involves arguments of this sort. But there is one class of moral disagreement that cannot be resolved in this way and that is when the disputants share a metaphysics and when it can be shown that they do not disagree in this regard in any significant way. How is this sort of moral dispute to be resolved? That is, what is the bottom line of appeal when, for example, two naturalists disagree on the morality of abortion? There is, I think, still another sort of interesting moral situation which cannot be warranted by appeal to a crucial description and that is when two moralists who adopt different metaphysical schemata come to the same moral conclusions: for example, when a naturalist and a super-naturalist both condemn the practice of abortion. Upon what do two moralists who adopt divergent metaphysics base their agreement? Generally, the answer to these sorts of questions has been that there are certain ultimate and obvious rights, goods or rules, which must be taken for granted – however arduously the moral philosopher has laboured to discover their obviousness. This style of final appeal keeps arguments within the explicitly moral domain; it says, in effect, 'look, morally speaking that's just the way things are'. Given these remarks, it is obvious that for rights, rule, or goodness moralities, the rights, the rules, or the goods are taken as ultimate and as giving final warrant to the moral philosophies for which they constitute the court of final appeal.

In modern moral philosophy, it is G. E. Moore's intuitionism that most clearly recognises that justificatory appeals are ultimately tied to some sort of direct apprehension. Historically, things would have gone better for moral philosophy if Moore's insight had been taken more seriously, and it seems to me that this insight can be taken seriously, however amusing it may be to recall that Moore's early disciples went around trying to intuit non-natural properties.[6] The problem with Moore's analysis was that it substituted the ultimate appeal to obvious cases for too much of the preliminary work of justification. If we avoid the difficulty of collapsing the distinction between ultimate and penultimate manoeuvres in moral reasoning, we remain safe in taking seriously what Moore has to teach us about the terminus of moral argument.

Two recent authors (Gass and Pincoffs) have tried to reinstate something like Moore's insight by arguing that what is wrong with modern moral philosophy is that it is preoccupied with extreme or ambiguous cases.[7] The merit of their somewhat different arguments is that they try to *begin* the work of moral philosophy with an appeal to obvious (though not ultimate) cases. Thus Gass, for example, observes that there is something obviously wrong with baking an 'obliging stranger' who agrees to let you use him in an experiment. Aristotelian moral philosophy involved a different sort of appeal to obvious cases insofar as it argued that in order to be a responsible Athenian one had merely to imitate the behaviour of the obviously good Athenian citizen. By showing the citizen what he was *for the most part* to do, Aristotle's ethics prepared individuals for action in extremis – though such was not its primary intent – by giving them confidence that they knew the right thing to do. The wisdom of Aristotle's approach – however provincial some of its specific recommendations – lies in that it clearly understands that one learns how to act by acting and that one first learns how to undertake *appropriate action* in everyday situations simply by observing how things are done.

I take it that Moore's recognition that we must appeal to something *ultimately* obvious and Gass and Pincoffs's injunction to begin with *initial* obvious cases are both salutary for moral philosophy. Taken together these recommendations show us a way beyond moral philosophy's preoccupation with appeals to the obviousness of rights, rules or goods; and they do this while making clear the necessity of an appeal to *some* sort of obvious case. The point is that it is *not* obvious that the only type of warrant to which one might make a final moral appeal is either a right, a rule or a good. And the further point is that it is obvious that in appealing to some final court of rights, goods or rules, moral philosophy is employing the criterion of obviousness. Thus this chapter offers as another possibility of ultimate moral appeal the moral obviousness of the character of the paradigmatic individuals. In that character the obviousness of the initial obvious cases is exemplified and we have at hand a way to retain both the objectivity of moral philosophy and the primacy of the moral agent.

The appeal to the character of paradigmatic individuals is itself, in some ways, a radically traditional sort of appeal. Underlying Plato's moral philosophy, for example, is his certainty that Socrates is a moral exemplar. All of Plato's dialogues may be read as an attempt to portray and defend the character of Socrates – whether he is searching for beauty, truth or virtue – in such a way that the reader will be led to imitate him. It is perhaps equally obvious that for Aristotle, Aristotle himself is the moral paradigm. Thus if we want to be virtuous citizens of an Aristotelian polis, we must act like Aristotle – or at least like an Aristotle with a sense of humour. Nietzsche in the nineteenth century portrays the character of Zarathustra as the paradigmatic philosophical individual and enjoins us, especially in part IV of *Thus Spake Zarathustra*, to *appropriately* imitate that character. For each of these philosophers, then, it is character that in some important senses is the bottom line of moral appeal. The appeal to character is, of course, even more central in the arguments and practices of the great religious traditions.

Nevertheless, however central the appeal to character has been in moral argument or however central I argue it ought to be, a first obligation of any argument such as this is to suggest some prima facie reasons as to *why* character is a more adequate final court of appeal in moral philosophy than either rights, goods or rules. Let me begin this argument with a discussion of Karl Jaspers' list of paradigmatic individuals in his book, *The Great Philosophers*.[8] Jaspers singles out Socrates, Buddha, Confucius and Christ as paradigmatic individuals, acknowledging that he might well have chosen Moses, Mohammed and Lao Tsu, among others. Jaspers' acknowledgement of a certain imprecision in his list seems to raise doubts about the possibility of any clear specification as to who counts as a paradigmatic individual. Would not, for instance, philosophers, poets, and mathematicians, as well as athletes and religious people, all come up with different lists of paradigmatic individuals and with different descriptions of exemplary moral character? And if they did, would this not itself count as a telling objection?

By way of a first general attempt to deflect such a line of argument, I want to say that it is not at all obvious that differences in such things as class, profession or talent, for example, would affect who gets named as a paradigmatic individual any more than they would affect what rights, rules or goods get named as obvious and fundamental on lists compiled by rights theorists, Kantians or utilitarians. In the second place, it is obvious that if class and professional differences do affect the compilation of rights, goods, rules or paradigmatic individuals, this itself would not yield a telling objection to the possibility of compiling non-provincial lists of goods, rights, rules or paradigmatic individuals. All it would do is show that such lists would initially have to cope with the biases reflected in class, profession, and so forth – although these biases are quite probably over-emphasised in the social sciences. The third and telling point, of course, is that from the fact that a group of people approve of a good, a right, a rule or a paradigmatic individual, it does not follow that such approval is justified. Jaspers' list of paradigmatic individuals thus merely provides us with a reasonable set of clues – the initial obvious cases – we need to get on with the argument.

Given these general remarks, I do have to argue that it is logically necessary to specify a common set of character traits which will be shared by all paradigmatic individuals, and I want to make this argument even while acknowledging that no such set of traits is to be found in this chapter. In arguing for a possible set of universally commendable character traits, I thus reject Jaspers' and Cua's assumptions that no such set can be described. My argument is itself, I think, not one whit more tenuous than the presumption in favour of the possibility of universal rights, goods or duties, a presumption made by every rights theorist, deontologist or utilitarian. Indeed, the sceptical presumption against the very possibility of such a specification of paradigmatic character traits seems to me little more than an *ad ignorantium* argument of modern relativism.

From a longer list by Jaspers, then, I have culled the following family of tentative identifying characteristics. In terms of these characteristics we can identify the paradigmatic individuals whose character provides us with the best clue for the description and ordering of those elusive dispositional traits, the virtues themselves.

1. They set norms by their attitudes and actions.
2. They *indicate* what is to be done and their demands are never fully expressed in instructions.
3. They possess great empathy.
4. All stress silence, speak in parables, and emphasise that their highest teachings can be expressed only indirectly.
5. They do not write.
6. They are preoccupied with overcoming death and suffering, and they themselves exemplify this overcoming.
7. They believe human love is universal and unlimited.

The most obvious result of this list of characteristics is that it clearly places the paradigmatic individual in the domain of praxis rather than in the domain of theory. The paradigmatic individuals thus exemplify Aristotle's insight that moral philosophy is a practical science, one to be learned by practising what certain key individuals do rather than by analysing what they say. This feature of the list itself yields a presumption in favour of taking the character of paradigmatic individuals as the final line of appeal in moral argument, and it does this because it helps make sense of the common charge made against philosophy that it is nothing but a matter of 'words, words, words'.

At no point in his own discussion of the paradigmatic individuals does Jaspers raise doubts about the possibility of recognising them as such: the cases of Buddha, Christ and Confucius make it clear that character is the final line of moral appeal in diverse moral traditions. This historical fact itself further indicates the prima facie cogency of taking the concept of paradigmatic character more seriously in moral philosophy, and it does this on the grounds that the task of philosophy is to clarify the practices of the everyday world and not to legislate them out of existence. The assumption that either rights or rules are logically prior to character in moral argument thus runs counter to the shared wisdom of the Buddhist, Christian and Confucian traditions. To make somewhat different use of this same point, the institutional and intellectual traditions derived from the four paradigmatic individuals constitute a rather rigorous test of their status as moral paradigms, however modern it may be to remember P. T. Barnum's sceptical observation that 'there's a sucker born every minute'. Thus to ignore these tests and to begin with the sceptical question 'but how do we know they are moral paradigms?' is to eschew what is obvious. Such scepticism begs the question against the actuality of the moral life as it is lived in diverse human traditions. The point here is that one can begin neither moral nor mathematical arguments with critics who doubt the possibility of such arguments. Traditional moral arguments are an existence proof for the possibility of such arguments.

In addition to its positive gains, Jaspers' discussion also raises two difficulties with the concept of the paradigmatic individual which are important for different reasons.

In the first place, we must acknowledge that the traditional practices established by the paradigmatic individuals differ in major respects, and this seems to raise the problem of Babel: should we try to imitate Buddha, Christ, Socrates, or some other moral exemplar? But this is a specious problem, for what is most obvious about the paradigmatic individuals – as with the great moral theories – is that there is a common core of moral behaviours endorsed by all of them. And it is with these obvious cases of obviously moral behaviour that we must begin our discussion, otherwise we merely, once again, accede to an unsubstantiated scepticism that seems utterly to relativise the domain of moral practices.

The 'obvious differences' in the Buddhist, Christian and Socratic traditions, for example, seem to me to stand in the character of their founders in somewhat the same way the reasons of traditional moral theory stand in their conclusions (i.e. rights, rules or goods): they are different kinds of pragmatic support for the same 'conclusions'. The differences in the moral philosophies of, for example, Kant and Mill, lie primarily in the reasons they give for their conclusions and not primarily in the conclusions themselves. So it is also with the differences in the paradigmatic individuals. Of course – and this is the key point – the kinds of 'reasons' (i.e. the traditions and practices) which support the characters of the paradigmatic individuals are of a different logical type than those which support the conclusions of rights and rule theories. And this means that the structures holding together a moral stance that takes the character of paradigmatic individuals as fundamental will be different from those of contemporary moral philosophy: they will be narrative and dramatic, rather than logical and deductive. This is a point to which I shall return in the next section.

The second difficulty Jaspers raises is that of deciding if a paradigmatic individual is being *appropriately* imitated. This I take it is an empirical and not a conceptual problem. That is, it is an empirical problem to decide if someone is meeting an agreed standard; whereas it is a conceptual problem to determine the meaning and adequacy of some standard. For example, consider a rather strange rule requiring everyone to high-jump nine inches, nine times, at nine a.m. The test of appropriate responsiveness in this case is relatively straightforward. One appeals to a ruler, to a clock and to arithmetic. (There also seem to be no serious conceptual problems with the meaning of this standard, though there do seem to be many concerning its adequacy.) Now if the test of appropriateness also includes the style or tone of the jump, then things get much more difficult. One might imagine appropriateness judges saying such things as: 'He had a bad attitude', or 'He seemed awkward', or 'He was bored when he jumped'. It is, of course, just the dispositional dimension of emulation that is the core of an appropriate imitation of any paradigmatic individual. And we should be surprised not that it is difficult to measure such things but that anyone would think otherwise.

The difficulty of appropriate imitation occurs first as an intra-traditional problem; it is, for example, the problem of how a Westerner appropriately imitates Christ, a problem addressed by Thomas à Kempis and resolved, however imperfectly, by the monastic tradition of Christianity. One knows that one appropriately imitates Christ if one lives as a viable member of a community whose task it is to know what 'appropriate' means in a tradition that takes such imitation as the bottom line of moral argument. The test is, of course, the same for the Buddhist, Confucian and even the Socratic traditions; and in all cases it is true that one never knows if the test of 'appropriateness' is perfectly met. But this sort of objection also holds for rights, rule or goodness theories: Have I really acted in such a way as to maximise utilitarian happiness? Have I really properly generalised some Kantian maxim? The odd result of this observation is that it becomes evident that moral philosophies which assume the character of paradigmatic individuals as the bottom line of argument are in a stronger position than contemporary moral philosophies on this point, for they have both traditional practices, as well as philosophical arguments, to employ in the tests of appropriateness; whereas contemporary moral philosophy has only the arguments of philosophers. Each of the monastic orders, churches and denominations, is then a mechanism for making the test of appropriate imitation, and it is no telling objection to this line of argument to say, 'Well, which one of them has got Christ right?'. The point, of course, is that we never know for sure. But more importantly it is the very dialogue between varying interpretations of Christ's character which keeps the question of 'appropriate imitation' open and rescues it from mere dogmatism.

The second focus of the problem of appropriate imitation is extra-traditional: Can, for example, a Westerner be a Buddhist? Of course he can if he knows the texts, traditions and institutional practices of Buddhism. But can he really know these things? And the answer is: of course he can if he knows the appropriate languages or if translations are commensurate with the original texts (and I think they certainly can be). Now saying these things is not meant to minimise difficulties; for it is difficult enough merely to learn a language and to get to know a different culture. How much more challenging it must be to get to understand the highest moral achievements of an alien tradition.

Having acknowledged the extra-traditional problem of appropriate imitation, I want, nonetheless, to argue that it is the attempt at such imitation and not the difficulties that accompany it which is interesting, for in an odd way the attempt is both supportive of the idea of the universality of the paradigmatic individuals and, at the same time, logically superfluous. That is, in the first place, if an 'alien' paradigmatic individual can be recognised as such, it must be because he illuminates certain features of the seeker's own experience. Otherwise why – assuming no mere preoccupation with the exotic – would he be sought? The ability to recognise alien paradigmatic individuals as such thus supports two important conclusions: there is such a thing as *human* experience, and the paradigmatic individuals manifest universally human character traits. This is the point at which the argument gets interesting; for if the alien paradigmatic individual can be recognised as such (e.g., Buddha), it is only because he is analogous to some other paradigmatic individual (e.g., Christ). In such a situation it is (for Westerners) Christ who is the explanatory term of the analogy and Buddha who is the unknown. Thus a Westerner can recognise an 'alien' paradigmatic individual only to the extent he knows the paradigmatic individual of his own tradition, but since paradigmatic individuals express fundamentally human truths, there is no reason to seek to know an alien paradigmatic individual. A Westerner can be a Buddhist, but why should he?

Now I understand there may be serious answers to this last question. For example, one might want to argue that in this epoch Buddhism and Christianity emphasise different aspects of the human predicament that need to be attended to, and therefore Westerners ought to learn those other aspects by becoming Buddhists. But this is not the sort of answer it seems to be, for what the answer really says is that no tradition is perfect and that traditions learn from each other. Thus what we are left with is an injunction to explore another tradition in order to 'perfect' our own, so that we may more adequately imitate our own traditional paradigmatic individual. The key part of all of this, however, is that insofar as traditions, institutions, practices, etc., are 'reasons' supporting the character of a paradigmatic individual, one will always be able to give better reasons for the imitation of an indigenous paradigmatic individual than one will for an alien; that is, one always has a better understanding of the nuances of one's native tradition. The imitation of alien paradigmatic individuals thus carries with it the greater risk of dogmatism and is therefore to that extent, at least, to be abjured.

This line of argument establishes a presumption in favour of the idea that paradigmatic individuals are universally accessible and that their character has transcultural significance. This does not, however, mean that I have shown that in all respects all paradigmatic individuals endorse the very same range of appropriate behaviours, so that all questions about conflict between paradigmatic individuals are eliminated. Nevertheless, my argument does make plausible the conclusion that the appeal to the character of paradigmatic individuals involves something more than a mere appeal to the contingencies of cultural practices. More strongly than this, Jaspers' list of identifying characteristics itself suggests that close attention to a comparative study of the paradigmatic individuals will show that there are no fundamental, irresolvable conflicts between their moral practices. Those conflicts that do exist will prove to be resolvable in terms of an account of being human that is neither merely provincial nor merely formal.[9]

Since the necessity of some universally human dimension of character is a central element of my argument I want to garner additional support for the existence of such a dimension from two other sources. First, it seems to me that this dimension is much more than hinted at in those great works of literature that can be read across major historical, linguistic and cultural divides. The access that all readers have to the universally accessible experiences of, for example, Oedipus, Quixote, Ishmael, Arjuna, Kokopeli or Beowulf yields such a strong presumption in favour of a shared dimension of character that probably only philosophers would ignore it in favour of the tidier, theoretical domains of rights, rules and goods. Indeed, the preoccupation of great dramatists, poets and novelists with re-telling these or similar tales is an effort to renew in the writer's own appropriate idiom the hero's quintessentially human struggle with the matters ideally resolved by the paradigmatic individuals. The great works of both Western and Eastern literature seem to me to provide a second obvious – perhaps banally so – set of clues to the *human* domain of experience which the paradigmatic individuals most perfectly exemplify. Having said this, it is beyond my present intentions to develop the connections between this set of clues and Heidegger's philosophical descriptions of the human dimension, a dimension whose existence I think the cases clearly indicate. Rather, I mean to take seriously the very style of philosophical argument which this chapter, following suggestions of MacIntyre and others, suggests has been somewhat neglected in moral philosophy – the presentation of clear and important cases – and, for the time being, to rest content with the promise made by my presentations.[10] Nonetheless, remembering Moore's premature appeal to obviousness, I would acknowledge the need to complete the presentations with further philosophical defence. Yet the presentations themselves have their own autonomy and it is with this in mind that I end this section with yet a third appeal to an obvious case of a different sort.

Sir Richard Francis Burton, the nineteenth-century scholar, geographer, soldier, anthropologist and linguist, provides an historical example that further supports the conclusion that there is a cross-cultural dimension of human character. Since Burton himself exemplifies the experience of the multitude of travellers who have been able to recognise character in individuals with whom they do not share primary cultural membership, his case is particularly decisive. In general, Burton, as many sources make clear, had the uncanny knack of being not only a virtuous Victorian (who always knew the right Victorian thing to do, though he did not always do it) but of also knowing in disparate, alien cultures what counted as appropriate behaviour. Given this knack, Burton was always recognised as a man of virtue; that is to say, he was able either to imitate appropriately the 'right' behaviour of worlds radically different from his own or, when failing this, he, nonetheless, was able to act in such a way as to be recognised as a man of character. Thus Burton, for example, successfully lived as an Indian native while spying for the British Army; more dramatically, while disguised as an Arab-speaking Persian he was one of the first Europeans to visit Mecca. By contrast, when Burton enters Dahome for the first time, knowing neither the language nor the standard behaviours, he is, at a crucial juncture, nonetheless perceived by King Gelele as a man of character.[11] Both Burton, the alien, and Gelele, the King, step outside their cultures to meet in the quintessentially human dimension.

Burton's arrival in Dahome became an occasion for Gelele to order the performance of the 'Ku To Man' ceremony. This ceremony had as its dramatic climax the ritual execution of a number of slaves, the number being determined by the importance of the event which occasioned it. Burton was appalled by the executions that took place, and he had the audacity to demand that the king release some of the prisoners and to insist that he, himself, be absent from all the killings. The king accepted Burton's admonitions, although he nonetheless executed twenty-three slaves in Burton's honour. Burton are a careful description of the grisly scene: the resigned and terrified victims, the execution platform, the mute testimony of the fresh corpses, and the bleached skulls of earlier 'messengers', which was how Gelele saw the people killed as part of the Ku To Man ceremony.

The point of these remarks is that King Gelele tolerated Burton's violations of well-established Dahomean customs and did so in such a way that rather than being offended he recognised that Burton was a man of character, who in some sense had done the right thing. But in what regard did Burton do the right thing? Surely no one would draw from this case a rule to the effect that one ought to rebuff the king's hospitality by correcting his royal etiquette, for it is clear that Burton's achievement lies precisely in his violation of standard behaviour. Thus what is communicated in this event is character and not a sensitivity to the rules of an alien etiquette. Burton *showed* Gelele that there was a dimension in which they could meet that was neither English nor Dahomean. With his typically dramatic sense of his own presence, Burton revealed that he was a brave and decisive man who would not easily abandon the moral demands of his own culture. To all of these roles the king responded with friendliness: he and Burton could meet outside the host-guest relationship because the king acknowledged a set of virtues which could be recognised across the boundaries of their cultures. The triumphant moment of this meeting took place when the king invited Burton to dance with him in a ritual dance, and there in the African bush two strangers shared a common and human meeting place. As a gleeful but somewhat awed Dahomean populace looked on, the king danced with an outsider. This experience of Richard Burton – one of many in his career – thus shows in a decisive way that there is a transcultural dimension of character which can be recognised without argument. It is this dimension that constitutes the human dimension of character, a dimension that is manifest in the heroes of literature and, in an ideal way, in the paradigmatic individuals. It is to this dimension that moral philosophy must make its final appeal.

## 3.

In this part of my argument I want to indicate what a moral philosophy, re-thought in the way I have argued is necessary, would look like. That is, I want to give a first indication of its conceptual terrain and thus also to develop a further set of arguments in its defence. In order to begin this discussion I want to separate my previous critique of goodness theories from my critique of law theories. I have to do this because I must now acknowledge that my earlier, apparently parallel, opposition to rules and goods theories seems to break down insofar as it is appropriate to deem this virtue theory itself a species of goodness theory. I am willing to so deem it with the proviso – as I argued in the preceding section – that there is a convincing prima facie warrant for taking the character of the paradigmatic individual as the highest good; no such warrant is available for any other conception of the good. Thus it seems to me to be utterly absurd to argue that there are ever circumstances under which paradigmatic character is morally undesirable. By contrast, it is not absurd to argue that under some circumstances neither pleasure nor the greatest happiness of the greatest number is morally desirable. The example of the indulgent libertine – for which the wealthy drug addict is the paradigm – establishes the case against the egoistic hedonist, and the example of the tyranny of a majority over a minority – for which there are all too many twentieth-century examples alone – makes the case against the altruistic utilitarian. Now, I realise that both the hedonist and the utilitarian have what they take to be forceful responses to these not altogether original objections, but it is not my goal here to try to rebuff their responses. My goal is rather more direct and I think more devastating for both the egoistic hedonist and the utilitarian: if – as I have argued – no similar, intuitively damning objections can even be formulated against the conclusion that in all circumstances paradigmatic character is a moral good, then this impossibility alone places all other goods in a secondary, provincial relationship to the universal good of virtuous character.

Given my argument that the good of character is logically fundamental, it follows that in several important senses rules, although at least heuristically helpful, are also conceptually secondary. It is to these various senses and to their ramifications that I now must attend. Let me begin this way: in being with a moral paradigm one learns to be virtuous the same way one learns to cook, dance, play football and so forth, and that is by imitating people who are good at those sorts of things. Since being moral means learning how to do the right thing, it seems to me not at all logically odd to argue that learning how to be moral is strictly analogous to all other cases of *learning how to*. Rules, then, are secondary in the first place insofar as they are not necessary to learn how to be moral. And this is true in the sense that an anthropologist would never learn how to behave appropriately in an alien community simply by asking for the rules of right behaviour. Rather he would do so by observing what people do and, in particular, by observing what the people do who are approved of by the culture. The rules might well *clarify* his practices, but they are *not* the point; just as they are neither necessary nor sufficient conditions of appropriate behaviour, as I shall argue below.

For neither the moral agent nor the anthropologist, then, can rules give an adequate orientation to all the nuances and contingencies of appropriate behaviour. What they both require is a certain character, a certain dispositional feel for things. Like children and anthropologists, then, moral agents learn best when they act like the people who exemplify what is expected of them. The difficulties of modern moral philosophy, given this remark, can be seen as analogous to the difficulties of the 'new math' insofar as it substitutes the rules of set theory for the praxis of ordinary arithmetical behaviour. The traditional teacher shows her pupils that you always write '1 + 1 = 2', and the pupils practise writing it. And they do so successfully to the extent that the teacher manifests the sort of disposition that motivates children to imitate her behaviour. Or, to introduce one more telling case, if it is impossible to teach a seven-year-old how to ride a bicycle by giving him the right set of rules, is it not absurd to think that a set of moral rules is sufficient to teach a person how to live a good life?

The secondary role of rules can be emphasised from another direction by calling attention to the shared conception that people who, for example, paint or dance by the rules are somehow missing the point of what they do. In these sorts of rule-following behaviour, the spirit or tone of the praxis which is to be learned is somehow missed and the behaviour is criticised as 'just going through the motions'. In the same sense, a sociopath who followed the rules of appropriate behaviour would be missing the point of the moral life. Kant, in drawing the distinction between 'acting in accordance with' and 'acting because of', shows that following the rules is not a sufficient condition of morality, although his own conception of 'acting because of' is itself misleading to the extent that it allows rule-following behaviour to be divorced from the development of desirable character traits.

Now although my interpretation holds that the concept of being moral is to be explicated in terms of the logic of acting like rather than in terms of the logic of rule following, it is nonetheless true that one can formulate rules for what one is doing when one imitates either a craftsman or a moral paradigm. But when someone (e.g., the craftsman) is in a position to formulate adequate rules, he no longer needs them. Thus, rules are superfluous for becoming like a craftsman (after all, he did it without them) and are unnecessary when one is a craftsman. Rules, as Collingwood observed, are late developments in the moral life.[12] Perhaps they are autobiographical footnotes which we have mistaken for the life itself?

Another limitation of rules is indicated from a different direction by Lawrence Becker when he calls attention to the problems rule theories have with the analysis of excuses or exceptions.[13] We are all familiar with the phenomenon of saying such things as 'even though he broke the rule he is still a good man'. According to Becker such occurrences indicate the need to supplement rule theories by reference to the character of moral agents. From my point of view, such occurrences indicate more fundamental problems since they show that character is logically prior to the obligation to follow some rule. It is, after all, always in the context of a justifying prior judgment that someone is of good character that we are willing to make exceptions, the point being that we recognise that for some people breaking the rules does not affect any judgment made about them. It would be conceptually odd to make exceptions if rules were logically fundamental.

The point I want to make here is the one Nietzsche made in *The Genealogy of Morals*: it is the character of certain persons that provides the warrant for following or not following rules and not the obviousness of some rules which justifies approving of the persons who follow those rules. Becker, in contrast, wants to say that the character of the moral agent has 'significant' impact on how we regard the morality of actions. I want to say that it is morally decisive. It is because of this decisiveness that we are willing to say that when, for example, two teachers strike a pupil under roughly the same circumstances that in one case the action is morally warranted (at least permissible) and in the other it is clearly not. This sort of judging of behaviour thus indicates not an inconsistent application of rules but rather an incisive perception of what is fundamental in moral arguments.

But, of course, there are rules and then there are rules, and the categorical imperative, as Kant made quite clear, is a rule unlike any other. What relationship does this most austere of all rules hold to paradigmatic character? The answer, it seems to me, is quite straightforward: the extent to which one can meet the challenge of the categorical imperative is a measure of one's moral character. That is, in the domain of moral praxis, the categorical imperative is a sort of litmus test for virtue, only an *indicator* and not the cause or justifying reason. Just as it would be odd to say, 'it is the redness of the litmus paper that causes the solution to be an acid', so also it is morally odd to say that adherence to the categorical imperative is a sufficient condition for justifying the claim that someone is a moral person. Kant, of course, recognised this in his distinction between acting in accordance with and acting because of. But the conceptual cut he makes does not accomplish what he thinks it does: the categorical imperative is also not a necessary condition. It is no condition at all but rather a highly fallible sign – as the case of the rule-following sociopath makes clear – of something else. By regarding all moral agents as Kantian ends-in-themselves, by refusing to objectify persons, the paradigmatic individual creates the very possibility of virtuous character. Strict adherence to the categorical imperative is thus a sign of the seriousness with which the paradigmatic individual regards character as the universal good. It is as if one is obliged to follow the rule of the categorical imperative only if one is committed to regarding virtuous character as the fundamental good.

Given the fundamental role of character in this re-visioned portrait of moral philosophy, the standards of formal completeness and consistency that hold for a Kantian rule theory cannot be applied to an ethics of virtue. The sorts of connections that hold between rules (deductive) are not those that hold between virtues or states of character. To put the point negatively, let me paraphrase Gödel and say that if a moral philosophy is deductively complete (a rule theory) it is substantively inadequate, and if it is substantively adequate (a virtue theory) it will necessarily be formally unsatisfactory. The point here is that although any virtue theory must necessarily be deductively inadequate, the canons of deductive completeness and consistency are simply inappropriate. Rather, the canon of completeness appropriate to this conception of an ethics of virtue is that of narrative completeness, and thus the appropriate structure of any possible substantively adequate moral philosophy must be more like the structure of a story than like the structure of a formal system. A narrative structure is, of course, complete only when it has told the story it means to tell.

The fundamental stories to be told in a virtue theory such as that envisioned here are about paradigmatic individuals. They are depictions of character revealed in action; and they will be complete only to the extent that they reveal what is morally essential in the praxis of some moral exemplar. It is thus from such character itself that we must derive the canon of narrative completeness. It is precisely because the virtues (i.e. the dispositional character traits) of a paradigmatic individual are not themselves deductively related that the parts of an adequate moral narrative are not to be deductively ordered. The problem of the unity of the virtues, which generally has been posed as a logical problem and which troubled scholastic philosophy, is instead a dramatic, human and narrative problem; and there is as much unity of the virtues as the character of some paradigmatic individual reveals – and no more and no less. It is for these reasons that only narrative portrayal can remain faithful to the standard of completeness that is manifest in the character of the paradigmatic individual.

This proposal for an appeal to the standards of narrative depiction in moral argument seems to me neither logically odd nor historically unusual. Traditionally, it is through biographical accounts, myths and fables that one is morally instructed. The universal use of story-telling as the vehicle of moral education increases the plausibility of this appeal to narrative as the most appropriate form of moral argument. Anthropology has taught us that cultures tend not to repeat forms that are dysfunctional. The Ashanti, the Lakota, and even the Californian, for example, are taught how to live through story-telling. Contemporary developments in philosophy and literary theory further stress the importance of narrative structure as a form of moral argument. In the nineteenth century, both Kierkegaard and Nietzsche paid considerable attention to the narrative depiction of character. In the twentieth century, Sartre in a major dimension of his *philosophical* activity wrote a series of highly acclaimed novels and dramas that focus on the agony of moral choice. Iris Murdoch writes novels of character that are essentially narrative moral arguments. The work of Martha Nussbaum powerfully develops the connections both between philosophy and literature and between literature and moral argument.[14] Plato, of course, in the beginning of our tradition, and in spite of himself, depends in great measure on the devices of story-telling. And this dependency is not just didactic, since it is only in terms of literary expression that a number of Plato's most essential insights can even be formulated.

It is, of course, not only within the tradition of philosophy itself that the appeal to literary depiction achieves a sort of historical warrant. All the major religious traditions are primarily concerned to portray the character of paradigmatic individuals: thus we have the Gospels in which Christ himself, at crucial moments, is portrayed as a teller of stories. We also have the Sutras of Buddhism and the narrative accounts of Mohammed's life in the Koran, which show them both to be essentially tellers of stories that are intended to portray their own character. Although the very fact that such appeals have been taken seriously is a presumption in their favour, the epistemological force of the appeal to narrative depiction is, nonetheless, something that must be isolated for philosophical analysis.[15] This force, it seems to me, as Aesop recognised, derives from the fact that telling a story is a more adequate way of getting through a moral crisis (or of expressing a moral point) than is citing a rule or specifying a good.[16]

The reconstruction of moral argument as the narrative depiction of character forces the conclusion that the major texts of traditional moral philosophy are either wrong-headed (Kant and Mill) or that in important ways they have been wrongly responded to (Aristotle). Such reconstruction also forces the conclusion that, to the extent that these texts *cannot* be read as narrative portraits, we must look elsewhere for the more fundamental texts of moral philosophy, the texts which reveal the central forum of moral argument. This forum I suggest, in addition to Aristotle, would necessarily include Thomas à Kempis' *On the Imitation of Christ*, Nietzsche's *Thus Spake Zarathustra*, and Thoreau's *Walden Pond*, to name but the most important. And the fundamental moral question would then be seen to be: which of these narratives tells the human tale most fully? Which of them – if any – gives the truest depiction of the ways in which people of good character resolve the inevitable conflicts of human life? The problem, then, is that of choosing between alternative characterisations of paradigmatic individuals. It is the problem of deciding when a moral tale is well told. And even though there is no algorithm for choosing between alternative moral narratives, this does not inhibit us from making the obvious sort of judgments that would exclude Hitler's *Mein Kampf* or Sade's *Philosophy in the Bedroom* from the arena of serious moral attention, any more than the absence of an adequate criterion for choosing between rules or goods inhibits us from recognising that some putative 'goods' (e.g., the masochist's pain) and rules (e.g., 'Children ought not to read until they have all their permanent teeth') are absurd. How does one choose between possible, alternative characterisations of paradigmatic character? One does so in exactly the same way that one chooses between rules or goods – very carefully.

To say that the characterisation of paradigmatic individuals is the point of moral philosophy is thus not to say that just any such characterisation will do. As with the mandating of rules or the specification of goods or rights, characterisations of paradigmatic individuals require support from the rest of philosophy; and thus we are led back to metaphysics, epistemology and the philosophy of literature. It is just such support that precludes our taking seriously as moral paradigms such obvious moral absurdities as the character of Charles Manson or the Nuremberg laws. Virtue theories, like axiological, deontological and rights theories are in need of good reasons. This view of moral philosophy, then, stresses its dependence on the rest of philosophy as, I would argue, would any close scrutiny of rights, rule or goodness theories. And it should be obvious that the point of my argument is not that with the turn towards the characterisation of paradigmatic individuals things become philosophically easier, but that they become morally and philosophically more adequate.

A crucial feature of this relative adequacy is the decision procedure that derives from construing moral philosophy in the way I have argued is necessary. In this view of things, determining what one ought to do in a specific instance of moral choice involves neither knowing and applying a rule nor specifying a good and predicting which course of action will most efficiently yield access to it. Rather, one resolves moral ambiguity and makes choices by emulating what some paradigmatic individual would do in the same situation; and knowing what he would do requires an imaginative experiment of envisioning him doing it (a Gedanken experiment). One might prepare for these imaginative experiments by, for example, living with the paradigmatic individual, by reading characterisations of his life, or by having personal contact with one of his disciples. In either case what one would try to do is to exemplify a certain character. Aristotle, as I have noted, recognised that one acquired virtuous character by acting like the person who has such character. There is then clearly a sort of circle involved in this decision procedure. The ordinary moral agent, not possessing paradigmatic character, must emulate the *actions* of some moral exemplar in order to acquire that character. But it is only when one possesses some specific character trait exemplified by a paradigmatic individual that one fully sees the point of what one is doing when one acts morally. In this the moral agent is like the new student in a physics course who must perform an experiment whose fundamental principle he does not understand. Much trial and error is required before one gets the thing right, and getting it right involves working on both the experiment and the principle at the same time. So it is also with the moral life.

Additional support for this decision procedure of emulation derives from the common moral experience of asking a trusted friend what he would do in some problematic situation. Such appeals, of course, might be justified by saying that we trust the friend to know the right rules or goods. Undoubtedly such explanations cover a large number of the cases, but they do not cover what I take to be the crucial feature of such appeals. In the first place, we would not ask the advice of someone – even thinking he knew the right rules or appropriate goods – if we doubted his character. For persons of bad character (perhaps lacking the virtue of empathy) cannot be trusted to hear one's intimate moral problems or to give good advice. A person of bad character might well know the right thing to do but deliberately give inappropriate advice. More decisively, the advice of a friend or trusted advisor is most important exactly under those conditions when, not being sure we see the point of his advice, we do what he recommends *because* he recommends it. The point of these remarks becomes particularly clear, I think, when we consider the sorts of moral quandary in which, having no one to consult, we conduct imaginative interior dialogues with absent friends or counsellors, asking ourselves what they might do in a difficulty like ours. In such cases we take up a line of action or judgment exactly because we think we can identify what some seeming moral exemplar would do (or would advise us to do) if he were only in our situation (or if he were available to advise us). In all such cases it is the character of the imagined friend or counsellor that provides the moral warrant for the decisions we make.

The difficulties that are endemic to this sort of decision procedure do not, at least, place it at any disadvantage with respect to the decision procedures of moral philosophies whose final appeal is to rules or other goods. Each of the decision procedures is apparently biased with respect to the possession of certain skills. As Alasdair MacIntyre has argued, Kant's moral philosophy can be most advantageously used by persons who are ingenious in describing cases and in generalising the maxims to be tested by the categorical imperative.[17] Logical and analytical skills permit a more subtle access to the highly formal decision procedure of the categorical imperative, and thus permit persons of great analytical skills to be more sophisticated Kantians. Such a decision procedure is clearly biased against poets and painters, for example. By contrast, the ability to use something like the hedonic calculus depends upon predictive skills that are not uniformly distributed through the population of moral agents. So also the ability to emulate the activity of a paradigmatic individual derives from the possession of the sorts of mimetic skills that great actors possess in abundance.

Nonetheless, since, as seems to be true, we all learn our first lessons through imitating the practices of mothers, fathers, family or friends, it follows that we all have something like an initial privileged access to the mimetic skill required to utilise the decision procedure of emulation, regardless of whether we are initially members of privileged or underprivileged, moral or immoral communities. And each of us in our own communities is equally dependent upon the exercise of this most fundamental skill. The acquisition of analytic or predictive skills presupposes the art of mimicry in communities where such skills are taken seriously as goods. Thus it seems that this mimetic skill is of a different sort than the predictive skills of the hedonic calculus or the analytic skills involved in the use of the categorical imperative. If as mature moral agents there seems to be an inequality in its distribution, this inequality would be the result not of a personal failure to acquire specialised techniques of analysis or prediction but of a communal failure to provide access to a human *techne* that we all necessarily possess as members of some community or other. Although the reasons for such failures are themselves important and interesting, it is enough for my current purposes to note that the imitative skills of the decision procedure of emulation seem to define the very minimal conditions of a community of moral agents.[18] Thus a moral philosophy that takes as its primitive notion the idea of a universally accessible realm of paradigmatic character yields a decision procedure that not only provides us with an explicit mechanism for judging the morality of specific actions – as must any adequate moral philosophy – but that also calls attention to the way in which the mechanism itself is clearly rooted in the original learning practices of all moral agents. Such a decision procedure is a constant reminder of that ideal community of moral agency that achieves its fullest expression in the lives of the paradigmatic individuals.

## 4.

In conclusion, I have argued that virtue (i.e. the character of paradigmatic individuals) is the primary moral category and that it is neither reducible to nor dependent upon either some rule or some other notion of the good. Rules and other notions of the good are, at best, either analytic clarifications of what we mean by virtuous character, maps which indicate how it might be acquired, or a sign that someone actually has it. Indeed, it is quite obvious that if the moral force of virtuous character is dependent upon following some rule or reducible to some other notion of the good or to some set of supposed rights, then there can be no independent virtue theory such as I have proposed here. I have tried to face this possibility while presenting a set of appeals that show why I think there are good grounds for defending a logically independent concept of virtuous character. In this, my essay is another essay in moral epistemology, one that claims we need to rewrite the standards of moral argument in the ways I have suggested. More importantly, this chapter has argued that the appropriate canons of adequacy in moral philosophy can first be glimpsed only in the context of an approach that clearly ties all moral discourse to the domain of moral agency, a domain ideally manifest in the praxis of the paradigmatic individuals. Without such a tie, moral discourse becomes merely formal and necessarily without significant reference to the domain of moral praxis it is meant to illuminate.

What is now needed – and it is a difficult set of needs to meet – is more complete analyses of the family of concepts that clusters around the notions of character and paradigmatic individual, concepts such as those of disposition, narrative completeness, and the logic of acting-like. So also, we need to map further the relationships between this family of concepts and those of rights, goods and law theories. I here have had to limit myself to a first sketch of these problems and to arguing that such analyses are necessary in order to rescue moral philosophy from its mostly technical preoccupations, preoccupations which do not reflect the actual practices of moral agents or important domains of moral tradition and reasoning. Such preoccupations cannot provide anything like an appropriate, rational terminus for moral arguments, a terminus that at one and the same time must be both objective (i.e. non-relative) and personal (i.e. focused on the attempts of ordinary moral agents to resolve the sorts of conflicts that lead one to do philosophical ethics). It is the task of ethics not to ignore the logic of traditional moral arguments but to clarify and evaluate them. In this claim, at least, I hope my argument is not without virtue.[19]

## ENDNOTES

1. G. E. M. Anscombe, 'Modern Moral Philosophy', *Philosophy*, 33, 124 (January 1958), 1–19. See also William Frankena, 'Prichard and the Ethics of Virtue: Notes on a Footnote', *Monist*, 54, 1 (January 1970), 1–7, and 'The Ethics of Love Conceived as an Ethics of Virtue', *Journal of Religious Ethics*, 1, 1 (1973), 21–36. Also in this connection see Philippa Foot, 'Moral Beliefs', *Proceedings of the Aristotelian Society*, 59 (1958–9), 83–104; Alasdair MacIntyre, *After Virtue*, Notre Dame, Indiana: University of Notre Dame Press (1981); Iris Murdoch, 'The Sovereignty of Good Over Other Concepts', *The Sovereignty of Good*, New York: Schocken Books (1971) and also 'Vision and Choice in Morality', *Christian Ethics and Contemporary Philosophy*, Ian Ramsey (ed.), New York: MacMillan (1966). This latter paper is an extended commentary on R. W. Hepburn's paper cited below (Endnote 16).

2. H. A. Prichard, 'Is Moral Philosophy Based on a Mistake?' *Mind* (1912), 21–37. This is the first essay in the twentieth century to raise the discussion of virtue theories.

3. MacIntyre, *After Virtue*, 70.

4. Op. cit., 6.

5. Aristotle's moral philosophy is properly to be construed as the first important virtue theory. However, insofar as the virtue of justice has generally been taken in isolation from the other virtues and regarded solely as a formal mechanism for deciding the proper distribution of goods, Aristotle's moral philosophy has been distorted and its character as a virtue theory thereby neglected. See Lawrence C. Becker, 'Axiology, Deontology and Agent Morality: The Need for Coordination', *The Journal of Value Inquiry*, 6, 3 (Autumn 1972), 213–20; *On Justifying Moral Judgment*, Atlantic Highlands, New Jersey: Humanities Press (1973); and 'The Neglect of Virtue', *Ethics*, 85, 2 (January 1975), 110–22. See also A. S. Cua, *Dimensions of Moral Creativity*, University Park: Pennsylvania State University Press (1978); Stanley Hauerwas, *Character and the Christian Life: A Story in Theological Ethics*, San Antonio: Trinity University Press (1975) and *Vision and Virtue, Essays in Christian Ethical Reflections*, Notre Dame: Fides Publishers, Inc. (1974); and Alasdair MacIntyre, *After Virtue*.

6. See J. M. Keynes' memoir published in *The Bloomsbury Circle*, ed. S. P. Rosenbaum, Toronto: University of Toronto Press (1975).

7. William H. Gass, 'The Case of the Obliging Stranger', *Philosophical Review*, 66 (1957), 193–204. See also Edmund Pincoffs, 'Quandary Ethics', *Mind*, 80, 320 (October 1971), 552–71.

8. Karl Jaspers, *The Great Philosophers*, New York: Harcourt, Brace & World (1962), especially 97–106. Cf. A. S. Cua, 'Morality and the Paradigmatic Individuals', in *Dimensions of Moral Creativity*.

9. Such an account is, I think, available in terms of Heidegger's description of being-in-the-world in *Sein und Zeit*. There we get a global portrayal of the human situation that yields criteria in terms of which we can identify different styles of moral agency without being overwhelmed by the apparently irreducible differences in cultures. Heidegger's work, in my view, thus supplies the basis for something like that 'philosophical psychology' which Anscombe ('Modern Moral Philosophy') has argued is needed to make sense of virtue theories. Such a philosophical psychology will have to take account of the theory of natural rights which is undergoing a sort of renaissance in contemporary moral philosophy. The relationship between natural rights and paradigmatic character is rooted in the assumption of a universally shared human condition, an assumption to which both rights theories and virtue theories such as this are committed. Cf. A. S. Cua, *Dimensions of Moral Creativity*, 77–8.

10. Philosophers from Socrates on have been aware of the usefulness of presenting clear examples in complex arguments. My point is that such presentations are the *focus* of philosophical argument and not mere supporting devices. In contemporary philosophy, the essays of Judith Jarvis Thomson exemplify the focal role of such presentations. Cf., for example, her 'The Right to Privacy', *Philosophy and Public Affairs*, 4 (Summer 1975), 295–314 and 'A Defense of Abortion', *Philosophy and Public Affairs*, 1 (Autumn 1971), 47–66.

11. Richard Francis Burton, *A Mission to Gelele, King of Dahome*, London: Routledge & Kegan Paul (1966).

12. Robin George Collingwood, *An Autobiography*, London: Oxford University Press (1939), especially 100–6.

13. Lawrence C. Becker, 'The Neglect of Virtue'.

14. See, for example, her *Love's Knowledge*, New York: Oxford University Press and *The Fragility of Goodness*, New York: Cambridge University Press.

15. This presumption is supported by the rather plausible belief that people keep doing something only if, in some sense or other, it works. Cf. Lawrence Sklar's treatment of this theme in 'Methodological Conservatism', *Philosophical Review*, 84, 3 ( July 1975), 374–400.

16. Cf. Alasdair MacIntyre, 'Epistemological Crises, Dramatic Narrative and the Philosophy of Science', *Monist*, 60 (October 1977), 453–72. See also MacIntyre's comments on narrative and story-telling in *After Virtue*, especially 135, 191–4 and 201–2. See also R. W. Hepburn's 'Vision and Choice in Morality', in *Christian Ethics and Contemporary Philosophy*, Ian Ramsey (ed.), New York: MacMillan (1966). Cf. Stanley Hauerwas, *Truthfulness and Tragedy*, Notre Dame, Indiana: University of Notre Dame Press (1977). See also my *Nietzsche's Gift*, Athens, Ohio: Ohio University Press (1977).

17. Alasdair MacIntyre, *A Short History of Ethics*, New York: MacMillan (1976), 197–8.

18. Imitative skills atrophy because of the nature of the communities in which those skills must be exercised. Thus, for example, in underprivileged Indian communities where children are used as professional beggars, the children's imitation of their given role-models necessarily truncates the development of the very imitative skills that permit them to become economically valuable members of their communities; for in all such situations what is lacking is the very sort of role-model in which the notion of moral autonomy is central. The failure of the exercise of original imitative skills is thus a failure of moral community. It is a failure of some group of moral agents to move from the idea of their community of interest to the idea of the human community of autonomous moral agents. Or, to put this discussion in terms of the virtue of empathy, the children's original disposition to identify with their role-models ceases because the very agents with whom the children identify use them as objects rather than teach them to be agents.

19. I am indebted to Lawrence Becker for early discussions of some of these themes and to both him and Roger Pilon for criticisms of an early draft of this chapter. I would also like to acknowledge the support of N. E. H. during the summer of 1978 when a very different first draft of this chapter was written in an N. E. H. seminar conducted by Alasdair MacIntyre. A second version was completed with the support of an N. E. H. Fellowship for College Teachers (1981–2) and originally published in the *Review of Metaphysics*. Additional revisions have been made for this printing.

# 9

# INTERNAL OBJECTIONS TO VIRTUE ETHICS

## David Solomon

### 1. WHAT IS AN ETHICS OF VIRTUE?

While there has been much talk recently about the revival of an ethics of virtue (EV), it is not always entirely clear what such a revival might entail. There are three quite different views expressed by contemporary moral philosophers that might be taken to point to such a revival. There is, first, the view that recent moral philosophy has not paid sufficient attention to moral criticism and deliberation that centrally involves virtue concepts. The charge has been often made, for example, that contemporary moral philosophers pay excessive attention to the most abstract terms involved in ethical thought and talk, terms like 'right', 'good', and 'ought', while largely ignoring richer and more concrete terms like 'sensitive', 'compassionate', and 'courageous'.[1] Since these latter terms typically refer to virtue-like aspects of human character, one might regard this charge as a gesture in the direction of an EV.

A second view associated with the 'revival' of virtue ethics holds that any developed ethical theory must include a *component* that deals with virtue. The thought here is that an ethical theory will be incomplete in an important sense if it does not have an account of virtue attached to it. William Frankena, for example, has argued forcefully that while an account of the virtues is not sufficient for an adequate ethical theory, any ethical theory which does not embody an account of the virtues will be importantly incomplete.[2] In introducing his own view of the virtues, he defends what we might call a 'double aspect theory of morality', according to which a theory of the virtues will always be one feature of an adequate ethical theory, but not the most basic feature. Similarly, John Rawls finds it necessary to incorporate an account of the virtues in his broadly deontological moral theory, but his account of the virtues, like Frankena's, has a decidedly inferior position within his overall political theory.[3]

There is, finally, a third and much stronger account of what is involved in the revival of an EV, according to which an EV entails the view that normative theory must have a structure such that assessment of human character is, in some suitably strong sense, more fundamental than either the assessment of the rightness of action or the assessment of the value of the consequences of action. There is much in this characterisation of an EV that needs clarification and expansion, but for our purposes we can pass over some of the deeper difficulties. It does presuppose that we can distinguish three features of any human action: that it is performed by some *agent*, that some particular *action* is performed, and that the action has certain determinate *consequences*. It is further presupposed that practical judgments typically take as their subject matter one of these three features of action. Either they are judgments of the agent, e.g., 'she is honest and just', or of the action, e.g., 'what he did was wrong', or of the consequences, e.g., 'the skyscraper that he built is bad for the downtown area'. The task of normative ethical theory – broadly conceived – is to order these kinds of practical judgments with the aim of showing that some practical judgments play a primary role in the overall justificatory structure of ethics. One looks for a foundation for ethics, such that foundational claims stand to other adequate moral judgments in a relation of justification or support.[4]

An EV, according to this third view, is a normative theory that takes the foundational moral claims to be claims about the agent, or about human character. It takes judgments of character or of agents as basic in that it construes the fundamental task of normative theory to be to depict an ideal of human character. The ethical task of each person, correspondingly, is to become a person of a certain sort where becoming a person of that sort is to become a person who has certain dispositions to respond to situations in a characteristic way. We recognise differences among persons of quite different kinds. Some people are shorter or fatter than others, some more or less intelligent, some better or worse at particular tasks, and some more courageous, just, or honest than others. These differences can be classified in various ways: physical versus mental differences, differences in ability versus differences in performance, etc. Those features of human beings on which virtue theories concentrate in depicting the ideal human being are states of character. Such theories typically issue in some list of virtues for human beings where these virtues are states of character which human beings must possess if they are to be successful as human beings, i.e., to reach the appropriate *telos* of human life.

Given this general characterisation, a virtue ethics will typically have three central goals:

1. to develop and defend some conception of the ideal person
2. to develop and defend some list of virtues that are necessary for being a person of that type
3. to defend some view of how persons can come to possess the appropriate virtues.

One can also characterise a virtue ethics by contrasting these sorts of goals with the goals typically attaching to normative theories that take judgments of each of the other two types as basic. A normative theory that takes judgments of *actions* as basic, a deontological theory, will typically have as its goals:

1. to formulate and defend a particular set of moral rules, or to defend some procedure for generating appropriate moral rules[5]
2. to develop and defend some method of determining what to do when the relevant moral rules come into conflict.

A normative theory which takes judgments of *consequences* of actions as fundamental, a consequentialist theory, will attempt:

1. to specify and defend some thing or list of things which are good in themselves
2. to provide some technique for measuring and comparing the amount of the relevant good thing (or things) that might be brought about
3. to defend some procedures for those cases where one is not in a position to determine which of a number of alternative actions will maximise the good thing or things.

The third view of what is entailed by a concern with virtue in ethics is clearly much stronger than the first two. It suggests not only that moral philosophers should 'pay attention' to virtue concepts and include a virtue component in a complete normative theory, but that the concept of a virtue is in important respects a more fundamental notion than the concepts of 'the right' or 'the good' where the good is seen as attaching to objects as possible consequences of our action. It is the third view of the importance of virtue in ethics that I will attend to in what follows.

## 2. OBJECTIONS TO VIRTUE ETHICS

The most striking feature of virtue ethics is the near universality of its rejection in contemporary ethical theory and in modern ethics generally. For the most part, the field has been left to broadly deontological normative theories and their consequentialist opponents. Both of these types of theories, while differing in many respects, find themselves in agreement on the inadequacy of an EV. There are undoubtedly a number of reasons for the widespread rejection of an EV but there is an important distinction among these reasons which I will mark by dividing them into two classes, *external* objections and *internal* objections.

By an external objection to an EV, I mean an objection that comes from outside ethics proper. Typically, such objections will raise broadly epistemological or metaphysical difficulties with an EV. The primary external objection to an EV claims that an EV cannot be sustained because a necessary condition for the success of such a theory is a certain metaphysical or theological underpinning which, given the rise of distinctively modern science and the decline of classical theology, is implausible.

From the metaphysical side it is argued that what is required to sustain a virtue ethics is a broadly teleological view of nature – a view according to which explanations in terms of final causes are legitimate and indeed necessary, for understanding nature.

Such a view underpins an EV in that it can provide a justification for supposing that normative questions about human action are ultimately to be settled by appealing to the contribution action may make to the movement of persons towards their metaphysically fixed end or telos. Character is a way a human being can *be*, and such a teleological view of nature underpins an EV in that it supports the view that human beings should *be* a certain way.

The rise of distinctively modern natural sciences is supposed to show that such a teleological view of human nature is implausible in that the history of science is alleged to show that the mysteries of nonhuman nature have only been revealed when such a teleological conception has been set aside. Modern science has mounted a relentless assault on such a teleological conception, and natural teleology has been defeated in every encounter. Since a large part of the justification for a teleological conception of human nature was always that such a conception was necessary for the understanding of nature in general, its failure in this latter respect makes it implausible to take it seriously in the former.

Some have attempted to salvage virtue ethics by substituting for natural teleology a theological account of teleology according to which the teleological structure of nature can be guaranteed by the purposive nature of God's creative activity. The difficulty with a theological underpinning for ethics is not so much that it has been undermined by modern conceptions of nature and our powers to uncover its mysteries (although this is part of the story); the main difficulty is that if we must rely on a particular theological account of human nature, then any ethical view which is based on this account will not have the universal appeal that we expect of a *moral* view. The theological account will support virtue ethics only for those who accept the relevant theological beliefs, but it is frequently alleged that an appropriate foundation for ethics must make a more general appeal. It is the hope of most people who do normative theory that ethical discourse will allow persons from different theological traditions to talk across these traditions – to rise above their theological differences. But if the structure of moral argument is itself grounded in one of these traditions then this goal will not be able to be satisfied.

Internal objections to virtue ethics differ from external objections in that they come from within ethical reflection itself. They claim that there are general considerations connected to the *point* of ethical theory or to the structure of the moral point of view that make a virtue ethics untenable. As a consequence of being internal they ultimately depend upon arguments that support the claim that ethics really is the way they say it is. There is always the possibility, given their internal character, that these objections can slip into being question-begging.

In setting out the most important of these objections, I am not going to locate them in particular writers. They seem to me, however, to be found in many modern ethical theorists of otherwise quite different persuasions. I think all of them, for example, are found in Kant, although some of them are more obviously there than others, and utilitarians also frequently have recourse to them. They express a set of assumptions which are taken seriously by many contemporary writers and thinkers about ethics.

There are three central internal objections to virtue ethics. The first objection, which I will call the 'self-centredness objection', alleges that an EV tends to focus too much attention on the agent. As we noted in discussing the structure appropriate to an EV, such theories demand a focus on the character of the individual agent. What gives point to the task of acquiring the virtues is that one supposes that one should become a person of a particular kind. One wants to change one's character from 'the way it is' to 'the way it ought to be', in the language of Alasdair MacIntyre.[6] This view demands that the moral agent keep his or her own character at the centre of his or her practical attention. To many persons this requirement that each agent keep his or her character as the central focus of practical thought seems to import an unjustifiable degree of self-centredness into ethics. If one supposes that the point of moral reflection essentially involves a concern for others (or at least a concern that the interests of others be taken into account in practical thought, or that one move away from a narrowly prudential view of one's action) then it may appear that an EV cannot satisfy this requirement.

This attitude towards an EV is reflected in the claims frequently made that Aristotle, Plato, and other classical virtue theorists are ethical egoists of some sort. The thought behind such claims seems to be that for classical virtue theorists, it is *rational* for an agent to acquire the virtues only insofar as it is a good for that agent that he or she acquire them. But if the rationality of virtue acquisition is thus grounded in the needs of the agent, so the argument goes, the needs, wants and desires of others have, from the point of view of morality, an insufficiently prominent status. Many twentieth-century Kantians have argued that this agent-centred feature of classical virtue theory makes it impossible for such theories to account for genuine moral obligation.[7]

The second internal objection, which I will call the 'action-guiding objection', alleges that an EV lacks the capacity to yield suitably determinate action guides. Normative ethics is undoubtedly supposed to have a practical point. We engage in it partly out of a disinterested pursuit of truth, but, like cookery and engineering, it would be misunderstood if its theoretical point were allowed to exclude all others. An important part of the practical aim of normative theory is that it can guide our actions in situations where we find ourselves in moral conflict because we feel required to perform each of two incompatible actions. Also, guidance seems appropriate in situations of moral indeterminacy where we are unclear what we should do because our deliberative apparatus does not appropriately cover a new case in our experience. Moral life sometimes seems almost exhausted by cases like these where we are plagued by moral conflict or moral indeterminacy. It is alleged by proponents of the action-guiding objection that normative ethics should help in each of these cases by providing principles or rules (action-guides generally) of a suitably algorithmic character which will help deliver us from our perplexity. Both deontological theories and consequentialist theories of the modern sort, it is argued, fare much better in this respect than do virtue theories. An EV, with its emphasis on the development of states of character, lacks the capacity for precision or determinateness found in the two alternative views. Critics of virtue ethics, in this respect, point to the failure of classical virtue theorists even to attempt to provide determinate guides to action. We are reminded that Plato and Aristotle seldom discuss moral quandaries and, when they do, the advice forthcoming (such as the advice to feel certain emotions 'at the right times, with reference to the right objects, towards the right people, with the right motive, and in the right way'[8]) has seemed egregiously unhelpful. The conclusion is drawn that it is in the very nature of an EV that it cannot provide the kind of determinate guidance for action that is required in an adequate normative ethics.[9]

The third type of internal objection, which I will call the 'contingency objection', is the most deeply Kantian objection of the three. It alleges that the moral goodness of an agent should be within his or her control at the moment of action. The spirit of this objection permeates much modern ethical thinking, I think, and it is largely responsible for some of the more notorious features of Kant's treatment of the concept of moral worth in the first section of the *Groundwork*. It is particularly evident in his discussion of naturally benevolent persons – persons who act benevolently solely because they are moved by feelings of care and concern for their fellow creatures.[10] Kant is quite clear that persons so motivated should get no moral credit for their otherwise morally praiseworthy benevolent actions. Kant does not mean, of course, as he is sometimes taken to mean, that we should seek to extirpate such feelings on the grounds that they may interfere with moral goodness. His view is rather that such feelings are, from the point of view of a moral evaluation of the agent, neutral. They count neither for nor against the moral goodness of the agent. And the reason they are morally irrelevant features of the agent is that they lie outside his rational control. Benevolent feelings towards others (as a species of what Kant called pathological desires) may have either of two sources – biological or social. Some persons, biologically or genetically, may be naturally disposed to care for others; others may have had inculcated in them by social training, either of an explicit or implicit sort, a tendency to have certain benevolent feelings towards others. In either case, the agent does not have it within his power upon the occasion of action to call up such feelings if they are not already there. If the presence of such feelings, or the disposition to have such feelings on certain occasions, is used as a determinate of moral goodness, then an agent's level of moral goodness will be, at least partly, a matter of luck. Perhaps Kant's deepest insight (or prejudice as it may seem) was that morality should not, in this respect, be a matter of luck.[11]

This argument is relevant to an EV in that moral character, if conceived as a bundle of dispositions to act or to have certain feelings about action, would surely be outside the control of the agent at the moment of action. Indeed, many aspects of an agent's character are surely not within his or her control at all. This contingency of moral goodness is reflected in a number of features of classical virtue theory, especially in the pessimism about moral conversion expressed by Aristotle and Plato and in their emphasis on moral education as a matter of forming habits in the service of shaping character. If the achievement of moral goodness must be within the power of every moral agent upon every occasion for action, then surely the critic here is right. An EV cannot satisfy that constraint.

## 3. RESPONSE TO THE OBJECTIONS

The objections to an EV set out above constitute a formidable challenge to anyone who hopes to revive an EV. It seems to me, however, that there is an important difference between the challenge set by the central external objection, and that set by the three internal objections. Any response to the external objection will have to involve one of two strategies, either of which will involve philosophical work on a grand scale. One might respond by attempting to resurrect Aristotelian natural teleology as a comprehensive theory of nature. I am sceptical about the prospects for the success of such a project, but am willing to wish those well who may want to attempt it. More promisingly, one might attempt to give an account of human social activity that, after the manner of A. MacIntyre or C. Taylor, aims to establish a teleological account of rational action.[12] The defence of such a 'local' teleology will surely present far fewer philosophical difficulties than the more ambitious Aristotelian project, but, as the recent work of MacIntyre and Taylor suggests, it remains a formidable project. Whatever strategy one might adopt in responding to the external objection to an EV, however, it is clear that the issues raised are of a level of complexity that makes it impossible to address them here.

Things seem to me otherwise, however, with regard to the internal objections to an EV. Although these objections have been widely used by the deontological and consequentialist opponents of an EV, each of them seems to me to fail to damage seriously the prospects for an adequate EV. And in the case of each of these objections, the failure is largely of the same nature. Each places demands on an EV which neither deontological nor consequentialist normative theories can satisfy. So while it may be true that an EV cannot meet the standards for a normative theory demanded by these objections, neither will the standard theoretical alternatives to an EV be able to meet these demands. While this 'partners in crime' strategy, if successful, will not show that these demands should not be placed on normative theories, it will at least place those defenders of consequentialist or deontological alternatives to an EV who wish to use them in a rhetorically awkward position. In the remainder of this chapter, I would like to sketch briefly how this strategy can be used with regard to each of these objections.

## 1. The self-centredness objection

It may appear that there is a quick response to the self-centredness objection available to the virtue theorist. He may point out that the objection fails to take account of an important distinction between two features of an EV. There is, first, the feature that the objector notices: the central place that one's own character plays in the practical thinking associated with an EV. But there is also within an EV the set of virtues that each agent aims to embody in his character. While the first feature of an EV may appear to render it excessively self-centred, the second feature is surely able to counteract that danger. The particular virtues characteristic of an EV may be as other-regarding as one might wish. While each agent may be expected to devote primary practical attention to the development of his or her own character, that attention may be required to turn the agent into a person fundamentally concerned with the wellbeing of others. Classical virtues like justice, Christian virtues like love or charity, and Alasdair MacIntyre's favorite modern virtue, Jane Austen's amiability, all have a predominantly other-regarding character.[13] They both restrict the attention I am allowed to pay to my own wants, needs and desires, and force me to attend to the wants, needs and desires of others.

This response may still appear insufficient, however, in that it allows the self-centredness objection to arise at a deeper level. At this deeper level, the objection points to an asymmetry that arises between an agent's regard for his own character and his regard for the character of others. The question raised here has this form: Since an EV requires me to pay primary attention to the state of my own character, doesn't this suggest that I must regard my own character as the ethically most important feature of myself? But, if so, and if I am suitably concerned about others, shouldn't my concern for them extend beyond a mere concern that their wants, needs and desires be satisfied, and encompass a concern for *their* character? Shouldn't I indeed have the same concern for the character of my neighbour as I have for my own?

Consider an example here. Suppose that I hold a virtue theory according to which Christian love or charity is the primary virtue. I believe, that is, that my fundamental ethical task is to become the sort of person who has towards others the attitudes we associate with Christian love. Then, it would seem that I must hold the view that my having this virtue is the most important thing for me; practically I must subordinate everything else to this. But – and this is the problem – Christian love does not require of me – that is, the developed virtue does not – that I bring it about that others around me possess Christian love. Rather, Christian love requires me to attend to the wants, needs and desires of others. But doesn't this suggest that I regard others as less morally important than myself? Satisfying their needs is good enough for them, but I require of myself that I become a loving person.

This asymmetry between my attitude towards my own character and my attitude towards the character of others is, it seems to me, ineliminable within virtue ethics. And this is why the virtue theorist must simply look for partners in crime – if, indeed, this is a crime. And, it can surely be shown that theories of the other two sorts equally fall prey to it. Consider Kant's claim in the Introduction to the *Doctrine of Virtue* that the distinction between duties to myself and duties to others lies in the fact that while I can only seek to make others happy, I must primarily seek to make myself good.[14] His claim here is that it is not a proper object of my action to try to bring it about that others do the right thing. (The Kantian slogan here might be, 'rightness for me, happiness for you'.) And it is surely not merely an accidental feature of Kant's particular deontological theory that an asymmetry similar to that characteristically found in an EV between concern for self and concern for others is found there. Deontological theories characteristically require that each agent regard his or her own actions in a different light from the actions of others.

Consider, for example, the fact that deontological theories typically forbid agents to perform one morally bad action, $A_1$, in order to prevent some other agent (or agents) from performing two or more actions, $A_2$–$A_n$, which are morally indistinguishable from $A_1$. The justification for this is surely not that deontological theories regard $A_1$

as somehow morally worse than $A_2$–$A_n$ taken together. Even the deontologist might be forced to admit that from a 'purely objective' standpoint, it is a morally 'worse' thing that several morally bad actions occur than that a single morally bad action occur. The reason deontological theories require the agent to avoid morally bad actions in these cases is that an agent's relation to his own actions is special in a way that his relation to the actions of others is not. We need not inquire here into the nature of this 'special relationship', since merely recognising that deontological theories are committed to it is sufficient to show that such theories will suffer from the same sort of 'self-centredness' that was alleged to be so damaging to an EV.

A similar kind of difficulty bedevils the history of utilitarianism.[15] In classical utilitarianism there is a tension between the kind of universally benevolent character I am required to develop in myself and the kind of requirements that constrain my activities towards others. The point is not that I am required to make myself benevolent, but only required to make others happy. Classical utilitarianism surely does require me (at least under normal conditions) to attempt to make others benevolent too. The point is rather that my concern for their benevolence can be at most an instrumental concern, while my concern for my own benevolence cannot be, at the deepest level, of this character. The benevolence of others is only of instrumental concern to the utilitarian, because all of his concerns with regard to others are guided ultimately by the single requirement to maximise human happiness. Under normal circumstances, inducing benevolence in others is a useful way of promoting that end. But the utilitarian's concern for his *own* benevolence cannot be in the same way a matter of merely instrumental concern. His own benevolence is, as it were, the perspective from which the benevolence of others attains a kind of (instrumental) moral significance; but his own benevolence cannot, itself, attain moral significance from this perspective, because it *is* the perspective. It is in this way that even for a utilitarian one's own character has a special status that is denied to others.

One might attempt to respond to this claim about utilitarianism by pointing out, what is surely true, that a utilitarian possessed of a suitably benevolent character may have good utilitarian reasons to change his character in such a way that he or she is no longer benevolent. For example, a utilitarian may decide that human happiness will be maximised if everyone, including himself, comes to have a character that is thoroughly selfish and mean-spirited. In such a case, a good utilitarian should set to work to root out his benevolent character and to replace it with a suitably selfish set of dispositions. This possibility may seem to suggest that, after all, the benevolent character of the utilitarian is only of instrumental concern to himself or herself after all. But this conclusion would be too hasty. What remains true is that there is never a moment at which the agent in question is both a utilitarian and such that he can regard his benevolence as a matter of merely instrumental concern. If he succeeds in his moral transformation, one can only conjecture what his attitude might then be towards his former benevolence. But his attitude after the transformation will, of course, be of no relevance to this argument, since after the transformation he will no longer be a utilitarian.

These remarks about utilitarian and deontological theories are intended to suggest that while an EV may require an asymmetry between an agent's attitude towards his own character and that of others, similar asymmetries are found in the two other types of normative theory. Both deontological theories and consequentialist theories require agents to treat their own actions or motivational structures differently from those of others. In this respect, it is difficult to see that the special features of the asymmetry in the case of an EV should constitute a serious objection to theories of that type.

## 2. The action-guiding objection

The virtue theorist's response to the action-guiding objection involves three claims. First, that an EV can guide action more successfully than the objection seems to recognise. Second, that the deontological and consequentialist alternatives to an EV are *less* successful at guiding action than the objection alleges. Third, that the demand for determinate action-guidingness as spelled out by these opponents involves more than one dubious claim about the relation between ethical theory and action.

With regard to the first point, it is important to note that it is simply false that virtue theories do not provide *any* guidance for action. Rather, they provide it at a place and in a manner that seem inappropriate to many modern ethical theorists. Virtue theorists suggest that the primary focus of moral evaluation is human character, and since character is a dynamic phenomenon the focus is on the whole life of a person. The moral life is not, on this view, best regarded as a set of episodic encounters with moral dilemmas or moral uncertainty (although anyone's moral life will certainly contain moments of this kind); it is rather a life-long pursuit of excellence of the person. The kind of guidance appropriate to such a pursuit will be quite different from that envisioned by many modern ethical theorists. An EV primarily helps us to answer questions like: What features of human life contribute essentially to human excellence? What character traits should one strive to develop? In taking such questions as primary, it will, of course, fall short of providing determinate guidance of action for the whole range of problematic situations in which human beings might find themselves. But it does not take this as its goal. The task of an EV is not determinately to guide action; that task is left to the virtues. Virtue theories do not propose algorithms for solving practical difficulties; they propose something more like a fitness program to get one ready to run a race. This does not mean, of course, that an EV is completely without resources in guiding particular actions. A just person does not seduce a good friend's wife or husband; a charitable person does not refuse to extend help to the needy; and a courageous person does not run when the first shot is fired.

This kind of guidance in what some might regard as 'easy' ethical cases is unlikely to satisfy the opponent of an EV, however. They will point out that their claim is not that a virtue theory is *useless* in guiding action; rather, it is that in the genuinely tough cases where we demand rules or principles, a kind of algorithm for right action, virtue ethics is found wanting. It does not provide what is provided by consequentialists in the principle of utility or by broadly deontological theories in principles like Kant's universal law formulation of the categorical imperative. But here the opponents of an EV have surely gone too far. If one examines the algorithmic moral principles put forward by philosophers of a consequentialist or deontological stripe, one seems always to find difficulties in applying these principles. Some of these difficulties are of a broadly theoretical sort like those utilitarians have in making sense of interpersonal comparisons of utility. But others involve more down to earth problems in applying principles to cases. These problems are reflected in the fact of practical disagreement among ethical theorists who agree on the alleged algorithmic principles. Many contemporary Kantians, for example, while largely agreeing with Kant's formulation of the fundamental principle of morality, are horrified at some of the conclusions he drew from it. Nor do they necessarily agree among themselves on what the results of such applications should be. Utilitarians similarly find themselves frequently in theoretical agreement, but practical disagreement. Both utilitarians and Kantians are frequently found on both sides of all of the most controversial moral issues in contemporary discussion. Positions on ethical theory do not typically fix practical attitudes on controversial issues involving abortion, the use of nuclear weapons, affirmative action, or the details of schemes for distributive justice.

The conclusion to be drawn from this ubiquitous practical disagreement is, I think, that the claims for the determinate action-guiding power of deontological and consequentialist normative theories are overstated. What seems to be the case is rather that each of these putative algorithmic principles requires a quality of judgment, not too unlike what classical virtue theorists called *phronesis*, for its application. Easy moral cases are easy for everyone – virtue theorists, deontologists and consequentialists; hard cases are also hard for everyone, demanding on all views, as it may seem, an exercise of practical wisdom that eludes being captured in a formula.

It still may be argued, of course, that deontological and consequentialist alternatives to an EV fare better with regard to action-guidingness than does an EV; and that to the extent that they do so they are to be preferred to an EV. To assess this claim, it would be necessary to be clearer both on what it is for a normative theory to be determinately action-guiding and also on why it is a good thing that normative theories should strive to maximise their action-guiding power. Both of these topics are enormously complicated and also much neglected in recent discussions of normative ethical theory.

With regard to the first topic, it is important to note that action-guidingness as a property of a normative theory is hardly a simple property. Although it seems clear that action-guidingness in this sense involves some relation between a normative theory and particular normative problems, the relation will involve a number of different aspects. For example, in attempting to measure the overall action-guiding power of a normative theory, one needs to distinguish at least three different senses in which one theory, $NT_1$, might be regarded as being more determinately action-guiding than another theory, $NT_2$. First, with regard to *breadth* of action-guiding power, $NT_1$ might yield solutions to a wider range of normative problems than does $NT_2$. Second, with regard to *specificity* of action-guiding power, $NT_1$ might yield more specific, or more narrowly circumscribed, solutions to particular normative problems than $NT_2$. Finally, with regard to *decisiveness* of action-guiding power, $NT_1$ might yield more decisive solutions, in the sense of solutions recommended with a higher degree of probability that they are correct, than $NT_2$. It is also important to see that these criteria could conflict in the case of comparisons of particular normative theories. Thus, in comparing $NT_1$ and $NT_2$, one might discover that $NT_1$ resolves a wider range of normative problems than $NT_2$, but that $NT_2$ resolves the problems it resolves either more decisively or more specifically. Other kinds of conflicts could also arise.

These distinctions are important in their own right, but they are especially important to the topics under discussion here because they point to difficulties in addressing the question of how to measure the overall action-guiding power of a normative theory. If there are a number of different senses in which one normative theory might be said to be more powerfully action-guiding than another, then it seems appropriate that the question about the relative action-guiding power of different types of theories will have to be asked with regard to each of these senses. In comparing the action-guiding power of an EV with the powers of its deontological and consequentialist opponents, then, one must compare them *at least* with regard to breadth, specificity and decisiveness.

Here I can only suggest what seems to me the likely outcome of such a comparison. With regard to breadth of action-guiding power, there seems no reason to suppose that the opponents of an EV will fare better than an EV. An EV can yield a set of virtues that will be relevant to choice in virtually every situation of choice in which an agent might find himself. If EVs are capable of such maximal breadth, then they are hardly likely to suffer in this regard from comparison with deontological and consequentialist theories. I suspect that opponents of an EV would agree with this point, and concentrate on deficiencies of an EV with regard to specificity and decisiveness. But at this point it is important to recall a point made above: that within an EV it is not the theory of the virtues which is supposed to be primarily action guiding, but rather the virtues themselves. It is not the theoretical account either of the point of the virtue of justice or of its role in the overall economy of practical thought that is supposed to guide action, but rather the virtue of justice itself. With this point in hand, however, the proponent of an EV can argue that it is not implausible that such a developed virtue can guide action with at least as much specificity and decisiveness as any rule or principle. An agent who embodies the virtue of justice may discern the justice of particular actions, projects, or institutions as specifically and decisively as some impersonally formulated rule or principle. Indeed, one might suppose that virtues might fare better than rules or principles with regard to specificity and decisiveness. It is because they embody a more complex capacity for discernment than do rules and principles that they defy formulation in rules or principles. In support of this claim, one can point to many examples of powers of discernment (e.g., in wine-tasters or art critics) where we do not suppose that inability to formulate powers of discernment in rules or principles need lead to lack of either specificity or decisiveness.

These general remarks about the relative action-guiding power of normative theories, of course, are of the most preliminary sort. Much more needs to be said both about the precise nature of the various measures of action-guiding power and about the structure of virtues which allows them to embody the relevant powers of discernment. But I hope that even these preliminary remarks make it clear that an EV is not without resources, and considerable resources at that, in combatting the claim that it suffers in a comparison of action-guiding power with deontological and consequentialist theories.

### 3. The contingency argument

We can again use a partners-in-crime strategy in formulating an initial response to the contingency argument. It can be shown, I think, that neither consequentialist nor deontological theorists can escape the charge that moral goodness on their view too is tainted with contingency. For utilitarianism, the argument is straightforward. Moral goodness, on this view, must be given either an objective or a subjective reading. If it is given an objective reading, then moral goodness will be determined by the value of the *actual consequences* of an agent's actions. But surely nothing could be less under the control of an agent. Typically the actual consequences of an action are influenced not only by the intention of the agent, but also by all of the natural contingencies of the world that intervene between the intention and the consequences. Efforts may be made by the agent, of course, to control these intervening factors, but no amount of effort can insure that the actual consequences of an action match the original intention.

For this reason, the utilitarian may reject the objective reading of moral goodness, and substitute a subjective view. But a subjective view fares little better. According to a subjective view, moral goodness will be determined by the *intended consequences* of an action. But surely whether one has sufficiently benevolent intentions to satisfy the strong requirements, say, of utilitarianism, is frequently going to be outside the control of the agent at the moment of action. I may, of course, frequently have it within my power to intend an action that is required by the principle of utility. But the subjective account of moral goodness requires more than this. It requires that I intend the action in question *as a means* to the greatest happiness of the greatest number, and it is surely far from clear that this intention is always within my power.[16]

Since Kant was so insistent on the contingency argument, one might suppose that his view, at least, escapes the charge. But it is far from clear that this is the case. Although Kant's account of the moral goodness of an agent is too complicated to discuss in detail here, the central idea of it is that an agent is morally good just in case he wills right actions because they are right. One's belief that an action is right need not be the sole motive for performing the action, but it must be a sufficient motive in the sense that if it were the sole motive then, other things being equal, it would move the agent to perform the action. Kant seems to think that his own account of moral goodness escapes the contingency objection in that he believes that agents always have the power to act conscientiously, where conscientious action is right action motivated by the belief that it is right. Kant admits, of course, that we may not always be able to call up feelings or desires for the end of our morally required action, but the bare ability to will what is right, because it is right, is supposed always to be available to us. Given the variety of ways in which human powers of choice may, however, be impaired, this view seems literally incredible. Kant seems never to have fully appreciated that the capacity for conscientious action is subject to the vagaries of socialisation and explicit training in a way similar to the capacity for benevolent action, although he implicitly admits this when in his metaphysical view he removes the will to the noumenal realm where it must be located if any taint of contingency is to be removed.

This brief attempt to demonstrate some difficulties both utilitarians and Kantians may have in removing contingency from attributions of moral goodness surely settles very little. It may be possible for the opponents of an EV to develop an account of moral goodness that escapes the difficulties above, and then one would have to examine such a view to determine if contingency does not sneak in in some other way. My suspicion is that it always would but, I know of no general argument to establish this. A more fruitful line of inquiry. I suspect, would pursue the question of why so many moral philosophers have sought an account of moral goodness that is free of contingency. Perhaps an understanding of the reasons for this quest would free us from the need to continue it.

## ENDNOTES

1. This charge has been made by a number of philosophers, but it is especially powerfully made in Elizabeth Anscombe, 'Modern Moral Philosophy', *Philosophy* 33 (1958), and in Julius Kovesi, *Moral Notions*, New York (1967).
2. William Frankena, *Ethics*, New Jersey, Englewood Cliffs (1973), 65–7.
3. John Rawls, *A Theory of Justice*, Cambridge, Massachusetts (1971). The inferior position Rawls attributes to the virtues is evident from his characterisation of virtues as 'sentiments, that is, related families of dispositions and propensities regulated by a higher-order desire, in this case a desire to act from the corresponding moral principles' (192).
4. I do not intend to suggest, however, that an EV need be a foundationalist theory in the sense in which such a theory is contrasted with a coherence theory. There is surely no reason why an EV could not be ultimately supported by a form of argument that is broadly coherentist.
5. This characterisation may need to be modified in certain respects to account for 'act deontological' views.
6. Alasdair MacIntyre, *After Virtue*, Notre Dame, Indiana: University of Notre Dame Press (1984), 67.
7. Perhaps the most powerful arguments of this sort are still to be found in Prichard's 'Does Moral Philosophy Rest on a Mistake?' reprinted in his *Moral Obligation* New York (1950).
8. Aristotle, *Nicomachean Ethics*, Ross translation, London (1966), 38.
9. This alleged inability of an EV to provide determinate action guides is one of the main motives of those who have claimed that an account of the virtues can at most provide one component of a normative ethical theory. Frankena, for example, is quite explicit in taking this as the main justification for his 'double aspect' normative theory.
10. Kant's discussion of the naturally benevolent person is found in Chapter 1 of the *Groundwork of the Metaphysics of Morals*.
11. One can arrive at this same Kantian thought, I think, by reflecting on the implications of his views on 'ought implies can'.
12. Cf. MacIntyre, *After Virtue*, and Charles Taylor, *The Explanation of Behaviour*, London (1964).
13. MacIntyre, *After Virtue*, 127.
14. Kant argues there that there are two ends 'which are at the same time duties': 'one's own perfection and the happiness of others. One cannot invert these and make, on the one hand, our own happiness and, on the other, the perfection of others, ends which should be in themselves duties for the same person'. *The Metaphysical Principles of Virtue*, translated by James Ellington, Indianapolis (1964), 43.
15. Although I develop this argument only in connection with classical utilitarianism, I think similar results would follow in considering any consequentialist view.

16. I do not mean to suggest here that classical utilitarians were unaware of these difficulties. Mill, indeed, goes to some lengths to combat them. He says in *Utilitarianism*, 'Then multiplication of happiness is, according to the utilitarian ethics, the object of virtue: the occasions on which any person (except one in a thousand) has it in his power to do this on an extended scale – in other words, to be a public benefactor – are but exceptional; and on these occasions alone is he called on to consider public utility; *in every other case, private utility, the interest or happiness of some few persons, is all he has to attend to,*' emphasis added ( J. S. Mill, *Utilitarianism*, Indianapolis, 1957, 25.) The question that Mill's position raises is, however, whether it can be reconciled with other features of his utilitarianism. I suspect it cannot.

# 10

# ON SOME VICES OF VIRTUE ETHICS

## *Robert B. Louden*

It is common knowledge by now that recent philosophical and theological writing about ethics reveals a marked revival of interest in the virtues. But what exactly are the distinctive features of a so-called virtue ethics? Does it have a special contribution to make to our understanding of moral experience? Is there a price to be paid for its different perspective, and if so, is the price worth paying?

Contemporary textbook typologies of ethics still tend to divide the terrain of normative ethical theory into the teleological and deontological. Both types of theory, despite their well-defined differences, have a common focus on acts as opposed to qualities of agents. The fundamental question that both types of theory are designed to answer is: What ought I to do? What is the correct analysis and resolution of morally problematic situations? A second feature shared by teleological and deontological theories is conceptual reductionism. Both types of theory start with a primary irreducible element and then proceed to introduce secondary derivative concepts which are defined in terms of their relations to the beginning element. Modern teleologists (the majority of whom are utilitarians) begin with a concept of the good – here defined with reference to states of affairs rather than persons. After this criterion of the good is established, the remaining ethical categories are defined in terms of this starting point. Thus, according to the classic maxim, one ought always to promote the greatest good for the greatest number. Duty, in other words, is defined in terms of the element of ends – one ought always to maximise utility. The concepts of virtue and rights are also treated as derivative categories of secondary importance, definable in terms of utility. For the classic utilitarian, a right is upheld 'so long as it is upon the whole advantageous to the society that it should be maintained', while virtue is construed as a 'tendency to give a net increase to the aggregate quantity of happiness in all its shapes taken together'.[1]

For the deontologist, on the other hand, the concept of duty is the irreducible starting point, and any attempt to define this root notion of being morally bound to do something in terms of the good to be achieved is rejected from the start. The deontologist is committed to the notion that certain acts are simply inherently right. Here the notion of the good is only a derivative category, definable in terms of the right. The good that we are to promote is right action for its own sake – duty for duty's sake. Similarly, the virtues tend to be defined in terms of pro-attitudes towards one's duties. Virtue is important, but only because it helps us do our duty.

But what about virtue ethics? What are the hallmarks of this approach to normative ethics? One problem confronting anyone who sets out to analyse the new virtue ethics in any detail is that we presently lack fully developed examples of it in the contemporary literature. Most of the work done in this genre has a negative rather than positive thrust – its primary aim is more to criticise the traditions and research programmes to which it is opposed rather than to state positively and precisely what its own alternative is. A second hindrance is that the literature often has a somewhat misty antiquarian air. It is frequently said, for instance, that the Greeks advocated a virtue ethics, though what precisely it is that they were advocating is not always spelled out. In describing contemporary virtue ethics, it is therefore necessary, in my opinion, to do some detective work concerning its conceptual shape, making inferences based on the unfortunately small number of remarks that are available.

For the purposes of illustration, I propose briefly to examine and expand on some key remarks made by two contemporary philosophers – Elizabeth Anscombe and Philippa Foot – whose names have often been associated with the revival of virtue movement. Anscombe, in her frequently cited article, 'Modern Moral Philosophy', writes: 'you can do ethics without it [viz., the notion of "obligation" or "morally ought"], as is shown by the example of Aristotle. It would be a great improvement if, instead of "morally wrong", one always named a genus such as "untruthful", "unchaste", "unjust"'.[2] Here we find an early rallying cry for an ethics of virtue programme, to be based on contemporary efforts in philosophical psychology and action theory. On the Anscombe model, strong, irreducible duty and obligation notions drop out of the picture, and are to be replaced by vices such as unchasteness and untruthfulness. But are we to take the assertion literally, and actually attempt to do moral theory without any concept of duty whatsoever? On my reading, Anscombe is not really proposing that we entirely dispose of moral oughts. Suppose one follows her advice, and replaces 'morally wrong' with 'untruthful', 'unchaste', etc. Isn't this merely shorthand for saying that agents *ought* to be truthful and chaste, and that untruthful and unchaste acts are *morally wrong* because good agents don't perform such acts? The concept of the moral ought, in other words, seems now to be explicated in terms of what the good person would do.[3]

A similar strategy is at work in some of Foot's articles. In the Introduction to her collection of essays, *Virtues and Vices and Other Essays in Moral Philosophy*, she announces that one of the two major themes running through her work is 'the thought that a sound moral philosophy should start from a theory of virtues and vices'.[4] When this thought is considered in conjunction with the central argument in her article, 'Morality

as a System of Hypothetical Imperatives', the indication is that another virtue-based
moral theory is in the making. For in this essay Foot envisions a moral community
composed of an 'army of volunteers', composed, that is, of agents who voluntarily
commit themselves to such moral ideals as truth, justice, generosity and kindness.[5]
In a moral community of this sort, all moral imperatives become hypothetical rather
than categorical: there are things an agent morally ought to do if he or she wants
truth, justice, generosity or kindness, but no things an agent morally ought to do if
he or she isn't first committed to these (or other) moral ideals. On the Foot model
(as presented in 'Morality as a System'), what distinguishes an ethics of virtue from its
competitors is that it construes the ideal moral agent as acting from a direct desire,
without first believing that he or she morally ought to perform that action or have
that desire. However, in a more recent paper, Foot has expressed doubts about her
earlier attempts to articulate the relationship between oughts and desires. In 'William
Frankena's Carus Lectures', she states that *'thoughts* [my emphasis] about what is
despicable or contemptible, or low, or again admirable, glorious or honourable may
give us the key to the problem of rational moral action'.[6] But regardless of whether she
begins with desires or with thoughts, it seems clear her strategy too is not to dispense
with oughts entirely, but rather to employ softer, derivative oughts.

In other words, conceptual reductionism is at work in virtue ethics too. Just as its
utilitarian and deontological competitors begin with primitive concepts of the good
state of affairs and the intrinsically right action respectively and then drive secondary
concepts out of their starting points, so virtue ethics, beginning with a root conception
of the morally good person, proceeds to introduce a different set of secondary
concepts which are defined in terms of their relationship to the primitive element.
Though the ordering of primitive and derivatives differs in each case, the overall
strategy remains the same. Viewed from this perspective, virtue ethics is not unique at
all. It has adopted the traditional mononomic strategy of normative ethics. What sets
it apart from other approaches, again, is its strong agent orientation.

So, for virtue ethics, the primary object of moral evaluation is not the act or its
consequences, but rather the agent. And the respective conceptual starting points of
agent and act-centred ethics result in other basic differences as well, which may be
briefly summarised as follows. First of all, the two camps are likely to employ different
models of practical reasoning. Act theorists, because they focus on discrete acts and
moral quandaries, are naturally very interested in formulating decision procedures
for making practical choices. The agent, in their conceptual scheme, needs a guide –
hopefully a determinate decision procedure – for finding a way out of the quandary.
Agent-centred ethics, on the other hand, focuses on long-term characteristic patterns
of action, intentionally downplaying atomic acts and particular choice situations in the
process. They are not as concerned with portraying practical reason as a rule-governed
enterprise which can be applied on a case-by-case basis.

Secondly, their views on moral motivation differ. For the deontological act theorist,
the preferred motive for moral action is the concept of duty itself; for the utilitarian
act theorist, it is the disposition to seek the happiness of all sentient creatures. But
for the virtue theorist, the preferred motivation factor is the virtues themselves (here

understood non-reductionistically). The agent who correctly acts from the disposition of charity does so (according to the virtue theorist) not because it maximises utility or because it is one's duty to do so, but rather out of a commitment to the value of charity for its own sake.

While I am sympathetic to recent efforts to recover virtue from its long-standing neglect, my purpose in this chapter is not to contribute further to the campaign for virtue. Instead, I wish to take a more critical look at the phenomenon, and to ask whether there are certain important features of mortality which a virtue-based ethics either handles poorly or ignores entirely. In the remainder of this chapter, I shall sketch some objections which (I believe) point to genuine shortcomings of the virtue approach to ethics. My object here is not to offer an exhaustive or even thoroughly systematic critique of virtue ethics, but rather to look at certain mundane regions of the moral field and to ask first what an ethics of virtue might say about them, and second whether what it says about them seems satisfactory.

## AGENTS VS ACTS

As noted earlier, it is a commonplace that virtue theorists focus on good and bad agents rather than on right and wrong acts. In focusing on good and bad agents, virtue theorists are thus forced to de-emphasise discrete acts in favour of long-term, characteristic patterns of behaviour. Several related problems arise for virtue ethics as a result of this particular conceptual commitment.

### 1. Casuistry and applied ethics

It has often been said that for virtue ethics the central question is not 'What ought I to *do*?' but rather 'What sort of person ought I to *be*?'.[7] However, people have always expected ethical theory to tell them something about what they ought to do, and it seems to me that virtue ethics is structurally unable to say much of anything about this issue. If I'm right, one consequence of this is that a virtue-based ethics will be particularly weak in the areas of casuistry and applied ethics. A recent reviewer of Foot's *Virtues and Vices*, for instance, notes that 'one must do some shifting to gather her view on the virtues'. 'Surprisingly', he adds, 'the studies of abortion and euthanasia are not of much use'.[8] And this is odd, when one considers Foot's demonstrated interest in applied ethics in conjunction with her earlier cited prefatory remark that a 'sound moral theory should start from a theory of virtues and vices'. But what can a virtues and vices approach say about specific moral dilemmas? As virtue theorists from Aristotle onwards have rightly emphasised, virtues are not simply dispositions to behave in specified ways, for which rules and principles can always be cited. In addition, they involve skills of perception and articulation, situation-specific 'know-how', all of which are developed only through recognising and acting on what is relevant in concrete moral contexts as they arise. These skills of moral perception and practical reason are not completely routinisable, and so cannot be transferred from agent to agent as any sort of decision procedure 'package deal'. Due to the very nature of the moral virtues, there is thus a very limited amount of advice on moral quandaries that one can reasonably expect from the virtue-oriented approach. We ought, of course, to do what the virtuous person would do, but it is not always easy to fathom what the hypothetical moral exemplar would do were he in our shoes, and sometimes even he will act out of character. Furthermore, if one asks him why he did what he did, or how he knew what to do, the answer – if one is offered – might not be very enlightening. One would not necessarily expect him to appeal to any rules or principles which might be of use to others.

We can say, à la Aristotle, that the virtuous agent acts for the sake of the noble (*tou kalou heneka*), that he will not do what is base or depraved, etc. But it seems to me that we cannot intelligently say things like: 'The virtuous person (who acts for the sake of the noble) is also one who recognises that all mentally deficient eight-month-old foetuses should (or should not) be aborted, that the doctor/patient principle of confidentiality must always (or not always) be respected, etc'. The latter simply sound too strange, and their strangeness stems from the fact that motives of virtue and honour cannot be fully routinised.

Virtue theory is not a problem-oriented or quandary approach to ethics: it speaks of rules and principles of action only in a derivative manner. And its derivative oughts are frequently too vague and unhelpful for persons who have not yet acquired the requisite moral insight and sensitivity. Consequently, we cannot expect it to be of great use in applied ethics and casuistry. The increasing importance of these two subfields of ethics in contemporary society is thus a strike against the move to revive virtue ethics.

## 2. Tragic humans

Another reason for making sure that our ethical theory allows us to talk about features of acts and their results in abstraction from the agent and his conception of what he is doing is that sometimes even the best person can make the wrong choices. There are cases in which a man's choice is grounded in the best possible information, his motives honourable and his action not at all out of character. And yet his best laid plans may go sour. Aristotle, in his *Poetics*, suggests that here lies the source of tragedy: we are confronted with an eminent and respected man, 'whose misfortune, however, is brought upon him not by vice (*kakia*) and depravity (*moktheira*) but by some error of judgment (*amartia*)'.[9] But every human being is morally fallible, for there is a little Oedipus in each of us. So Aristotle's point is that *regardless of character*, anyone can fall into the sort of mistake of which tragedies are made. Virtue ethics, however, since its conceptual scheme is rooted in the notion of the good person, is unable to assess correctly the occasional (inevitable) tragic outcomes of human action.

Lawrence Becker, in his article 'The Neglect of Virtue', seems at first to draw an opposite conclusion from similar reflections about virtue theory and tragedy, for it is his view that virtue ethics makes an indispensable contribution to our understanding of tragedy. According to him, 'there are times when the issue is not how much harm has been done, or the value to excusing the wrongdoer, or the voluntary nature of the offending behaviour, but rather whether the sort of character indicated by the behaviour is "acceptable" or not – perhaps even ideal – so that the "wrongful" conduct must be seen simply as an unavoidable defect of it'.[10] As Becker sees it, Oedipus merely comes off as a fool who asked too many questions when viewed from the perspective of act theories. Only a virtue ethics, with its agent perspective, allows us to differentiate tragic heroes from fools, and to view the acts that flow from each character type in their proper light. And the proper light in the case of tragic heroes is that there are unavoidable defects in this character type, even though it represents a human ideal. Becker's point is well taken, but its truth does not cancel out my criticism. My point is that virtue ethics is in danger of blinding itself to the wrongful conduct in Oedipal acts, simply because it views the Oedipuses of the world as honourable persons *and* because its focus is on long-term character manifestations rather than discrete acts. To recognise the wrong in Oedipal behaviour, a theory with the conceptual tools enabling one to focus on discrete acts is needed. (Notice, incidentally, that Becker's own description does just this.)

### 3. Intolerable actions

A third reason for insisting that our moral theory enables us to assess acts in abstraction from agents is that we need to be able to identify certain types of action which produce harms of such magnitude that they destroy the bonds of community and render (at least temporarily) the achievement of moral goods impossible. In every traditional moral community one encounters prohibitions or 'barriers to action' which mark off clear boundaries in such areas as the taking of innocent life, sexual relations, and the administration of justice according to local laws and customs.[11] Such rules are needed to teach citizens what kinds of actions are to be regarded not simply as bad (a table of vices can handle this) but as intolerable.[12] Theorists must resort to specific lists of offences to emphasise the fact that there are some acts which are absolutely prohibited. We cannot articulate this sense of absolute prohibition by referring merely to characteristic patterns of behaviour.

In rebuttal here, the virtue theorist may reply by saying: 'Virtue ethics does not need to articulate these prohibitions – let the law do it, with its list of do's and don't's'. But the sense of requirement and prohibition referred to above seems to me to be inescapably moral rather than legal. Morality can (and frequently does) invoke the aid of law in such cases, but when we ask *why* there is a law against, for example, rape or murder, the proper answer is that it is morally intolerable. To point merely to a legal convention when asked why an act is prohibited or intolerable raises more questions that it answers.

### 4. Character change

A fourth reason for insisting that a moral theory be able to assess acts in abstraction from agents and their conception of what they're doing is that people's moral characters may sometimes change. Xenophon, towards the beginning of his *Memorabilia* (I.II.21), cites an unknown poet who says: 'Ah, but a good man is at one time noble *(esthlos)*, at another wicked *(kakos)*'. Xenophon himself agrees with the poet: '. . . many alleged *(phaskonton)* philosophers may say: A just *(dikaios)* man can never become unjust; a self-controlled *(sophron)* man can never become wanton *(hubristes)*; in fact no one having learned any kind of knowledge *(mathesis)* can become ignorant of it. I do not hold this view . . . For I see that, just as poetry is forgotten unless it is often repeated, so instruction, when no longer heeded, fades from the mind'.[13]

Xenophon was a practical man who was not often given to speculation, but he arrived at his position on character change in the course of his defence of Socrates. One of the reasons Socrates got into trouble, Xenophon believed, was due to his contact with Critias and Alcibiades during their youth. For of all Athenians, 'none wrought so many evils to the *polis*'. However, Xenophon reached the conclusion that Socrates should not be blamed for the disappearance of his good influence once these two had ceased their close contact with him.

If skills can become rusty, it seems to me that virtues can too. Unless we stay in practice we run the risk of losing relative proficiency. We probably can't forget them completely (in part because the opportunities for exercising virtues are so pervasive in everyday life), but we can lose a certain sensitivity. People do become morally insensitive, relatively speaking – missing opportunities they once would have noticed, although perhaps when confronted with a failure they might recognise that they had failed, showing at least that they hadn't literally 'forgotten the difference between right and wrong'. If the moral virtues are acquired habits rather than innate gifts, it is always possible that one can lose relative proficiency in these habits. Also, just as one's interests and skills sometimes change over the course of a life as new perceptions and influences take hold, it seems too that aspects of our moral characters can likewise alter. (Consider religious conversion experiences.) Once we grant the possibility of such changes in moral character, the need for a more 'character free' way of assessing action becomes evident. Character is not a permanent fixture, but rather plastic. A more reliable yardstick is sometimes needed.[14]

## 5. Moral backsliding

Finally, the focus on good and bad agents rather than on right and wrong actions may lead to a peculiar sort of moral backsliding. Because the emphasis in agent ethics is on long-term, characteristic patterns of behaviour, its advocates run the risk of overlooking occasional lies or acts of selfishness on the ground that such performances are mere temporary aberrations – acts out of character. Even the just man may on occasion act unjustly, so why haggle over specifics? It is unbecoming to a virtue theorist to engage in such pharisaic calculations. But once he commits himself to the view that assessments of moral worth are not simply a matter of whether we have done the right thing, backsliding may result: 'No matter how many successes some people have, they still feel they "are" fundamentally honest'.[15] At some point, such backsliding is bound to lead to self-deception.

I have argued that there is a common source behind each of these vices. The virtue theorist is committed to the claim that the primary object of moral evaluation is not the act or its consequences but rather the agent – specifically, those character traits of the agent which are judged morally relevant. This is not to say that virtue ethics does not ever address the issue of right and wrong actions, but rather that it can only do so in a derivative manner. Sometimes, however, it is clearly acts rather than agents which ought to be the primary focus of moral evaluation.

## WHO IS VIRTUOUS?

There is also an epistemological issue which becomes troublesome when one focuses on qualities of persons rather than on qualities of acts. Baldly put, the difficulty is that we do not seem to be able to know with any degree of certainty who really is virtuous and who vicious. For how is one to go about establishing an agent's true moral character? The standard strategy is what might be called the 'externalist' one: we try to infer character by observing conduct. While not denying the existence of some connection between character and conduct, I believe that the connection between the two is not nearly as tight as externalists have assumed. The relationship is not a necessary one, but merely contingent. Virtue theorists themselves are committed to this claim, though they have not always realised it. For one central issue behind the 'Being vs. Doing' debate is the virtue theorist's contention that the moral value of Being is not reducible to or dependent on Doing; that the measure of an agent's character is not exhausted by or even dependent on the values of the actions which he may perform. On this view, the most important moral traits are what may be called 'spiritual' rather than 'actional'.[16]

Perhaps the most famous example of a spiritual virtue would be Plato's definition of justice (*dikaiosunē*). Plato, it will be remembered, argued that attempts to characterise *dikaiosunē* in terms of an agent's conduct are misguided and place the emphasis in the wrong place. *Dikaiosunē* for Plato is rather a matter of the correct harmonious relationship between the three parts of the soul: 'It does not lie in a man's external actions, but in the way he acts within himself (*tēn entos*), really concerned with himself and his inner parts (*peri eauton kai ta eautou*)'.[17] Other spiritual virtues would include such attitudes as self-respect and integrity. These are traits which do have a significant impact on what we do, but whose moral value is not wholly derivable from the actions to which they may give rise.

If there are such spiritual virtues, and if they rank among the most important of moral virtues, then the externalist strategy is in trouble. For those who accept spiritual virtues, the Inner is not reducible to or dependent on the Outer. We cannot always know the moral value of a person's character by assessing his or her actions.

But suppose we reject the externalist approach and take instead the allegedly direct internalist route. Suppose, that is, that we could literally 'see inside' agents and somehow observe their character traits first-hand. (The easiest way to envision this is to assume that some sort of identity thesis with respect to moral psychology and neurophysiology is in principle correct. Lest the reader object that this is only a modern materialist's silly pipe dream, I might add that at least one commentator has argued that Aristotle's considered view was that the presence of the virtues and vices depends on modifications of the brain and nervous system; and that the relevant mental processes in ethics have accompanying bodily states.)[18] Here the goal will be to match specific virtues with specific chemicals, much in the manner that identity theorists have sought to match other types of mental events with other specific neurophysiological events. However, even on this materialistic reading of the internalist strategy, nothing could be settled about virtues by analysing chemicals without first deciding who has what virtue. For we would first need to know who possessed and exhibited which virtue, and then look for specific physical traces in him that were missing in other agents. But as indicated earlier in my discussion of the externalist strategy, this is precisely what we don't know. An analogy might be the attempt to determine which objects have which colours. Regardless of how much we know about the physical make-up of the objects in question, we must first make colour judgments. However, at this point the analogy breaks down, for the epistemological problems involved in making colour judgments are not nearly as troublesome as are those involved in making virtue judgments.[19]

To raise doubts about our ability to know who is virtuous is to bring scepticism into the centre of virtue ethics, for it is to call into question our ability to identify the very object of our inquiry. This is not the same scepticism which has concerned recent writers such as Bernard Williams and Thomas Nagel, when they reflect on the fact that 'the natural objects of moral assessment are disturbingly subject to luck'.[20] Theirs is more a scepticism *about* morality, while mine is a scepticism *within* morality. The son of scepticism to which I am drawing attention occurs after one has convinced oneself that there are genuine moral agents who really do things rather than have things happen to them. As such, my scepticism is narrower but also more morality-specific: it concerns not so much queries about causality and free will as doubts about our ability to know the motives of our own behaviour. As Kant wrote, 'the real morality of actions, their merit or guilt, even that of our own conduct . . . remains entirely hidden from us'.[21] Aquinas too subscribed to a similar scepticism: 'Man is not competent to judge of interior movements, that are hidden, but only of exterior acts which are observable; and yet for the perfection of virtue it is necessary for man to conduct himself rightly in both kinds of acts.'[22]

Now it may be objected here that I am making too much of this epistemological error, that no one actually 'lives it' or contests the fact that it is an error. But I think not. To advocate an ethics of virtue is, among other things, to presuppose that we can clearly differentiate the virtuous from the vicious. Otherwise, the project lacks applicability.

Consider for a moment the Aristotelian notion of the *spoudaios* (good man) or *phronimos* (man of practical wisdom) – two essentially synonymous terms which together have often been called the touchstone of Aristotle's ethics. Again and again in the *Nicomachean Ethics* the *spoudaios/phronimos* is pointed to as the solution to a number of unanswered problems in Aristotle's ethical theory. For instance, we are told to turn to the *spoudaios* in order to learn what really is pleasurable.[23] And we must turn to an actual *phronimos* in order to find out what the abstract and mysterious *orthos logos* really is (right reason or rational principle – a notion which plays a key role in the definition of virtue).[24] Even in discussing the intellectual virtue of *phronèsis* or practical wisdom,

Aristotle begins by announcing that 'we shall get at the truth by considering who are the persons we credit with it' (1140a24).[25] But who are the *phronimoi*, and how do we know one when we see one? Aristotle does say that Pericles 'and men like him' are *phronimoi*, 'because they can see what is good for themselves and what is good for men in general' (1140b8–10).[26] However, beyond this rather casual remark he does not give the reader any hints on how to track down a *phronimos*. Indeed, he does not even see it as a problem worth discussing.

The reasons for this strange lacuna, I suggest, are two. First, Aristotle is dealing with a small face to face community, where the pool of potential *phronimoi* generally come from certain well established families who are well known throughout the *polis*. Within a small face to face community of this sort, one would naturally expect to find wide agreement about judgments of character. Second, Aristotle's own methodology is itself designed to fit this sort of moral community. He is not advocating a Platonic ethics of universal categories.

Within the context of a *polis* and an ethical theory intended to accompany it, the strategy of pointing to a *phronimos* makes a certain sense. However, to divorce this strategy from its social and economic roots and to then apply it to a very different sort of community – one where people really do not know each other all that well, and where there is wide disagreement on values – does not. And this, I fear, is what contemporary virtue ethicists have tried to do.[27]

## STYLE OVER SUBSTANCE

In emphasising Being over Doing, the Inner over the Outer, virtue theorists also lay themselves open to the charge that they are more concerned with style than with substance. For, as I argued earlier, virtue theorists are committed to the view that the moral value of certain key character traits is not exhausted by or even dependent on the value of the actions to which they may give rise. When this gulf between character and conduct is asserted, and joined with the claim that it is agents rather than actions which count morally, the conclusion is that it is not the substance of an agent's actions which is the focus of moral appraisal. The implication here seems to be that if you have style, i.e. the style of the virtuous person, as defined in the context of a concrete moral tradition, it doesn't matter so much what the results are. ('It's not whether you win or lose, but how you play the game that counts.') As Frankena remarks, in a passage which underscores an alleged basic difference between ancient and contemporary virtue ethics:

> The Greeks held . . . that being virtuous entails not just having good motives or intentions but also doing the right thing. Modern views typically differ from Greek views here; perhaps because of the changed ways of thinking introduced by the Judeo-Christian tradition, we tend to believe that being morally good does not entail doing what is actually right . . . even if we believe (as I do) that doing what is actually right involves more than only having a good motive or intention. Today many people go so far as to think that in morality it does not matter much *what* you do; all that matters, they say, is *how* you do it. To parody a late cigarette

advertisement; for them it's not how wrong you make it, it's how you make it wrong.[28]

But it is sophistry to claim that the consequences of the lies of gentlemen or Aristotelian *kaloikagathoi* aren't very important, or that the implications of their rudeness are somehow tempered by the fact that they are who they are. This line of thought flies in the face of our basic conviction that moral assessment must strive towards impartiality and the bracketing of morally irrelevant social and economic data.

It seems to me that this particular vice of virtue ethics is analogous to the Hegelian 'duty for duty's sake' critique of formalist deontologies. Virtue-based and duty-based theories are both subject to the 'style over substance' charge because their notion of ends is too weak. Both types of theory speak of ends only in a derivative sense. For the duty-based theorist, the good is an inherent feature of dutiful action, so that the only proclaimed end is right action itself. For the virtue-based theorist, the good is defined in terms of the virtuous agent. ('Virtue is its own reward.') Aristotle, as noted earlier, in distinguishing the true from the apparent good, remarks that 'that which is in truth an object of wish is an object of wish to the good man (*spoudaios*), while any chance thing may be so to the bad man'.[29]

While no one (except the most obstinate utilitarian) would deny these two respective ends their place in a list of moral goods, it appears that there is another important type of end which is left completely unaccounted for. This second type of end is what may be called a *product-end*, a result or outcome of action which is distinct from the activity that produces it. (An example would be a catastrophe or its opposite.) Virtue-based and duty-based theories, on the other hand, can account only for *activity-ends*, ends which are inherent features of (virtuous or dutiful) action. Virtue-based theories then, like their duty-based competitors, reveal a structural defect in their lack of attention to product-ends.[30]

Now it might be said that the 'style over substance' charge is more appropriately directed at those who emphasize Doing over Being, since one can do the right things just to conform or for praise. One can cultivate the externalities, but be inwardly wretched or shallow. I grant that this is a problem for act theorists, but it is a slightly different criticism than mine, using different senses of the words 'style' and 'substance'. 'Style', as used in my criticism, means roughly: 'morally irrelevant mannerisms and behaviour', while 'substance', as I used it, means something like: 'morally relevant results of action'. The 'substance' in this new criticism refers to good moral character and the acts which flow from it, while 'style' here means more 'doing the right thing, but without the proper fixed trait behind it'. However, granted that both 'style over substance' criticisms have some validity, I would also argue that mine points to a greater vice. It is one thing to do what is right without the best disposition, it is another not to do what is right at all.

## UTOPIANISM

The last vice I shall mention has a more socio-historical character. It seems to me that there is a bit of utopianism behind the virtue theorist's complaints about the ethics of rules. Surely, one reason there is more emphasis on rules and regulations in modern society is that things have grown more complex. Our moral community (insofar as it makes sense to speak of 'community' in these narcissistic times) contains more ethnic, religious and class groups than did the moral community which Aristotle theorised about. Unfortunately, each segment of society has not only its own interests but its own set of virtues as well. There is no general agreed and significant expression of desirable moral character in such a world. Indeed, our pluralist culture prides itself on and defines itself in terms of its alleged value neutrality and its lack of allegiance to any one moral tradition. This absence of agreement regarding human purposes and moral ideals seems to drive us (partly out of lack of alternatives) to a more legalistic form of morality. To suppose that academic theorists can alter the situation simply by re-emphasising certain concepts is illusory. Our world lacks the sort of moral cohesiveness and value unity which traditional virtue theorists saw as prerequisites of a viable moral community.[31]

The table of vices sketched above is not intended to be exhaustive, but even in its incomplete state I believe it spells trouble for virtue-based moral theories. For the shortcomings described are not esoteric – they concern mundane features of moral experience which any minimally adequate moral theory should be expected to account for. While I do think that contemporary virtue theorists are correct in asserting that any adequate moral theory must account for the fact of character, and that no ethics of rules, pure and unsupplemented, is up to this job, the above analysis also suggests that no ethics of virtue, pure and unsupplemented, can be satisfactory.

My own view (which can only be stated summarily here) is that we need to begin efforts to coordinate irreducible or strong notions of virtue along with irreducible or strong conceptions of the various act notions into our conceptual scheme of morality. This appeal for coordination will not satisfy those theorists who continue to think in the single-element or mononomic tradition (a tradition which contemporary virtue-based theorists have inherited from their duty-based and goal-based ancestors), but I do believe that it will result in a more realistic account of our moral experience. The moral field is not unitary, and the values we employ in making moral judgments sometimes have fundamentally different sources. No single reductive method can offer a realistic means of prioritising these different values. There exists no single scale by means of which disparate moral considerations can always be measured, added and balanced.[32] The theoretician's quest for conceptual economy and elegance has been won at too great a price, for the resulting reductionist definitions of the moral concepts are not true to the facts of moral experience. It is important now to see the ethics of virtue and the ethics of rules as adding up, rather than as cancelling each other out.[33]

## ENDNOTES

1. The rights definition is from Bentham's 'Anarchical Fallacies', reprinted in A. I. Melden (ed.), *Human Rights*, Belmont: Wadsworth (1970), 32. The virtue definition is from Bentham's 'The Nature of Virtue', reprinted in Bhiku Parekh (ed.), *Bentham's Political Thought*, New York: Barnes and Noble (1973), 89.
2. G. E. M. Anscombe, 'Modern Moral Philosophy', *Philosophy*, Vol. 33 (1958), 1–19; reprinted in J. J. Thomson and G. Dworkin (eds), *Ethics*, New York: Harper & Row (1968), 196.

3. Anscombe appears to believe also that moral oughts and obligations only make sense in a divine law context, which would mean that only divine command theories of ethics employ valid concepts of obligation. I see no reason to accept such a narrow definition of duty. See pp. 192, 202 of 'Modern Moral Philosophy'. For one argument against her restrictive divine law approach to moral obligation, see Alan Donagan, *The Theory of Morality*, Chicago: University of Chicago Press (1977), 3.

4. Philippa Foot, *Virtues and Vices and Other Essays in Moral Philosophy*, Berkeley and Los Angeles: University of California Press (1978), xi.

5. Foot, 'Morality as a System of Hypothetical Imperatives', *The Philosophical Review*, Vol. 81 (1972), 305–16; reprinted in *Virtues and Vices*, 157–73. See especially the long concluding footnote, added in 1977.

6. Foot, 'William Frankena's Carus Lectures', *The Monist*, Vol. 64 (1981), 311.

7. For background on this 'Being vs. Doing' debate, see Bernard Mayo, *Ethics and the Moral Life*, London: Macmillan & Co., Ltd. (1958) 211–14, and William K. Frankena, *Ethics*, 2nd edn, Englewood Cliffs, New Jersey: Prentice Hall (1973), 65–6.

8. Arthur Flemming, 'Reviving the Virtues'. Review of Foot's *Virtues and Vices* and James Wallace's *Virtues and Vices. Ethics*, Vol. 90 (1980), 588.

9. Aristotle, *Poetics* (1453a8–9).

10. Lawrence Becker, 'The Neglect of Virtue', *Ethics*, Vol. 85 (1975), 111.

11. Stuart Hampshire (ed.), *Private and Public Morality*, New York: Cambridge University Press (1978), 7.

12. Alasdair MacIntyre, *After Virtue*, Notre Dame: University of Notre Dame Press (1981), 142.

13. It is curious to note that contemporary philosophers as different as Gilbert Ryle and H. G. Gadamer have argued, against Xenophon and myself, that character cannot change. See H. G. Gadamer, 'The Problem of Historical Consciousness', p. 140 in P. Rabinow and W. M. Sullivan (eds), *Interpretive Social Science*, Berkeley and Los Angeles: University of California Press (1979), and Gilbert Ryle, 'On Forgetting the Difference Between Right and Wrong', in A. I. Melden (ed.), *Essays in Moral Philosophy*, Seattle: University of Washington Press (1958).

14. One possibility here might be to isolate specific traits and then add that the virtuous agent ought to *retain* such traits throughout any character changes. (E.g.: 'The good man will not do what is base, regardless of whether he be Christian, Jew, or atheist'.) However, it is my view that very few if any moral traits have such a 'transcharacter' status. The very notion of what counts as a virtue or vice itself changes radically when one looks at different traditions. (Compare Aristotle's praise for *megalopsuchia* or pride as the 'crown of the virtues' with the New Testament emphasis on humility.) Also, one would expect basic notions about what is base or noble to themselves undergo shifts of meaning as they move across traditions.

15. Becker, 'The Neglect of Virtue', 112.

16. I have borrowed this terminology from G. W. Trianosky-Stillwell, *Should We Be Good? The Place of Virtue in Our Morality*, Doctoral Dissertation, University of Michigan (1980).

17. Plato, *Republic* (443d).

18. W. F. R. Hardie, *Aristotle's Ethical Theory*, 2nd edn, Oxford: Clarendon Press (1980), Chapter VI, esp. 111–13.

19. I am indebted to Bill Robinson for help on this criticism of the internalist strategy.

20. Thomas Nagel, 'Moral Luck', in *Mortal Questions*, New York: Cambridge University Press (1979), 28. See also Bernard Williams, 'Moral Luck', in *Moral Luck: Philosophical Papers 1973–1980*, New York: Cambridge University Press (1981).

21. Kant, *Critique of Pure Reason*, A552 = B580, n. 1.

22. Thomas Aquinas, Saint. *Summa Theologica*, I–II Q. 91, a. 4.

23. Aristotle, *Nicomachean Ethics* (1113a26–8).

24. Op. cit. (1107a2, 1144b24).

25. Op. cit. (1140a24).

26. Op. cit. (1140b8–10).

27. I would like to thank Arthur Adkins for discussion on these points.

28. William K. Frankena, *Thinking About Morality*, Ann Arbor: University of Michigan Press (1980), 52–3.

29. Op. cit. (1113a26–8).

30. My own position on this topic is contra that of utilitarianism. I believe that activity-ends are clearly the more important of the two, and that most product-ends ultimately derive their moral value from more fundamental activity-ends. (The importance of saving lives, for instance, borrows its value from the quality of life it makes possible. 'Life at any price' is nonsense.) But I also believe, contra deontology and virtue ethics, that any adequate moral theory must find room for both types of ends.

31. For similar criticism, see Mayo, *Ethics and the Moral Life*, 217; and MacIntyre, *After Virtue*.

32. See Thomas Nagel, 'The Fragmentation of Value', 131–2, 135 in *Mortal Questions*, New York: Cambridge University Press (1979). A similar position is defended by Charles Taylor in his essay 'The Diversity of Goods', in A. Sen and B. Williams (eds), *Utilitarianism and Beyond*, New York: Cambridge University Press (1982).

33. Earlier versions of this essay were read at the 1982 American Philosophical Association Pacific Division Meetings, and at the 1981 Iowa Philosophical Society Meeting at Grinnell College. I am very grateful for useful criticisms and suggestions offered on these occasions. I would also like to thank Marcia Baron, Lawrence Becker, James Gustafson, W. D. Hamlyn, Bob Hollinger, Joe Kupfer, and Warner Wick for criticisms of earlier drafts. Portions of the present version are taken from my doctoral dissertation, *The Elements of Ethics: Toward a Topography of the Moral Field*, University of Chicago (1981).

# 11

# VIRTUE ETHICS: A QUALIFIED SUCCESS STORY

## *Phillip Montague*

Proponents of virtue ethics (VE) are unanimous in decrying the extent to which 'modern moral philosophy' has been concerned with examining the moral status of acts, but they are far from being agreed about how moral philosophy *should* be done. According to some VE advocates, claims about the rightness, wrongness, obligatoriness, etc., of acts are either incoherent or pernicious, and should therefore be ignored entirely by ethical theory. These philosophers recommend that moral philosophers concern themselves exclusively with questions about personal worth and about virtue and the like.[1] Less radical versions of VE regard the morality of acts as a legitimate area of inquiry for ethical theory, but they treat act-appraisals as explicable in terms of more basic person-appraisals. This chapter will be concerned exclusively with these latter versions of VE.

Now, it seems plain that VE advocates are correct in emphasising the philosophical importance of person-appraisals, and that they are also justified in criticising certain ethical theories as too narrowly focused on act-appraisals. It will be argued here, however, that VE fails as a comprehensive account of the respective roles of act-appraisal and of person-appraisal in moral theory. In the course of criticising VE, some suggestions will be offered regarding how the relation between act- and person-appraisals *should* be understood.

### 1.

According to VE, person-appraisals are (explanatorily) more basic than act-appraisals. In order to evaluate this idea, certain distinctions must be drawn within the area of person-appraisal.

Some person-appraisals are judgments of persons *as agents*: they are judgments of people *for acting* or *for refraining*. Person-appraisals of this type (a type which includes judgments of blameworthiness and of praiseworthiness) will be referred to as 'deontic'. Deontic person-appraisals stand in sharp contrast to those which will be called 'aretaic'. In aretaic appraisals, people are judged not as agents, but *as persons*: aretaic appraisals are concerned not with how people have acted or refrained from acting on particular occasions, but with their overall moral worth.

One difference between deontic and aretaic person-appraisals is that the former presuppose act-appraisals in a way that the latter do not. Thus, for example, you deserve moral criticism for performing some action only if the action is somehow morally defective; but your being a morally bad person does not depend on your having acted immorally on some particular occasion. Similarly, if you deserve moral credit for acting, then your action has some positive moral feature; whereas your being morally good is independent of whether you have performed some specific good or right action.

A second difference between deontic and aretaic person-appraisals is that, while both imply propositions about the mental lives of those at whom they are directed, deontic appraisals are connected with propositions about transitory motives, whereas aretaic appraisals imply propositions about settled character traits. That is, although propositions about the motives with which someone performs a specific act can be directly relevant to whether that person is blameworthy or praiseworthy for acting, and while they may provide evidence of the presence of features on which the person's moral goodness depends, they themselves have no direct bearing on that individual's worth as a person. If, for example, some act of mine is motivated by a fleeting desire to harm you, then this fact is relevant to whether I am blame-worthy for acting. It also provides some reason to believe that my character is flawed, and is therefore one bit of indirect evidence that I am a bad person. By itself, however, my acting on such a desire has no *direct* bearing on my overall moral worth. Conversely, facts about a person's character – facts on which the person's overall moral worth depends – are by themselves irrelevant to whether the person is blameworthy or praiseworthy for performing particular actions.[2]

Given how deontic person-appraisals presuppose act-appraisals, the former cannot reasonably be regarded as explanatorily more basic than the latter. In other words, VE almost certainly fails if interpreted as a thesis about the relation between act-appraisals and *deontic* person-appraisals. Now, this is not to suggest that VE proponents have had deontic appraisals in mind in presenting and defending their view. Quite the contrary: those who endorse VE have probably been concerned (at least primarily) with aretaic person-appraisals. All too often, however, the distinction between deontic and aretaic appraisals is completely overlooked by both proponents and opponents of VE, with the result that discussions of VE are sometimes flawed in ways which are easily avoidable.

At any rate, VE will be interpreted here as a view about the relation between act-appraisals on the one hand, and aretaic person-appraisals on the other. Assuming the latter appraisals are somehow connected with propositions about character traits, VE includes a view about the relation between act-appraisals and trait-appraisals. If we adopt the conventional view which equates '(moral) virtue' with '(morally) good character trait', we can interpret VE as the thesis that all act-appraisals are explicable in terms of more basic appraisals of persons or of traits – that the moral status of acts depends entirely on whether they would be performed by morally good persons or are manifestations of virtue. VE's opposite number – the thesis that act-appraisals are explanatorily more basic than person- and trait-appraisals – will be referred to as 'duty ethics' (DE).

## 2.

As VE and DE have been characterised, they are concerned with the relation between moral appraisals of acts on the one hand, and moral appraisals of *persons or of traits* on the other. This tendency to lump person-appraisals together with trait-appraisals not only reflects the way these two types of appraisals are typically treated in the literature, but also helps explain why some writers regard DE as obviously mistaken. For if person- and trait-appraisals are casually grouped together, then the idea that trait-appraisals can somehow *mediate* inferences from act- to person-appraisals is unlikely to be afforded the attention it deserves. And, consequently, DE may well *appear* to imply that a person's overall moral worth depends directly and entirely on how the person acts on particular occasions. Such a result would cast considerable doubt on DE since it seems clear that personal moral worth depends not on *what* acts are performed, but on certain considerations relevant to *why* they are performed.

If there are problems here, however, then they arise not from the proposition that act-appraisals are more basic than person-appraisals, but rather from a failure adequately to explain how person-appraisals differ from trait-appraisals, and how appraisals of these two types are related to each other and to act-appraisals. If trait-appraisals are indeed capable of mediating inferences from act-appraisals to person-appraisals, then one can acknowledge that act-appraisals are more basic than person-appraisals while denying that the overall moral worth of individuals depends in any direct way on what they do. One can claim, in other words, that the overall moral worth of persons depends directly on their possessing good character traits; that the goodness of traits depends on their being suitably related to acts of certain sorts; and that matters of overall personal worth are therefore related only *indirectly* to propositions about the morality of acts. In any case, it is of the utmost importance when attempting to assess VE and DE to separate person- from trait-appraisals, and to explain how these types of appraisals are related to each other.

Two different explanations of this relation spring quickly to mind. It might be claimed, on the one hand, that trait-appraisals are explicable in terms of person-appraisals, or, on the other hand, that the latter appraisals are explicable in terms of the former. Plato evidently subscribes to the first view, since he maintains that good persons are those whose souls are in harmony, and that virtues are traits which manifest or enhance this harmony. In contrast, Hume seems to regard judgments of personal worth as explicable in terms of propositions about virtue (although the latter are not themselves treated as *basic*). Thus, he maintains that a person's worth depends on his having a 'propensity to the tender passions' – which include, among other traits, generosity, compassion and fidelity.[3]

If the moral goodness of traits depends on whether their possession enhances (manifests, etc.) the goodness of those whose traits they are, then – contrary to what many philosophers have accepted as a truism – possessing virtues cannot be a criterion of personal moral worth. And if we do deny that being a good person depends on possessing good traits, then we are faced with the task of producing alternative criteria of personal moral worth, or of demonstrating that there is no need for such criteria.

There is good reason to think that this task is hopeless, and it is not one which very many philosophers have even attempted to accomplish. Various neo-Aristotelian theories may *seem* to provide plausible alternatives to the idea that being morally good depends on possessing virtues, but a close look at such theories reveals that they do not in fact do so. Some elaboration of this remark will be useful.

The neo-Aristotelians referred to above are nicely exemplified by Rosalind Hursthouse, who takes the basic question of ethics to be 'How should/ought/must I live in order to live the best life/flourish/be successful?'[4] She also emphasises that flourishing is not itself a *moral* concept, although being morally good is in some sense *part of* flourishing. People flourish from the moral standpoint when they live according to the moral virtues – where virtues are understood as character traits of a certain sort. But what determines whether some particular trait is a moral virtue?

Hursthouse answers this question by maintaining that morally good traits are (or incorporate) settled inclinations to pursue intrinsically worthwhile ends, and to do so for the 'right reason'. Of course, this idea immediately raises the question of what counts as an intrinsically worthwhile end pursued for the right reason. If this question is answered by appealing to the concept of flourishing, then the theory has come full circle; and yet it is difficult to see what alternative answers are available to Hursthouse. Certainly it would be contrary to the spirit of her view to explain virtue in terms of the notion that there are ends the pursuit of which is required by morality, since such an explanation would implicitly contravene the central neo-Aristotelian presupposition that person- and trait-appraisals are more basic than act-appraisals.

*Perhaps* it is possible to develop a moral theory based on individual flourishing or some other concept of person-appraisal which provides a plausible alternative to the idea that personal moral worth depends on possessing morally good character traits. No such alternative seems available, however; nor is it easy to produce very good reasons for doubting that person-appraisals rest on trait-appraisals.[5]

Indeed, it does not seem at all unreasonable to regard virtues as *by their very nature* traits on whose possession the moral worth of their possessors depends. Accordingly, it will be assumed henceforth that propositions concerning the goodness of traits provide criteria for appraising the moral worth of persons: the moral goodness of persons is determined by the virtues they possess.

The preceding discussion seems to suggest that the traits whose possession determines the moral worth of their possessors are many and varied; but one might well reject such a suggestion by maintaining that there is some single virtue the possession of which is necessary and sufficient for a person to be morally good. That is, one might acknowledge that personal moral worth depends on the possession of morally good traits and go on to claim either (a) that there is only one virtue, or (b) that although there is more than one virtue, whether people are morally good depends entirely on whether they possess some particular virtue (Kantian conscientiousness, say).

Having mentioned (a) as a possible component of an account of virtue, it can be set aside without further ado. Clearly, if there are any morally good character traits at all, then such traits are numerous and diverse; and (certain claims about 'the unity of the virtues' notwithstanding) there is no very good reason to regard these diverse character traits as manifestations or aspects of some single virtue. Position (b) is only marginally more plausible than (a), and is effectively disposed of by arguments advanced by a number of VE philosophers – arguments which need not be repeated here.[6]

Let us say, then, that personal moral worth depends on the possession of good traits, and also that there are many such traits, no one of which is preeminent. We are now confronted with the problem of identifying criteria of *trait*-appraisal – considerations which determine whether traits are morally good and therefore count as moral virtues.

We *might* attempt to solve this problem by embracing DE, according to which trait-appraisals are based on *act*-appraisals. But DE is a correct approach to moral theory only if VE is not; and as yet no reason has been given here for rejecting VE. We also must devote some attention to an account of the relation between trait- and act-appraisals which differs from those of both DE and VE – namely, the idea that whether traits are good is explanatorily unrelated to whether acts are obligatory, right, etc. If either this 'explanatory independence' view (EI) or VE is true, then DE is mistaken; and if DE is mistaken, then our attempt to determine what makes character traits morally good is returned to square one. However, let us now consider some reasons for thinking that neither VE nor EI is correct under the unqualified interpretations given them here.

According to VE, act-appraisals must be based on appraisals of persons or of traits. But since we are assuming that the goodness of persons depends on the goodness of traits, we can interpret VE as implying that act-appraisals are based (ultimately) on *trait*-appraisals. Moreover, the idea that act-appraisals are based on trait-appraisals is open to at least these two distinct interpretations: (i) whether a specific act is (say) morally obligatory depends entirely on whether it manifests specific traits of its agent; or (ii) whether a specific act is obligatory depends on whether it is of a general type which is obligatory, and the obligatoriness of an act-type is explicable in terms of claims about the virtues.

Versions of VE based on (i) are very different from those which accept (ii). Thus, suppose (i) is true. Then, for example, whether I am obligated to keep a particular promise depends on my actually possessing an appropriate virtue – fidelity, presumably. If (ii) is true, however, then although the moral status of a specific act would be *ultimately* explicable by appealing to virtue considerations, no reference need be made to the actual character of the agent of that act. Given (ii), the obligatoriness of my act of promise-keeping would be explained by appealing to the principle that promise-keeping is obligatory (and any other principles of obligation which applied to my act), together with the claim that promise-keeping is obligatory because fidelity is a virtue.[7]

The distinction between versions of VE based on (i) and those based on (ii) closely parallels the distinction between 'act' and 'rule' forms of other ethical theories – between act and rule utilitarianism, act and rule egoism, etc. For this reason, the expressions '*act VE*' and '*rule VE*' will be used to refer to forms of VE which accept (i) and (ii) respectively.[8]

Suppose now that act VE is true, and consider the implications of this supposition for judgments about the obligatoriness of specific acts. According to act VE, a specific act is obligatory just in case it manifests good traits in its agent; and this construal of the obligatoriness of specific acts is surely mistaken. To see this, we need only note that people sometimes incur obligations by performing actions of certain widely varied sorts – by making promises, vandalising property, etc.; and that the existence of these 'special obligations' cannot be explained entirely in terms of references to the character traits of those who are obligated (and can probably be explained without any such references).[9]

Rule VE cannot be disposed of quite so easily, but is seriously problematic in important respects. In this connection, we can consider certain difficulties that arise when rule VE is applied to act-types whose moral status is unclear.

Consider beneficence, for example. Some philosophers are convinced that 'pure' beneficence – improving the relatively good conditions of others (as opposed to preventing others from being harmed, alleviating their suffering, etc.) – is *not* obligatory, and that the moral significance of beneficence should perhaps be explained by appealing in an appropriate way to the concept of supererogation.[10] Other philosophers disagree, maintaining (or at least implying) that even pure beneficence is obligatory. How might we try to resolve this dispute? According to rule VE, we should look to the virtues; and, in this case, we should presumably look to the virtue of benevolence. But even assuming that benevolence is a virtue and that it is related in some way to beneficence, we have no basis at all on which to decide whether pure beneficence is morally obligatory. We clearly have no more basis on which to claim that pure beneficence is *obligatory* because benevolence is a virtue than we have for maintaining that pure beneficence is *supererogatory* because benevolence is a virtue.

Moreover, we appear to be no better off when we attempt to apply rule VE to act-types whose moral status is quite clear. For example, how does rule VE say we should explain the obligatoriness of promise-keeping? We assumed above that, according to rule VE, promise-keeping is obligatory because fidelity is a virtue. But if (as is commonly claimed) making promises confers rights on promisees, then promise-keeping may more appropriately be related to justice than to fidelity. Granted, there is no obvious reason why the obligatoriness of an act-type cannot be explained by appealing to several virtues. But in the case of promise-keeping at least, the order of explanation is from act-type to trait-type rather than vice versa as would be the case if rule VE were true.

It seems fair to say that, by and large, the distinction between act VE and rule VE has been ignored in discussions of virtue ethics. It seems too that, once act and rule VE are separated from each other, good reasons are revealed for rejecting both – and hence for rejecting virtue ethics itself. Let us now turn our attention to EI – to the proposition that trait-appraisals are explanatorily unrelated to act-appraisals.

Some writers interpret virtues as dispositions to perform (or refrain from performing) actions which are determined independently to be right, good, obligatory, etc. If this were a correct interpretation of the nature of virtue, then moral trait-appraisals would be explicable in terms of moral act-appraisals, and EI would be mistaken. However, to equate virtues with dispositions to act is to paint an over-simplified picture of the nature of morally good character traits.

There are morally good traits – or at least components of such traits – which cannot adequately be accommodated by purely dispositional accounts of virtue like those we are considering. The character traits being referred to here comprise a disparate collection, all of which seem clearly to be morally good, but none of which can reasonably be equated with dispositions to perform or to refrain from performing actions of any sort. For example, someone with a settled inclination to view situations from the standpoints of others involved in those situations evidently possesses a morally good character trait. And at least some virtues incorporate beliefs about the worth of others, concern for their welfare, etc. Since such beliefs, inclinations and concerns are not themselves dispositions to perform or refrain from performing any sort of action, EI cannot be jettisoned on the basis of dispositional accounts of virtue like those we have been considering.

But EI implies that trait-appraisals are *entirely* independent of act-appraisals, and in this unqualified form, the view seems clearly to be mistaken. Certainly, the goodness of *some* traits depends on their being (or incorporating) dispositions to do what is obligatory, right, etc. For example, the goodness of honesty arises from its containing a disposition to refrain from lying; and the virtue of justice includes a disposition to treat people according to their rights and deserts. EI cannot accommodate such virtues (call them 'actional virtues'[11]), and therefore does not provide an adequate comprehensive account of what makes traits morally good.

Reasons have now been offered for rejecting both VE and EI – reasons for doubting both that the morality of acts depends solely on their being suitably related to good traits, and that the goodness of traits is entirely independent of the rightness, obligatoriness, etc., of acts. We are therefore returned to DE as a potential account of what makes character traits morally good. As it turns out, however, even if VE and EI are shown to be mistaken, DE is not thereby established as unqualified true.

Recall that, according to DE, the goodness of traits depends *entirely* on their being suitably related to acts of certain sorts; and my discussion of EI indicates one reason why this unqualified version of DE should be rejected. It should be rejected because the goodness of at least some traits does *not* depend on their being related to acts which are obligatory, right, good, etc. Indeed, even the virtues referred to here as 'actional' should not be *identified* with the disposition they incorporate.[12] Thus, for example, while people who possess the virtue of honesty are characteristically disposed to refrain from lying, one lacks the virtue of honesty if his characteristic disinclination to lie arises from a belief that liars are disliked and a desire to be liked by others.

## 3.

According to the account of virtue and personal moral worth which has been presented here, the moral goodness of persons depends on their possessing morally good traits; and the moral goodness of some traits – viz., the actional virtues – depends at least partly on their containing dispositions to perform acts of certain diverse types. The discussion which follows will be concerned exclusively with actional virtues, and will begin with an attempt to answer this question: Of what, in addition to settled dispositions, are the actional virtues composed?

A natural answer to this question consists in the idea that people who possess actional virtues necessarily accept general (and true) principles concerning the rightness, wrongness, obligatoriness, etc., of act-types which correspond appropriately to the various dispositional components of the virtues. For example, corresponding to its contained disposition to refrain from lying, the virtue of honesty apparently includes the belief that lying is wrong; and, associated with the dispositions included in justice, would seem to be beliefs about what rights people have, together with the belief that rights should be respected. Since the beliefs purportedly associated with actional virtues would be aspects of the *characters* of people, they would have to be construed as relatively stable and firmly entrenched states of those people.

The idea, then, is that actional virtues include dispositions to perform acts of certain types, together with appropriate beliefs about the obligatoriness, rightness, etc., of acts of those types (and perhaps other things as well). While this idea may hold true for certain of the actional virtues, however, it seems not to be true of all such virtues. In particular, it seems not to be true of the *other-interested* actional virtues such as kindness, compassion and generosity.

The idea that other-interested virtues need not be associated with beliefs about the obligatoriness or rightness of act-types has been espoused by a number of philosophers, although its proponents do not entirely agree as to how it should be developed. Thus, according to Lester H. Hunt, 'virtue is a trait of character in which one acts on some principle which is true';[13] but Hunt maintains that certain other-interested virtues (generosity in particular) are associated with 'axiological principles', while other virtues are related either to 'act-necessitating principles' or to 'limiting principles'. Whereas act-necessitating principles 'enjoin actions'[14] and a limiting principle limits 'the importance of some end of action',[15] axiological principles 'commit the agent to seek certain goods'.[16] When the virtues governed by axiological principles are *other-interested* in nature, they carry with them the idea that 'the good of others is important or worthwhile'.[17]

James D. Wallace offers a somewhat different version of the idea that other-interested virtues need not be associated with beliefs about the rightness, wrongness, etc., of act-types. Wallace distinguishes virtues which are 'forms of conscientiousness' from those which are 'forms of benevolence'.[18] He explains this distinction by stating that 'Actions fully characteristic of virtues that are forms of conscientiousness are the sort that moral philosophers regard as manifesting a sense of duty or obligation';[19] whereas virtues that are forms of benevolence manifest not a sense of duty, but rather 'a direct concern for the happiness and well-being of others'.[20]

Hunt and Wallace seem right in suggesting that other-interested virtues need not incorporate normative moral beliefs, and in emphasising that such virtues include valuing the good of others. Moreover, there is considerable plausibility in Wallace's opinion that other-interested virtues *cannot* incorporate normative moral beliefs – that people who perform other-interested acts from a sense of duty are not manifesting any other-interested virtue. These views can be taken a step further, however, so that they not only allow other-interested virtues to be unrelated to beliefs about moral rightness or wrongness, but also imply that other-interested virtues need not incorporate any *moral* beliefs at all. The suggestion is that, while other-interested virtues contain beliefs about the value of promoting or protecting the good of others, these beliefs can concern *non-moral* value.

The view being proposed here arises in large part from a consideration of cases like Jonathan Bennett's well-known Huck Finn example.[21] As Bennett characterises the case, Huck helps his slave friend Jim escape even though Huck's moral beliefs require him *not* to assist Jim in any way. He renders assistance not because of what his moral beliefs dictate, but rather out of feelings of friendship and sympathy for Jim. Assuming that Huck has a settled disposition to act on such feelings, and that the feelings themselves are components of his character, it seems reasonable to infer that he possesses an other-interested actional virtue. And if we accept this conclusion, we must deny that, over and above dispositions to perform certain types of acts, other-interested virtues must also contain beliefs that these act-types are morally right, good, etc.

To be sure, one might insist that people who behave as Huck does in similar circumstances actually do manifest firmly held (even if inchoate and deeply buried) beliefs about the morality of helping friends in distress. The idea would be that such people choose not between feelings of sympathy on the one hand and moral principles on the other, but between moral beliefs held in two very different ways, or at two very different levels. But even if this is a possible characterisation of situations like Huck's, there is no reason to accept it as the *only* possible characterisation. It is worth emphasising too that the purpose for which Bennett's example is being used here almost certainly differs from his. That is, we are *not* concerned with whether moral beliefs can conflict with sympathetic *feelings*, or with how such conflicts should be resolved if they do occur. It is merely being suggested that Bennett's example serves to illustrate how people manifest morally good character traits in performing other-interested acts without being moved to act by moral beliefs of any sort. The idea, then, is that other-interested actional virtues contain settled dispositions to perform acts of certain types, together with general (and perhaps non-moral) evaluative beliefs.

We now have a partial account of where aretaic person-appraisals fit into moral theory: they are explicable in terms of trait-appraisals in the sense that one's overall moral worth depends on possessing morally good character traits; and trait-appraisals of at least one important sort (viz., those concerned with actional virtues) are grounded in act-appraisals. According to this account, DE holds for the actional virtues (i.e., for character traits whose moral value depends partly on their relation to acts of certain kinds) – although it gives only a partial explanation of these virtues. In other words, DE is true, but only under the following qualified interpretation: the goodness of some (*but not all*) traits depends partly (*and only partly*) on their containing dispositions to perform acts which are right, good, etc. DE is rather less interesting with these qualifications than without them; but if it is correct even in this qualified form, then VE is seriously mistaken in its view of the respective roles of act-appraisal and of person-appraisal in moral theory.

## ENDNOTES

1. See, for example, G. E. M. Anscombe, 'Modern Moral Philosophy', *Philosophy*, Vol. 33 (1958), 1–19; Michael Stocker, 'The Schizophrenia of Modern Ethical Theories', *The Journal of Philosophy*, Vol. 14 (1976), 453–66; Bernard Williams, *Ethics and the Limits of Philosophy*, Cambridge: Harvard University Press (1985), passim; Richard Taylor, 'Ancient Wisdom and Modern Folly', in Peter A. French, Theodore E. Uehling and Howard K. Wettstein (eds), *Midwest Studies in Philosophy*, Vol. XIII, *Ethical Theory: Character and Virtue*, Notre Dame: University of Notre Dame Press (1988), 54–63; and Alasdair MacIntyre, *After Virtue*, 2nd edn, Notre Dame, Indiana: Notre Dame University Press (1984).
2. A certain connection is here being assumed between one's overall moral worth and the state of one's character. This assumption will be examined below.
3. David Hume, *A Treatise of Human Nature*, L. A. Selby-Bigge (ed.), Oxford: The Clarendon Press (1960), 603f.
4. Rosalind Hursthouse, *Beginning Lives*, Oxford: Basil Blackwell (1987), Chapter 6.
5. The account developed by Alasdair MacIntyre in *After Virtue* (loc. cit.) is also a neo-Aristotelian version of VE, and suffers from some of the same infirmities as do other forms of neo-Aristotelianism. In particular, MacIntyre's account (like Hursthouse's) raises the question of how to develop a genuinely *moral* theory from claims that are non-moral in character – a problem which, in MacIntyre's case, consists in basing morality on the notion of the narrative unity of a life (203, 218f.). It is worth emphasising that the point here has nothing to do with whether an 'is' (or a 'fact') can be derived from an 'ought' (or a 'value') – a question which MacIntyre answers affirmatively (58f.). Even if MacIntyre's answer is correct, he needs to show that the kind of value derivable from factual claims about narrative unity is *moral* value. And this he does not do.

    MacIntyre's account will not be examined at any length here because, rather than attempting to explain central components of existing morality in terms of the concepts of personal worth and of virtue, he recommends replacing existing morality with a certain kind of ethics of virtue. As was indicated at the outset of this discussion, such replacement views are not being considered.
6. See Stocker, loc. cit.; and N. J. H. Dent, *The Moral Psychology of the Virtues*, Cambridge: Cambridge University Press (1984), 27f.
7. Stocker's account (loc. cit.) seems clearly to focus on (i), while Hursthouse (loc. cit.) argues for an instance of (ii).

    An account which does not fit neatly into either category is developed by Edmund L. Pincoffs in *Quandaries and Virtues*, Lawrence, Kansas: University of Kansas Press (1986). In some places (on p. 102, for example) Pincoffs suggests that the moral status of an act depends on whether it is performed with motives reflective of virtues in its agent – a claim which corresponds to (i). But in defending a form of perfectionism, Pincoffs seems to espouse (ii). For example, he maintains that 'it is a necessary and sufficient condition of the moral acceptability of an action or a course of action that it not violate the requirements of the relevant set of virtue considerations' (103). The precise nature of Pincoffs' position is difficult to determine, and he might very well not vacillate between (i) and (ii) as has been suggested. It does seem in any case, however, that his view would be clearer if it were formulated with the distinction between (i) and (ii) in mind.
8. For example, just as rule utilitarians commonly regard the actual consequences of specific acts as irrelevant to the morality of those acts, so a proponent of rule VE might maintain that the actual possession of virtues by particular individuals has no bearing on the morality of specific acts performed by those individuals.
9. Even Pincoffs might agree with this claim, but then go on to insist that the *moral acceptability* of an act depends entirely on the motives with which it is performed. On his view it seems possible for an act to be both morally obligatory and morally unacceptable (or morally

prohibited and morally acceptable) – an idea that is puzzling enough to require much more in the way of supporting arguments than Pincoffs provides.

10. See Joel Feinberg's discussion in Chapter IV of *Harm to Others*, New York: Oxford University Press (1984); and also Phillip Montague, 'Acts, Agents, and Supererogation', *American Philosophical Quarterly*, Vol. 26 (1989), 101–12.

11. This expression is borrowed from Gregory Trianosky. See his 'Virtue, Action, and the Good Life: Toward a Theory of the Virtues', *Pacific Philosophical Quarterly*, Vol. 68 (1987), 124–47.

12. One way in which the idea that actional virtues are more than mere dispositions might be justified would be by way of a general view of the nature of character traits – a view which denies that *any* character traits are equivalent to dispositions. (In this connection, see Lester H. Hunt, 'Character and Thought', *American Philosophical Quarterly*, Vol. 15 (1978), 177–90.

13. Lester H. Hunt, 'Generosity and the Diversity of the Virtues', in Robert B. Kruschwitz and Robert C. Roberts (eds), *The Virtues*, Belmont: Wadsworth Publishing Co. (1987), 227.

14. Ibid., 220.

15. Ibid., 226.

16. Ibid., 226.

17. Ibid., 224.

18. James D. Wallace, *Virtues and Vices*, Ithaca: Cornell University Press (1978), Chapters IV, V.

19. Ibid., 90–1.

20. Ibid., 128.

21. Jonathan Bennett, 'The Conscience of Huckleberry Finn', *Philosophy*, Vol. 49 (1974), 123–34.

# CORPORATE ROLES, PERSONAL VIRTUES: AN ARISTOTELIAN APPROACH TO BUSINESS ETHICS

## *Robert C. Solomon*

Each of us is ultimately lonely. In the end, it's up to each of us and each of us alone to figure out who we are and who we are not, and to act more or less consistently on those conclusions.
       Tom Peters, 'The Ethical Debate', *Ethics Digest*, December 1989, 2.

We are gratefully past that embarrassing period when the very title of a lecture on 'business ethics' invited – no, required – those malapert responses, 'sounds like an oxymoron' or 'must be a very short lecture'. Today, business ethics is well-established not only in the standard curriculum in philosophy in most departments but, more impressively, it is recommended or required in most of the leading business schools in North America, and it is even catching on in Europe (one of the too rare instances of intellectual commerce in that direction). Studies in business ethics have now reached what Tom Donaldson has called 'the third wave', beyond the hurried-together and overly-philosophical introductory textbooks and collections of too-obvious concrete case studies, too serious engagement in the business world. Conferences filled half-and-half with business executives and academics are common, and in-depth studies based on immersion in the corporate world, e.g. Robert Jackall's powerful *Moral Mazes*, have replaced more simple-minded and detached glosses on 'capitalism' and 'social responsibility'. Business ethics has moved beyond vulgar 'business as poker' arguments to an arena where serious ethical theory is no longer out of place but seriously sought out and much in demand.

The problem with business ethics now is not vulgar ignorance but a far more sophisticated confusion concerning exactly what the subject is supposed to do and how (to employ a much overworked contrast) the theory applies to the practice of business. Indeed, a large part of the problem is that it is by no means clear what a theory in business ethics is supposed to look like or whether there is, as such, any such theoretical enterprise. It has been standard practice in many business ethics courses and – whether cause or effect – most standard textbooks, to begin with a survey of ethical theory. This means, inevitably, a brief summary of Kant and deontological ethics, a brief survey of utilitarianism with a note or two about John Stuart Mill and a distinction or two between act and rule, pleasure versus preference utilitarianism and some replay of the much-rehearsed contest between the two sorts of theories. Given the business context, libertarianism or some form of contractualism is often included as a third contender. 'Justice' is a natural introductory section, and John Locke on natural property rights is an appropriate inclusion too. But is this the theory of business ethics? Not only is the application to concrete business situations in question – and then the message to students is too often an unabashed relativism ('if you are a utilitarian, you'll do this, if you're a Kantian, you'll do that') – but it is not even clear whether there is, then, anything distinctive about *business* ethics. There is just ethics, or rather ethical theory, whatever that may be. Indeed, one is almost tempted to retreat to the tongue-in-cheek advice of Robert Townsend, former CEO of Avis and author of *Up the Organization,* that if a company needs a corporate code of ethics, it should tack up the Ten Commandments. And so with its success assured, at least for the time being, business ethics faces both a crisis of theory and a pragmatic challenge, that is, what is to count as a theory in business ethics and how that theory applies and can be used by flesh-and-blood managers in concrete, real life ethically-charged situations.

One possibility, of course, is that the theory of business ethics is really the philosophy of economics, that is, economics as ethics, social-political philosophy with an emphasis on economic justice. Thus the theoretical questions of business ethics are those raised by John Rawls in his *Theory of Justice* in 1971 and by his colleague Robert Nozick in *Anarchy, State and Utopia* in 1974. The questions of business ethics are those posed repeatedly by Amartya Sen and Jon Elster in their various books and articles and in a more informal way by John Kenneth Galbraith and Lester Thurow in the pages of the *New York Review.* This, of course, is rich and promising territory. The theories are well developed and, though they may take Kant, Locke and Mill as their precursors, they raise concerns that are particular to economic concerns and ask, with regard to the system as a whole as well as particular practices within it, whether the free-market is indeed a just and fair mechanism for the distribution of goods in a grossly inegalitarian world. The theories here are well-developed and impressively formalised – in the sophisticated techniques of game theory, social choice theory and all of those other accoutrements that make theories look like *theory,* in other words, adequate for publication in the most serious professional journals and conducive to a positive tenure decision.

Such theorising is, however, utterly inaccessible to the people for whom we supposedly do business ethics, our students and the executives and corporations we talk to and write for. Here, especially, the pragmatic problem comes back to haunt us; how do these grand theories of property rights and distribution mechanisms, these visionary pronouncements on the current economy apply to people on the job? Of course, one could argue that this is the case in any science – and not just in the sciences either.

The hard part of any academic teaching is taking very sophisticated theoretical material and 'watering it down' for the hoi poloi, or more modestly, making it intelligible in not overly over-simplified terminology. But quite apart from the offensive patronizing presumed by this view – especially in the so-called liberal arts, it is inadequate for a more theoretical reason as well. The grand theories of the philosophy of economics, however intriguing they may be in their own right, are not adequate for business ethics, and for many of the same reasons that the classic theories of Kant, Locke and Mill are inadequate. The theories themselves are incomplete, oblivious to the concrete business context and indifferent to the very particular roles that people play in business. Their inaccessibility and/or inapplicability to the ordinary manager in the office or on the shop floor is not just a pragmatic problem but a failure of theory as well. At any rate, that is what I would like to argue here. Business ethicists (like some country folk singers) have been looking for theory in the wrong place and, consequently, they have been finding and developing the wrong theories.

## THE ARISTOTELIAN APPROACH TO BUSINESS ETHICS

Economists and economic theorists naturally tend to look at systems and theories about systems, while ethicists tend to look at individual behaviour, its motives and consequences. Neither of these approaches is suitable for business ethics. One of the problems in business ethics, accordingly, is the *scope* and *focus* of the disciplines and the proper *unit* of study and discourse. Much of the work in business ethics courses and seminars centers around 'case studies', which almost always involve one or several particular people within the realm of a particular corporation in a particular industry facing some particular crisis or dilemma. Individual ethical values are, of course, relevant here, but they are rarely the focus of attention. Economics, of course, is essential to the discussion – since the realm of the corporation is, after all, a business, but the desire to show a profit is virtually taken for granted while our attention is drawn to other values. Insofar as business ethics theories tend to be drawn from either individualistic ethics or economics they remain remote from the case study method which often seems so inadequate with regard to more general implications and conclusions in business and is the reason why business ethics theory lags so far behind theory in both ethics and economics. In this chapter, I want to begin to develop a more appropriate focus for business ethics theory, one that centres on *the individual within the corporation*. For reasons that should be evident to anyone who has had the standard Philosophy 102 History of Ethics course, I call this the Aristotelian Approach to Business Ethics.

In a book *It's Good Business*, I once distinguished between macro-, micro- and molar-ethics, and within this limited dichotomy it should be evident that I am going to argue for the neglected importance of micro-business ethics – the concepts and values that define individual responsibilities and role behaviour as opposed to the already well-developed theories of macro-business ethics – the principles and policies that govern or should govern our overall system of (re-)distribution and reward. (In ethics as such, one might argue, the neglect has taken the opposite twist, ignoring the larger social anthropological setting in favour of individual autonomy, rights and wellbeing.) The distinction between micro and macro is borrowed from and intended to be parallel to a similar dichotomy in economics. (I have elsewhere argued that economics is a branch of ethics, but that is another story.[1]) That distinction, however, is left over from the ancient days of Lord Keynes and is also inadequate. The integral or 'molar' unit of commerce today is neither the individual entrepreneur or consumer nor the all-embracing system that still goes by the antiquated nineteenth-century name 'capitalism'. It is the *corporation*, a type of entity mentioned by Adam Smith in a few dismissive sentences (and of minimal interest even to Keynes). While I will continue to hold that the existential unit of responsibility and concern is and remains the individual, the individual in today's business world does not operate in a social vacuum. He or she is more likely than not an employee – whether in the stockroom or as Chief Financial Officer – and our basic unit of understanding has to be the company whose perceived primary purpose is 'to make money'. Theory in business ethics thus becomes the theory – that is, description and contemplation about – individuals in (and out) of business roles as well as the role of business and businesses in society. People in business are ultimately responsible as individuals, but they are responsible as individuals in a corporate setting where their responsibilities are at least in part defined by their roles and duties in the company and, of course, by 'the bottom line'. Businesses in turn are defined by their role(s) and responsibilities in the larger community, where the bottom line is only an internal concern (if the business is to stay in business and the shareholders are to hold onto their shares) but for everyone else may be a minimal consideration.

A different way of putting this central point is to point out that much of business ethics today focuses on questions of *policy* – those large questions about government regulation and the propriety of government intervention, e.g. in failing industries and affirmative action programmes, and in very general business practices and problems, e.g. pollution control, opacity and lying in advertising, employee due process and the social responsibilities of companies to their surrounding communities. All of this, of course, is perfectly proper for philosophers and other social observers who have the luxury of standing outside the pressures of the business world to survey the larger scenery, and I am not for a minute suggesting that we abandon our interest in policy questions in favour of an atomistic and perhaps narcissistic concern for person integrity. But I do think that we have employed policy talk as an exclusionary practice in our effort to provide impersonal solutions to large and seemingly impersonal questions. To this end, traditional theories of ethics – especially Kantian deontology and utilitarianism have been called in to support one or another concern beyond or contrary to the bottom line. (Where business profits and public policy agree, of course, there's not much call for debate.[2]) But what gets left out of these well-plumbed studies and arguments is an adequate sense of *personal* values and involvement. Too much of our emphasis in our courses on business ethics is on policy disputes and the grand theories that support one position or another. But the practical problem with such policy disputes is that few people in the business world and even fewer of our students have any real sense of what to do with them, except to argue about them and, perhaps, become aware of the possibility that they may well become the victims of one policy or another. The Chairman of the Board may have a very real and tangible interest in discussing and resolving policy issues, and so too the members of this or that governmental commission. But policy disputes don't have very much to say to the ordinary manager, or for that matter, the ordinary executive, much less the ordinary business student. What is missing from much of business ethics is an adequate account of the *personal* dimension in ethics. Accordingly, I want to defend business ethics as a more personally oriented ethics, not just as public policy, 'applied' abstract philosophy or a byproduct of the social sciences. But business ethics so conceived is not 'personal' in the sense of 'private' or 'subjective'; it is rather self-awareness writ large, a sense of oneself as an intimate (but not inseparable) part of the business world with a keen sense of the virtues and values of that world. This is an ethics that involves not personal values as such but rather one's values as a member of a possibly humongous organisation to which one has pledged one's loyalty and in which one's honour as well as one's potential for success is at stake. It is an Aristotelian ethics precisely because it is membership in a community, a community with collective goals and a stated mission – to produce quality goods and/or services and make a profit for the stockholders.

Aristotle is the philosopher who is best known for this emphasis on the cultivation of the virtues. But isn't it inappropriate if not perverse to couple Aristotle and business ethics? True, he was the first economist. He had much to say about the ethics of exchange and so might well be called the first (known) business ethicist as well. But Aristotle distinguished two different senses of what I call economics, one of them '*oecinomicus*' or household trading, which he approved of and thought essential to the working of any even modestly complex society, and '*chrematisike*', which is trade for profit. Aristotle declared that latter activity wholly devoid of virtue and called those who engaged in such purely selfish practices 'parasites'. All trade, he believed, was a kind of exploitation. Such was his view of what I call 'business'. Indeed, Aristotle's attack on the unsavoury and unproductive practice of 'usury' and the personal vice of avarice held force virtually until the seventeenth century. Only outsiders at the fringe of society, not respectable citizens, engaged in such practices. (Shakespeare's Shylock, in *The Merchant of Venice*, was such an outsider and a usurer, though his idea of a forfeit was a bit unusual.) It can be argued that Aristotle had too little sense of the importance of production and based his views wholly on the aristocratically proper urge for acquisition, thus introducing an unwarranted zero-aim thinking into his economics.[3] And, of course, it can be charged that Aristotle, like his teacher Plato, was too much the spokesman for the aristocratic class and quite unfair to the commerce and livelihoods of foreigners and commoners.[4] It is Aristotle who initiates so much of the history of business ethics as the wholesale attack on business and its practices. Aristotelian prejudices underlie much of business criticism and the contempt for finance that preoccupies so much of Christian ethics even to this day, avaricious evangelicals notwithstanding. Even defenders of business often end up presupposing Aristotelian prejudices in such Pyrrhonian arguments as 'business is akin to poker and apart from the ethics of everyday life'[5] (Alfred Carr) and 'the [only] social responsibility of business is to increase its profits' (Milton Friedman).[6] But if it is just this schism between business and the rest of life that so infuriated Aristotle, for whom life was supposed to fit together in a coherent whole, it is the same holistic idea – that business people and corporations are first of all part of a larger community, that derives business ethics today. I can no longer accept the amoral idea that 'business is business' (not a tautology but an excuse for insensitivity). According to Aristotle, one has to think of oneself as a member of the larger community, the *Polis*, and strive to excel, to bring out what was best in ourselves and our shared enterprise. What is best in us – our virtues – are in turn defined by that larger community, and there is therefore no ultimate split of antagonism between individual self-interest and the greater public good. Of course, there were no corporations in those days, but Aristotle would certainly know what I mean when I say that most people in business now identify themselves – if tenuously – in terms of their companies, and corporate policies, much less corporate codes of ethics, are not by themselves enough to constitute an ethics. But corporations are not isolated city-states, not even the biggest and most powerful of the multi-nationals (contrast the image of 'the sovereign state of ITT'). They are part and parcel of a larger global community. The people that work for them are thus citizens of two communities at once, and one might think of business ethics as getting straight about that dual citizenship. What I need to cultivate is a certain way of thinking about ourselves in and out of the corporate contest and this is the aim of ethical theory in business, as I understand it. It is not, I insist, anti-individualistic in any sense of 'individualism' that is worth defending. The Aristotelian approach to business ethics rather begins with the idea that it is individual virtue and integrity that counts: good corporate and social policy will follow: good corporate and social policy are both the preconditions and the result of careful cultivation and encouragement.

With what is this Aristotelian approach to be contrasted? First of all, I want to contrast it with the emphasis on public policy that has preoccupied our subject. In Texas, to take one provincial example, the business school can't quite give itself over to the idea of a business ethics course, and my own business ethics course in philosophy was (until this year) cross listed with the management department as a public and social policy course. There is nothing wrong with policy studies, of course, and I don't for a moment suggest that they be replaced or discarded. But policy decisions aren't usually made by folks like us. We rarely even get to vote or speak for them. For the ordinary line manager, or even most executives, policy questions are, for the most part, something to debate over lunch, usually by way of reaction to some *fait accompli*. And there is something missing from policy decisions that is absolutely central to ethics on virtually any account, and that is, personal responsibility. The ethical problems that the average manager faces on the job are personnel and routine administrative decision-making problems, not policy problems. Some of those problems have to do with temptations – in attractive competing offer, a convenient kick-back, personal relationship or prejudice against an employee. Some have to do with conflicts of duties, mixed messages, crossed loyalties. Business ethics begins, for most of us, in some conflict of roles within an organisation, implementing policies or decisions not of our own making and often against our better judgment. Whatever else business ethics may involve and however sophisticated its theories may become, it means knowing that even such decisions (and their consequences) are nevertheless one's own to live with. Ethics is not just a subject for executive boards, planning committees and government overseers but for all of us, in the details as well as the larger dramas of our everyday lives.

The Aristotelian approach is also to be contrasted with that two-hundred-or-so-year-old obsession in ethics that takes everything of significance to be a matter of *rational principles*, 'morality' as the strict Kantian sense of duty in the moral law. This is not to say, of course, that Aristotelian ethics dispenses with rationality, or for that matter with principles or the notion of duty. But Aristotle is quite clear about the fact that it is cultivation of character that counts, long before we begin to 'rationalise' our actions, and the formulation of general principles (in what he famously but confusingly calls his 'practical syllogism') is not an explicit step in correct and virtuous behaviour as such but rather a philosopher's formulation about what it means to act rationally.[7] And, most important for our purposes here, duties too are defined by our roles in a community, e.g. a corporation, and not by means of any abstract ratiocination, principle of contradiction or *a priori* formulations of the categorical imperative. Kant, magnificent as he was a thinker, has proved to be a kind of disease in ethics. It's all very elegant, even brilliant, until one walks into the seminar room with a dozen or so bright, restless corporate managers, waiting to hear what's new and what's relevant to them on the business ethics scene. And then we tell them: don't lie, don't steal, don't cheat – elaborated and supported by the most gothic non-econometric construction ever allowed in a company training centre. But it's not just its impracticality and the fact that we don't actually do ethics that way; the problem is that the Kantian approach shifts our attention away from just what I would call the 'inspirational' matters of business ethics (its 'incentives') and the emphasis on 'excellence' (a buzz-word for Aristotle as well as Tom Peters and his millions of readers). It shifts the critical focus from oneself as a full-blooded person occupying a significant role in a productive organisation to an abstract role-transcendent morality that necessarily finds itself half empty-handed when it comes to most of the matters and many of the motives that we hear so much about in any corporate setting.

The Aristotelian approach is also to be contrasted with that rival ethical theory that goes by the name of 'utilitarianism'. I have considerably more to say about utilitarianism, its continued vulgarisation and its forgotten humanistic focus in John Stuart Mill, but not here. For now, I just want to point out that utilitarianism shares with Kant that special appeal to anal compulsives in its doting over principles and rationalisation (in crass calculation) and its neglect of individual responsibility and the cultivation of character. (John Stuart Mill exempted himself from much of this charge in the last chapter of *Utilitarianism*, but I promised not to talk about that here.) But I can imagine a good existentialist complaining quite rightly that the point of all such 'decision procedures' in ethics is precisely to neutralise the annoyance of personal responsibility altogether, appealing every decision to 'the procedure' rather than taking responsibility oneself, Of course, I am not denying the importance of concern for the public good or the centrality of worrying, in any major policy decision, about the number of people helped and hurt. But I take very seriously the problems of meas-urement and incommensurability that have been standard criticisms of utilitarianism ever since Bentham, and there are considerations that often are more basic than public utility – if only because, in most of our actions, the impact on public utility is so small in contrast to the significance for our personal sense of integrity and 'doing the right thing' that it becomes a negligible factor in our deliberations.

I would also distinguish the Aristotelian approach to business ethics from all of those approaches that primarily emphasise rights, whether the rights of free enterprise as such, the rights of the employee, the customer or the community and even civil rights. Again, I have no wish to deny the relevance of rights to ethics or the centrality of civil rights, but I think that we should remind ourselves that talk about rights was never intended to eclipse talk about responsibilities and I think the emphasis in business ethics should move from *having* rights oneself to *recognising* the rights of others, but then, I'm not at all sure that all of this couldn't just as well or better be expressed by saying that there are all sorts of things that a virtuous person should or shouldn't ever do to others.[8] Of course, Aristotle's defence of slavery in his *Politics* should be more than enough to convince us that we would still need the language of rights even with a fully-developed language of the virtues. The problem with virtue ethics is that it tends to be provincial and ethnocentric. It thereby requires the language of rights and some general sense of utility as a corrective.

It will be evident to most of you that I am arguing – or about to argue – for a version of what has recently been called 'virtue ethics', but I do want to distance myself from much of what has been defended recently under that title. First of all, I want to reject those versions of ethics that view the virtus as no more than particular instantiations of the abstract principles of morality. This is an analysis that has been argued at some length, for instance, by William Frankena and Kurt Baier, both distinguished defenders of 'the moral point of view'.[9] But if, for example, being an honest man or woman is nothing other than obeying the general Kantian-type principle 'do not lie', if being respectful is a conscientious application of the 'ends' formulation of the categorical imperative (not even Kant held this), if one's sense of public service is an expression of the utilitarian principle, then it is emphatically not what I have in mind, nor did Aristotle. To be witty or magnificent (two Aristotelian virtues not taken seriously enough by our contemporaries) is surely not to express or apply certain principles, but neither is courage, temperance, nor even justice (contrary to Rawls and many of our finest social thinkers today). To imagine our good existentialist here again, one can hear him saying, presumably in French, that one's personal judgments precede rather than follow one's abstract ethical pronouncements. Of course, this isn't exactly Aristotelian (Aristotle was no existentialist), but modified it makes a good Aristotelian point: choice and character get cultivated first, philosophical ethics – if one is lucky enough to study in the right academy – afterwards. Theory in business ethics consists in part of just such reflection on the cultivation of the right virtues and their nature.

I also want to distance myself from some of the now-familiar features of what is being defended as virtue ethics, in particular the rather dangerous nostalgia for 'tradition' and 'community' that is expressed by Alasdair MacIntyre and Charles Taylor among others.[10] Of course, the Aristotelian approach does presuppose something of sense of community that I particularly want to emphasise. But there is a difference between the more or less singular, seemingly homogeneous, autonomous (and very élite) community that Aristotle simply took for granted and the nostalgic (I think purely imaginary) communities described or alluded to by recent virtue ethicists, often defined by a naive religious solidarity and unrealistic expectation of communal consensus. No adequate theory of ethics today can ignore or wish away the pluralistic and culturally diverse populations that make up almost every actual community. Even the smallest corporation will be rent by professional and role-related differences as well as divided by cultural and personal distinctions. Corporate cultures like the larger culture(s) are defined by their differences and disagreements as well as by any shared purpose or outside antagonist or competition, and no defence of the concept of corporate culture can or should forget that corporations are always part of a larger culture and not whole cultures themselves. And yet, in place of the abstract nostalgia that defines much of the current fascination with 'communities', many modern corporations would seem to represent just such a community. They enjoy a shared sense of *telos* as many communities do not. They invoke an extraordinary, almost military emphasis on loyalty and, despite the competitive rhetoric, they first of all inspire and require team-work and cooperation. Corporations are real communities, neither ideal nor idealised, and therefore the perfect place to start understanding the nature of the virtues.

There has been some suggestion in the literature that virtue ethics is a more 'feminine' ethics than Kantian or utilitarian rule-bound ethics. I disagree. I thus want to distance myself from some recent feminist writings – including the work of one of my own best students – who have drawn a sharp contrast between the good, warm, feminine virtues of caring and concern and the oppressive, impersonal, war-mongering masculine principles of justice and duty.[11] I certainly agree with the shift in emphasis, from Kantian justice to compassion and caring, but it is not my intention to supply one more weapon in the perennial war between the sexes, and it seems to me that Aristotle – certainly no feminist – has much to say about the virtues that has little or nothing to do with the (admittedly not unimportant) fact that one is a male or female. It may be, as some writers have recently argued, that the increasing numbers of women in significant executive positions will change the dominant ethic of corporate America. I do not yet see much evidence of this promising proposition, but I think the importance of emphasising the virtues (including the so-called 'feminine' virtues) should not be held captive to gender distinctions.

## THE SIX DIMENSIONS OF VIRTUE ETHICS

So what defines the Aristotelian approach to business ethics? What are its primary dimensions? There is a great deal of ground to be covered, from the general philosophical questions 'what is a virtue?' and 'what is the role of the virtues in ethics and the good life?' to quite specific questions about virtues and supposed virtues in business, such as loyalty, dependability, integrity, shrewdness and 'toughness'. But I can only begin to answer these general questions or speak much of these particular virtues here; however, what I want to do first is very briefly to circumscribe the discussion of the virtues in business ethics with a few considerations not usually so highlighted in the more abstract and principle-bound discussions of ethics nor so personalised in the policy discussions that so dominate the field. These considerations make up the framework of virtue ethics in business, and for the sake of brevity I simply call them *community, excellence, role identity, holism, integrity, judgment.*

## Community

The Aristotelian approach and, I would argue, the leading question for business in the 1990s begins with the idea that the corporation is first of all a community. We are all individuals, to be sure, but we find our identities and our meanings only within communities, and for most of us that means at work in a company or an institution. The philosophical myth that has grown almost cancerous in many business circles, the neo-Hobbesian view that 'it's every man[sic] for himself' and the newer Darwinian view that 'it's all a jungle out there' are direct denials of the Aristotelian view that we are all *first of all* members of a community and our self-interest is for the most part identical to the larger interests of the group. Our individuality is socially constituted and socially situated. Furthermore, our seemingly all-important concept of competition presumes, it does not replace, an underlying assumption of mutual interest and cooperation. Whether we do well, whether we like ourselves, whether we lead happy productive lives, depends to a large extent on the companies we choose. As the Greeks used to say, 'to live the good life one must live in a great city'. To my business students today, who are all too prone to choose a job on the basis of salary and start-up bonus alone, I always say, 'to live a decent life choose the right company'. In business ethics the corporation is one's community, which is not to deny, of course, that there is always a larger community – as diverse as it may be – that counts even more.

## Excellence

The Greek *'arete'* is often translated as either 'virtue' or 'excellence', as opposed to the rather modest and self-effacing notion of 'virtue' that we inherited from our Victorian ancestors (indeed, even Kant used the term). The dual translation by itself makes a striking point. It is not enough to do no wrong. 'Knowingly do no harm' (*Primus non nocere*) is *not* the end of business ethics (as Peter Drucker suggests[12]). The hardly original slogan I sometimes use to sell what I do, 'ethics and excellence', is not just a tag-along with Peters and Waterman. Virtue is doing one's best, excelling, and not merely 'toeing the line' and 'keeping one's nose clean'. The virtues that constitute business ethics should not be conceived as purely ethical or moral virtues, as if (to come again) business ethics were nothing other than the general application of moral principles to one specific context (among others). Being a 'tough negotiator' is a virtue in business but not in babysitting. It does not follow, however, that the virtues of business are therefore opposed to the ordinary virtues of civilised life – as Alfred Carr famously argued in his *Harvard Business Review* polemic of several years ago. The virtues of business ethics are business virtues but they are nonetheless virtues, and the exercise of these virtues is aimed at both 'the bottom line' and ethics.

### *Role Identity*

Much has been written, for example, by Norman Bowie in his good little book *Business Ethics*, on the importance of 'role morality' and 'My Position and its Duties'.[13] It is the situatedness of corporate roles that lends them their particular ethical poignancy, the fact that an employee or an executive is not just a person who happens to be in a place and is constrained by no more than the usual ethical prohibitions. To work for a company is to accept a set of particular obligations, to assume a *prima facie* loyalty to one's employer, to adopt a certain standard of excellence and conscientiousness that is largely defined by the job itself. There may be general ethical rules and guidelines that cut across most positions but as these get more general and more broadly applicable they also become all but useless in concrete ethical dilemmas. Robert Townsend's cute comment that 'if a company needs an ethical code, use the Ten Commandments' is thus not only irreverent but irrelevant too.[14] The Aristotelian approach to business ethics presumes concrete situations and particular people and their place in organisations. There is little point to an ethics that tries to transcend all such particularities and embrace the chairman of the board as well as a middle manager, a secretary and a factory worker. All ethics is contextual, and one of the problems with all of those grand theories is that they try to transcend context and end up with vacuity. The problem, of course, is that people in business inevitably play several roles ('wear several hats') at once, and these roles may clash with one another as they may clash with more personal roles based on family, friendship and personal obligation. This, I will argue, is the pervasive problem in micro-business ethics, and it is the legitimacy of roles and their responsibilities, and the structures of the corporation that defines those roles and their responsibilities, that ought to occupy a good deal more of our time and attention.

### *Integrity*

Integrity, accordingly, is the key to Aristotelian ethics, not, perhaps, as a virtue as such but rather as the linchpin of all of the virtues, the key to their unity or, in conflict and disunity, an anchor against personal disintegration. 'Integrity' is a word, like 'honor' – its close kin – that sometimes seems all but archaic in the modern business world. To all too many business executives, it suggests stubbornness and inflexibility, a refusal to be a 'team player'. But integrity seems to have at least two divergent meanings, one of them encouraging conformity, the other urging a belligerent independence.[15] Both of these are extreme and potentially dangerous. The very word suggests 'wholeness', but insofar as one's identity is not that of an isolated atom but rather the product of a larger social molecule, that wholeness includes – rather than excludes – other people and one's social roles. A person's integrity on the job typically requires him or her to follow the rules and practices that define that job, rather than allow oneself to be swayed by distractions and contrary temptations. And yet, critical encounters sometimes require a show of integrity that is indeed antithetical to one's assigned role and duties. At that point some virtues, notably moral courage, become definitive and others, e.g. loyalty, may be jettisoned. (In other cases, of course, it is loyalty that might require moral courage.) But in harmony or in conflict, integrity represents the integration of one's roles and responsibilities and the virtues defined by them.

## Judgment (phronesis)

The fact that our roles conflict and there are often no singular principles to help us decide on an ethical course of action shifts the emphasis away from our calculative and ratiocinative faculties and back towards an older, often ignored faculty called 'judgment'. Against the view that ethics consists primarily of general principles that are applied to particular situations, Aristotle thought that it was 'good judgment' or *phronesis* that was of the greatest importance in ethics. Good judgment (which centred on 'perception' rather than the abstract formulation and interpretation of general principles) was the product of a good upbringing, a proper education. It was always situated, perhaps something like Joseph Fletcher's still much referred-to notion of a 'situation ethics', and took into careful account the particularity of the persons and circumstances involved. But I think the real importance of *phronesis* is not just its priority to ethical deliberation and ratiocination; it has rather to do with the inevitable conflicts of both concerns and principles that define almost every ethical dilemma. Justice, for example, may sound (especially in some philosophers) as if it were a monolithic or hierarchically layered and almost mechanical process. But, as I have argued elsewhere, there are a dozen or more different considerations that enter into most deliberations about justice, including not only rights and prior obligations and the public good but questions of merit (which themselves break down into a variety of sometimes conflicting categories) and responsibility and risk.[16] I won't go into this here but the point is that there is *no* (non-arbitrary) mechanical decision procedure for resolving most disputes about justice, and what is required, in each and every particular case, is the ability to balance and weigh competing concerns and come to a 'fair' conclusion. But what's fair is not the outcome of one or several pre-ordained principles of justice; it is (as they say) a 'judgment call', always disputable but nevertheless well or badly made. I have often thought that encouraging abstract ethical theory actually discourages and distracts us from the need to make judgments. I have actually heard one of my colleagues say (without qualms) that, since he's been studying ethical theory, he no longer has any sense of ethics. And if this sounds implausible, I urge you to remember your last department or faculty senate meeting, and the inverse relationship between high moral tone of the conversation and ridiculousness of the proposals and decisions that followed.

## Holism

It more or less follows from what I've said above that one of the problems of traditional business thinking is our tendency to isolate our business or professional roles from the rest of our lives, a process that Marx following Schiller described as 'alienation'. The good life may have many facets, but they are facets and not mere components. Despite the tiresome emphasis on tasks, techniques and 'objectives', a manager's primary and ultimate concern is *people*. It has become trite, but as I watch our more ambitious students and talk with more and more semi-successful but 'trapped' middle managers and executives, I become more and more convinced that the tunnel-vision of business life encouraged by the too narrow business curriculum and the daily rhetoric of the corporate community is damaging and counter-productive. Good employees are good people, and to pretend that the virtues of business stand isolated from the virtues of the rest of our lives – and this is not for a moment to deny the particularity of either our business roles or our lives – is to set up that familiar tragedy in which a pressured employee violates his or her 'personal values' because, from a purely business point of view, he or she 'didn't really have any choice'. It is the integration of our roles – or at least their harmonisation – that is our ideal here, and that integration should not be construed as either the personal yielding to the corporate or the corporate giving in to the personal. The name of that integration is *ethics*, construed in an Aristotelian way.

## BUSINESS AND THE VIRTUES

Business ethics is too often conceived as a set of impositions and constraints, obstacles to business behaviour rather than the motivating force of that behaviour. So conceived, it is no surprise that many people in business look upon ethics and ethicists with suspicion, as antagonistic if not antithetical to their enterprise. But properly understood, ethics does not and should not consist of a set of prohibitive principles or rules, and it is the virtue of an ethics of virtue to be rather an intrinsic part and the driving force of a successful life well-lived. Its motivation need not depend on elaborate soulsearching and deliberation but in the best companies moves along with the easy flow of interpersonal relations and a mutual sense of mission and accomplishment.

'The virtues' is a short-hand way of summarising the ideals that define good character. There are a great many virtues that are relevant to business life, in fact, it would be a daunting task to try to even list them all. Just for a start, we have honesty, loyalty, sincerity, courage, reliability, trustworthiness, benevolence, sensitivity, helpfulness, cooperativeness, civility, decency, modesty, openness, cheerfulness, amiability, tolerance, reasonableness, tactfulness, wittiness, gracefulness, liveliness, magnanimity, persistence, prudence, resourcefulness, cool-headedness, warmth and hospitality.[17] Each of these has subtle sub-traits and related virtues, and there are a great many virtues of strength, energy and skill as well as attractiveness, charm and aesthetic appeal that I have not yet mentioned. There are 'negative' virtues, that is, virtues that specify the absence of some annoying, inefficient or anti-social trait, such as non-negligence, non-vengefulness, non-vindictiveness and non-pretentiousness, and there are virtues of excess and superiority, such as super-conscientiousness and super-reliability. Then there are those virtues that seem peculiar (though not unique) to business, such as being shrewd and ruthless and 'tough', which may well be vices in other aspects of life.

From the variety of virtues, one of the most important conclusions to be drawn immediately is the impoverished nature of ethical language when it limits itself to such terms as 'good' and 'bad', 'right' and 'wrong'. To be sure, most of the virtues are 'good' and lead to 'right' action, and most of the contrary vices are 'bad' and lead to 'wrong'-doing. But not only does such ethical language lead us to ignore most of what is significant and subtle in our ordinary ethical judgments, it tends to lead us away from just that focus on personal character that is most essential to most of our interpersonal decisions, whether it is to trust a colleague, make a new friend, hire or fire a new assistant, respect a superior or invite the boss over to the house for dinner. Ethics is not the study of right and wrong, any more than art and aesthetics are the study of beauty and ugliness.[18] Ethics (like art and aesthetics) is a colourful, multifaceted appreciation and engagement with other people in the world. In business ethics, it is only the extreme and sinister misdeed that we label simply 'wrong'; more often, we invoke an artist's palette of imaginative descriptions such as 'sleazy' and 'slimy'. Even the phrase 'good character' (or 'good person') strikes us as uninteresting and vacuous; it is the details that count, not the gloss. And there are many, many details, any of which might become more or less significant in some particular situation.

A virtue, according to Aristotle, is an excellence. It is not, however, a very specialised skill or talent (like being good with numbers or a brilliant researcher) but an exemplary way of getting along with other people, a way of manifesting in one's own thoughts, feelings and actions the ideals and aims of the entire community. Thus honesty is a virtue not because it is a skill necessary for any particular endeavour or because it is 'the best policy' in most social situations, but because it represents the ideal of straight dealing, fair play, common knowledge and open inquiry. What is public is probably approved of and what is hidden is probably dangerous. So, too, courage is a virtue not just because it requires a special talent or because 'somebody's got to do it' but because we all believe (with varying degrees of commitment) that a person should stand up for what he or she cares about and what he or she believes in. But not all virtues need be so serious or so central to our idea of integrity. Aristotle listed charm, wit and a good sense of humour as virtues, and with corporate life in particular I think that we would probably agree. To be sure, the circumstances in which congeniality is a central virtue and in which courage becomes cardinal will be very different, but it is a troubled organisation that requires the more heroic virtues all the time and does not have the relative security and leisure to enjoy those virtues that make life worthwhile rather than those that are necessary for mere survival. Indeed, part of the folly of the familiar military, machine and jungle metaphors in business is that they all make business life out to be something threatening and relentless. But the truth (even in the military and in the jungle) is that there are long and sometimes relaxed respites and a need for play and playfulness as well as diligence. There is welcome camaraderie and the virtues of 'getting along' are just as important to group survival as the coordination needed for fighting together. There are reasons why we want to survive – apart from sheer Darwinian obstinacy – and the fact that we relish and enjoy the social harmony of our life and our jobs is one of them. One of the most powerful but most ignored arguments against hostile takeovers and unfriendly mergers is the desire on the part of the members of a corporate community to maintain that community, and this is not the same as executives 'fighting to keep their jobs'.

The fact that many of the virtues are social virtues of congeniality suggests that we should not insist on virtue as a particularly 'moral' category, nor is it obvious that we should draw a sharp distinction between moral virtues (such as honesty) and non-moral virtues (such as wit). Many virtues (e.g. loyalty and generosity) seem to be ambiguous in terms of morality, and the very notion of 'morality' has been so distorted by a century or two of conflation with a very specialised and overly principled conception of morals and confusion with very narrow questions of behaviour (particularly sexual behaviour) that it is, perhaps, no longer a useful term for understanding the subtleties of social harmony. What is important is rather the place of a virtue (along with other virtues) in the living of a meaningful, fulfilling life, and what is important for a business virtue is its place in a productive, meaningful life in business. And this does not simply mean, 'how does it contribute to the bottom line?' but rather, does it contribute to the social harmony of the organisation? Does it manifest the best ideals of the organisation? Does it render an employee or manager 'whole' or does it tear a person to pieces, walling off one aspect of a personality from another and leaving one part to apologise or feel ashamed before the other?

We might speculate that the more 'moral' virtues are those which, when violated, put one in a position of 'disgrace' in the eyes of his or her peers. (Having a lousy sense of humour, on the other hand, is certainly undesirable but hardly a disgrace.) But this is largely negative characterisation of character, and note that the very word 'dis-*grace*' suggests the religious origins of much of our conception of morality. Nevertheless, disgrace is not an adequate test even for the moral virtues however essential it may be to the moral life.[19] It would probably be better to emphasise the importance of the virtues rather than their violation. Despite the insistence of many moralists to the contrary, it would seem that the congenial virtues are just as essential to corporate wellbeing as the more moral virtues. We typically forgive a certain amount of exaggeration and fictionalisation for the sake of humour, and we recognise in Shakespeare's Falstaff, for instance, the convincing principle that a display of humour can sometimes take priority over valour. We tend to be overly absolutist about certain moral principles and the cost of that absolutism is the neglect of the congenial virtues and a consequent dreariness in both social life and ethical discourse.

If business life was like the brutal and heroic world of Homer's *Iliad*, corporations in mortal conflict with one another, we would expect the business virtues to be those warrior virtues most closely associated with combat, not only strength and prowess but courage, imperviousness to pain or pity, frightfulness (that is, causing fright in others, not being frightened oneself). We would expect the warrior to have an appropriately insensitive personality, rather clumsy social habits, and an enormous ego. Not surprisingly, these are precisely the virtues often praised and attributed to top business executives, summarised (badly) in the single word, 'toughness'. But, of course, warrior metaphors depend on a war-like situation, but business ethicists have taken considerable pains to dismiss that picture of corporate business life as pathological and misleading. Most CEOs, however 'tough', do not fit this picture at all. Consider, instead, a very different and usually more representative picture of the corporation, the corporation as a wealthy and prosperous 'polis', a free and sophisticated city-state with considerable pride in its products, philosophy and corporate culture. There will still be external threats and an occasional battle, but this is not the day-to-day concern of the community. Courage might still be an important virtue, but most of the other warrior virtues and the typical characteristics of the warrior personality will seem boorish and bullish, inappropriate in most social settings and downright embarrassing in some. The virtues, in such a society, will tend to be the genteel, congenial virtues, those which lubricate a rich, pleasant social life. And these will be just as applicable to the CEO as to the boy at the loading dock or the teller at the check-out window.

Aristotle, who lived in a military society, nevertheless lived a long time after the heroic times depicted by Homer. Aristotle's list of virtues, accordingly, does not include the military virtues, except for courage, which he describes as an occasionally necessary virtue but hardly the central one. Far more important is the virtue of justice – which in the warrior mentality means simply 'to the victor go the spoils' but in genteel society involves complicated deliberations about merit, need, status, equality and fairness. Of paramount importance too is honour, which is not so much a virtue in its own right as it is the sum of the virtues, one's character as a virtuous person. To be sure, a warrior might fight for his honour, but we usually take this to mean some challenge to his fighting ability or his willingness or readiness to fight. Honour for Aristotle has much more to do with one's status in society, being recognised as a just and generous and not a miserly man, for example, and not humiliating oneself with lewd displays or excess of food, song or drink. Taken as a description not of the Greek city-state but of the corporation, we can recognise here too many of the virtues ascribed to the best executives, who are moderate and often surprisingly modest, generous with their time and money, concerned first and foremost with their and the company's reputation (honour) and loathe to risk any action that might be humiliating. So, too, such virtues as charm, wit and friendliness are recognised as extremely important. Probably no one has reached the executive floor by wit alone, but few have succeeded without it. It is necessary to lead and to lead effectively, of course, but it is more important to lead not as an Achilles or an Agamemnon, charging ahead on his own through the scattering Trojans, but as an admirable, inspiring human being. Best-selling books to the contrary, Ghengis Khan and Attila the Hun would not be successful corporate leaders today, nor would the successful executive find that much to learn from Machiavelli. Tom Watson, Lee Iacocca and James Burke are much more the model, and in their very different ways exemplify the fact that the Aristotelian society, of course, and the corporation is not simply a *polis*. The Homeric world of the warrior is over three thousand years old, and the world of Aristotle well over two thousand. Since then, a great deal has happened in the world, and as social circumstances have changed so have our conception of the virtues. And what has happened, to condense millions of events and pages into a phrase or two, is the domination of Christianity and the rise of the individual. Put these two together (in fact our concept of the 'individual' largely originated in the Christian conception of the individual soul) and one finds, among many other aspects of the modern world, John Calvin's conception of individual salvation and its manifestations in worldly success and Adam Smith's revolutionary notion of individual enterprise serving the social good. Calvin incorporated in his philosophy a good many of the traditional Christian virtues, even as he altered the world-view of that religion to make ample room for business. Adam Smith, of course, was a good Christian too. At the foundation of his free enterprise model lay a conception of human nature that was deeply social and sympathetic, and he too was much concerned with the Christian virtues and how they might be made to fit into the rapidly expanding economy of the eighteenth century. But these virtues, although appropriately genteel for a gentlemanly Scottish bourgeoisie, were no longer Aristotelian virtues. The warrior virtues had all but disappeared (courage was now strictly a domestic virtue, and one given more lip-service than attention), the congenial virtues were demoted to a kind of second place, and what we now call the *moral* virtues had become primary.

Aristotle used the word 'moral' simply to mean 'practical'. But with the Judaeo-Christian tradition the words 'moral', 'morals' and 'morality' came to take on weighty, even cosmic meanings. Morality was that code given to us (or imposed on us) by God. Morality referred not to the things that make life pleasant or congenial but to a small set of essentials, rules that are not to be broken under any circumstances. Morality was cut off from its social base, the *polis* presumed by Aristotle, and became more and more a concern of God and the individual, only secondarily of society. Thus the virtues came to be identified with individual morality and, by the end of the eighteenth century, increasingly with the abstract rules of reason that dictated universal morality, a nature development of the ethics of the Ten Commandments. And, like the Ten Commandments, the virtues came to be more concerned with abstinence than excellence and more concerned with 'being a good person' than congeniality. A good person, depending on the severity of one's moral and religious upbringing, doesn't lie, doesn't cheat, doesn't do anything dishonest, doesn't drink or eat to excess – not only to avoid social humiliation but to avoid displaying that lack of control or self-indulgence that is the sure sign of a weak or corrupted personality. And here too, we see the virtues upon which a great many of the chief executives of our largest corporations pride themselves.

One might insist, just to waylay the argument I seem to be developing here, that warrior virtues, congeniality (Aristotelian) virtues and moral virtues are in fact quite compatible, and there is no reason why a James Burke or a Warren Buffett, for example, can't display warrior toughness, Aristotelian gentility and Christian righteousness. And indeed, this is the case. But my argument is not that these three sets of virtues are incompatible as such, but rather that they present us with three quite distinct contexts and three different ethical frameworks, and to understand business ethics is to understand the confluence, the priorities and the potential conflicts between these. Excessive attention paid to a corporation may become a screaming alliance of desperation and one's personal sense of integrity can be threatened or fatally damaged. Excessive attention to the congenial virtues may in fact 'soften' a company so that it becomes less competitive, and an exaggerated sense of righteousness to the detriment of congeniality and competitiveness may well cause a company to shatter into a thousand rigid little moralists, incapable of working together. But the Aristotelian framework tells us that it is cooperation and not an isolated individual sense of self-worth that defines the most important virtues, in which the warrior virtues play an essential but diminished role, in which the wellbeing of the community goes hand in hand with individual excellence, not by virtue of any 'invisible hand' but precisely because of the social consciousness and public spirit of each and every individual.

Almost all of Aristotle's virtues are recognisable as business virtues, and this is, of course, not surprising. Business is, above all, a social activity, involving dealing with other people in both stressful and friendly situations (and trying to make the former into the latter). Despite our emphasis on hard-headedness and the bottom line, we do not praise and often despise tight-fistedness and we do praise great-souled generosity ('magnificence'). But such virtues may be misleading for us. We would not praise an executive who 'gave away the store'; we would rather think that executive mentally un-hinged. But the virtues for Aristotle do not involve radical demands on our behaviour, and the sort of fanaticism praised if not preached in many religions ('give away all of your worldly goods') is completely foreign to Aristotle's insistence on 'moderation'. Thus the generous or 'magnificent' person gives away only as much of wealth as will increase his or her status in the community. Here we would encounter the familiar charge that such giving is not true generosity, for it involves no personal sacrifice and includes a 'selfish' motive, the quest for self-aggrandisement. But Aristotle would refuse to recognise this opposition between enlightened self-interest and virtue, and we continue to enforce it at our peril. The argument here, of course, is exactly the sceptical argument levelled against generous corporations when they give to the arts, to education, to social welfare programmes: 'They're only doing it for the PR'. But here executives (and everyone else) would be wise to follow Aristotle and reject the notion that 'true' generosity is self-sacrifice and self-benefiting generosity is only PR'. There are occasions that call for self-sacrifice, but to insist that such extreme action is essential to the virtues is to deny the virtues their relevance to business (and most of) life.

This brings us to the perhaps most misunderstood virtue in business life, the virtue of *toughness*. The word 'tough' is typically used by way of admiration, though often coupled with a shake of the head and an expression of frustration. Sometimes, it is used as a euphemism, in place of or in conjunction with various synonyms, for a nasty or odious human being. Not infrequently, it simply means stubborn, impossible or mean-spirited. But toughness is generally and genuinely perceived as virtue, albeit a virtue that is often misplaced and misconceived. Insofar as business consists of bargaining and dealing with other people, toughness is essential, and its opposite is not so much weakness as incompetence. But much of what is called toughness is neither a virtue nor a vice. It is not a character trait so much as it is a skill, whether cultivated or 'natural'. In certain central business practices, notably negotiating, toughness is not so much a personal virtue as it is a technique or set of techniques, an acquired manner and an accomplished strategy, 'knowing when to hole 'em, knowing when to fold 'em'. Toughness includes knowing how to bluff and when to keep silent, when to be cooperative and when not to be. But such a skill is not, contra Carr, unethical or divorced from ordinary morals; it is a legitimate part of a certain kind of obviously legitimate activity. Yet, as a specific skill or set of skills, being a tough negotiator is not sufficiently personal or general to count as a virtue, which is not to say, of course, that it is not therefore admirable or necessary.

Very often, what toughness means is simply 'smart', that is, knowing the business, knowing one's competitors and dealings, knowing how to get things done. Again, this is an admirable and necessary set of business qualifications, but not a virtue as such. But toughness also means perseverance, which is a personal as well as a business virtue. As always, Aristotle's standard of moderation comes into play here, for there is such a thing as too much perseverance, which then becomes mere obstinacy or stubbornness. Of course, what seemed like obstinacy to those of little faith may well turn out to be richly rewarded by the results, and what was indeed healthy perseverance may nevertheless turn to failure in the vicissitudes of the market. But too little 'stick-to-it-iveness' makes success virtually impossible and makes life intolerable for those investors, employees and other stockholders who naturally depend on a full-blooded effort rather than a half-hearted try. Toughness as perseverance means nothing other than having a goal and a purpose, seeing its worthiness and pursuing it to the end. What makes it 'tough' is facing up to set-backs and obstacles that would discourage lesser beings; indeed, it is only in the face of failure that such toughness is truly tested, for it is no virtue to 'persevere' when the market is handing you nothing but success.

Toughness in an executive also has an ethically painful element. Sometimes it is necessary to do something wrong in order to do what is right. Powerful politicians, of course, face such dilemmas all the time, giving rise to a substantial literature on the controversial virtues of toughness and 'ruthlessness' and the allegedly opposed domains of public and private morality.[20] Sometimes, to reach a higher goal, one must do what one otherwise would not and should not even consider. For example, in the face of debts or deficiencies that will very likely capsise the company, a chairman may need to let go perfectly qualified, hard-working loyal employees. Viewed as an action isolated from the circumstances, letting people go for no reason whatever, that is, for no fault of their own, would be the height of injustice. But if it is a matter of saving the company, then this otherwise unjust act may nevertheless be necessary. Toughness is being able and willing to undertake such measures. This is not to say, however – and this cannot be emphasised enough – that such decisions can or should be made without guilt or pain or bad feelings. It does not mean that what one has done is not, despite its necessity, wrong. The chief executive of a large corporation once told me that 'down-sizing' his company was the most painful thing he had ever had to do. His toughness lay not in callousness or indifference but in his willingness to do what was necessary and in his insistence on doing it as humanely as possible. Indeed, callousness and indifference are not themselves signs of toughness but the very opposite, indications of that form of weakness that can face moral issues only by denying them. Toughness is a virtue, but callousness and indifference are not, and the two should never be confused.

In politics, toughness is the phenomenon that is sometimes called 'dirty hands'.[21] It is the need to do what is painful or awful, even (in a smaller frame of reference) immoral in order to do what is right or necessary. One chief executive was asked point-blank by an elderly stockholder if his holdings in the company were safe and secure. The CEO, knowing full well that a slash in the dividend would be announced later that week, could not help but tell a lie, or, at least, seriously circumnavigate the truth. Again, his personal pain and guilt were considerable, but prevarication was unavoidable. Of course, profits alone are not sufficient as an excuse, and one might thus understand the popularity and indignation surrounding Michael Moore's movie *Roger and Me*, about the closing of the Flint, Michigan GM plants. If the reasons were company survival, combined with some well-publicised cutbacks in executive positions, perks and salaries, such closings would have hardly made a movie. But when profits and perks are the motivation, toughness is not a virtue or, alternatively, this isn't toughness but callousness.

Like almost all of the virtues, toughness is not simply self-interested, but neither can it be considered an altruistic or self-sacrificing trait of character. Toughness is ultimately having a vision and persevering in the long term plans and strategies necessary to achieve that vision. It means not being dissuaded by threats and temptations. But it does not mean an easy willingness to step on other people or violate the basic rules of morality or sacrifice the other basic virtues of business. Like all virtues, toughness has its place in the constellation of virtues, and sometimes toughness needs to yield to compassion or generosity, to trust or fairness. Again, this is no defence of naivety, but what toughness certainly does not mean – and is far too often taken to mean – is mean-spiritedness and indifference, lack of care and concern for others. Toughness is a true business virtue, and in tough business it may even emerge as the primary business virtue, but it is not opposed to integrity. Toughness is a proper sense of purpose, insulated against greed as well as weakness. As such, much of what is called toughness might better be called moral courage.

## THE BOTTOM LINE (CONCLUSION)

The bottom line of the Aristotelian approach to business ethics is that we have to get away from both traditional individualistic ethics and 'bottom line' thinking. This does not in any way imply that the individual 'checks in his or her values at the office door' nor does it suggest that, except in the unusual and unfortunate case, there will be any thorough-going disharmony or incompatibility between one's personal and professional values. Quite to the contrary, the point of what I am arguing is that we are, as Aristotle famously insisted, social creatures who get our identity from our communities and measure our worth accordingly. And as much as many employees may feel the need to divorce themselves from their work and pretend that what they 'do' is not indicative of their true selves, the truth is that most adults spend literally half of their waking adult life on the job, in the office, in the role or position that defines them as a citizen of the corporation. The Aristotelian approach to business ethics ultimately comes down to the idea that, while business life has its specific goals and distinctive practices and people in business have their particular concerns, loyalties, roles and responsibilities, there is no 'business world' apart from the people who work in business and the integrity of those people determines the integrity of the organisation as well as vice versa. The Aristotelian approach to business ethics is, perhaps, just another way of saying that people come before profits.

* Earlier versions of this chapter were presented at a number of conferences, the

Ruffin conference at the University of Virginia, the Applied Ethics conference at the University of British Columbia and (with Nick Imparato) the International Association of Business and Society conference in Sundance, Utah, the Center of Ethics conference at the University of Melbourne. Some parts of this chapter have been published in some of the proceedings of those conferences and I have benefited from comments and criticism from my colleagues there, most notably, from Patricia Werhane, Peter French, Ed Freeman and Tony Coady. Parts of this chapter also appear in my book, *Ethics and Excellence*, Oxford: Oxford University Press (1992).

## ENDNOTES

1. *Business and Society Review* (1984). Solomon and Hanson, *It's Good Business*, New York: Atheneum (1985).
2. Indeed, the most serious single problem that we find in the teaching of business ethics is the insistence on a false antagonism between profits and social responsibility, perhaps (on the part of philosophers) in order to keep the debate going. A far more productive route would be the search for profit-making solutions, but this would require a major step down from the abstractions of theory into the messy world of details, technology, marketing and politics. It is the same old problem of egoism in ethics (as in Hobbes and Butler three centuries ago) revised on the corporate level. It presupposes an artificial opposition between the self-interest and shared interest and then finds it impossible to locate the motivation for mutually inherited action.
3. Anthony Flew, 'The Profit Motive', in *Ethics*, Vol. 86 (July 1976), 312–22.
4. Manuel Velasquez, comment on Joanne Ciulla, Ruffin lectures, 1989.
5. Alfred Carr, 'Is Business Bluffing Ethical?' *Harvard Business Review* (Jan–Feb, 1968).
6. Milton Friedman, 'The Social Responsibility of Business is to Increase its Profits', *The New York Times Magazine* (1971).
7. This has been the topic of considerable debate. See, notably, G. E. M. Anscombe, *Intentionality*, Oxford: Basil Blackwell and John Cooper, *Reason and Human Good in Aristotle*, Cambridge: Massachusetts: Harvard University Press (1975).
8. Elizabeth Wolgast, *A Grammar of Justice*, Cornell: Cornell University Press (1989).
9. William Frankena, *Ethics*, 10th edn, New Jersey: Prentice-Hall (1987).
10. Alasdair MacIntyre, *After Virtue*, 2nd edn, Notre Dame: University of Notre Dame Press (1981).
11. Cheshire Calhoun, 'Justice, Care and Gender Bias', *Journal of Philosophy* (1988).
12. Peter Drucker, *Management*, Harper & Row (1973), 366f.
13. Norman Bowie, *Business Ethics*, New Jersey: Prentice-Hall (1982), 1–16.
14. Peter Townsend, *Up the Organization*.
15. Lynne McFall, 'Integrity', in *Ethics* (October 1987).
16. Robert C. Solomon, *A Passion for Justice*, New York: Addison-Wesley (1989).
17. A complex taxonomy of the virtues is in Edmund Pincoffs, *Quandaries and Virtues*, Kansas (1986), 84.
18. See Frithjof Bergmann, 'The Experience of Values', in Hauerwas and MacIntyre (eds), *Divisions*, Notre Dame: University of Notre Dame Press (1983), 127–59.
19. Aristotle does give us an elaborate discussion of the 'quasi-virtue' of *shame*. The point is not that it is desirable to be ashamed, of course, but rather that the capacity to be shamed is essential to having a virtuous character in the first place. As the Ethiopian proverb goes, where there is no shame, there is no honour'. The difference between shame and disgrace, however, is significant here. Disgrace suggests dishonour before God. Shame is secular and suggests rather a 'letting down' of your colleagues and others who trusted or depended on you.
20. See, for example, Stuart Hampshire (ed.), *Public and Private Morality*, Cambridge: Cambridge University Press (1978) and his own *Innocence and Experience*, Cambridge: Harvard University Press (1989). See also Bernard Williams, 'Politics and Moral Character' in his *Moral Luck*, Cambridge: Cambridge University Press (1981) and Thomas Nagel, 'Ruthlessness in Public Life' in the Hampshire collection.

21. The need to do wrong in order to do good was one of the enduring obsessions of the great German sociologist Max Weber. See his 'Politics as a Vocation', in H. Gerth and C. Mills (eds), *From Max Weber: Essays in Sociology*, New York: Oxford University Press (1946). The term 'dirty hands' was popularised by Jean-Paul Sartre in his play of that name. It can be found in the volume *No Exit and Three Other Plays*, New York: Vintage (1946). See also Michael Stocker on 'The Problem of Dirty Hands', in his *Plural and Conflicting Values*, Oxford: Oxford University Press (1990).

# 13

# VIRTUE THEORY AND ABORTION

## Rosalind Hursthouse

The sort of ethical theory derived from Aristotle, variously described as virtue ethics, virtue-based ethics, or neo-Aristotelianism, is becoming better known, and is now quite widely recognised as at least a possible rival to deontological and utilitarian theories. With recognition has come criticism, of varying quality. In this chapter I shall discuss nine separate criticisms that I have frequently encountered, most of which seem to me to betray an inadequate grasp either of the structure of virtue theory or of what would be involved in thinking about a real moral issue in its terms. In the first half I aim particularly to secure an understanding that will reveal that many of these criticisms are simply misplaced, and to articulate what I take to be the major criticism of virtue theory. I reject this criticism, but do not claim that it is necessarily misplaced. In the second half I aim to deepen that understanding and highlight the issues raised by the criticisms by illustrating what the theory looks like when it is applied to a particular issue, in this case, abortion.

### VIRTUE THEORY

Virtue theory can be laid out in a framework that reveals clearly some of the essential similarities and differences between it and some versions of deontological and utilitarian theories. I begin with a rough sketch of familiar versions of the latter two sorts of theory, not, of course, with the intention of suggesting that they exhaust the field, but on the assumption that their very familiarity will provide a helpful contrast with virtue theory. Suppose a deontological theory has basically the following framework. We begin with a premise providing a specification of right action:

P.1. An action is right iff it is in accordance with a moral rule or principle.

This is a purely formal specification, forging a link between the concepts of *right action* and *moral rule*, and gives one no guidance until one knows what a moral rule is. So the next thing the theory needs is a premise about that:

P.2. A moral rule is one that . . .

Historically, an acceptable completion of P.2 would have been

(i) is laid on us by God

or

(ii) is required by natural law.

In secular versions (not, of course, unconnected to God's being pure reason, and the universality of natural law) we get such completions as

(iii) is laid on us by reason

or

(iv) is required by rationality

or

(v) would command universal rational acceptance

or

(vi) would be the object of choice of all rational beings

and so on. Such a specification forges a second conceptual link, between the concepts of *moral rule* and *rationality*.

We have here the skeleton of a familiar version of a deontological theory, a skeleton that reveals that what is essential to any such version are the links between *right action, moral rule* and *rationality*. That these form the basic structure can be seen particularly vividly if we lay out the familiar act-utilitarianism in such a way as to bring out the contrasts.

Act-utilitarianism begins with a premise that provides a specification of right action:

P.1. An action is right iff it promotes the best consequences.

It thereby forges the link between the concepts of *right action* and *consequences*. It goes on to specify what the best consequences are in its second premise:

P.2. The best consequences are those in which happiness is maximised.

It thereby forges the link between *consequences* and *happiness*.

Now let us consider what a skeletal virtue theory looks like. It begins with a specification of right action:

P.1. An action is right iff it is what a virtuous agent would do in the circumstances.[1]

This, like the first premises of the other two sorts of theory, is a purely formal principle, giving one no guidance as to what to do, that forges the conceptual link between *right action* and *virtuous agent*. Like the other theories it must, of course, go on to specify what the latter is. The first step towards this may appear quite trivial, but is needed to correct a prevailing tendency among many critics to define the virtuous agent as one who is disposed to act in accordance with a deontologist's moral rules.

> P.1a. A virtuous agent is one who acts virtuously, that is, one who has and exercises the virtues.

This subsidiary premise lays bare the fact that virtue theory aims to provide a nontrivial specification of the virtuous agent *via* a nontrivial specification of the virtues, which is given in its second premise:

> P.2. A virtue is a character trait a human being needs to flourish or live well.

This premise forges a conceptual link between *virtue* and *flourishing* (or *living well* or *eudaimonia*). And, just as deontology, in theory, then goes on to argue that each favoured rule meets its specification, so virtue ethics, in theory, goes on to argue that each favoured character trait meets its.

These are the bare bones of virtue theory. Following are five brief comments directed to some misconceived criticisms that should be cleared out of the way.

First, the theory does not have a peculiar weakness or problem in virtue of the fact that it involves the concept of *eudaimonia* (a standard criticism being that this concept is hopelessly obscure). Now no virtue theorist will pretend that the concept of human flourishing is an easy one to grasp. I will not even claim here (though I would elsewhere) that it is no more obscure than the concepts of *rationality* and *happiness*, since, if our vocabulary were more limited, we might, *faute de mieux*, call it (human) *rational happiness*, and thereby reveal that it has at least some of the difficulties of both. But virtue theory has never, so far as I know, been dismissed on the grounds of the *comparative* obscurity of this central concept; rather, the popular view is that it has a problem with this which deontology and utilitarianism in no way share. This, I think, is clearly false. Both *rationality* and *happiness*, as they figure in their respective theories, are rich and difficult concepts – hence all the disputes about the various tests for a rule's being an object of rational choice, and the disputes, dating back to Mill's introduction of the higher and lower pleasures, about what constitutes happiness.

Second, the theory is not trivially circular; it does not specify right action in terms of the virtuous agent and then immediately specify the virtuous agent in terms of right action. Rather, it specifies her in terms of the virtues, and then specifies these, not merely as dispositions to right action, but as the character traits (which are dispositions to feel and react as well as act in certain ways) required for *eudaimonia*.[2]

Third, it does answer the question 'What should I do?' as well as the question 'What sort of person should I be? (That is, it is not, as one of the catchphrases has it, concerned only with Being and not with Doing.)

Fourth, the theory does, to a certain extent, answer this question by coming up with rules or principles (contrary to the common claim that it does not come up with any rules or principles). Every virtue generates a positive instruction (act justly, kindly, courageously, honestly, etc.) and every vice a prohibition (do not act unjustly, cruelly, like a coward, dishonestly, etc.). So trying to decide what to do within the framework of virtue theory is not, as some people seem to imagine, necessarily a matter of taking one's favoured candidate for a virtuous person and asking oneself, 'What would they do in these circumstances?' (as if the raped fifteen-year-old girl might be supposed to say to herself, 'Now would Socrates have an abortion if he were in my circumstances?' and as if someone who had never known or heard of anyone very virtuous were going to be left, according to the theory, with no way to decide what to do at all). The agent may instead ask herself, 'If I were to do such and such now, would I be acting justly or unjustly (or neither), kindly or unkindly [and so on]?'. I shall consider below the problem created by cases in which such a question apparently does not yield an answer to 'What should I do?' (because, say, the alternatives are being unkind or being unjust); here my claim is only that it sometimes does – the agent may employ her concepts of the virtues and vices directly, rather than imagining what some hypothetical exemplar would do.

Fifth (a point that is implicit but should be made explicit), virtue theory is not committed to any sort of reductionism involving defining all of our moral concepts in terms of the virtuous agent. On the contrary, it relies on a lot of very significant moral concepts. Charity or benevolence, for instance, is the virtue whose concern is the *good* of others; that concept of *good* is related to the concept of *evil* or *harm*, and they are both related to the concepts of the *worthwhile*, the *advantageous* and the *pleasant*. If I have the wrong conception of what is worthwhile and advantageous and pleasant, then I shall have the wrong conception of what is good for, and harmful to, myself and others, and, even with the best will in the world, will lack the virtue of charity, which involves getting all this right. (This point will be illustrated at some length in the second half of this article; I mention it here only in support of the fact that no virtue theorist who takes her inspiration from Aristotle would even contemplate aiming at reductionism.[3])

Let me now, with equal brevity, run through two more standard criticisms of virtue theory (the sixth and seventh of my nine) to show that, though not entirely misplaced, they do not highlight problems peculiar to that theory but, rather, problems that are shared by familiar versions of deontology.

One common criticism is that we do not know which character traits are the virtues, or that this is open to much dispute, or particularly subject to the threat of moral scepticism or 'pluralism'[4] or cultural relativism. But the parallel roles played by the second premises of both deontological and virtue theories reveal the way in which both sorts of theory share this problem. It is at the stage at which one tries to get the right conclusions to drop out of the bottom of one's theory that, *theoretically*, all the work has to be done. Rule deontologists know that they want to get 'don't kill', 'keep promises', 'cherish your children' and so on as the rules that meet their specification, whatever it may be. They also know that any of these can be disputed, that some philosopher may claim, of any one of them, that it is reasonable to reject it, and that at least people claim that there has been, for each rule, some culture that rejected it. Similarly, the virtue theorists know that they want to get justice, charity, fidelity, courage, and so on as the character traits needed for *eudaimonia*; and they also know that any of these can be disputed, that some philosopher will say of any one of them that it is reasonable to reject it as a virtue, and that there is said to be, for each character trait, some culture that has thus rejected it.

This is a problem for both theories, and the virtue theorist certainly does not find it any harder to argue against moral scepticism, 'pluralism', or cultural relativism than the deontologist. Each theory has to stick out its neck and say, in some cases, 'This person/these people/other cultures are (or would be) in error', and find some grounds for saying this.

Another criticism (the seventh) often made is that virtue ethics has unresolvable conflict built into it. 'It is common knowledge', it is said, 'that the requirements of the virtues can conflict; charity may prompt me to end the frightful suffering of the person in my care by killing him, but justice bids me to stay my hand. To tell my brother that his wife is being unfaithful to him would be honest and loyal, but it would be kinder to keep quiet about it. So which should I do? In such cases, virtue ethics has nothing helpful to say'. (This is one version of the problem, mentioned above, that considering whether a proposed action falls under a virtue or vice term does not always yield an answer to 'What should I do?')

The obvious reply to this criticism is that rule deontology notoriously suffers from the same problem, arising not only from the fact that its rules can apparently conflict, but also from the fact that, at first blush, it appears that one and the same rule (e.g., preserve life) can yield contrary instructions in a particular case.[5] As before, I agree that this is a problem for virtue theory, but deny that it is a problem peculiar to it.

Finally, I want to articulate, and reject, what I take to be the major criticism of virtue theory. Perhaps because it is *the* major criticism, the reflection of a very general sort of disquiet about the theory, it is hard to state clearly – especially for someone who does not accept it – but it goes something like this.[6] My interlocutor says:

> Virtue theory can't *get* us anywhere in real moral issues because it's bound to be all assertion and no argument. You admit that the best it can come up with in the way of action-guiding rules are the ones that rely on the virtue and vice concepts, such as 'act charitably', 'don't act cruelly', and so on; and, as if that weren't bad enough, you admit that these virtue concepts, such as charity, presuppose concepts such as the *good*, and the *worthwhile*, and so on. But that means that any virtue theorist who writes about real moral issues must rely on her audience's agreeing with her application of all these concepts, and hence accepting all the premises in which those applications are enshrined. But some other virtue theorist might take different premises about these matters, and come up with very different conclusions, and, within the terms of the theory, there is no way to distinguish between the two. While there is agreement, virtue theory can repeat conventional wisdom, preserve the status quo, but it can't get us anywhere in the way that a normative ethical theory is supposed to, namely, by providing rational grounds for acceptance of its practical conclusions.

My strategy will be to split this criticism into two: one (the eighth) addressed to the virtue theorist's employment of the virtue and vice concepts enshrined in her rules

– act charitably, honestly, and so on – and the other (the ninth) addressed to her employment of concepts such as that of the *worthwhile*. Each objection, I shall maintain, implicitly appeals to a certain *condition of adequacy* on a normative moral theory, and in each case, I shall claim, the condition of adequacy, once made explicit, is utterly implausible.

It is true that when she discusses real moral issues, the virtue theorist has to assert that certain actions are honest, dishonest, or neither; charitable, uncharitable, or neither. And it is true that this is often a very difficult matter to decide; her rules are not always easy to apply. But this counts as a criticism of the theory only if we assume, as a condition of adequacy, that any adequate action-guiding theory must make the difficult business of knowing what to do if one is to act well easy, that it must provide clear guidance about what ought and ought not to be done which any reasonably clever adolescent could follow if she chose. But such a condition of adequacy is implausible. Acting rightly *is* difficult, and *does* call for much moral wisdom, and the relevant condition of adequacy, which virtue theory meets, is that it should have built into it an explanation of a truth expressed by Aristotle,[7] namely, that moral knowledge – unlike mathematical knowledge – cannot be acquired merely by attending lectures and is not characteristically to be found in people too young to have had much experience of life. There are youthful mathematical geniuses, but rarely, if ever, youthful moral geniuses, and this tells us something significant about the sort of knowledge that moral knowledge is. Virtue ethics builds this in straight off precisely by couching its rules in terms whose application may indeed call for the most delicate and sensitive judgment.

Here we may discern a slightly different version of the problem that there are cases in which applying the virtue and vice terms does not yield an answer to 'What should I do?'. Suppose someone 'youthful in character', as Aristotle puts it, having applied the relevant terms, finds herself landed with what is, unbeknownst to her, a case not of real but of apparent conflict, arising from a misapplication of those terms. Then she will not be able to decide what to do unless she knows of a virtuous agent to look to for guidance. But her quandary is (*ex hypothesi*) the result of her lack of wisdom, and just what virtue theory expects. Someone hesitating over whether to reveal a hurtful truth, for example, thinking it would be kind but dishonest or unjust to lie, may need to realise, with respect to these particular circumstances, not that kindness is more (or less) important than honesty or justice, and not that honesty or justice sometimes requires one to act unkindly or cruelly, but that one does people no kindness by concealing this sort of truth from them, hurtful as it may be. This is the *type* of thing (I use it only as an example) that people with moral wisdom know about, involving the correct application of *kind*, and that people without such wisdom find difficult.

What about the virtue theorist's reliance on concepts such as that of the *worthwhile*? If such reliance is to count as a fault in the theory, what condition of adequacy is implicitly in play? It must be that any good normative theory should provide answers to questions about real moral issues whose truth is in no way determined by truths about what is worthwhile, or what really matters in human life. Now, although people are initially inclined to reject out of hand the claim that the practical conclusions of a normative moral theory have to be based on premises about what is truly worthwhile, the alternative, once it is made explicit, may look even more unacceptable. Consider what the condition of adequacy entails. If truths about what is worthwhile (or truly good, or serious, or about what matters in human life) do *not* have to be appealed to in order to answer questions about real moral issues, then I might sensibly seek guidance about what I ought to do from someone who had declared in advance that she knew nothing about such matters, or from someone who said that, although she had opinions about them, these were quite likely to be wrong but that this did not matter, because they would play no determining role in the advice she gave me.

I should emphasise that we are talking about real moral issues and real guidance; I want to know whether I should have an abortion, take my mother off the life-support machine, leave academic life and become a doctor in the Third World, give up my job with the firm that is using animals in its experiments, tell my father he has cancer. Would I go to someone who says she has *no* views about what is worthwhile in life? Or to someone who says that, as a matter of fact, she tends to think that the only thing that matters is having a good time, but has a normative theory that is consistent both with this view and with my own rather more puritanical one, which will yield the guidance I need?

I take it as a premise that this is absurd. The relevant condition of adequacy should be that the practical conclusions of a good normative theory *must* be in part determined by premises about what is worthwhile, important, and so on. Thus I reject this 'major criticism' of virtue theory, that it cannot get us anywhere in the way that a normative moral theory is supposed to. According to my response, a normative theory that any clever adolescent can apply, or that reaches practical conclusions that are in no way determined by premises about what is truly worthwhile, serious, and so on, is guaranteed to be an inadequate theory.

Although I reject this criticism, I have not argued that it is misplaced and that it necessarily manifests a failure to understand what virtue theory is. My rejection is based on premises about what an adequate normative theory must be like – what sorts of concepts it must contain, and what sort of account it must give of moral knowledge – and thereby claims, implicitly, that the 'major criticism' manifests a failure to understand what an *adequate normative theory* is. But, as a matter of fact, I think the criticism is often made by people who have no idea of what virtue theory looks like when applied to a real moral issue; they drastically underestimate the variety of ways in which the virtue and vice concepts, and the others, such as that of the *worthwhile*, figure in such discussion.

As promised, I now turn to an illustration of such discussion, applying virtue theory to abortion. Before I embark on this tendentious business, I should remind the reader of the aim of this discussion. I am not, in this chapter, trying to solve the problem of abortion; I am illustrating how virtue theory directs one to think about it. It might indeed be said that thinking about the problem in this way 'solves' it by *dis*solving it, insofar as it leads one to the conclusion that there is no single right answer, but a variety of particular answers, and in what follows I am certainly trying to make that conclusion seem plausible. But, that granted, it should still be said that I am not trying to 'solve the problems' in the practical sense of telling people that they should, or should not, do this or that if they are pregnant and contemplating abortion in these or those particular circumstances.

I do not assume, or expect, that all of my readers will agree with everything I am about to say. On the contrary, given the plausible assumption that some are morally wiser than I am, and some less so, the theory has built into it that we are bound to disagree on some points. For instance, we may well disagree about the particular application of some of the virtue and vice terms; and we may disagree about what is worthwhile or serious, worthless or trivial. But my aim is to make clear how these concepts figure in a discussion conducted in terms of virtue theory. What is at issue is whether these concepts are indeed the ones that should come in, that is, whether virtue theory should be criticised for employing them. The problem of abortion highlights this issue dramatically since virtue theory quite transforms the discussion of it.

## ABORTION

As everyone knows, the morality of abortion is commonly discussed in relation to just two considerations: first, and predominantly, the status of the foetus and whether or not it is the sort of thing that may or may not be innocuously or justifiably killed; and second, and less predominantly (when, that is, the discussion concerns the *morality* of abortion rather than the question of permissible legislation in a just society), women's rights. If one thinks within this familiar framework, one may well be puzzled about what virtue theory, as such, could contribute. Some people assume the discussion will be conducted solely in terms of what the virtuous agent would or would not do (cf. the third, fourth and fifth criticisms above). Others assume that only justice, or at most justice and charity,[8] will be applied to the issue, generating a discussion very similar to Judith Jarvis Thomson's.[9]

Now if this is the way the virtue theorist's discussion of abortion is imagined to be, no wonder people think little of it. It seems obvious in advance that in any such discussion there must be either a great deal of extremely tendentious application of the virtue terms *just, charitable*, and so on or a lot of rhetorical appeal to 'this is what only the virtuous agent knows'. But these are caricatures; they fail to appreciate the way in which virtue theory quite transforms the discussion of abortion by dismissing the two familiar dominating considerations as, in a way, fundamentally irrelevant. In what way or ways, I hope to make both clear and plausible.

Let us first consider women's rights. Let me emphasise again that we are discussing the *morality* of abortion, not the rights and wrongs of laws prohibiting or permitting it. If we suppose that women do have a moral right to do as they choose with their own bodies, or, more particularly, to terminate their pregnancies, then it may well follow that a *law* forbidding abortion would be unjust. Indeed, even if they have no such right, such a law might be, as things stand at the moment, unjust, on impractical, or inhumane: on this issue I have nothing to say in this chapter. But, putting all questions about the justice or injustice of laws to one side, and supposing only that women have such a moral right, *nothing* follows from this supposition about the morality of abortion, according to virtue theory, once it is noted (quite generally, not with particular reference to abortion) that in exercising a moral right I can do something cruel, or callous, or selfish, light-minded, self-righteous, stupid, inconsiderate, disloyal, dishonest – that is, act viciously.[10] Love and friendship do not survive their parties' constantly insisting on their rights, nor do people live well when they think that getting what they have a right to is of preeminent importance; they harm others, and they harm themselves. So whether women have a moral right to terminate their pregnancies is irrelevant within virtue theory, for it is irrelevant to the question 'In having an abortion in these circumstances, would the agent be acting virtuously or viciously or neither?'.

What about the consideration of the status of the foetus – what can virtue theory say about that? One might say that this issue is not in the province of *any* moral theory; it is a metaphysical question, and an extremely difficult one at that. Must virtue theory then wait upon metaphysics to come up with the answer?

At first sight it might seem so. For virtue is said to involve knowledge, and part of this knowledge consists in having the *right* attitude to things. 'Right' here does not just mean 'morally right' or 'proper' or 'nice' in the modern sense; it means 'accurate, true'. One cannot have the right or correct attitude to something if the attitude is based on or involves false beliefs. And this suggests that if the status of the foetus is relevant to the rightness or wrongness of abortion, its status must be known, as a truth, to the fully wise and virtuous person.

But the sort of wisdom that the fully virtuous person has is not supposed to be recondite; it does not call for fancy philosophical sophistication, and it does not depend upon, let alone wait upon, the discoveries of academic philosophers.[11] And this entails the following, rather startling, conclusion: that the status of the foetus – that issue over which so much ink has been split – is, according to virtue theory, simply not relevant to the rightness or wrongness of abortion (within, that is, a secular morality).

Or rather, since that is clearly too radical a conclusion, it is in a sense relevant, but only in the sense that the familiar biological facts are relevant. By 'the familiar biological facts' I mean the facts that most human societies are and have been familiar with – that, standardly (but not invariably), pregnancy occurs as the result of sexual intercourse, that it lasts about nine months, during which time the foetus grows and develops, that standardly it terminates in the birth of a living baby, and that this is how we all come to be.

It might be thought that this distinction – between the familiar biological facts and the status of the foetus – is a distinction without a difference. But this is not so. To attach relevance to the status of the foetus, in the sense in which virtue theory claims it is not relevant, is to be gripped by the conviction that we must go beyond the familiar biological facts, deriving some sort of conclusion from them, such as that the foetus has rights, or is not a person, or something similar. It is also to believe that this exhausts the relevance of the familiar biological facts, that all they are relevant to is the status of the foetus and whether or not it is the sort of thing that may or may not be killed.

These convictions, I suspect, are rooted in the desire to solve the problem of abortion by getting it to fall under some general rule such as 'You ought not to kill anything with the right to life but may kill anything else'. But they have resulted in what should surely strike any nonphilosopher as a most bizarre aspect of nearly all the current philosophical literature on abortion, namely, that, far from treating abortion as a unique moral problem, markedly unlike any other, nearly everything written on the status of the foetus and its bearing on the abortion issue would be consistent with the human reproductive facts (to say nothing of family life) being totally different from what they are. Imagine that you are an alien extraterrestrial anthropologist who does not know that the human race is roughly 50 per cent female and 50 per cent male, or that our only (natural) form of reproduction involves heterosexual intercourse, viviparous birth, and the female's (and only the female's) being pregnant for nine months, or that females are capable of childbearing from late childhood to early middle age, or that childbearing is painful, dangerous and emotionally charged – do you think you would pick up these facts from the hundreds of articles written on the status of the foetus? I am quite sure you would not. And that, I think, shows that the current philosophical literature on abortion has got badly out of touch with reality.

Now if we are using virtue theory, our first question is not 'What do the familiar biological facts show – what can be derived from them about the status of the foetus?' but 'How do these facts figure in the practical reasoning, actions and passions, thoughts and reactions, of the virtuous and the nonvirtuous? What is the mark of having the right attitude to these facts and what manifests having the wrong attitude to them?'. This immediately makes essentially relevant not only all the facts about human reproduction I mentioned above, but a whole range of facts about our emotions in relation to them as well. I mean such facts as that human parents, both male and female, tend to care passionately about their offspring, and that family relationships are among the deepest and strongest in our lives – and, significantly, among the longest-lasting.

These facts make it obvious that pregnancy is not just one among many other physical conditions; and hence that anyone who genuinely believes that an abortion is comparable to a haircut or an appendectomy is mistaken.[12] The fact that the premature termination of a pregnancy is, in some sense, the cutting off of a new human life, and thereby, like the procreation of a new human life, connects with all our thoughts about human life and death, parenthood and family relationships, must make it a serious matter. To disregard this fact about it, to think of abortion as nothing but the killing of something that does not matter, or as nothing but the exercise of some right or rights one has, or as the incidental means to some desirable state of affairs, is to do something callous and light-minded, the sort of thing that no virtuous and wise person would do. It is to have the wrong attitude not only to foetuses, but more generally to human life and death, parenthood, and family relationships.

Although I say that the facts make this obvious, I know that this is one of my tendentious points. In partial support of it I note that even the most dedicated proponents of the view that deliberate abortion is just like an appendectomy or haircut rarely hold the same view of spontaneous abortion, that is, miscarriage. It is not so tendentious of me to claim that to react to people's grief over miscarriage by saying, or even thinking, 'What a fuss about nothing!' would be callous and light-minded, whereas to try to laugh someone out of grief over an appendectomy scar or a botched haircut would not be. It is hard to give this point due prominence within act-centred theories, for the inconsistency is an inconsistency in attitude about the seriousness of loss of life, not in beliefs about which acts are right or wrong. Moreover, an act-centred theorist may say, 'Well, there is nothing wrong with *thinking* "What a fuss about nothing!" as long as you do not say it and hurt the person who is grieving. And besides, we cannot be held responsible for our thoughts, only for the intentional actions they give rise to'. But the character traits that virtue theory emphasises are not simply dispositions to intentional actions, but a seamless disposition to certain actions and passions, thoughts and reactions.

To say that the cutting off of a human life is always a matter of some seriousness, at any stage, is not to deny the relevance of gradual foetal development. Notwithstanding the well-worn point that clear boundary lines cannot be drawn, our emotions and attitudes regarding the foetus do change as it develops, and again when it is born, and indeed further as the baby grows. Abortion for shallow reasons in the later stages is much more shocking than abortion for the same reasons in the early stages in a way that matches the fact that deep grief over miscarriage in the later stages is more appropriate than it is over miscarriage in the earlier stages (when, that is, the grief is solely about the loss of *this* child, not about, as might be the case, the loss of one's only hope of having a child or of having one's husband's child). Imagine (or recall) a woman who already has children; she had not intended to have more, but finds herself unexpectedly pregnant. Though contrary to her plans, the pregnancy, once established as a fact, is welcomed – and then she loses the embryo almost immediately. If this were bemoaned as a tragedy, it would, I think, be a misapplication of the concept of what is tragic. But it may still properly be mourned as a loss. The grief is expressed in such terms as 'I shall always wonder how she or he would have turned out' or 'When I look at the others, I shall think, "How different their lives would have been if this other one had been part of them."' It would, I take it, be callous and light-minded to say, or think, 'Well, she has already *got* four children; what's the problem?'; it would be neither, nor arrogantly intrusive in the case of a close friend, to try to correct prolonged mourning by saying, 'I know it's sad, but it's not a tragedy; rejoice in the ones you have'. The application of *tragic* becomes more appropriate as the foetus grows, for the mere fact that one has lived with it for longer, conscious of its existence, makes a difference. To shrug off an early abortion is understandable just because it is very hard to be fully conscious of the foetus's existence in the early stages and hence hard to appreciate that an early abortion is the destruction of life. It is particularly hard for the young and inexperienced to appreciate this, because appreciation of it usually comes only with experience.

I do not mean 'with the experience of having an abortion' (though that may be part of it) but, quite generally, 'with the experience of life'. Many women who have borne children contrast their later pregnancies with their first successful one, saying that in the later ones they were conscious of a new life growing in them from very early on. And, more generally, as one reaches the age at which the next generation is coming up close behind one, the counterfactuals 'If I, or she, had had an abortion, Alice, or Bob, would not have been born' acquire a significant application, which casts a new light on the conditionals 'If I or Alice have an abortion then some Caroline or Bill will not be born'.

The fact that pregnancy is not just one among many physical conditions does not mean that one can never regard it in that light without manifesting a vice. When women are in very poor physical health, or worn out from childbearing, or forced to do very physically demanding jobs, then they cannot be described as self-indulgent, callous, irresponsible, or light-minded if they seek abortions mainly with a view to avoiding pregnancy as the physical condition that it is. To go through with a pregnancy when one is utterly exhausted, or when one's job consists of crawling along tunnels hauling coal, as many women in the nineteenth century were obliged to do, is perhaps heroic, but people who do not achieve heroism are not necessarily vicious. That they can view the pregnancy only as eight months of misery, followed by hours if not days of agony and exhaustion, and abortion only as the blessed escape from this prospect, is entirely understandable and does not manifest any lack of serious respect for human life or a shallow attitude to motherhood. What it does show is that something is terribly amiss in the conditions of their lives, which make it so hard to recognise pregnancy and childbearing as the good that they can be.

In relation to this last point I should draw attention to the way in which virtue theory has a sort of built-in indexicality. Philosophers arguing against anything remotely resembling a belief in the sanctity of life (which the above claims clearly embody) frequently appeal to the existence of other communities in which abortion and infanticide are practised. We should not automatically assume that it is impossible that some other communities could be morally inferior to our own; maybe some are, or have been, precisely insofar as their members are, typically, callous or light-minded or unjust. But in communities in which life is a great deal tougher for everyone than it is in ours, having the right attitude to human life and death, parenthood, and family relationships might well manifest itself in ways that are unlike ours. When it is essential to survival that most members of the community fend for themselves at a very young age or work during most of their waking hours, selective abortion or infanticide might be practised either as a form of genuine euthanasia or for the sake of the community and not, I think, be thought callous or light-minded. But this does not make everything all right; as before, it shows that there is something amiss with the conditions of their lives, which are making it impossible for them to live really well.[13]

The foregoing discussion, insofar as it emphasises the right attitude to human life and death, parallels to a certain extent those standard discussions of abortion that concentrate on it solely as an issue of killing. But it does not, as those discussions do, gloss over the fact, emphasised by those who discuss the morality of abortion in terms of women's rights that abortion, wildly unlike any other form of killing, is the termination of a pregnancy, which is a condition of a woman's body and results in *her* having a child if it is not aborted. This fact is given due recognition not by appeal to women's rights but by emphasising the relevance of the familiar biological and psychological facts and their connection with having the right attitude to parenthood and family relationships. But it may well be thought that failing to bring in women's rights still leaves some important aspects of the problem of abortion untouched.

Speaking in terms of women's rights, people sometimes say things like, 'Well, it's her life you're talking about too, you know; she's got a right to her own life, her own happiness'. And the discussion stops there. But in the context of virtue theory, given that we are particularly concerned with what constitutes a good human life, with what true happiness or eudaimonia is, this is no place to stop. We go on to ask, 'And is this life of hers a good one? Is she living well?'.

If we are to go on to talk about good human lives, in the context of abortion, we have to bring in our thoughts about the value of love and family life, and our proper emotional development through a natural life cycle. The familiar facts support the view that parenthood in general, and motherhood and childbearing in particular, are intrinsically worthwhile, are among the things that can be correctly thought to be partially constitutive of a flourishing human life.[14] If this is right, then a woman who opts for not being a mother (at all, or again, or now) by opting for abortion may thereby be manifesting a flawed grasp of what her life should be, and be about – a grasp that is childish, or grossly materialistic, or shortsighted, or shallow.

I said '*may* thereby': this *need* not be so. Consider, for instance, a woman who has already had several children and fears that to have another will seriously affect her capacity to be a good mother to the ones she has – she does not show a lack of appreciation of the intrinsic value of being a parent by opting for abortion. Nor does a woman who has been a good mother and is approaching the age at which she may be looking forward to being a good grandmother. Nor does a woman who discovers that her pregnancy may well kill her, and opts for abortion and adoption. Nor, necessarily, does a woman who has decided to lead a life centred around some other worthwhile activity or activities with which motherhood would compete.

People who are childless by choice are sometimes described as 'irresponsible', or 'selfish', or 'refusing to grow up', or 'not knowing what life is about'. But one can hold that having children is intrinsically worthwhile without endorsing this, for we are, after all, in the happy position of there being more worthwhile things to do than can be fitted into one lifetime. Parenthood, and motherhood in particular, even if granted to be intrinsically worthwhile, undoubtedly take up a lot of one's adult life, leaving no room for some other worthwhile pursuits. But some women who choose abortion rather than have their first child, and some men who encourage their partners to choose abortion, are not avoiding parenthood for the sake of other worthwhile pursuits, but for the worthless one of 'having a good time', or for the pursuit of some false vision of the ideals of freedom or self-realisation. And some others who say 'I am not ready for parenthood yet' are making some sort of mistake about the extent to which one can manipulate the circumstances of one's life so as to make it fulfil some dream that one has. Perhaps one's dream is to have two perfect children, a girl and a boy, within a perfect marriage, in financially secure circumstances, with an interesting job of one's own. But to care too much about that dream, to demand of life that it give it to one and act accordingly, may be both greedy and foolish, and is to run the risk of missing out on happiness entirely. Not only may fate make the dream impossible, or destroy it, but one's own attachment to it may make it impossible. Good marriages, and the most promising children, can be destroyed by just one adult's excessive demand for perfection.

Once again, this is not to deny that girls may quite properly say 'I am not ready for motherhood yet', especially in our society, and, far from manifesting irresponsibility or light-mindedness, show an appropriate modesty or humility, or a fearfulness that does not amount to cowardice. However, even when the decision to have an abortion is the right decision – one that does not itself fall under a vice-related term and thereby one that the perfectly virtuous could recommend – it does not follow that there is no sense in which having the abortion is wrong, or guilt inappropriate. For, by virtue of the fact that a human life has been cut short, some evil has probably been brought about,[15] and that circumstances make the decision to bring about some evil the right decision will be a ground for guilt if getting into those circumstances in the first place itself manifested a flaw in character.

What 'gets one into those circumstances' in the case of abortion is, except in the case of rape, one's sexual activity and one's choices, or the lack of them, about one's sexual partner and about contraception. The virtuous woman (which here of course does not mean simply 'chaste woman' but 'woman with the virtues') has such character traits as strength, independence, resoluteness, decisiveness, self-confidence, responsibility, serious-mindedness and self-determination – and no one, I think, could deny that many women become pregnant in circumstances in which they cannot welcome or cannot face the thought of having *this* child precisely because they lack one or some of these character traits. So even in the cases where the decision to have an abortion is the right one, it can still be the reflection of a moral failing – not because the decision itself is weak or cowardly or irresolute or irresponsible or light-minded, but because lack of the requisite opposite of these failings landed one in the circumstances in the first place. Hence the common universalised claim that guilt and remorse are never appropriate emotions about an abortion is denied. They may be appropriate, and appropriately inculcated, even when the decision was the right one.

Another motivation for bringing women's rights into the discussion may be to attempt to correct the implication, carried by the killing-centred approach, that insofar as abortion is wrong, it is a wrong that only women do, or at least (given the preponderance of male doctors) that only women instigate. I do not myself believe that we can thus escape the fact that nature bears harder on women than it does on men,[16] but virtue theory can certainly correct many of the injustices that the emphasis on women's rights is rightly concerned about. With very little amendment, everything that has been said above applies to boys and men too. Although the abortion decision is, in a natural sense, the woman's decision, proper to her, boys and men are often party to it, for well or ill, and even when they are not, they are bound to have been party to the circumstances that brought it up. No less than girls and women, boys and men can, in their actions, manifest self-centredness, callousness, and light-mindedness about life and parenthood in relation to abortion. They can be self-centred or courageous about the possibility of disability in their offspring; they need to reflect on their sexual activity and their choices, or the lack of them, about their sexual partner and contraception; they need to grow up and take responsibility for their own actions and life in relation to fatherhood. If it is true, as I maintain, that insofar as motherhood is intrinsically worthwhile, being a mother is an important purpose in women's lives, *being a father* (rather than a mere generator) is an important purpose in men's lives as well, and it is adolescent of men to turn a blind eye to this and pretend that they have many more important things to do.

## CONCLUSION

Much more might be said, but I shall end the actual discussion of the problem of abortion here, and conclude by highlighting what I take to be its significant features. These hark back to many of the criticisms of virtue theory discussed earlier.

The discussion does not proceed simply by our trying to answer the question 'Would a perfectly virtuous agent ever have an abortion and, if so, when?'; virtue theory is not limited to considering 'Would Socrates have had an abortion if he were a raped, pregnant fifteen-year-old?' nor automatically stumped when we are considering circumstances into which no virtuous agent would have got herself. Instead, much of the discussion proceeds in the virtue- and vice-related terms whose application, in several cases, yields practical conclusions (cf. the third and fourth criticisms above). These terms are difficult to apply correctly, and anyone might challenge my application of any one of them. So, for example, I have claimed that some abortions, done for certain reasons, would be callous or light-minded; that others might indicate an appropriate modesty or humility; that others would reflect a greedy and foolish attitude to what one could expect out of life. Any of these examples may be disputed, but what is at issue is, should these difficult terms be there, or should the discussion be couched in terms that all clever adolescents can apply correctly? (Cf. the first half of the 'major objection' above.)

Proceeding as it does in the virtue- and vice-related terms, the discussion thereby, inevitably, also contains claims about what is worthwhile, serious and important, good and evil, in our lives. So, for example, I claimed that parenthood is intrinsically worthwhile, and that having a good time was a worthless end (in life, not on individual occasions); that losing a foetus is always a serious matter (albeit not a tragedy in itself in the first trimester) whereas acquiring an appendectomy scar is a trivial one; that (human) death is an evil. Once again, these are difficult matters, and anyone might challenge any one of my claims. But what is at issue is, as before, should those difficult claims be there or can one reach practical conclusions about real moral issues that are in no way determined by premises about such matters? (Cf. the fifth criticism, and the second half of the 'major criticism'.)

The discussion also thereby, inevitably, contains claims about what life is like (e.g., my claim that love and friendship do not survive their parties' constantly insisting on their rights; or the claim that to demand perfection of life is to run the risk of missing out on happiness entirely). What is at issue is, should those disputable claims be there, or is our knowledge (or are our false opinions) about what life is like irrelevant to our understanding of real moral issues? (Cf. both halves of the 'major criticism'.)

Naturally, my own view is that all these concepts should be there in any discussion of real moral issues and that virtue theory, which uses all of them, is the right theory to apply to them. I do not pretend to have shown this. I realise that proponents of rival theories may say that, now that they have understood how virtue theory uses the range of concepts it draws on, they are more convinced than ever that such concepts should not figure in an adequate normative theory, because they are sectarian, or vague, or too particular, or improperly anthropocentric, and reinstate what I called the 'major criticism'. Or, finding many of the details of the discussion appropriate, they may agree that many, perhaps even all, of the concepts should figure, but argue that virtue theory gives an inaccurate account of the way the concepts fit together (and indeed of the concepts themselves) and that another theory provides a better account; that would be interesting to see. Moreover, I admitted that there were at least two problems for virtue theory: that it has to argue against moral scepticism, 'pluralism', and cultural relativism, and that it has to find something to say about conflicting requirements of different virtues.

Proponents of rival theories might argue that their favoured theory provides better solutions to these problems than virtue theory can. Indeed, they might criticise virtue theory for finding problems here at all. Anyone who argued for at least one of moral scepticism, 'pluralism', or cultural relativism could presumably do so (provided their favoured theory does not find a similar problem); and a utilitarian might say that benevolence is the only virtue and hence that virtue theory errs when it discusses even apparent conflicts between the requirements of benevolence and some other character trait such as honesty.

Defending virtue theory against all possible, or even likely, criticisms of it would be a lifelong task. As I said at the outset, in this chapter I aimed to defend the theory against some criticisms which I thought arose from an inadequate understanding of it, and to improve that understanding. If I have succeeded, we may hope for more comprehending criticisms of virtue theory than have appeared hitherto.

* Versions of this chapter have been read to philosophy societies at University College, London, Rutgers University, and the Universities of Dundee, Edinburgh, Oxford, Swansea and California–San Diego; at a conference of the Polish and British Academies in Cracow in 1988 on 'Life, Death and the Law', and as a symposium paper at the Pacific Division of the American Philosophical Association in 1989. I am grateful to the many people who contributed to the discussions of it on these occasions, and particularly to Philippa Foot and Anne Jaap Jacobson for private discussion.

## ENDNOTES

1. It should be noted that this premise intentionally allows for the possibility that two virtuous agents, faced with the same choice in the same circumstances, may act differently. For example, one might opt for taking her father off the life-support machine and the other for leaving her father on it. The theory requires that neither agent thinks that what the other does is wrong (see note 4 below), but it explicitly allows that no action is uniquely right in such a case – both are right. It also intentionally allows for the possibility that in some circumstances – those into which no virtuous agent could have got herself – no action is right. I explore this premise at greater length in 'Applying Virtue Ethics', in a *festschrift* for Philippa Foot.

2. There is, of course, the further question of whether the theory eventually describes a larger circle and winds up relying on the concept of right action in its interpretation of *eudaimonia*. In denying that the theory is trivially circular, I do not pretend to answer this intricate question. It is certainly true that virtue theory does not claim that the correct conception

of *eudaimonia* can be got from 'an independent "value-free" investigation of human nature' (John McDowell, 'The Role of *Eudaimonia* in Aristotle's Ethics', in *Essays on Aristotle's Ethics*, Amelie Rorty (ed.), Berkeley and Los Angeles: University of California Press (1980). The sort of training that is required for acquiring the correct conception no doubt involves being taught from early on such things as 'Decent people do this sort of thing, not that' and 'To do such and such is the mark of a depraved character' (cf. *Nicomachean Ethics*, 1110a22). But whether this counts as relying on the concept of right (or wrong) action seems to me very unclear and requiring much discussion.

3. Cf. Bernard Williams' point in *Ethics and the Limits of Philosophy*, London: William Collins (1985) that we need an enriched ethical vocabulary, not a cut-down one.

4. I put *pluralism* in scare quotes to serve as a warning that virtue theory is not incompatible with all forms of it. It allows for 'competing conceptions' of *eudaimonia* and the worthwhile, for instance, in the sense that it allows for a plurality of flourishing lives – the theory need not follow Aristotle in specifying the life of contemplation as the only one that truly constitutes *eudaimonia* (if he does). But the conceptions 'compete' only in the sense that, within a single flourishing life, not everything worthwhile can be fitted in; the theory does not allow that two people with a correct conception of *eudaimonia* can disagree over whether the way the other is living constitutes flourishing. Moreover, the theory is committed to the strong thesis that the same set of character traits is needed for *any* flourishing life; it will not allow that, for instance, soldiers need courage but wives and mothers do not, or that judges need justice but can live well despite lacking kindness. (This obviously is related to the point made in note 1 above.) For an interesting discussion of pluralism (different interpretations thereof) and virtue theory, see Douglas B. Rasmussen, 'Liberalism and Natural End Ethics', *American Philosophical Quarterly* 27 (1990), 153–61.

5. E.g., in Williams' Jim and Pedro case in J. J. C. Smart and Bernard Williams, *Utilitarianism: For and Against*, London: Cambridge University Press (1973).

6. Intimations of this criticism constantly come up in discussion; the clearest statement of it I have found is by Onora O'Neill, in her review of Stephen Clark's *The Moral Status of Animals*, in *Journal of Philosophy* 77 (1980), 440–6. For a response I am much in sympathy with, see Cora Diamond, 'Anything But Argument?' *Philosophical Investigations* 5 (1982), 23–41.

7. Aristotle, *Nicomachean Ethics*, 1142a12–16.

8. It seems likely that some people have been misled by Foot's discussion of euthanasia (through no fault of hers) into thinking that a virtue theorist's discussion of terminating human life will be conducted exclusively in terms of justice and charity (and the corresponding vice terms) (Philippa Foot, 'Euthanasia', *Philosophy & Public Affairs* 6, No. 2 [Winter 1977], 85–112). But the act-category *euthanasia* is a very special one, at least as defined in her article, since such an act must be done 'for the sake of the one who is to die'. Building a virtuous motivation into the specification of the act in this way immediately rules out the application of many other vice terms.

9. Judith Jarvis Thomson, 'A Defense of Abortion', *Philosophy & Public Affairs* 1, No. 1 (Autumn 1971), 47–66. One could indeed regard this article as proto-virtue theory (no doubt to the surprise of the author) if the concepts of callousness and kindness were allowed more weight.

10. One possible qualification: if one ties the concept of justice very closely to rights, then if women do have a moral right to terminate their pregnancies it *may* follow that in doing so they do not act unjustly. (Cf. Thomson, 'A Defense of Abortion'.) But it is debatable whether even that much follows.

11. This is an assumption of virtue theory, and I do not attempt to defend it here. An adequate discussion of it would require a separate article, since, although most moral philosophers would be chary of claiming that intellectual sophistication is a necessary condition of moral wisdom or virtue, most of us, from Plato onward, tend to write as if this were so. Sorting out which claims about moral knowledge are committed to this kind of élitism and which can, albeit with difficulty, be reconciled with the idea that moral knowledge can be acquired by anyone who really wants it would be a major task.

12. Mary Anne Warren, in 'On the Moral and Legal Status of Abortion', *Monist* 57 (1973), sec. 1, says of the opponents of restrictive laws governing abortion that 'their conviction (for the most part) is that abortion is not a *morally* serious and extremely unfortunate, even though sometimes justified, act, comparable to killing in self-defense or to letting the violinist die,

but rather is closer to being a *morally neutral* act, like cutting one's hair' (italics mine). I would like to think that no one *genuinely* believes this. But certainly in discussion, particularly when arguing against restrictive laws or the suggestion that remorse over abortion might be appropriate, I have found that some people *say* they believe it (and often cite Warren's article, albeit inaccurately, despite its age). Those who allow that it is morally serious, and far from morally neutral, have to argue against restrictive laws, or the appropriateness of remorse, on a very different ground from that laid down by the premise 'The foetus is just part of the woman's body (and she has a right to determine what happens to her body and should not feel guilt about anything she does to it)'.

13. For another example of the way in which 'tough conditions' can make a difference to what is involved in having the right attitude to human life and death and family relationships, see the concluding sentences of Foot's 'Euthanasia'.

14. I take this as a premise here, but argue for it in some detail in my *Beginning Lives*, Oxford: Basil Blackwell (1987). In this connection I also discuss adoption and the sense in which it may be regarded as 'second best', and the difficult question of whether the good of parenthood may properly be sought, or indeed bought, by surrogacy.

15. I say 'some evil has probably been brought about' on the ground that (human) life is (usually) a good and hence (human) death usually an evil. The exceptions would be (a) where death is actually a good or a benefit, because the baby that would come to be if the life were not cut short would be better off dead than alive, and (b) where death, though not a good, is not an evil either, because the life that would be led (e.g., in a state of permanent coma) would not be a good. (See Foot, 'Euthanasia'.)

16. I discuss this point at greater length in *Beginning Lives*.

# 14

# CONTEMPORARY VIRTUE ETHICS AND ARISTOTLE

## Peter Simpson

Moral philosophy has long been dominated by two basic theories, Kantianism or deontology on the one hand, and utilitarianism or consequentialism on the other. Increasing dissatisfaction with these theories and their variants has led in recent years to the emergence of a different theory, the theory of virtue ethics.[1] According to virtue ethics, what is primary for ethics is not, as deontologists and utilitarians hold, the judgment of acts or their consequences, but the judgment of agents. The good person is the fundamental category for moral philosophy, and the good person is the person of good character, the person who possesses moral virtue.[2]

Virtue ethics, according to its authors, is not a new theory. Not only are its origins very old,[3] but Aristotle is still held to be its finest exponent. Some contemporary virtue theorists in fact call themselves neo-Aristotelians. They are Aristotelians because they accept Aristotle's fundamental ideas; they are neo-Aristotelians because they reject some of his conclusions, notably about manual labor, slavery and women.[4] But neo-Aristotelians depart from Aristotle in more ways than those they expressly admit, notably over the connection between ethics and politics. The work of Aristotle that is most used and referred to by these theorists is the *Nicomachean Ethics*. The *Politics* is seldom if ever mentioned. This is not because such theorists are unaware of the connection between the *Nicomachean Ethics* and the *Politics*; rather they do not pay it much attention. Some do explicitly acknowledge the political context of Aristotle's ethics and even endorse this fact themselves,[5] but when they do so they do not give the reasons Aristotle gives. This is clear from their neglect of the central text of Aristotle on this question, namely the last chapter of the *Ethics*.[6]

## 1.

Aristotle opens this chapter by asking whether the chosen project of the *Nicomachean Ethics* has been completed. His answer is no because in practical matters the end is not to theorise but to do, not to know virtue but to possess and exercise it. The first task may have been accomplished, but the second has not. It is this second task, the task of coming to possess and exercise virtue, and the questions it raises, that occupy the rest of the chapter. Aristotle's answers to these questions force him into the discussion of political regimes and hence directly into the subject of the *Politics*.[7]

One should not, however, hurry over the beginning of the chapter and the distinction between theory and practice. Drawing such a distinction has now become standard in moral philosophy. Apart from works on the theories of ethics, which used to be virtually the whole of the academic study of ethics, there now abound works on practical ethics, such as biomedical ethics, business ethics, and so on. Broadly stated, this contemporary distinction between theory and practice is a distinction between the general and the particular, between propounding a general theory and applying it to, or testing it against, particular cases. The aim of the practical side of this exercise is to work out, as far as possible, whether and in what circumstances the particular issue in question, euthanasia say, is morally right or wrong.

This distinction between theory and practice is not the same as Aristotle's. His is not a distinction between the general and the particular but between knowing what is right and wrong on the one hand, and actually doing the right and avoiding the wrong on the other. The modern distinction passes over Aristotle's distinction and ignores his practical concern. Conversely, Aristotle's distinction passes over the modern one. If our modern distinction contains nothing corresponding to Aristotle's practice, however, we do have what he calls practice. We just do not include it under ethics, but under psychology, therapy, counselling, and the like. Still, it is striking that Aristotle includes this sort of thing under politics. As he goes on to argue, getting people actually to be virtuous is the job of political authority.[8] Further, though Aristotle does not note the difference between general theory and particular applications, he surely recognises it. The *Ethics* seems to be full of both: general theory of virtue and particular accounts of its exercise. This indeed is why virtue theorists turn to Aristotle. He provides them with a model of what such a theory should look like.

So what should virtue theory look like? Presumably it should at least be a theory that gives us a reasoned account of what virtue in general is and why it is necessary to be virtuous, or why being virtuous is good. More specifically, it should give us a reasoned account of what the number and kinds of the particular virtues are, why each one of these is good, and what acts they issue in. The general strategy of virtue theorists in response to these questions is to appeal, in the way they say Aristotle first did, to human happiness or flourishing. The virtues are those qualities of character the possession and exercise of which make human beings flourish. Flourishing is a good, perhaps the greatest good. Thus, given the proper account of flourishing, the argument goes, it should be possible to establish which qualities of character contribute to it, and so are virtues, and which do not, and so are vices. These qualities of character will then provide the key to determining good and bad action. A lot of debate about virtue ethics has therefore not surprisingly focused on this question of human flourishing, and whether an account can be given of it that will do the job required.[9]

One might think that if Aristotle is such a fine exponent of virtue ethics this is where his writings should be of special help. One would accordingly expect virtue theorists to take over his notion of flourishing to explain and justify the virtues. Unfortunately this turns out not to be such a good idea. Aristotle's notion of flourishing, or *eudaimonia*, seems, on the one hand, not to be a unified whole, since he recognises two different forms of it, and, on the other hand, to be too narrow and élitist. Only philosophers, according to Aristotle, those few who devote themselves to the theoretical life, flourish in the best way, while the politicians, or those who devote themselves to the practical life, flourish in a secondary and lesser way. Everyone else, presumably the vast majority, do not flourish at all. This is therefore one of those places where neo-Aristotelians find themselves forced to be more 'neo' than Aristotelian.[10]

There is a more serious difficulty than this to taking Aristotle as a guide to human flourishing, however. According to virtue theorists, one is supposed to use the concept of flourishing to develop an account and justification of the virtues. Flourishing is the prior notion and the virtues are to be understood in terms of it. But Aristotle's understanding of the relation between flourishing and the virtues is the opposite of this. Aristotle does not argue to the virtues from some prior notion of flourishing, nor does he even attempt to do this. The virtues fall into the definition of *eudaimonia*, but *eudaimonia* does not fall into the definition of the virtues. *Eudaimonia* is defined as activity of soul along with virtue, while the virtues are defined as various habits of choice, lying in a mean relative to us, and determined by reason. What falls into the definition of a thing is prior to that thing and has to be understood before that thing can be understood. So the notion of virtue must be prior to the notion of *eudaimonia* and must be understood before *eudaimonia* can be understood.[11] Accordingly, the long discussion of the virtues that follows the definition of *eudaimonia* in *Nicomachean Ethics* 1, their general definition, their number, their detailed descriptions, must all be understood as a commentary on the original definition. This is confirmed by the way Aristotle returns to the definition in the final book of the *Ethics*. He picks it up more or less where he left it in book 1 and then, using the account of the virtues he has just given in the intermediate books, finally determines what the flourishing life is. In other words, whereas the first book gives only a formal and general definition of *eudaimonia*, the last book gives the detailed and explicit definition.

If this is true, then any theorists who want to follow Aristotle in this respect are going to face a serious problem. Surely, to use the virtues to define flourishing instead of using flourishing to define the virtues begs all the important questions. The job of ethics is to give an account and justification of why such and such is good or bad, virtuous or vicious, right or wrong. It is not its job to assume this in advance and then use it to tell us what to do or how to live. To think this would be to think that the job of ethics is simply to tell us what we are already supposed to know, and that is not only useless, but completely misses the point. It is because we do not know, or are unsure about, what we should do or how we should live that we turn to ethics in the hope of finding answers. This is what the standard modern theories of ethics, utilitarianism and Kantianism, attempt to do; it is, moreover, what contemporary virtue theorists profess to do. If this were not so their theory could not be put forward as a serious rival to the others.

What about Aristotle himself? If he does not derive the virtues from the notion of flourishing, whence does he derive them? What other justification does he give in their defence? To the question of whence he derives the virtues, there seems to be a very simple answer: From common opinion. The virtues Aristotle lists, and the descriptions he gives of them and of their possessors, are taken from the common experience and opinions of the citizens of the day. 'Everyone in Aristotle's Athens knew who the virtuous citizens were; everyone could recognise courage or magnanimity.'[12] If this answers the question of derivation, however, it can hardly answer the question of justification. Merely because something is commonly believed to be a virtue does not mean that it is so. But perhaps it was enough for Aristotle that everyone would agree that these were the virtues. What need of proof is there if everyone already knows?

Is it true, though, that everyone did know or that everyone would agree? Surely we learn enough from the sophists and from the dialogues of Plato to know that the Athenians were very far from agreeing about the good and about virtue. Aristotle himself concedes that the many do not think that virtue is good or makes one flourish, but rather that the sensual pleasures do. So if Aristotle relies on common opinion, this is not the opinion of the many. It can only be the opinion of the few. We do not have to go far to find out who these few are. It is necessary, declares Aristotle, that those who are going to study ethics should be well trained in their habits; for the first principles of this study are the facts, and such persons already have or will easily accept these first principles. But those who neither know the facts, nor will believe someone who tells them, are, in the words of Hesiod, 'good-for-nothing'.[13] What are the facts? They are the facts about the just and the beautiful, as the context makes clear. Those who possess these facts are certainly not the many, who are, says Aristotle, anything but well trained in their habits, since they in fact follow their passions and have no sense at all of the beautiful. They must rather be those who call themselves, and are called by Aristotle, 'the beautiful and the good'.[14] Our English words imitate the Greek in this respect, for we speak of 'gentlemen', 'nobles' and 'aristocrats'.

Gentlemen have few doubts about what is good and beautiful. They are confident that they both know it and possess it.[15] Aristotle evidently agrees with them; for one of the notorious problems in Aristotle's ethical theory concerns the criterion for determining what is virtuous and what is vicious.[16] We know that each virtue is a mean between two vicious extremes, and we know the names for the virtues and the vices, but how are we to determine in each case where the mean lies, or how are we to determine about this particular action whether it is an act of virtue or not? This is where Aristotle appeals to the virtue of prudence (*phronesis*). The mean is what prudence determines to be the mean. This doctrine has struck many readers as signally unhelpful. What we want is not a discussion of the faculty which does the deciding but of the criterion by reference to which it does so.

Aristotle is, despite appearances, not quite as vague as this. He says on more than one occasion that prudence is perception. It operates in the here and now, for it decides what is the virtuous thing to do here and now; and judging the here and now is the work of perception. He also refers to prudence as a sort of 'eye'.[17] Prudence judges where the mean of virtue lies in the here and now, not by referring back to some criterion or measure, but directly by 'seeing' this mean in the here and now. In other words, prudence does not *reason* about virtue, it directly *intuits* it. So to look for a criterion of virtue which prudence is to follow must be mistaken. To think a criterion is necessary is to think that prudence is some sort of reasoning faculty which subsumes particular cases under general rules or applies general rules to particular cases. But if prudence intuits, rather than reasons out, this is precisely what it will *not* do.[18]

The great problem with appeals to intuition, of course, is that different people have different intuitions, so they will never give the same answer about what it is right to do. Aristotle would have no problem with this though. He would reply that not everyone's intuitions count as instances of prudence; only the intuitions of the virtuous do. Those who lack virtue necessarily lack the right sort of intuition. The 'eye' of their soul is blind.[19] This reply, however, is circular. If we ask who the virtuous are we are told they are those who have right intuition; if we ask who those with right intuition are we are told they are the virtuous.

Is this circle all Aristotle leaves us with? He does offer hints about acquiring the necessary prudence. He counsels us, for instance, to steer away from the extreme that is more contrary to the mean. He says we should guard against our natural tendencies as regards pleasures and pains. He says we should cling to the unproved sayings of the old and wise, and gives us instances of acts that are vicious, such as adultery, murder and theft; or bestial, such as homosexuality, cannibalism and fear of the sounds of mice.[20] What help do these sorts of remarks really provide? For Aristotle never bothers to give us any reason *why* adultery or murder is wrong. This is just asserted as a fact. They are presumably the sort of facts that Aristotle requires the hearers of his *Ethics* already to know, since those who do not know them are good-for-nothings. Thus we come back to where we were before, to 'the beautiful and the good', to the gentlemen and the sons of gentlemen. They will not be troubled by Aristotle's circle because they are already inside it. If not yet fully virtuous, they are on the way there. They certainly know and accept the necessary facts. Their intuitions are basically right. So the circle in Aristotle's theory may be a problem for everyone else; it is not a problem for the gentlemen.

If all this is correct, then Aristotle's theory of virtue has an altogether striking character. First, it does not seem to be a moral theory at all, at least not in the sense of moral theory that we standardly recognise. What we want from a moral theory is some overall account of moral goodness and badness which we can then use to show why this or that particular act is right or wrong. So the Kantian explains the right and wrong in terms of agreement with the categorical imperative, and the utilitarian in terms of promotion of the general welfare. Aristotle indeed has a general account of virtue, that it is a mean between two extremes, and so on. This general account, however, cannot be used to show that something is an act of virtue or something else an act of vice. The truth about such particulars is not shown by theory; it is perceived by prudence. In fact, the truth of Aristotle's general theory is shown from the particulars rather than vice versa; for when Aristotle wants to confirm that virtue is a mean between extremes he looks to particular virtues and particular acts to do this. It is, one may say, because his hearers already recognise particular virtues and vices and their corresponding acts that they are able to see, when Aristotle makes it explicit, that in each case virtue is a mean and vice an extreme.[21]

So Aristotle does not have a moral theory in the typically modern sense. Consequently he does not offer a good place for contemporary virtue ethicists to start if they want to develop such a theory. A striking contrast between them and Aristotle can be noted here. It is one of the chief concerns of virtue ethicists to establish that the virtues really are virtues or really are goods worth having.[22] This, however, is never a concern of Aristotle's. He never bothers to argue that justice or courage are goods worth having. These are givens of his argument, not conclusions. This is clear in the definition of *eudaimonia* as excellent activity of soul; for that the virtues he goes on to list are the excellences is taken as manifest. This is indeed manifest to those Aristotle is addressing, the well-educated gentlemen. It is not manifest, by contrast, to the many. Contemporary virtue ethicists seem to agree with the many, for they do not take this as manifest either.[23]

Another striking character of Aristotle's theory of virtue follows from this. It now looks as if Aristotle's theory is not only not a moral theory, it is not even a piece of moral philosophy. When it comes to particular judgments about good and bad, Aristotle's court of appeal is not reason or argument but opinion – and not the opinion of all, but only of a few.[24] These few turn out to be generally identifiable with a particular social class, the class of gentlemen. Aristotle's ethics is an ethics of and for gentlemen. It is prejudice, not philosophy.[25]

## 2.

Aristotle's position is not so crude, as a further look at the last chapter of the *Nicomachean Ethics* will reveal.[26] Having made the distinction between knowing virtue and getting it, Aristotle turns to consider how to get it. If words were sufficient for this, he says, we should provide them, but as it is, words seem only able to make the true lover of beauty able to possess virtue. The many will not be affected in this way; words cannot turn them towards the beautiful and the good. The many have no sense of the beautiful and avoid baseness through fear and punishment, not through shame. The many are clearly in need of something else to make them virtuous. What might this something else be? Aristotle mentions three things through which we become good: nature, habit and teaching. There is nothing we can do to ensure the presence of the first. That belongs to the truly fortunate through some divine causality. As regards the third, teaching, this will only be effective with those whose soul has been prepared in its habits to enjoy and hate in a beautiful way. Teaching, therefore, requires prior habituation, the second of the three things Aristotle mentions. The hearer's character must first be disposed to virtue and already be in love with the beautiful if teaching is to have its effect. But the only way to achieve this is through proper training from youth up, and that, in turn, cannot be achieved without the right laws.[27]

Words, it is now evident, are sufficient for no one except the divinely fortunate. The beauty-loving youth for whom they were first said to be sufficient only become beauty-loving through discipline. Once habituation under coercive laws has preceded, then words can have their effect and convert law-generated love of beauty into fully fledged virtue. So how will the many become good? Aristotle's silent answer is that they cannot become good. The necessary love of beauty has not been generated in them, and all that the laws are able to do is keep them in check through force.[28]

Aristotle's denial that the many can become virtuous goes along with his earlier refusal to pay their opinions about good and bad any attention. His preference for the gentlemen is consistent; but this preference is not prejudice. As this passage indicates, Aristotle's views about gentlemen and beauty-loving youth are tied up with his views about the soul and its parts. Aristotle outlines his theory of the soul at the end of the first book of the *Nicomachean Ethics*. There are three parts to the soul, but only two are relevant to ethics: desire or passion, and reason. Desire ought by nature to obey reason, for reason is what makes humans to be human and not just animal.[29] This does not happen automatically, however. This is manifest in the akratic or weak-willed, whose reason tells them to do the best, but whose passions drag them in the opposite direction. In the continent, by contrast, and especially in the virtuous, reason has the upper hand and the desires yield to reason. Clearly what is decisive for virtue and its development is the subordination of desire to reason. Experience teaches that such subordination comes about by habituation, not teaching. Experience further teaches that if passion gets the upper hand, appeals to reason are useless. Appeals to reason could only work if reason were in control, but in such cases reason is, *ex hypothesi*, not in control.[30]

Reason and desire are in agreement in the vicious as well as in the virtuous. In the vicious, however, this agreement is the wrong way around. Reason is here subordinate to passion, not passion to reason. That is why, as Aristotle says, bad habits corrupt not only desire, so that one does not love beauty, but also reason, so that one has no knowledge of or appreciation for beauty. Bad habits blind one to the moral facts and make think that vice is good and to be pursued, and virtue bad and to be avoided. In such people the first principles have been lost.

Aristotle's doctrine of prudence is tied up with this psychology. Prudence is the perception or intuition that the virtuous have; but the virtuous are those in whom reason rules, and rules without opposition. Their perception is therefore the perception of reason. What this perception perceives is the mean, and the mean is what agrees with reason. Prudence, the finding of the virtuous mean, is reason finding what accords with reason. As and when each situation arises, a finely attuned reason, unclouded by the distractions of passion, will simply sense what is right, what goes too far and what does not go far enough. We sometimes talk about things 'feeling right', meaning typically what feels right to affections and emotions. We could, with not too much licence, talk also about what 'feels right' to reason.[31] If we did, this would bring us close to the perceiving that is Aristotle's prudence. Not everyone is going to be good at feeling what is right to reason, but only those in whom reason rules and whose feeling is therefore the feeling of reason. Those who are dominated by passion will not be good at this because their feelings will either be those of their passions or will be too influenced by their passions. They will not be competent judges, and their opinions about what is virtuous and vicious will be without authority.[32]

Aristotle's psychology and ethics are closely tied together. Both are also closely tied to observation: the observation of human souls in action, in particular the observation of how passion and reason interact, and of how passion will dominate reason if nothing is done early in life to prevent it. The importance for Aristotle of such observation of souls can be seen also in this other way. When he first broaches the question of what flourishing or happiness is, he mentions three kinds of lives: the lives of indulgence, of politics, and of philosophy. These are the only candidates for happiness. All others reduce to these.[33] This claim is part of what we might call Aristotle's response to cultural and ethical relativism. Aristotle denies that the variety of opinions and practices in human life is as various as is often thought. He also denies that there is no way to reduce them to basic types. On the contrary, it is quite possible to do this, and the types are the three mentioned; for only those lives are to be considered that have a claim to being called happy. Many lives are devoted to things necessary, such as a life of business or of the mechanical arts, and not to a free and leisured happiness.[34]

Given that only these three lives are worth considering when it comes to the happy life, it is easy to show that only two are worth considering seriously. The life of indulgence, of sensual pleasure, is not a human life, and so is not a life of human happiness. The happy life must indeed be pleasant, but not, or not simply, with the physical pleasures. The ox worshipped in Egypt as the god Apis, notes Aristotle drily, has a greater abundance of such pleasures than many monarchs.[35] This leaves only the lives of politics and philosophy. But if the political life is really to denote a distinct kind of life, and constitute a third possibility, it must be understood as the life that those lead who devote themselves to politics for the sake of performing beautiful and virtuous deeds. Many politicians enter politics for the sake of gain. Their kind of political life is no different from the life of others who live for gain.[36] The life of gain is either not a happy life, for it is subject to necessity, or it reduces to the life of indulgence. The truly political life is the life devoted to moral and political virtue. This sort of politics is readily identifiable as the sort that gentlemen practise and strive to practise. The history of ancient Athens, to say nothing of the history of other places, provides us with plenty of examples.[37]

The life of philosophy too is a life of virtue, though a life of theoretical virtue. Unlike politicians, philosophers prefer to avoid the fully practical life in order to devote themselves to contemplation. Still, they do not ignore the moral and political virtues. They will practise these virtues when the occasion demands. Consequently, as regards these virtues, the philosophers will not differ from the gentlemen. The only serious question in ethics, therefore, about what life to lead concerns the political and philosophic lives. The other contender, the life of indulgence, has already been declared defeated because it is not human. From this it follows necessarily that the happy life must be the life of virtue in the sense in which virtue means the moral virtues of gentlemen and the theoretical virtues of philosophers. So if Aristotle prefers the gentleman, and if his theory of moral virtue is class-based, this is not a result of prejudice. He has reasons for his preference based on empirical observations of human souls, and human lives, and of the conditions and nature of each.

Many will still say that Aristotle was wrong in his preferences even if he was not simply prejudiced. Some want to explain this error in terms of history. Aristotle was not able, they say, to think beyond the limits of his time. If his views apply, they apply only to the ancient Greeks. This explanation is false for two reasons. First, Aristotle's ethical views apply not to all the ancient Greeks, but to a limited group of them, the noble few. There were plenty of Greeks who would have rejected his views.[38] Second, this group of people, while always limited *at* any particular time, has never been limited *to* any particular time. There were gentlemen, and people Aristotle would have recognised as gentlemen, both before his time and for many centuries after it. Such people still exist. They may not have much political influence, but that is not new, for in fact they did not have much political influence in Aristotle's time either. This is something he complains about. Moreover, Aristotle's other class, the many, seems to be as timeless as his class of gentlemen. The many are predominantly the *démos*, the mass of the poor – but not just the poor. Most of the rich will fall into the same group. For though the class of the rich and the class of the poor are different and in more or less perpetual conflict, this opposition is of no consequence for the analysis of virtue. The poor and the rich share the same views about the good life, except that the rich have this life and want to keep it, while the poor do not have it and want to get it.

### 3.

If Aristotle takes his bearings by gentlemanly opinions, he does not simply follow them; for these opinions, though sound, may, when examined by a philosopher, be seen to point beyond themselves. For example, the opinions about virtue point to the fact that virtue is a mean between extremes. That fact may not be fully articulated, however, and some virtues may be contrasted by existing opinion with only one vice and not two. Again, the opinions about virtue point to the fact that there are several virtues, because there are several distinct areas of human feeling and action, and all of them are handled well or badly according to the presence or absence of the relevant habit.[39] But this fact too may not be fully articulated, and some areas of human life, those that come less to attention, may have been passed over by opinion in the assignment of virtues. So the philosopher must come to the aid of opinion in these respects and complete it where it is still lacking.

All this supposes, of course, that gentlemanly opinion is getting hold of genuine facts about human life and how it is to be led, but getting hold of them imperfectly. That there are facts here, and that gentlemanly opinion does get hold of them (whereas the opinion of the many does not), is a doctrine that Aristotle has maintained from the beginning of the *Nicomachean Ethics*. That gentlemanly opinion is imperfect in getting hold of these facts, and so needs supplementing and correcting, is revealed by Aristotle as his analysis proceeds. This supplementing and correcting will, in turn, help to improve practice, at least of those who are ready to listen. Thus, for a suitably prepared audience, well brought up and in love with the beautiful, the words that will help to make them more fully virtuous will include Aristotle's own *Nicomachean Ethics*.

This leaves, therefore, the task of suitably preparing an audience. The task of doing that is what Aristotle takes up in the remaining sections of the last chapter of the *Ethics*. He has just argued that preparing a suitable audience for ethical teaching, since of necessity it is itself not a task of teaching, is a task of forced training. This training should begin as early in youth as possible. It must begin in the family; but the family is not sufficient for this. One father's command, taken on its own in separation from the political community, does not have the necessary strength. It needs to be backed up by the political community, by the city. The city has more force and more authority, and the exercise of its power is less resented. The city, then, should undertake this task of training the young. If, however, the city does not do this, and of course many do not, then one must try to do it as best as one can in one's own family. Since to do this is to become a lawgiver in one's own home, one can only do it well by becoming in effect a lawgiver altogether. The serious educator must learn the art of legislation. This requires a study and investigation of the laws and of the regimes which express and support the laws, and especially a study of the best regime and the best laws. Such a study and investigation, says Aristotle, does not yet exist. It needs to be provided. This is what the *Politics* is for.

The *Politics*, therefore, is devoted to finding regimes best suited to education in virtue, and its audience is legislators, potential or actual, who have an interest in such education – predominantly the heads of gentlemanly families. It should occasion no surprise that the fundamental themes of the *Politics*, even in the books where this seems least obvious, are education and the best regime.[40] It should also occasion no surprise that Aristotle's preference for the gentlemen remains as pervasive in the *Politics* as it was in the *Nicomachean Ethics*. This preference for gentlemen in the *Politics*, however, has the same features as the preference for gentlemen in the *Ethics*. It is a philosophically motivated and discriminating preference. As in the *Ethics*, so in the *Politics*, Aristotle corrects gentlemanly opinion even as he follows it. This is noticeable, for instance, in the case of slavery. Contrary to existing practice and belief, but in a way drawing out the implications of existing practice and belief, Aristotle shows that just slavery reduces to natural slavery; that natural slavery refers to facts of the soul, not to facts of national origin (except incidentally); that slavery is a mutually beneficial service, not the extortion of a hostile servitude; and that slaves are human, even capable of a species of virtue, and are not brute animals.[41]

That slaves can be virtuous is not what the *Nicomachean Ethics* would have led us to expect, where virtue seems attainable only by gentlemen. But the *Politics* introduces additions to Aristotle's theory of virtue that are of great interest.[42] Virtue comes in more than one form, not just in the sense that there are several kinds of virtue, as courage, moderation, and so on, but also in the sense that there are several kinds of these kinds. In the case of the family, for instance, there is a courage of the man, another of the woman, another of children, and another of slaves. The case is similar with moderation and justice. The ruler of the family, however, will have perfect virtue, while the others will have as much of virtue as falls to them according to their work.

These virtues differ, nevertheless, in kind, because ruler and ruled differ in kind.[43] Aristotle returns to this same point later when he argues that the virtue of the good man and the good citizen need not be the same. The goodness of good citizens varies from regime to regime, but the goodness of the good man is always one and the same. The goodness of the good man and the good citizen will only be identical where the good citizen is the ruler of a good city. The reason is that the ruler needs prudence in order to govern well, while the citizen who is ruled needs only right opinion.[44] Prudence makes the difference between the perfect virtue of the good man and the various kinds of virtue of the various kinds of good citizen. Already in the *Ethics* the importance of prudence was stressed, and virtue was denied to anyone who did not possess it;[45] but prudence was there distinguished into various kinds.

There is prudence about one's own affairs and about the city. Of the latter there is first legislative prudence, which is architectonic prudence, and then practical and deliberative prudence. There is also prudence about the household. Aristotle is obscure about the first kind of prudence, prudence about one's own affairs. He suggests that it is not possible for one's own affairs to be in good order without a household and a city, but he leaves this point aside for later consideration.[46] This later consideration is taken up in the last chapter of the *Nicomachean Ethics* and in the *Politics*. The supremacy of legislative prudence and its necessity for the wellbeing of one's own affairs is expressly argued in that last chapter of the *Ethics*; to provide the materials for such prudence is the specific task of the *Politics*. Aristotle is evidently indicating that no kind of prudence can exist, not excluding prudence about one's own affairs, without architectonic legislative prudence. This does not mean that everyone who is prudent in any sense must be prudent in the legislative sense. It need only mean that those who are prudent in the subordinate senses need others who are prudent in the legislative sense, so that they could not be prudent in those subordinate senses without the guidance and rule of those who are prudent in the legislative sense.

In the *Politics*, then, Aristotle is both relaxing and tightening the conditions for virtue. He is relaxing them because he is allowing that the virtues discussed in the *Nicomachean Ethics* come in many kinds and that these kinds can be spread over all members of a household and all members of a city. He is tightening them because he is now saying that only those really have prudence; and hence really have virtue, who have legislative prudence; and such people are likely to be few, even within the class of gentlemen itself.

Nevertheless, this all neatly fits Aristotle's teaching in the *Politics* about the virtue of the good man and the virtue of the good citizen. The picture we get is of a moral and political hierarchy. At the top of this hierarchy stand the simply good men who possess virtue in the highest sense and prudence in the highest sense. They are also the rulers. Below them in descending orders and dependencies come the various kinds of good citizen and good members of households. Some of these good citizens and members of households may be in the process of rising up the hierarchy, and will themselves some day achieve the highest eminence and become simply good. Others may be rising higher but will not reach the highest, while yet others may already have reached their upper limit. All, if not good simply, will be good in their degree and according to their capacity. At least this would be the case in the best governed city; and the best governed city, and hence the training of the sort of men who could establish and govern it, is Aristotle's primary and ultimate concern in the *Politics*.

Such a hierarchical picture enables us to see better the character of Aristotle's ethical theory and the role played in it by his preference for the gentlemen. This preference does not exclude other classes altogether, for virtue in its subordinate forms can be attained by nongentlemen.[47] This is only possible, however, in a certain political context. The development and perfection of virtuous life is not something that can be abstracted from the development and perfection of politics. Virtue, both in its subordinate and its highest forms, is the product of a good regime, and a good regime is one where gentlemen are dominant. Even so, the gentlemen themselves are not self-sufficient. They have need of someone to point out to them the true bearing of their opinions and to teach them how to reach higher levels of virtue and prudence. This someone else is the philosopher; for unlike Plato's Socrates, Aristotle does not require the philosophers to rule. He only requires the rulers to listen to the philosophers.[48] Aristotle is concerned with philosophers as well as with gentlemen. That is why he includes, both in the *Nicomachean Ethics* and the *Politics*, appeals to the philosophic life. These appeals are not obtrusive; they are moderate both in expression and in length. They appear, nevertheless, in both works at the important points.[49] The philosophic life is an alternative happy life to the practical, political life prized by gentlemen. Indeed, it is an alternative happier life. This does not deny the significance nor integrity of the political life of gentlemen. It merely sets it in its place.

### 4.

Viewed in the light of the *Politics*, Aristotle's ethical theory is inseparable not only from the opinions of gentlemen, but also from the politics of gentlemen. Virtue exists fully in aristocratic regimes, and elsewhere only in isolation. Since contemporary virtue ethicists have no intention whatsoever of tying their theory to gentlemanly opinions, let alone gentlemanly politics, their theory is not, and could never be, Aristotelian. The 'neo' in their title destroys the 'Aristotelian' to which it is attached. Of course, this does not tell us much about whether their theory is plausible, defensible, or true. It does tell us, however, that whatever their theory is, it is not a continuation of something old.[50] On the contrary, it is quite new. Getting clear about this newness, however, while it may prohibit easy appeals on the part of such theorists to the thought of the Stagirite, will have the advantage of keeping separate things separate.[51] This will benefit both the understanding of Aristotle and the understanding of modern virtue ethics; for there will be less risk that our study of the one will be distorted by irrelevant echoes from the other.

### ENDNOTES

1. G. E. M. Anscombe led the way with her 'Modern Moral Philosophy', *Philosophy* 33 (1958), 1–19. She has been followed in particular by Philippa Foot, *Virtues and Vices*, Berkeley: University of California Press (1978); Peter Geach, *The Virtues*, Cambridge: Cambridge

University Press (1977); Alasdair MacIntyre, *After Virtue*, Notre Dame: University of Notre Dame Press (1984). See also Michael Slote, *Goods and Virtues*, Oxford: Oxford University Press (1983); Bernard Williams, *Moral Luck*, Cambridge: Cambridge University Press (1984); and Bernard Williams, *Ethics and the Limits of Philosophy*, Cambridge: Cambridge University Press (1985). The literature on virtue ethics is now extensive. Volume 13 of *Midwest Studies in Philosophy*, Peter A. French, Theodore E. Uehling, Jr. & Howard K. Wettstein (eds), Notre Dame: University of Notre Dame Press (1988), was devoted to the topic, and a representative selection of essays with a large bibliography can be found in *The Virtues: Contemporary Essays on Moral Character*, Robert B. Kruschwitz and Robert C. Roberts (eds), Belmont, California: Wadsworth Publishing Company (1987).

2. Louis P. Pojman, *Ethics: Discovering Right and Wrong*, Belmont, California: Wadsworth Publishing Company (1990), 119–23; David Solomon, 'Internal Objections to Virtue Ethics', *Midwest Studies in Philosophy*, Vol. 13, 428–9.

3. MacIntyre traces back the virtues to Homer's heroes; *After Virtue*, 121–30.

4. See Rosalind Hursthouse, *Beginning Lives*, Oxford: Basil Blackwell (1987), 220, 236; MacIntyre, *After Virtue*, 159.

5. MacIntyre is the most obvious instance here; *After Virtue*, 146–64. See also Martha Nussbaum, *The Fragility of Goodness*, Cambridge: Cambridge University Press (1986), 343–53; and her 'Non-Relative Virtues: An Aristotelian Approach', *Midwest Studies in Philosophy*, Vol. 13, 32–53.

6. The *Eudemian Ethics* and the *Magna Moralia* (which is Aristotelian if not written by Aristotle) have no equivalent of this chapter. For some interesting speculations on what this might mean as regards the *Eudemian Ethics*, see Günther Bien, 'Das Theorie-Praxis Problem und die politische Philosophie bei Platon und Aristoteles', *Philosophisches Jahrbuch* 76 (1968/9), 304.

7. There is some dispute as to whether the summary at the end of the *Nicomachean Ethics* can be made to fit our text of the *Politics*. As against W. L. Newman, *The Politics of Aristotle*, Oxford: Oxford University Press (1887), Vol. 1, 2–3; and Carnes Lord, 'The Character and Composition of Aristotle's *Politics*', *Political Theory* 9 (1981), 472–4, who think it cannot, I agree with Terence Irwin, who thinks it can. See Irwin, *Aristotle's First Principles*, Oxford: Clarendon Press (1988), 603–4, n. 13.

8. This is not a view of politics popular today, and there is not much sign that virtue ethicists want to revive it. See Ruth Putnam, 'Reciprocity and Virtue Ethics', *Ethics* 98 (1988), 381. MacIntyre might be something of an exception, but for reasons having to do with his historicism, not for the reasons Aristotle gives.

9. See Sarah Conly, 'Flourishing and the Failure of the Ethics of Virtue', *Midwest Studies in Philosophy*, Vol. 13, 83–96; Nussbaum, 'Non-Relative Virtues'; Hursthouse, *Beginning Lives*, 226–37.

10. See Hursthouse, *Beginning Lives*, 236; MacIntyre, *After Virtue*, 159. For some discussions of the problem of the two happinesses in Aristotle see J. L. Ackrill, 'Aristotle on Eudaimonia', in *Essays on Aristotle's Ethics*, Amélie O. Rorty (ed.), Berkeley: University of California Press (1980), 15–33; John M. Cooper, *Reason and Human Good in Aristotle*, Cambridge, Massachusetts: Harvard University Press (1975), Part 3; W. F. R. Hardie, *Aristotle's Ethical Theory*, Oxford: Oxford University Press (1980), Chapters 2, 16; Richard Kraut, *Aristotle on the Human Good*, Princeton: Princeton University Press (1989), Chapter 1; Nussbaum, *The Fragility of Goodness*, 373–7.

11. *Nicomachean Ethics* 1098a16–18, 1106b36–1107a1. The priority of the virtues to *eudaimonia* in Aristotle's thought, while required by the logic of his definitions, has not always been acknowledged by scholars. Hardie, for instance, argues that the account of human ends or of *eudaimonia* in *Nicomachean Ethics* 1, and the list of virtues in books 3 and 4, are not 'integrated', and their mutual relations 'are not made clear'; *Aristotle's Ethical Theory*, 122. This is false, however, for it is made very clear that the virtues constitute *eudaimonia*. What Hardie was really pointing to, and what he really should have said, is that there is no justification given by Aristotle for the move from the definition of *eudaimonia* to the particular virtues. This is indeed true, for the movement of thought is the other way round: the virtues are the way to understand *eudaimonia*; *eudaimonia* is not the way to understand the virtues. Complaints similar to Hardie's by Cooper (*Reason and Human Good*, 146–7) and by A. W. H. Adkins ('The Connection Between Aristotle's *Ethics* and *Politics*', *Political Theory* 12, 1984, 29–49, esp. p. 33) can be answered in the same way. Irwin and Kraut see the correct order of priority but

do not dwell sufficiently on the implications of the fact that the virtues are independently identifiable, and their goodness independently recognisable; Irwin, *Aristotle's First Principles*, Chapters 17, 18; Kraut, *Aristotle on the Human Good*, 323–7. Myles Burnyeat is much better in this regard; see his 'Aristotle on Learning to be Good', in *Essays on Aristotle's Ethics*, 69–92. That virtue is also said in the *Ethics* to be what makes those who possess it and their work good (1106a15–17) only confirms this order of priority. Virtue makes one good in the same way that health makes one healthy, not because it *causes* goodness, but because it *is* goodness. That is why *eudaimonia* is defined by reference to virtue and not vice versa. Virtue and its exercise are what essentially constitute the goodness of *eudaimonia*.

12. Putnam, 'Reciprocity and Virtue Ethics', 380. See also Adkins, 'The Connection Between Aristotle's *Ethics* and *Politics*'; and Hardie, *Aristotle's Ethical Theory*, 119–20. Hardie quotes T. H. Green, W. D. Ross and Bertrand Russell to the same effect.

13. *Nicomachean Ethics*, 1095b3–13. On this passage see in particular Burnyeat, 'Aristotle on Learning to be Good', 71–2.

14. The Greek word is καλοικάγαθοί *Nicomachean Ethics* 1099a6, 1124a4, 1179b10. There is a long discussion of καλοκάγαθία in the last chapter of the *Eudemian Ethics*. Notice also the contrast between οἱ χαρίεντες 'the refined', and 'the many' at 1095a18–20. Lord's remarks in this regard are apposite; see his 'Politics and Education in Aristotle's *Politics*', in *Aristoteles' Politik: Akten des XI Symposium Aristotelicum*, Günther Patzig (ed.), Göttingen: Vandenhoeck and Ruprecht (1990), 202–15, esp. p. 213.

15. Cf. Friedrich Nietzsche, *Beyond Good and Evil*, Part 9, 'What is Noble?'

16. For just a few of the discussions of this question, see Ackrill, 'Aristotle on Eudaimonia', 15, 30–1; Cooper, *Reason and Human Good*, 101–33; Hardie, *Aristotle's Ethical Theory*, Chapter 11; J. L. Mackie, *Ethics: Inventing Right and Wrong*, New York: Penguin (1977), 186; Nussbaum, *The Fragility of Goodness*, Chapter 10.

17. *Nicomachean Ethics*, 1109b20–23, 1126b2–4, 1142a23–30, 1143a32–b17, 1144a29–31.

18. For some discussion of intuition in Aristotle see Hardie, *Aristotle's Ethical Theory*, 232–4; Cooper, 58–76; and in particular Sandra Peterson's excellent article, '*Horos* (Limit) in Aristotle's *Nicomachean Ethics*', *Phronesis* 33 (1988), 233–50.

19. *Nicomachean Ethics*, 1144a29–36.

20. Ibid., 1109a30–b26, 1143b11–13, 1107a8–15, 1148b19–1149a20.

21. Aristotle gives general considerations to show virtue is a mean, but he does not put much confidence in such 'common' arguments. Where actions are concerned, the particulars are truer and the general account has to be shown to harmonise with the particulars. Aristotle does just that. He appeals directly to his list of particular virtues and shows from them, not from the common arguments just given, that virtues are means between extremes. He uses, in other words, a sort of proof by ostension, see *Nicomachean Ethics* 1106b28–34.

22. This is particularly obvious in Foot, *Virtues and Vices*, and Hursthouse, *Beginning Lives*, 226–37.

23. Cf. Robert B. Louden, 'On Some Vices of Virtue Ethics', *American Philosophical Quarterly* 21 (1984), 227–36; and Pojman, *Ethics: Discovering Right and Wrong*, 123–4. As far as Aristotle is concerned, Burnyeat's remarks are exact; see Burnyeat, 'Aristotle on Learning to be Good', 81.

24. This might seem to conflict with Aristotle's stated dialectical method of getting after the truth by examining the opinions (*Nicomachean Ethics* 1145b2–7), since he would, in the case of virtue, be ignoring some of these opinions and opinions held by a great many. On this point see Jonathan Barnes, 'Aristotle on the Methods of Ethics', *Revue Internationale de Philosophie* 34 (1980), 490–511. A passage from Barnes explaining Aristotle's position is worth quoting: 'We must distinguish between οἱ πολλοί and οἱ πολείστοι: opinions held by most men are indeed ἔνδοξα [that is, to be taken seriously]; but opinions peculiar to οἱ πολλοί, the vulgar herd, should be ignored' (p. 504).

25. Cf. Hursthouse's remark about Aristotle's 'lamentable parochialism'; *Beginning Lives*, 236. See also Nussbaum, 'Non-Relative Virtues', 34; Williams, *Ethics and the Limits of Philosophy*, 34–6; Stuart Hampshire, *Morality and Conflict*, Cambridge, Massachusetts: Harvard University Press (1983), 149–53. That Aristotle's moral and political thought is mere ideology is a view long held by Marxists, but it is insinuated already by Hobbes, *Leviathan*, Chapter 15.

26. On this part of the text see Burnyeat, 'Aristotle on Learning to be Good'. Burnyeat's conclusions are basically correct, but they need to be pushed much further; see Lord, 'Politics and Education', esp. 208, n. 14.

27. *Nicomachean Ethics*, 1179b4–1180a5.
28. Cf. the remarks at ibid., 1144a13–17.
29. This is part of the point of the famous 'function' argument in ibid., 1.7.
30. Cf. the remarks about children and self-control at the end of book 3, 1119b5–18.
31. In the Penguin translation of the *Nicomachean Ethics* (rev. edn, Harmondsworth: Penguin Books, 1976, 110), H. Tredennick correctly notes the following: 'A person of good character *feels* that he is getting too angry; he does not, in a particular case, refer to a general principle of ethics'. Kraut argues that there is a principle the person of good character refers to, namely, promoting a life of excellent theoretical and practical reasoning; *Aristotle on the Human Good*, 335–8. This interpretation, however, is based on a bizarre reading of the phrase 'right reason' in *Ethics* 1138b18–34, as if it meant right reason in the sense of giving the right reason for doing something, rather than in the sense of describing the condition the faculty of reason is in when it is right, that is, when it judges rightly (see 1144b21–28). Admittedly the goal of excellent reasoning is served when reason rightly judges the mean; but this is because, in the case of practical reason, rightly judging the mean *is* excellent reasoning (that is, excellent exercise of reason), not because rightly judging the mean has the promotion of excellent reasoning as its criterion or measure.
32. On this point see Burnyeat, 'Aristotle on Learning to be Good', 73, 81. Some contemporary virtue ethicists show signs of wanting to follow Aristotle in holding that there are moral truths that one cannot perceive if one does not have the requisite character. The full implications of this, however, they have yet to draw out; see Hursthouse, *Beginning Lives*, 232–3.
33. This point is made very clear in *Eudemian Ethics*, 1.4–5 (1215a20–1216a36). The parallel chapter in the *Nicomachean Ethics* is briefer and less fully argued (1095b14–1096a10).
34. This is a point made in *Eudemian Ethics*, 1215a26–33.
35. *Eudemian Ethics*, 1216a1–2.
36. Ibid., 1216a23–27.
37. Several gentlemen-politicians, or καλοικάγαθοί, are referred to as such in the Aristotelian *Athenaion Politeia*, most notably in Chapter 28, where there is also a sharp contrast drawn between these and the vulgar politicians, the demagogues. On whether Aristotle is the author of this book, and for a commentary on this particular chapter of it, see P. J. Rhodes, *A Commentary on the Aristotelian Athenaion Politeia*, Oxford: Clarendon Press (1981), 58–63, 344–61.
38. That Aristotle's moral and political views were a minority view and not shared by everyone in ancient Greece has long been recognised by historians, if not always by historicist-minded philosophers. For a recent discussion see Cynthia Farrar, *Inventing Politics: The Origins of Democratic Thinking*, Cambridge: Cambridge University Press (1988).
39. Cf. Nussbaum, 'Non-Relative Virtues', 34–6.
40. See Lord, 'Politics and Education'; Lord, *Education and Culture in the Political Thought of Aristotle*, Ithaca: Cornell University Press (1982); and Pierre Pellegrin, 'La Politique d'Aristote: Unité et Fractures', *Revue Philosophique de la France et de l'Étranger* 177 (1987), 129–59.
41. *Politics*, 1.4–6, 1.13.
42. Some hints can be found already in *Nicomachean Ethics*, 9.9–13.
43. *Politics*, 1260a20–24.
44. Ibid., 3.4.
45. *Nicomachean Ethics*, 6.12–13.
46. *Nicomachean Ethics*, 1141b23–1142a11.
47. This is Aristotle's answer, if there is one, to the question of how the many can become virtuous.
48. Aristotle frag. 647 Rose.
49. *Nicomachean Ethics*, 10.7; *Politics*, 7.2–3.
50. Cf. Adkins, 'The Connection Between Aristotle's *Ethics and Politics*', 47–8. MacIntyre's insistence on the role of historical traditions makes him more Aristotelian than most, but he still rejects what is decisive for Aristotle. Insofar as virtue ethics is dependent on the opinions embodied in the traditions, MacIntyre follows Aristotle. Insofar as the traditions are subordinate to history and there is no abiding class of gentlemen, whether actual or possible, by which to take one's bearings, MacIntyre entirely rejects him.
51. Some have wanted to suggest Hume as an alternative historical inspiration for contemporary virtue ethics. But Hume's dependence on gentlemanly opinion for what counts as 'personal merit', and hence for the content of ethics, seems, if we attend to his examples and sources, very evident; see *An Enquiry Concerning the Principles of Morals*, L. A. Selby-Bigge (ed.), Oxford: Clarendon Press (1962), §138.

# 15

# DOES ARISTOTLE HAVE A VIRTUE ETHICS?

## Gerasimos X. Santas

The question may seem purely rhetorical. After all, it may be replied to equally rhetorically, if Aristotle does not have a virtue ethics, who does? Surprisingly, recent literature shows that neither the question nor the retort are idle: some writers have suggested that Aristotle does not have a virtue ethics, but that Plato does; while most writers in the historical tradition seem to have Aristotle in mind when criticising or defending a virtue ethics.[1] This division of opinion may reflect unclarity or at least controversy on the answers to two fundamental questions: what is a virtue ethics? and, what is the structure of Aristotle's ethical theory? Some philosophers[2] have recently tackled the first question, while a number of philosophers and classicists[3] have wrestled with the second.

I begin with a discussion of what is a virtue ethics. This will serve as a helpful preliminary to the historical and contemporary controversies about the structure of Aristotle's ethical theory.

## 1. WHAT IS A VIRTUE ETHICS?

There is general agreement among friends and foes of virtue ethics that there are significant contrasts between an ethics of virtue and an ethics of principles (rules, laws, acts).[4] The complaints about the neglect of virtues and vices in modern and contemporary moral philosophy, voiced by P. Foot, G. H. von Wright and others, certainly presuppose some significant contrasts. What are they?

The strongest contrasts have been isolated recently by G. Trianosky and Gary Watson. A '*pure* ethics of virtue', Trianosky says, makes two claims: 1. at least some judgments about virtue can be validated independently of any appeal to judgments about the rightness of actions'; and 2. it is this antecedent goodness of traits which ultimately makes any right act right'.[5] Trianosky claims that Plato, in his definition of soul justice in Republic IV, satisfies both these conditions and so has a pure virtue ethics; and Aristotle 'might be read' so as to satisfy them.

The Platonic view to which Trianosky refers is worth exploring briefly. The passage is *Republic* 443E–444A: the man who has attained order and harmony[6] (i.e. justice) in his soul will 'then and only then turn to practice . . . in the getting of wealth or the tendance of the body or in political action or private business, in all such doing believing and naming the just and honorable action to be that which preserves and helps to produce this condition of soul, and wisdom the science that presides over such conduct . . . and the unjust action to be that which tends to overthrow this spiritual constitution. . . .' (Shorey translation). Earlier Plato had defined justice in the soul (as a virtue of individuals) without reference to some prior notion of right conduct, indeed without reference to conduct at all, as a state in which each of the three parts of the soul is performing its own optimal function: reason rules the entire soul, spirit helps to defend by obeying the commands of reason, and appetite obeys in matters of bodily needs. So here we do indeed seem to have the two conditions of a pure virtue ethics satisfied. And though this may not be an adequate interpretation of Plato's theory of justice,[7] it can serve here as an example of a 'pure virtue ethics'.

In an ambitious article Watson tries to isolate a virtue ethics which falls outside the modern conceptual framework of teleological and deontological ethical theories. As expressed by John Rawls, for example, this modern framework recognises three main ethical concepts, the concepts of the right, the good, and of moral worth (or goodness of character, or moral virtue as a disposition); with the last of these concepts being derivative from the other two. Moreover, the structure of an ethical theory depends on how the right and the good are related: in teleological theories the good is conceived independently of the right and then the right is defined as what maximises the good, while deontological theories deny one or both of these two conditions.[8] In this framework, essentially the same as that of Sidgwick a century earlier, teleologists and deontologists agree that moral worth or moral virtue (as a state of character or disposition) is derived from, or defined in terms of, the right and/or the good.

Watson seeks to show that this framework is inadequate by isolating a virtue ethics in which this derivation is reversed (or at least does not obtain): the right and/or the good (at least what Watson calls good states of affairs or good outcomes) are to be derived from the virtues. If he is correct, his view is of some historical as well as theoretical interest, since several recent writers have held that Aristotle's theory is neither teleological nor deontological, as these structures are conceived by the moderns.[9] Perhaps Watson has succeeded in identifying a structure which fits and illuminates Aristotle's theory.

The conceptual schema defining this Watsonian ethics of virtue is as follows:

1. Living a characteristically human life (functioning well as a human being) requires possessing and exemplifying certain traits, T. 2. T are therefore human excellences and render their possessors to that extent good human beings. 3. Acting in a way W is in accordance with T (exemplifies or is contrary to T). 4. Therefore, W is right (good, or wrong).[10]

It appears from 3 and 4 (as well as from Trianosky's 2) that in a virtue ethics right conduct is defined in terms of, or derived from, or validated, or explained, by reference to the virtues.[11] And this appears contrary to the way modern non-virtue ethics theorists have proceeded, from Grotius to Rawls. Rawls' characterisation of 'the fundamental moral virtues' as 'the strong and normally effective desires to act on the basic principles of right',[12] is essentially the same in the relevant respect as that of Grotius;[13] not to speak of writers such as John Locke who make the matter explicit: 'By whatever standard soever we frame in our minds the ideas of virtues or vices . . . their rectitude . . . consists in the agreement with those patterns prescribed by some Law'.[14]

This contrast is thus an essential difference between a virtue ethics and modern ethical theories which give primacy to moral laws, principles, or rules. Of course we must be careful about what the contrast is. It is not as if according to a virtue ethics a virtuous person would not do what is right. On either theory s/he would. Rather the issue concerns whether goodness of character or rightness of actions is more 'basic' or more 'fundamental' in some broad sense. The writers we have reviewed do not say explicitly enough what notion of more basic or more fundamental they have in mind. Trianoski speaks of judgments about virtue being 'validated' independently of judgments about the rightness of actions, and about the goodness of traits 'making' right acts right; Watson speaks of 'explanatory primacy'; Locke and possibly Rawls could be interpreted as offering definitional remarks. In Aristotle, *one* way the issue could be posed is by using his notion of *priority in definition*: Aristotle's idea is that one thing is prior in formula (definition) to another if and only if the one is mentioned in the definition of the other but not the other in the definition of the one.[15] If, for example, Locke were to define a just person as one who has strong and normally effective desires to act according to principles of justice, and in his statement of principles of justice he made no reference to just persons, then in his theory just principles would be prior in definition to just persons. So *one* contrast between a virtue ethics and an ethics of principles may be about what is prior in the Aristotelian sense of priority of definition: whether the virtues as traits of character are to be defined in terms of principles of right conduct, as Grotius, Locke and Rawls might be read to be saying, or whether principles of right or right conduct are to be defined in terms of the virtues, as the virtue theorists would have it.

We must note at once that in his ethics Aristotle seeks *real* definitions of the good (or happiness), virtue and acting rightly; not nominal definitions (whether lexical or stipulative). It is priority in real definitions of things that we are speaking of here: and this depends on the nature of these things and how they are related, not on how we use words or define words lexically or stipulatively. The dispute is not about words.

The issue of which is more basic or fundamental, the virtues or principles of conduct (or, judgments about good character or the rightness of acts), might also be cast not in terms of priority of definition but in terms of logical derivability. In Plato's *Republic*, for example, we find parallel and elaborate constructions of *two* definitions of justice, one of a just city-state and one of a just person; neither definition makes reference to, or mentions the concepts of, the other. But Plato in fact derives the definition of just person from the definition of a just city, the assumption being that a just city and a just person do not differ at all with respect to justice, and that the tripartite division of the soul is parallel to the tripartite division of the city. So what is more basic or fundamental here, the notion of a just person or that of a just city? To find out, we may have to look at whole theories, their definitions, their assumptions and their arguments. In Aristotle's case, we have to look at the relevant arguments, not only the definitions he constructs.

There may also be other relations between the virtue of persons and the rightness of their acts, which may be relevant to our issue: for example, causal relations, ontological relations and relations of 'finality' – what is desired and pursued for the sake of what. The Aristotelian texts are full of remarks about such relations, and we must be sensitive to them.

In trying to understand an ethics of virtue there is, however, a second question to be answered, besides the relation between the goodness of character and the rightness of acts, perhaps more difficult and controversial: what is the relation between virtue and good?

Watson admits that his schema for a virtue ethics appeals 'to several notions of good: to functioning well as a human being, to being a good human being, to being a human excellence (perhaps also to being good for one as a human being)'. But, he claims, there is no 'essential appeal to the idea of a valuable state of affairs or outcome from which the moral significance of everything (or anything) else derives'.[16] It is not entirely clear what is this notion of a good state of affairs or a good outcome, other than the notions of good Watson has listed as being appealed to. Why, for example, is functioning well not an example – even a paradigmatic one – of a good outcome?

Watson distinguishes his virtue ethics from 'character utilitarianism', which he believes is not a virtue ethics. According to this theory, (1) the virtues are human traits that promote human happiness (the good) more than alternative traits; and in turn, (2) right conduct is defined as conduct which is contrary to no virtue and wrong conduct as conduct contrary to some virtue. Because of (1) Watson calls this character utilitarianism an 'ethics of outcome' rather than a virtue ethics, even though by (2) it satisfies the first condition by which we isolated a virtue ethics (the priority of virtue over right conduct); and indeed it appears to satisfy the two conditions by which Trianosky isolated a 'pure virtue ethics'.[17]

Can character utilitarianism be accommodated within the modern ethical conceptual framework and characterised as a teleological ethical theory? Here the good is defined independently of the right;[18] and there is a principle of maximising the good, but it is applied directly to the virtues and only indirectly to right conduct via the virtues. So, even though the virtues are still derivative from the good and the good is defined independently of the virtues, it is not true that the right is *defined* as what maximises the good; *if* by the right we mean right conduct or principles of right conduct, as seems to be the case in the modern conceptual framework. However, if maximising is a transitive relation, as it appears to be (since 'producing more or greater good' is transitive), then it will logically follow from the two propositions defining character utilitarianism that right conduct does indeed maximise the good. So right conduct being conduct which maximises the good will appear as a *theorem* in the system, rather than as a definition.[19] But except for this difference the theory will be teleological. We have our three main concepts, and virtue is derived from at least one of the other two. The order of the definitional/logical priorities is: the good, virtue, right conduct.

In any case, character utilitarianism gives a more prominent role to the virtues than do rule or act utilitarian theories or deontological theories: the virtues *are* primary over right conduct. It may also have the distinctive problems of traditional virtue ethics when trying to derive right conduct from the virtues; for example, insufficient practical content – a main modern objection to an Aristotelian ethics, as we shall see below. So perhaps it should not be dismissed as a virtue ethics. It occupies an interesting intermediate position between theories Watson is willing to call an ethics of virtue and ethics of principles. Watson refuses to consider it a virtue ethics because 'the facts it takes to be morally basic are not facts about virtue'.[20] That is, in character utilitarianism virtue is logically posterior to happiness or the good. But character utilitarianism does pose a significant contrast to a morality in which laws or principles or rules are primary over the virtues; and it would be difficult to find a historical or contemporary theory of virtue in which virtue does not exhibit some dependence on good.[21] So far as Aristotle's ethics is concerned at least, character utilitarianism is a live option for the structure of his ethical theory.

There is a third view, distinct from character utilitarianism, which, Watson says, is 'naturally called an ethics of virtue'. According to it, (1) right conduct is defined in terms of the virtues (the same as character utilitarianism); but (2) the virtues are either the sole or the primary *constituents* of the good (or happiness), this being its essential difference from character utilitarianism which seems to take the virtues as instrumental to happiness.[22] Here it would appear that both right conduct and the good are defined in terms of the virtues; so it would be difficult indeed to see how this fails to be an ethics of virtue. Watson doubts that it falls outside the Rawlsian framework, but it is not clear why he thinks so; perhaps, I suggest, because so far the relation between virtue and good is not clear enough. Let us use a simplistic illustration.

Suppose we have a definition of intrinsic goods (or it could be, 'things good in themselves') as, for example, things which are desired for themselves and *would* be desired even if nothing resulted from them; and a definition of *the* good as composed entirely of all (at least com-possible) intrinsic goods. Then we have arguments (made up from the definitions and further independent premises) for the conclusion that all the virtues and only the virtues are intrinsic goods. From the definition of the good and the last proposition it would follow that the good is composed exclusively of all the virtues. Finally, we define right conduct as conduct contrary to no virtue and wrong conduct as conduct contrary to some virtue.

Now this is in fact a sketch of the view Aristotle works out in the first five chapters of *Nicomachean Ethics*, what we called elsewhere his *orectic* theory of the good; it is not his final view but one he tries to reconcile with his own functional theory.[23]

Does an ethical theory having this structure fall within the Rawlsian framework? If so, is it teleological? And is it a virtue ethics?

It is clear enough here that virtue is definitionally prior to right conduct. But the relations between virtue and good are more complex and still not entirely in sight.

To begin with, intrinsic good is defined independently of virtue, so it is certainly not definitionally posterior to virtue. What about virtue and *the* good? The *formal* definition of the good, as composed exclusively of all intrinsic goods, is also independent of the virtues. A full (form *and* content) characterisation of the good, to be sure, would say that it is composed entirely and exclusively of the virtues. But the content of the characterisation would be the logical result of the formal definition of the good and further premises about the virtues; it would be a theorem in the system, not a definition.

It would seem then that the theory satisfies one condition of a teleological theory, the independence of the good from the right. And virtue is not derivative from right conduct but the very reverse; so the theory also satisfies one condition of a virtue ethics. But what is still not completely in sight is the relation of virtue to good: because we do not have yet the definitions of virtue and of the individual virtues, nor the arguments by which the good is said to be composed exclusively of all the virtues. What is it about the virtues that makes them desired and desirable for themselves? And why should they be the exclusive content of the good? If the virtues are constituents of the good because they are traits of character which are intrinsically good (or good in themselves), then even though they are not in an instrumental maximising relation to the good, they have been defined, insofar as they are virtues, in terms of good. So definitionally/logically the relation among our three concepts here is the same as in character utilitarianism: *good*, virtue, right conduct. Well, not quite: the character utilitarianism order was: *the* good, virtue, right conduct. Plainly we need a finer analysis which distinguishes, as one should anyway, between good and *the* good; as well as the arguments by which virtue is related to both good and the good.

In *sum*, we have three different theories which might be counted as a virtue ethics: Watson's theory, character utilitarianism and the constitutive theory. What all three share in common is the definitional priority of virtue over right conduct. Where they differ is in the relation of virtue to good or to the good; but this relation, we have seen, is not completely clear till a theory of virtue is in place, and possibly a definition of good.

If Aristotle's ethical theory has any of these three structures it is a meaningful candidate for an ethics of virtue. So does it?

Before we can answer this question, we must consider a significant and much neglected possibility. Our investigation so far presupposes that whatever analysis of virtue Aristotle has, it is the same for all the virtues. But this overlooks the possibility that *some* virtues, such as generosity and benevolence, are susceptible to a virtue ethics analysis; while others, such as justice, are not. This is a possibility for any ethical theory. I believe it is also a live possibility for Aristotle's theory and one which, so far as I know, has not been examined.

In an illuminating modern historical sketch, J. B. Schneewind discusses the contemporary complaint, made by such writers as P. Foot and G. H. von Wright, that modern moral philosophers have neglected the virtues.[24] Schneewind reviews such founders of modern moral philosophy as Grotius, Locke, Hume, Kant and Adam Smith. He makes out a plausible (to me, pretty convincing) case that these writers did not neglect the virtues; indeed Hume might well be thought of as a virtue ethics theorist; and

Kant certainly devoted much analysis to the virtues, though not in the most widely read of his moral writings, the *Groundwork*. Rather, Schneewind finds, these writers were pretty much in agreement that an Aristotelian virtue ethics is not adequate for such virtues as justice; to analyse justice, even in Hume, we need a principles or laws centred framework. Schneewind further argues that these writers used the distinction between perfect and imperfect duties – in Hume the analogous distinction between natural and artificial virtues – to give a limited role to a virtue ethics analysis. Such virtues as generosity and benevolence receive virtue ethics analysis; their duties are 'imperfect', indefinite; it is up to the agent to decide when, to what extent and towards whom to be generous. But justice, whose duties are 'perfect', definite or specific in all these respects, and enforceable, requires reference to principles and/or laws in its analysis. A virtue ethics analysis, all these writers agree, is inadequate for the 'artificial' virtue of justice and its 'perfect' duties. The misfortune of virtue was not its neglect, Schneewind argues, but the finding in modern times that a virtue ethics analysis is inadequate for a central part of morality, such as justice.

It is not within the scope of this chapter to discuss the accuracy of Schneewind's thesis; so far as I know it seems correct. However, both Schneewind and the writers he examines appear to presuppose that Aristotle had a virtue ethics for *all* the virtues. This is the common understanding of Aristotle, the received opinion. I believe that this is incorrect. It is one of the theses of this chapter that Aristotle may have had a virtue ethics analysis for *some* of the virtues, such as generosity and magnificence; but definitely *not* for the virtue of justice. For such virtues as temperance and courage, the picture is ambiguous and unclear.

We shall now examine Aristotle's analyses of the virtues, concentrating on two questions: (1) On the thesis which all three virtue ethics have in common, namely the logical primacy of virtue over right conduct, what is Aristotle's view? (2) On the unclarity which all three virtue ethics share, namely the relation between virtue and good, what is Aristotle's view?

## 2. VIRTUE AND FUNCTIONING WELL

There is a central passage in Aristotle's *Nicomachean Ethics* with which we must begin if we are to find answers to these questions. It is the famous function argument in Book I, Chapter 7, until recently neglected, but now acknowledged as governing Aristotle's theory.[25]

It comes at the end of a discussion (Chapters 1, 2, 4, 5) in which Aristotle, relying on what people desire, pursue and say about the good, has determined that the good has three formal features: it is an ultimate end, a single end of all our actions (i.e. there is only one such end and it is the end of all our voluntary actions) and a self-sufficient end. But Aristotle does not think he can determine what the content of the good is by simply relying on such data: for men disagree in what they say about the content of this good, and in what they desire and pursue as the single, ultimate and self-sufficient end of their lives; even though they verbally agree that it is happiness. Some say that happiness is (a life whose single ultimate end is) pleasure, others honour, others wealth, others virtue, others reason; and they pursue one or another of these accordingly. Within this *orectic* concept of the good, Aristotle himself argues that virtue and reason, unlike the other candidates, are desired and desirable for themselves as well as for the sake of happiness, so they would appear to be constituents of the good rather than necessary conditions or instruments. This view would appear to have the form of what we earlier called a constituent virtue ethics.

But Aristotle does not think that he can settle the disagreements about the content of the good within the orectic concept of good; nor is he content to leave it at that, as our contemporaries are.[26] So he brings in the function argument to try to support his own functional-perfectionist account.

Aristotle's function argument, given in *Nicomachean Ethics*, I, 7, 1097b22–a18, is notoriously compressed and obscure. The clearest and most detailed interpretation known to me is by David Keyt, who reconstructs it as a valid deductive argument, drawing from other writings of Aristotle to fill in and clarify various premises.[27]

1. In the animate world there are four general functions: to use food and reproduce, to perceive, to move from one place to another, and to think. (The second and third functions are seen as almost coextensive and are collapsed into one.) Accordingly, there are three general forms of life: the nutritive and reproductive, shared by all animate things, the perceptive, shared by all animals, and the life of reason, practical and theoretical, which is special to man (*De Anima*, I, 1, II, 4, III, 9; *Politics*, VII, 13).
2. One form of life is lower than another if and only if normal members of the first lack a function that normal members of the second possess. Thus plants are lower than animals, animals with fewer sense modalities lower than those with more, and non-human animals lower than man (*De Anima*, II, 2, III, 12).
3. A form of life or an activity of the soul is the distinctive function of a kind of living thing if and only if every normal member of this kind and no member of a lower kind can perform it (*Nicomachean Ethics*, I, 7).
4. The distinctive function of man is theoretical and practical activity of reason (*NE* I, 7).
5. A good member of a kind is one that performs the distinctive function of that kind well (as compared to other members of the kind) (*NE*, 1, 7).
6. Hence, a good man is one who performs well the activities of practical and theoretical reason, i.e. one who deliberates well about what to do and reasons well about what is true (From 4 and 5).
7. A member of a kind performs its distinctive function well if and only if it performs it according to (or 'by') the virtue or excellence appropriate to that kind (*NE*, I, 7, II, 6).
8. The good of a member of a kind is to be a good member of that kind. (Supplied premise, possibly in the text of *NE*, I, 7.)
9. Hence, 'human good (the good for man) is (rational) activity of soul according to virtue, and if there is more than one virtue, in accordance with the best and most complete (perfect)'.

The function argument has a formal and a material part, a concept and a conception. The formal part we may call the functional theory of good and virtue; the material part, which seems to be based on Aristotle's psychology and biology, gives some of Aristotle's theory of human nature, and in particular it specifies essential and distinctive functions of human beings.

Since part of our concern is issues of structure, we can look first at the formal part of the argument, the theory of good and virtue. On the basis of the argument and the analogies Aristotle gives in the passage,[28] we can set out his general formal theory of good and virtue. We can then look to this general formal theory for clues of the structure and procedure in Aristotle's application of it to man. The central question here is what concepts are the most fundamental, or, in Aristotle's terms, what is prior in definition to what.

The formal theory seems to contain at least the following propositions:

1. An F does well as an F iff it performs well the function of Fs.
2. A good F is an F which performs well the function of Fs.
3. The good of an F 'depends' on its performing well the function of Fs.
4. The virtue of an F is that by (the presence of) which it (a) is a good F and (b) performs well the function of Fs. (See also *NE*, II, 6.)
5. A good F (is an F which) has the virtue of an F. (From 2 and 4.)
6. The virtue of an F is good for an F. (From 3 and 4.)

The last two propositions can be derived from the others (perhaps with some reformulations). Propositions 1 and 3 capture Aristotle's remark in the function passage that 'the well and the good' of a thing reside and/or depend on its function. The analogies[29] might be thought of as inductive evidence for the main propositions of the theory, 1–4. But when applied to man all these propositions become controversial, with 3 and 6 the centre of controversy.

The most fundamental concept here seems to be that of function, since reference to it seems to be made directly (1, 2, 3, 4) or indirectly (5, 6) in all the propositions of the theory. And the most fundamental *normative* concept seems to be that of functioning well, since reference to it is made in the explications of other main normative concepts of the theory, the good of an F, a good F, and the virtue of an F, but not conversely. So functioning well is prior in definition to virtue.

We obtain the same result from Aristotle's metaphysical view that actuality is both more final and prior in definition to potentiality. The virtues are first actualities of inborn human potentialities, the exercise of the virtues second actualities; and second actualities are both more final than, and prior in definition to, first actualities.[30] A courageous action, for example, is a second actuality and so it is more final and prior in definition to the virtue of courage, the disposition, which is a first actuality of the potential for courage humans are born with. Similarly, functioning well in the activities of eating, drinking and sexual conduct, stands to the virtue of temperance as second to first actuality, and so it is more final and prior in definition to the disposition.

So both the formal part of the function argument and Aristotle's metaphysical views support the conclusion that Aristotle does not have a virtue ethics, since the necessary condition we found in all virtue ethics – the priority in definition of states of character over conduct – is denied here.

When we next look at the material part of the argument, we see that the conclusion of the argument seems to define the good for man by reference to virtue; so, on the face of it, the good is not defined independently of the right, and one condition of a teleological ethical theory seems to fail.

We must note at once, though, that the virtue referred to may be the *intellectual* virtue of theoretical wisdom, *or* the 'ethical' virtues of character, *or* both in some ordered relation. Especially since Hardie introduced the distinction between dominant and inclusive ends, there has been hot controversy among Aristotle's commentators, whether the conclusion of the function argument is to be given an exclusionary or inclusive interpretation.[31] On an inclusive interpretation, the good or happiness is an inclusive end and the reference to 'complete virtue' is a reference to all the virtues, intellectual and ethical. On the exclusionary interpretation the good or happiness is a dominant end and it includes as a constituent *only* the intellectual virtue of theoretical wisdom.

The exclusionary interpretation is an interesting possibility, because it opens the way to Aristotle's theory being teleological in a straightforward way and to possibly being a case of character utilitarianism. If happiness consists entirely in the exercise of theoretical wisdom, as the exclusionary interpretation has it, then the ethical virtues can be instrumental goods insofar as they promote theoretical wisdom,[32] and the role of practical wisdom will be to determine this instrumentality. If so, Aristotle's ethical theory might have the form of character utilitarianism, if the ethical virtues are conceived as traits of character which maximise theoretical wisdom, *and* conduct is judged right if it is not contrary to any such traits. That the ethical virtues might be thought of as maximising theoretical wisdom is by no means implausible. According to Aristotle, ethical virtues are acquired by 'habituation'; the feelings these virtues are concerned with – fear and confidence, greed, the pleasures of touch, and so on – need to be trained and educated so that at the very least they do not interfere with the deliberative functions of practical reason; and insofar as they do *that*, they also make the functions of theoretical reason easier to exercise. The temperate, courageous and just person can think better, practically and theoretically, because s/he is least susceptible to the disturbances of greed, fear and the pleasures of touch. The ethical virtues give us a certain kind of inner freedom to control feelings and emotions. Thus the exclusionary interpretation of the good is possibly Aristotelian character utilitarianism. Of course, we have not shown that the second necessary condition also obtains, namely, that right conduct is defined by reference to the states of character which constitute the ethical virtues. We shall see that this is certainly *not* true of justice.

However, there is no agreement on the exclusionary interpretation, so we cannot ignore the inclusive interpretation, which makes the ethical virtues constituents of happiness. Here we seem to have another of our possibilities, that Aristotle has a constituent virtue ethics.

We may begin by noting that the reference to virtue in the conclusion of the function argument is ambiguous: virtue may refer to a standard of excellence by which performance is judged, or to the disposition which causes and promotes well functioning.

The phrase 'according to virtue' in the conclusion of the function argument seems to support the standard of performance interpretation; while virtue as 'that *by which* a thing performs its function well' in Book II, 6, seems to refer to the disposition, and this supports the causal interpretation.

The causal interpretation fits the case of the arts and organs, where a virtue (in the most general sense) is a skill, a trained ability, an educated talent, or, in the case of organs, a structure/composition which causes well functioning.[33] The builder's skill or *techne* can be defined in terms of producing good buildings, and reference to such skill need not enter into the definition of a good building; 'right' action for a builder is whatever contributes to the production of good buildings, and reference to such action need not enter the explication of good building. A good building in turn will be explicated in terms of the function of buildings. But of course these are cases of *production*, in which Aristotle explicitly recognises the logical independence of the product from the process. Aristotle says that the case of the virtues is different: 'But for actions expressing [according to] virtue to be done temperately or justly [and hence well] it does not suffice that they are themselves in the right state. Rather, the agent must also be in the right state when he does them. First, he must know [that he is doing virtuous actions]; second he must decide on them, and decide on them for themselves; and third he must also do them from a firm and unchanging state. As conditions for having a craft, these three [conditions] do not count, except for the knowing itself. As a condition for having virtue . . . the knowing . . . counts for very little . . . whereas the other two conditions are . . . all important.' (*NE*, II, 4, Irwin translation, brackets his except for the first.) This passage is perhaps somewhat ambiguous: are the three conditions conditions for an action being just or temperate, or only for the agent being just or temperate? We shall see that at least in the case of justice, the latter interpretation can be the only correct one.

On the other hand, the standard of performance interpretation seems deontological, seeming to introduce into the concept of the good for man a moral standard by which functioning is to be evaluated. Courage is to be thought of as a standard by which the performance of a soldier is evaluated: to perform the function of a soldier well is to act courageously, that is, as a courageous person would. Here functioning well as a soldier seems to be referred back to a moral virtue. And when Aristotle seems to make the virtuous man a standard of what is good and pleasant, as in the case of temperance (*NE*, Bk X, 3), he seems to be using virtue as the fundamental notion, not functioning well. All this coheres well with virtue being a subordinate good and thus part or constituent of the good for man.

But what exactly is part of the good or happiness? There is another ambiguity, parallel to the ambiguity between virtue as cause and as standard of performance, which we need to take into account here. Though the genus of virtue is disposition, references to virtue may be to the *disposition* (state of character), which is a first actuality, *or* to *activity* or action which is the exercise of the disposition and is a second actuality. It would be natural to interpret references to virtue as a standard of performance to be references to activity and to conduct, rather than to the disposition: it is courageous acts or temperate *acts* that can be standards of performance, not in any direct way the disposition; it is a record performance in track and field that can be a standard for runners, not in any direct way the skill and talent involved (the skill might be shown in the *form* the runner displays in running, but that is the form of an activity). When Aristotle makes the virtuous man a standard of what is virtuous, he presumably means that it is his conduct, his choices, not just the disposition, which is the standard. And when he says, in the conclusion of the function argument, that happiness is activity of the soul 'according to virtue', he must be referring to the exercise of the disposition, the second actuality, if he is referring to a standard of performance.

We can reach the same conclusion by considering what sort of thing can be part of happiness and what sort desired for itself. Is it the disposition or the activity which is part of happiness and is desired for itself? It is not virtue as a disposition that is part of happiness, but the exercise of the disposition, which is activity. Happiness is activity. How could a disposition be part of activity? The relation of first to second actuality is not that of part to whole in any plausible sense.[34] Virtuous activities can be part of happiness in a straightforward sense: the activity which is happiness can be literally made up of virtuous activities. Moreover, it is virtuous activity that is to be pursued for its own sake, the cultivation of the disposition being pursued because of what it enables us to *do*; for the first actuality is for the sake of the second actuality, which of course is more final.[35]

So the reference to virtue in the conclusion of our argument must be a reference to activity, *if* it is virtuous *activity* which is desired for itself and is part of happiness or the good, and *if* the reference is to a standard of performance. Virtue the disposition can be defined by a causal or enabling relation to that activity. There is no conflict between *NE*, I, 7 and *NE*, II, 6: 'according to virtue' in the former refers to virtuous activity, 'by which it functions well' in the latter refers to the disposition.

If we are correct so far, the definition of happiness at the conclusion of the function argument can be rephrased as follows: happiness is activity of soul which manifests reason and which is virtuous (and if there is more than one kind of virtuous activity the best and most complete [perfect]). Here the reference is explicitly to activity, not to disposition.

But how are we to explicate virtuous activity? Isn't there a reference back to the disposition? To say that an activity is virtuous is to say that the functioning which constitutes the activity is performed well. The second analogy by which virtue is introduced in the function argument indeed says just this: 'virtue being added with respect to superiority in the performance of function'. And so does the immediate hypothetical before the conclusion: 'and if the function of a good man is to do these things well and nobly,[36] and if this is done well by its appropriate virtue'. To be sure, reference to the disposition, in the statement 'So and so acted (say) courageously', is not totally eliminable; because on Aristotle's view the man must act knowingly, rather than in ignorance or accidentally, he must choose the act for its own sake, and he must act from a firm state of character. But none of this re-introduces the disposition as a standard of performance. The firm state of character is a reference to the state of the relevant feelings which enable the person to do the act reason selects; 'for its own sake' means something like, 'because it is a courageous thing to do', rather than, say, 'because it will bring me a fortune if I win';[37] and knowledge (here practical wisdom) refers to knowledge of the circumstances and objects of the act, what is at stake, what is to be feared, what might be won, as well as determination of the mean. Aristotle is not appealing to the dispositional elements to discover what act, among the various options, would be the right thing to do; *that* is the function of reason, as Aristotle tells us in the very definition of virtue. How reason is supposed to do that remains to be seen; but it is not supposed to do it by reference back to the disposition.[38]

Aristotle's analysis of virtuous action, as making ineliminable reference to the cognitive and motivational state of the agent, is shared by theorists who do not have a virtue ethics, writers who take laws or rules as primary over a virtuous disposition. W. D. Ross's distinction between *action* and *act* illustrates the point: virtuous act refers to the rightness of the act, virtuous action to right act done from a virtuous motive; but on his view it is not the motive that makes the act right, it is what makes the agent virtuous. We have a similar distinction in Kant, acts according to duty, and dutiful acts done from duty. We can strengthen this interpretation by looking at Aristotle's theory of the mean.

## 3. ETHICAL VIRTUE, THE MEAN, AND PRACTICAL WISDOM

The theory of the mean is supposed to provide a standard for functioning well. The theory is brought in after Aristotle has determined the genus of ethical virtue as a state of character concerned with choice, and he is now looking for the differential.[39] He begins with a restatement of his theory of function and virtue: 'every virtue causes its possessors to be in a good state and to perform their function well . . . If this is true in every case, the virtue of a human being will likewise be the state that makes a human being good and makes him perform his function well' (*NE*, II, 6, Irwin translation). But what is functioning well for a human being? Relying on the analogies Aristotle had already introduced in the first mention of the mean (*NE*, II, 2), namely practices about eating and exercise in medicine and physical training, he continues: 'every scientific expert avoids excess and deficiency and seeks and chooses what is intermediate – but intermediate relative to us, not in the object. This then is how each science produces its product well, by focusing on what is intermediate and making the product conform to that . . . And since virtue, like nature, is better and more exact than any craft, it will also aim at what is intermediate' (*NE*, II, 6, Irwin translation). Next Aristotle makes it clear that he is speaking of ethical virtue (rather than intellectual virtue), which is concerned with feelings and actions, both of which admit of excess and deficiency, and concludes the discussion as follows:

> Now virtue is concerned with feelings and actions, in which excess and deficien-
> cy are in error and incur blame, while the intermediate condition is correct and
> wins praise, which are both proper features of virtue. Virtue, then, is a mean, in
> so far as [because] it aims at what is intermediate.

Here the theory of the mean is applied to three sorts of entities, actions, feelings and states of character: and states of character which fall between extremes are said to be virtues because, or in so far as, they enable the person to have feelings between extremes and to choose actions between extremes. Once more, first actualities (states of character) are explicated in part at least by second actualities (the actions); and because the actions constitute well functioning, the states of character are said to be virtues.

The definition of moral virtue which comes at the end of this discussion should be read accordingly: 'Virtue then is a state of character concerned with choice, lying in the mean, i.e. the mean relative to us, this being determined by a principle, as the man of practical wisdom would determine it' (1107a, Ross). It is of course rather remarkable that feelings are not explicitly mentioned in this definition; but they come in implicitly when we recall Aristotle's earlier explication of a state of character as 'what we have when we are well or badly off in relation to feelings' (*NE*, II, 5, Irwin translation). Thus in the explication of temperance, for example, which is concerned with well functioning in the activities and pleasures of eating, drinking and having sex, Aristotle tells us that the temperate person finds 'no pleasure in all the wrong things . . . [but] if something is pleasant and conducive to health or fitness, he will desire this moderately and in the right way' (*NE*, III, 11, Irwin translation).

In sum, the fundamental notion here, what is prior in definition, is well functioning as activity intermediate between extremes of excess and deficiency. This intermediate activity is something which practical reason discovers when it has the intellectual virtue of practical wisdom. The intermediate in feelings has value because it allows – even leads – the person to act as practical reason bids. And the intermediate in states of character, produced by habituation, has value because it enables the person to have such intermediate feelings.[40]

This interpretation of the theory of the mean, though, has two problems, both of which are relevant to the issue of whether Aristotle has a virtue ethics.

First, the definition of ethical virtue makes reference to practical wisdom; but in Book VI, when practical wisdom is distinguished from cleverness, we have reference back to ethical virtue: apparently, practical wisdom is knowledge of efficient means to *virtuous* ends, whereas cleverness is knowledge of efficient means to *any* ends a person has. This procedure appears circular: it looks as if functioning well and choosing the mean are not explicated independently of the state of character which is ethical virtue.

Why does Aristotle refer back to ethical virtue in his distinction between practical wisdom and cleverness, and what sort of reference is it?

In Book VI Aristotle sets out to distinguish practical wisdom from other intellectual virtues, to delineate what wisdom is about and to determine the contribution practical wisdom makes to the life of virtue and happiness. Some of this is reflected in his definition of practical wisdom in Book VI, 5: 'Practical wisdom is a state grasping the truth, involving reason, concerned with action about what is good or bad for a human being'.

Here there is no reference to the state of character which is ethical virtue. The context of this cryptic definition explains its main elements. All wisdoms and arts are virtues by which we grasp the truth of something; practical wisdom, unlike theoretical, is that by which we can grasp the variable truths about effective means, and by which we can reason truly from ends to effective means. The contribution practical wisdom makes is in the deliberation through which we discover the best means; it enables us to perform well the function of deliberating. Since deliberating well is necessary for attaining any ends, it is necessary for attaining the subordinate and ultimate ends which constitute the good for man. And since deliberating about means is an exclusive and essential function of man, deliberating well, besides enabling us to discover correct means to ends, is also a subordinate end and part of the good for man. As Aristotle says in Book VI, 12, practical wisdom is desirable for itself and also for the effects it produces.

But Aristotle also wishes to distinguish practical wisdom from cleverness. The latter seems to be what the moderns, Hume and Rawls for example, call practical rationality – taking effective means to one's ends, *no matter what one's ends are*. Aristotle wishes to distinguish the two because, for him, cleverness or Humean rationality is not a virtue: a virtue enables us to function well, choosing cleverly does not necessarily do so. Whether with respect to behaviour towards one's self or towards others, one can choose effective means to bad ends, and in neither case is one functioning well. So Aristotle has practical wisdom beginning with good ends, apparently ends supplied by the ethical virtues. And so we seem to have a reference back to the ethical dispositions.

But this is misleading. What Aristotle is worrying about here (*NE*, VI,12) is not distinguishing the virtuous man from the wrong-doer, but the virtuous man from the man who does the right thing wrongly, i.e. 'unwillingly' or 'in ignorance', or 'for the sake of something else and not for itself' (see 1144a15–25). Here the man is hitting the mean, but not from choice, perhaps accidentally, or only for some end beyond the act itself. Because of this the man's 'wisdom' is only cleverness, though in hitting the mean it resembles practical wisdom. But the good man does the same thing (hits the mean) 'from choice' and 'for the sake of the acts themselves' (1144a20–25). And it is precisely these two elements that ethical virtue, the state of character insofar as it is a state of feeling, supplies: not some ends other than what practical wisdom sets, but a firm inclination to choose the mean for its own sake as well as for its results. In the case of temperance, for example, which is concerned with functioning well physically and with the rational regulation of (some of our) animality, functioning well consists in choosing the mean with respect to the pleasures of food, drink and sex, i.e. the animal pleasures: practical wisdom determines this mean, while the emotional element of the ethical virtue of temperance inclines us to choose that mean and choose it for its own sake. To be sure, some of Aristotle's remarks seem to imply that ethical virtue sets ends such as health, or deliberating well, or theorising well, or in the case of temperance the proper 'mixture' of reason to animality; but this does not mean that ethical virtue without wisdom does that, but only that a properly educated and habituated person has these built into her as ends, and so in any situation she seeks these as if by her 'second nature', and practical wisdom then finds the mean in the particular circumstances.

Aristotle of course needs to distinguish not only the man who does the right thing from a good motive from the man who does the right thing wrongly; but also the virtuous man from the wrong-doer. He does this ultimately by the function argument: for this argument determines ultimate (and perhaps subordinate) ends, and it is the work of reason, both practical and theoretical. The material part of the argument determines the ultimate ends of man, and it is the work of theoretical reason since the discovery of the distinctive functions of man comes from biology and psychology. This argument rules out, for example, pleasure and wealth as ultimate, or even subordinate, ends of human beings. Means to the wrong ultimate ends, say, pleasure or wealth, might occasionally fall on the mean, and in this case the clever man and the man of practical wisdom will choose the same act; but often the means to wealth or pleasure, taken as ultimate ends, will be intemperate or unjust acts.

The second problem is that the theory of the mean does not seem specific enough, it does not have sufficient practical content for guiding choices. Many have made this objection, including Sidgwick, who complains that all the mean tells us is that virtue lies somewhere between two kinds of bad. Grotius and Adam Smith make similar charges.[41] The complaint is familiar and notorious: when we ask what is the rational principle(s) by which we are to choose the mean, we get no answer in Book VI.

I think that for such virtues as temperance and courage and generosity Aristotle is unable to give any formulation of the mean which would allow us to derive rules of what constitutes temperate or courageous or generous acts. One reason Aristotle gives for this inability is that the mean is relative to the individual, taking this apparently to mean that it varies too much to receive quantitative formulation. And so he says it is a matter of 'perception', meaning not necessarily sense perception but intuitive judgment of what individual action is correct, what the mean relative to us is in the particular circumstances we find ourselves in. Or, he cites the virtuous man as the model to follow. The reference to the virtuous man and the man of practical wisdom is an individual model device in the absence of measurability and a mathematical formula.

Aristotle, though, is perfectly aware of this lack of exactness in his theory of the mean.[42] Indeed he prefaces his first discussion of the mean with the remark that matters of conduct have nothing fixed or invariable about them, 'but the agents themselves have to consider what is suited to the circumstances on each occasion, just as is the case with the art of medicine and navigation' (1104a5–10). The reference to medicine is crucial. As D. S. Hutchinson has recently shown,[43] this lack of exactness was standard theory in medicine. Thus the author of *Regimen* tells us:

> If . . . it were possible to discover for the constitution of each individual a due proportion of food to exercise, with no erring either of excess or insufficiency, one would have discovered exactly how to make men healthy. But . . . this discovery cannot be made . . . There are many things to prevent this [such a discovery]. First, the constitutions of men differ . . . then the various ages have different needs. Moreover there are situations of districts, the shifting of winds, the changes of the seasons, and the constitution of the year. Foods themselves exhibit many differences . . . all these factors prevent its being possible to lay down rigidly precise rules in writing. (I, 2 and III, 67, Jones translation.)

The author appears to be saying that there are too many – perhaps an indefinite number – of variables involved in the choice of the mean in eating and exercise, and thus no hope of an exact mathematical formulation of such a mean. Significantly, he goes on to say that if a doctor were constantly present when the patient exercised and ate, the doctor would be able to find the mean in exercise and food; perhaps because in the particular circumstances of a particular patient the doctor has to watch out for only a small number of actual variables at work, out of the indefinitely large set of possible variables. So the absence of a mathematical formulation, and even its alleged impossibility, did not keep doctors from successfully finding the mean for particular patients in their particular circumstances. Aristotle was simply taking over both parts of this theory of the mean in medicine: its theoretical lack of precision and mathematical formulation, and its success in practice for the expert doctors. The parallel for ethics is a theoretical lack of precision and mathematical formulation, and the success in practice for men of practical wisdom.

## 4. JUSTICE

For the controversies over virtue ethics, there is no more instructive case than Aristotle's analysis of justice, the very virtue ironically neglected in contemporary discussions of virtue ethics. The case of justice is crucial, for it is a big and central part of virtue and rightness, whether in Aristotle or in Rawls. What Aristotle calls *general* justice includes all the moral virtues insofar as they are concerned with our behaviour towards others; and his *particular* justice (a part of his general justice) includes what we call distributive justice – what Rawls' theory of justice is all about – and the justice of restitution and punishment. So general justice takes up all of rightness, and particular justice a central part of it. If Aristotle explicates general and particular justice as a personal virtue in terms of the justice of laws and constitutions, then he does not have an ethics of virtue for justice. And if his account of the justice of constitutions is sufficiently detailed then his theory of justice does not suffer from a paucity of practical content, an answer to a stock objection to virtue ethics.

Let us look briefly at Aristotle's procedure for defining justice. Here we are concerned with the bare essentials, for we are concerned mainly with the structure of his theory; though some detail will come in to show there is no paucity of content.

He begins with a characterisation of justice the disposition: 'Now we observe that everyone means by justice the disposition which makes us doers of just actions, that makes us do what is just and wish what is just. In the same way we mean by injustice the state that makes us do injustice and wish what is unjust' (*NE*, V, 1, 1129a, Irwin). This is a partial explication of justice the disposition in terms of just actions; already this is some evidence away from a virtue ethics, since it makes the justice of actions definitionally prior to justice the disposition.

The rest of Aristotle's procedure is 1. to explicate general justice in terms of lawful actions and particular justice in terms of proportional equality in the distribution of certain kinds of goods; 2. to explicate just laws and just proportional equality in terms of just constitutions; and finally 3. just constitutions in terms of the contribution which a particular kind of distribution makes to the end or the good of the state.

Having noted that justice and injustice are expressed in many ways, Aristotle begins with the unjust man, and notes that one can be said to be unjust both in the general sense of being lawless (acting contrary to laws) and in the particular sense of 'having more'; and from this he infers to the contrary. 'Hence what is just will be what is lawful and what is equal' (1129b). Accordingly, he identifies *general* justice with what is lawful in all our behaviour towards others and calls it 'complete virtue' (1129b31); and one kind of *particular* justice with the distribution of 'honor [offices], wealth, and the other divisible assets [or '*goods of fortune*'], of the community, which may be allotted among its members in equal or unequal shares' (1131b);[44] the other kind of particular justice being corrective (not to be discussed here). Moreover, Aristotle argues that particular justice is part of (or a species of) general justice (1130b); so particular justice will also be explicated in terms of laws.

The explication of general justice in terms of law is very strong evidence for a negative answer to the question of whether Aristotle has a virtue ethics: Aristotle does not have a virtue ethics for all the virtues, since this explication makes law the immediate standard of just acts. Three times in the first two chapters of *NE* Book V Aristotle explicates just conduct terms of lawful actions; even in the case of courage and temperance, which, insofar as they are concerned with our relation to others are parts of general justice, and in which the doctrine of the mean is pre-eminent, he gives some rules of action specific enough to guide choice: 'But the law also prescribes certain conduct: the conduct of a brave man, for example, not to desert one's post, not to run away, not to throw down one's arms ... that of the temperate man, for example, not to commit adultery or outrage; that of a gentle man, for example, not to strike, not to speak evil ... and so with the actions exemplifying the rest of the virtues and vices, commanding these and forbidding those – rightly if the law has been rightly enacted, not so well if it has been made at random' (1129b20–30).

There is no relevant difference between this view and Locke's or Grotius' definitions of justice by appeal to laws. The Cambridge tutor who proposed as Aristotle's definition of virtue 'a constant disposition of the soul to live according to law', whom Schneewind quotes to show how act-centred theorists misinterpreted even Aristotle, was in fact correct![45]

Aristotle is aware that laws themselves may be correct or incorrect, more or less just or unjust (*NE*, V, 1129b29–30, *Politics*, Book III, Chapter 11). And in the next stage of his analysis he gives a criterion for judging the justice of laws, a criterion which on the face of it seems teleological: 'Now in every matter they deal with, the laws aim either at the common benefit of all, or at the benefit of those in control, whose control rests on virtue or on some other such basis. And so in one way what we call just is whatever produces and maintains happiness and its parts for a political community' (*NE*, V, 2, 1129b, Irwin, and *Politics*, III, 7). Here he seems to be saying clearly that the justice of laws depends on their promoting the good of the whole community, clearly a version of a universalist or non-egoistic teleological ethical theory; *or*, the good of those who make the laws, a version of egoistic teleological ethical theory, earlier expounded by Plato's Thrasymachus; constitutions of this latter type Aristotle in the *Politics* calls 'deviant' or 'perversions' of right constitutions.[46]

In the *Politics*, Book III, the position concerning particular justice is similar: just laws are laws 'constituted in accordance with right constitutions' (1282b); and the rightness of constitutions is then determined by how far they promote the *common* interest rather than the interest of the rulers (1279a).

Thus, in both the *Ethics* and the *Politics*, and for both general and particular justice, we have accounts of justice which on the surface are teleological ethical theories which are not virtue ethics. But we must remember that Aristotle's order of analysis has several stages, in this respect closer to rule rather than act teleological theories: dispositions, actions, laws, constitutions, the good.

Returning to particular justice, the next question Aristotle takes up is, what distribution of the divisible goods of offices, wealth and safety, is just distribution? He reasons that since the unjust man is the man who 'has or takes more', that is, more of the divisible goods or less of the bad things, the just man must be the one who has and takes something between the more and the less, and that is in some sense the equal. And since the equal is somewhere between the extremes of the more and the less, he also brings in his theory of the mean and says that the equal is a mean (*NE*, V, 3).[47]

What happens next is instructive. In the case of the other virtues, Aristotle was content to argue that virtuous acts, courageous, temperate, or generous, fall on the mean; there was no further analysis of the mean in terms of rules for determining the mean. But in the case of particular justice the mean is said to be the equal, between the extremes of the more and the less, *and* we get a mathematical analysis of the equal.[48] Everyone agrees, Aristotle says, that the equality in question is in proportion to worth (*axian*) of some sort, and that this is a geometrical, as distinct from an arithmetical, proportion. Accordingly, a distribution is just to the extent that the value of the things (the divisible goods) it assigns to one person stands to the value of the things it assigns to another as the worth of the one person stands to the worth of the other.[49]

People agree on the value of the things distributed, but they disagree on what this worth should be. 'All agree that the just in distribution must be according to worth of some sort, though all do not recognize the same sort of worth; but democrats say it is freedom, oligarchs wealth, and aristocrats virtue' (*NE*, V, 3, 1131a25–9). Accordingly, we have three different conceptions of distributive justice, under the same concept. In the *Politics* Aristotle gives us a detailed analysis of different constitutions based on different conceptions of distributive justice; and of the institutions which embody these different constitutions. Thus a democratic constitution, according to which all free-born citizens should have an equal share of political authority since they are all equally free, includes several institutions and rules which embody this democratic political egalitarianism: universal membership of free men in the assembly, rotation in other offices, terms of office, selection by lot and by election, and so on. (*Politics*, VI, 1–3.)

These are certainly specific enough to provide plenty of practical content and a guide to choice. And almost the same is true of Aristotle's discussion of oligarchic constitutions, according to which a distribution of political offices is just to the extent that the share of political office it assigns to one person stands to the share of political office it assigns to another as the wealth of the one person stands to the wealth of the other; thus it is just that persons of equal wealth have equal shares of political office, and persons of unequal wealth (e.g. double) proportionately unequal (e.g. double) (*Politics*, IV, 9, VI, 6). Here also there is no paucity of practical content. Rules and devices can be easily thought of which would be specific enough to determine what is just in particular cases. For example, one could have a rule weighing votes by wealth, as is done with stockholders in a company: one vote for each share of stock, rather than one vote for each person.[50] Thus, when we look at Aristotle's discussion of just constitutions in the *Politics*, we find a wealth of practical content, something certainly not indicative of a virtue ethics.

In the final stage of his argument, *Politics*, Book III, Aristotle tries to resolve the disagreement among the different conceptions of particular distributive justice. He begins by arguing that it cannot be superiority in any respect whatsoever (for example, a person's height) that is a ground for distributing greater shares in offices; he gives a *reductio ad absurdum* to rule out this possibility.[51] It must rather be something which is related to the office, such as fitness for the office or contribution to the end for the sake of which the office exists that is a ground for distribution (*Politics*, III, 12). But this does not settle the matter; for one thing, free birth, wealth and virtue all make some contribution; for another, each of the three proponents, democrat, oligarch or aristocrat, can still claim that their attribute makes the greatest or only contribution. Who is correct, Aristotle says, depends on what the function or the end of the state is (*Politics*, III, 13). For example, 'If property were the end for which men came together and formed an association, then men's share [in the offices and honours] of the state would be proportionate to their share of property; and in that case the argument of the oligarchical side . . . would appear to be a strong argument' (III, 9, 1280a, Barker translation). To resolve the matter, we need to know what the function or the end of the state is, towards the realisation of which contributions are made (*Politics*, III, 13). As is well known, Aristotle argues that property is not the (complete) end of the state. The end of the state is not only life (survival) or a shared life: it is primarily 'a good life' or a 'fine or noble life' or 'a perfect and self-sufficient life' (*Politics*, III, 9, 13). And for that end, Aristotle argues, superiority in free birth and wealth are not enough for distributing shares of office but virtue must above all be included.[52] The fitness for the job (*ergon*) criterion and the flute-player analogy ('nobody will play better for being better born', 1282b) assure us, I think, that the criterion is proposed with a view to assuring the performing well of the function. Whatever the correct end or the function of the city is, Aristotle is saying, shares of offices should be assigned with a view to performing that function or serving that end well. And this is a maximising principle: for the good of the city and the performing well of the functions of the city are identical. The teleological character of his argument comes out also in the crucial opening lines of *Politics*, III, 12, in which he takes up where he left off in the discussion of justice in the *Ethics*:

In all arts and sciences the end in view is some good. In the most sovereign of
all the arts and sciences – and this is the art and science of politics – the end in
view is the greatest good and the good which is most pursued. The good in the
sphere of politics is justice; and justice consists in what tends to promote the
common interest.

The last statement is one that J. S. Mill (and every non-egoistic teleologist) could
have written, though the common good might be different.[53]

## 6. JUSTICE AND THE OTHER ETHICAL VIRTUES

All three interpretations of the concept of distributive justice in the *Politics* provide
plenty of practical content. From the analysis of the justice of a democratic constitution, for example, it follows that it would be unjust to deprive someone, both of whose
parents were free and citizens, of the right to participate and vote in the Assembly;
unjust not to give someone his rotating share in office in the Council and the Courts;
unjust not to have limits to terms of office, and so on. In general, as Keyt has shown,[54]
Aristotle's four-step procedure (just person–just action, just action–lawful action,
lawful action–just laws, just laws–just constitution) will give us a lot of standards by
which to judge individual conduct, though of course not perfectly so.

But we have no such richness of practical content in Aristotle's analysis of courage,
temperance, or generosity. The theory of well functioning and the mean seems to
give us very different results in the case of justice and the other ethical virtues: that
is, it is much more specific and fruitful in choice-guiding in the case of justice. Part
of the reason for this is perhaps that in the case of distributive justice Aristotle was
able to give a mathematical formulation to 'the equal', geometrical proportion, and
was also able to specify several different bases for the proportionally equal distribution
of the goods of office, wealth and safety. He thought that the view of distributive
justice as proportional equality was generally agreed on; he was able to give it a
mathematical formulation, and simply superimposed his theory of the mean on it.
In addition, justice is a virtue that applies to institutions as well as to individuals, as
John Rawls has so forcibly reminded us. And institutions almost by definition have
rules. So Aristotle was able to rely on institutional rules – such as rules of election
to office, terms of office, rotation in office, and so on – which can serve as guides
to action.

In sum, in the case of at least particular justice, Aristotle was aided by the established
relation of justice to equality – which is susceptible to mathematical analysis – and by
the institutional and lawful nature of justice.

But temperance, courage and generosity are not institutional virtues. Moreover, in
the case of temperance the inexactness of the medical theory of the mean was of direct
relevance, since temperance is concerned with the rational regulation of the activities
and pleasures of eating, drinking and sex, where health or physical well functioning is
one of the standards of temperate behaviour. Courage is further away from medical
cases, and the difficulties of finding the mean here are even greater. And generosity
may be further away yet.

The difficulties of mathematical formulation and an exact account of the mean, or alternatively, of rules of conduct for *these* virtues, are still with us. Have we done any better at all in specifying rules for temperance, courage, generosity or benevolence? Sidgwick had certainly not done any better in his analysis of these virtues a century ago. And when Rawls characterises the moral virtues as 'strong and normally effective desires to act on the basic principles of right', what principles of right has he identified for courage, temperance, generosity or benevolence?[55]

But here we have another possibility, brought out in Schneewind's sketch: the 'duties' of courage, temperance, generosity, benevolence or love are all imperfect duties. The problem here is not an epistemic one, lack of knowledge of principles or rules, which is responsible for the indefiniteness of these duties; it is not that we have not yet discovered rules of how much, when and towards whom to be generous. It is the nature of these duties to be indefinite. Their nature allows for discretion, the moderns would say. Aristotle might say that their nature calls for special expertise in the art of living, namely practical wisdom, which cannot be quantified but is rather like the wisdom of the physician.

## 7. CONCLUSION

The widespread belief that Aristotle had a virtue ethics is false of his analysis of justice, and perhaps false of his analyses of the other virtues. This is confirmed by the fact that Aristotle's theory of distributive justice does not lack sufficient practical content, a stock objection to virtue ethics. His analyses of other virtues, such as courage, temperance, or generosity, do not have such richness of practical content and offer much less of a guide to choice; but this may be due to the nature of these virtues rather than to a defect of his analysis. The contemporary complaint of the friends of virtue that, unlike Aristotle and Plato, the moderns have neglected virtue ethics in favour of the ethics of laws and principles of conduct, may be false of the moderns; but in any case it is at best misleading about the ancients, insofar as it presupposes false beliefs about Aristotle's theory of justice.[56]

### ENDNOTES

1. For the first set of writers see M. Slote, *Goods and Virtues*, New York: Oxford University Press (1989); G. Trianosky, 'What is Virtue Ethics All About?', *American Philosophical Quarterly*, 1990; G. Watson, 'On the Primacy of Character', in A. Rorty (ed.), *Identity, Character, and Morality*, MIT (1990); for the second set see Grotius, G. H. von Wright, P. Foot and others in J. B. Schneewind, 'The Misfortunes of Virtue', *Ethics*, October, 1990, 42–63.
2. See Schneewind, op. cit., Trianosky, op. cit., and Watson, op. cit.
3. See, for example, H. Sidgwick, *Methods of Ethics*, London: Macmillan, 7th edn (1981), Introduction, Part I, Chapters 9 and 13; W. D. Ross, *Aristotle*, London: Methuen (1923), and John Cooper, *Reason and Human Good in Aristotle*, Cambridge, Massachusetts: Harvard University Press (1975), 87–8, 125–35.
4. In Schneewind's modern historical sketch the contrast is clear from Grotius to Rawls. R. B. Brandt and W. Frankena also agree; see Brandt, 'W. K. Frankena and the Ethics of Virtue', *Monist*, Vol. 64, 271–92. Watson too can admit some contrast, especially on the issue of derivability or primacy discussed below.
5. Trianosky, op. cit., 336. Similar contrasts are made by W. Frankena and R. Brandt; see Brandt, op. cit.

6. There is a widespread misconception that Platonic individual justice is 'psychic harmony': this is psychic temperance, not justice; the latter consists in each part of the soul performing its own optimal function; harmony is agreement among the parts of the soul on this order, and is a further property. See my 'Justice and Democracy in Plato's *Republic*', in *Antike Rechts und Sozialphilosophie*, O. Gigon and M. W. Fischer (eds), New York: Peter Lang (1988).

7. Writers who cite this passage ignore the fact that Plato also has a concept of social justice, which is defined in terms of principles of conduct and from which psychic justice is derived via the assumption of isomorphism between social and psychic justice. So the Platonic case is far more complicated. In his actual procedure Plato derives psychic justice from the definition of social justice and the assumption of isomorphism. For the derivation see 'Justice and Democracy', op. cit.

8. John Rawls, *A Theory of Justice*, Cambridge, Massachusetts: Harvard University Press (1971), 24–5.

9. See, e.g., J. Annas, *An Introduction to Plato's Republic*, New York: Oxford University Press (1981), 60–4, and John Cooper, op. cit.

10. Watson, op.cit., 459. Watson's 'in accordance with T' 'contrary to T' might be too weak. A more specific relation would be Plato's 'actions which produce and/or preserve T', and 'actions which destroy T'.

11. Brandt and Schneewind are also in agreement here.

12. Rawls, op. cit., 436.

13. Schneewind, op. cit., 46–8.

14. John Locke, *An Essay on Human Understanding*, Oxford: Clarendon Press (1975), 358.

15. For a recent account of Aristotle's notion of priority in definition, see M. Ferejohn, 'Aristotle on Focal Meaning and the Unity of Science', *Phronesis*, Vol. XXV, No. 2 (1980), 117–28, and D. Keyt, 'Three Basic Theorems in Aristotle's *Politics*', in *A Companion to Aristotle's Politics*, D. Keyt and F. Miller (eds), Oxford: Basil Blackwell (1991), 126. For example, right angle is prior in definition to acute angle, since an acute angle is an angle that is less than a right angle; again, in Euclid's *Elements*, breadth and length are prior in definition to line because they are mentioned in Euclid's definition of line, as length without breadth, but line is not mentioned in their definitions (if any).

16. Watson, 'On the Primacy of Character', 459.

17. Trianosky's two conditions say nothing about the relation of virtue to the good; they can be true and it can also be true that the goodness of virtues derives from their maximising happiness – Trianosky takes up these matters later in his article.

18. In Character Utilitarianism the good can, at any rate, be defined as happiness in the sense of pleasure, or as the satisfaction of rational desire, or as well functioning; there is no reason inherent in this theory for supposing there is danger of a circle between the definitions of the right and the good.

19. Strictly, the maximising principle is not applied twice; the relations of conduct to the virtues as dispositions are 'not contrary to any virtue' and 'contrary to some virtue'. But perhaps right conduct maximising the good can still be deduced from the other propositions. In any case, we can have a version of Character Utilitarianism in which we do have two maximising principles: right conduct is conduct which maximises the virtues as dispositions, and the virtues are the dispositions which maximise happiness. So why can it not be accommodated within the modern framework?

20. Watson, 457.

21. See, e.g., Aristotle's definition of practical wisdom in terms of good, and Sidgwick's discussion, op. cit., Part I, Chapter VIII.

22. Watson, 457.

23. See my 'Desire and Perfection in Aristotle's Theory of the Good', *Apeiron*, Vol. XXII, No. 2 (1988).

24. Schneewind, op. cit.

25. For a review of this, see 'Desire and Perfection in Aristotle's theory of the Good', op. cit.

26. The so-called 'liberal state' in current democratic theory is neutral on 'comprehensive conceptions' of the individual's good. See John Rawls, 'Social Unity and Primary Goods', in *Utilitarianism Beyond*, A. Sen and B. Williams (eds), Cambridge: Cambridge University Press (1988). The point is elaborated in *Political Liberalism*.

27. David Keyt, 'Intellectualism in Aristotle', in *Essays in Ancient Philosophy*, Vol. II, John Anton and A. Preus (eds), Albany (1983), 366–8.

28. Aristotle uses analogies during the function argument – once at the outset illustrating the relevance of function to the good of man, once near the end introducing and illustrating the relevance of virtue to the good for man. Since he never gives arguments for the analogical cases themselves, Aristotle apparently believes that the functional theory of good and virtue is true and uncontroversial in such cases. The first analogy: 'As in the case of the flute player and the sculptor and every artist, and in all cases where there is a function and action, the good and the [doing] well is thought to depend on [see 'reside in' – Irwin note] its function, so it may be thought in the case of man, if there is a function in his case'. The second analogy: '. . . if, as we say, the function of a man and of a good man is the same in genus (as of the harpist and of a good harpist, and so in general), virtue being added with respect to superiority in [the performance of] function (for, of the harpist [the function is] to play the harp and of the good harpist to play well), and the function of man is a certain life, activity and actions of soul according to reason, [then] the function of a good man is to do these things well and nobly, and [if] each thing performs its function well according to its proper virtue, then the good for man is activity of soul according to virtue'. The third relevant use of analogy is in Book II, Chapter 6: 'It should be said that every virtue makes its possessor be in a good state and perform its function well; for example, the virtue of the eye makes the eye good and its functioning good (for it is by the virtue of the eye that we see well); and similarly the virtue of a horse makes it a good horse and good at galloping, carrying its rider, and facing the enemy. If this is true in every case, then the virtue of a man will be the disposition or state by which one becomes a good man and by which one performs his function well'.

29. See note 25 below.

30. See *De Anima*, Book II, Chapter 4, and W. D. Ross's notes in *Aristotle's De Anima*, Oxford: Oxford University Press (1961), 224–5. See also T. Irwin's helpful discussion of first and second actualities in his *Aristotle, Nicomachean Ethics*, Irwin, Indianapolis: Hackett (1985), 385–6.

31. W. F. R. Hardie, 'The Final Good in Aristotle's Ethics', in J. M. E. Moravcsik (ed.), *Aristotle*, Garden City, New York: Doubleday (1967). See also J. L. Ackrill, 'Aristotle on *Eudaimonia*', in A. O. Rorty (ed.), *Essays on Aristotle's Ethics*, Berkeley: University of California Press; David Keyt, op. cit.; R. Kraut, *Aristotle on the Human Good*, Princeton: Princeton University Press (1989); T. Irwin, 'The Structure of Aristotelian Happiness', *Ethics*, January 1991; John Cooper, 'Contemplation and Happiness: A Reconsideration', in *Synthese*, 72 (1987); and S. Brodie, *Ethics with Aristotle*, New York: Oxford University Press (1991). The most recent illuminating discussion known to me is Roger Crisp's 'Aristotle's Inclusivism', *Oxford Studies in Ancient Philosophy*, Vol. XII (1994). Kraut and Crisp give more complete bibliographies of the dispute.

32. On some versions of the exclusionary interpretation, the highest happiness consists of theoretical wisdom, but a second-grade happiness, available to the common man, consists of moral virtue. See R. Kraut, op. cit. Here there might still be a circle between virtue and happiness, relative to the second-grade happiness.

33. The relations between structure and function in Aristotle are discussed in several articles in *Philosophical Issues in Aristotle's Biology*, ed. A. Gotthelf and J. Lennox, Cambridge (1987), for example M. Furth, 'Aristotle's Biological Universe'.

34. See 'part' in Aristotle's *Metaphysics*, Book V, 25.

35. See, e.g., *De Anima*, Book II, Chapters 1, 4.

36. 'Nobly' or 'finely' may be thought to introduce circularity because we now seem to have a restriction pertaining to the rightness of the act, restricting 'functioning well'. But as Irwin notes, 'nobly' normally indicates or makes reference to promotion of the good of others. See *NE*, I, 2, 1094b, where Aristotle says that it is 'finer' or 'nobler' to preserve the good of the city than the good of an individual, apparently on the ground that the good of a whole city is greater than that of any individual in it.

37. What 'for its own sake' means is not always clear in Aristotle. Sometimes it may mean 'because the act is *kalon*', as in *NE*, III, 9, where the courageous man will face death and wounds because 'it is noble to do so or base not to do so' (see *EE*, 1229a, for a similar statement); and it may be *kalon* because it promotes some good greater that the agent's personal good

at risk; thus an act may be *kalon* if it promotes the good of the city at the risk to one's own good, and it is *kalon* because the good of the city is greater than that of the agent. In this case, *kalon* has a teleological interpretation. See also T. Irwin, *Aristotle*, op. cit., 401ff.

38. As in the case of Plato we discussed earlier, where just action was defined as what produces and preserves justice in the soul.

39. Aristotle's first discussion of the mean occurs in the passages on how we acquire the ethical virtues, and it is rather ambiguous on whether he has a virtue ethics. On the one hand, he says that the ethical virtues are acquired by habituation: we become just by doing just acts, temperate by temperate acts: 'In a word the dispositions are formed by performing similar activities' (*NE*, II, 1). This seems to presuppose that we can know what acts are temperate or just independently of the dispositions by which we so act. On the other hand, when he tries to determine what 'right principle' is, according to which acts are to be chosen, he says that we cannot be very exact in ethics, but we can start with the idea that 'ethical dispositions are so constituted as to be destroyed by excess and by deficiency, as we see is the case with bodily strength and health' (*NE*, II, 2). This might be taken to mean that we determine what excess and deficiency are in actions by seeing what destroys the disposition.

40. For an illuminating account of the different possible relations of practical reason to feelings in Aristotle, all consistent with my general statement, I believe, see Christine Koorsgaard, 'Aristotle on Function and Virtue', *History of Philosophy Quarterly*, Vol. 3, No. 3, July 1986.

41. Sidgwick, op. cit, 376, and Schneewind, op. cit., 46–7.

42. For a study of Aristotle's views about inexactness in ethics see Georgios Anagnostopoulos, *Aristotle on the Goals and Exactness of Ethics*, Los Angeles: University of California Press (1993), Chapter V.

43. 'Doctrines of the Mean and the Debate Concerning Skills in Fourth Century Medicine, Rhetoric and Ethics', in *Method, Medicine, and Metaphysics*, R. J. Hankinson (ed.), Edmonton, Alberta (1988), 18–24.

44. Another such good, security, was mentioned earlier at 1130b; see also 1129b. As Keyt notes, though, what in fact Aristotle takes up for distribution in the *Politics* is offices. In any case, wealth would be a problematic case for oligarchy, since wealth in that case is the *basis* of the distribution; it would be difficult to apply a formula which directs us to distribute offices *and wealth* on a proportionally equal basis to wealth.

45. Schneewind, 45–6.

46. 'Deviant' constitutions, against which Aristotle argues, seem to be versions of egoism Rawls calls 'first person dictatorship', which is: 'Everyone is to serve my interests', where 'my' refers to the ruler(s). Aristotle, *Politics*, III, 7, and Rawls, op. cit., 124.

47. See Charles Young, 'Aristotle on Justice', forthcoming, and Grotius in Schneewind, op. cit., for criticism of the application of the theory of the mean to justice.

48. We shall concentrate on the proportional equality which constitutes just distribution; we take the theory of the mean in the case of justice to be derivative from that of proportional equality: that is, the mean in the case of particular distributive justice is whatever the theory of justice as proportional equality says it is. This is consistent with what the theory of the mean is supposed to accomplish: provide some guide for choice of actions; in the theory of distributive justice the mean is *further* explicated in terms of proportional equality; whereas in the case of the other virtues there is no further explication. Is Aristotle in effect giving up his theory of the mean in the case of justice, as in effect Grotius claims, since allegedly Aristotle switches from applying the concept of the mean to states of character, feelings and actions, to applying it to goods? Actually Aristotle literally applies it not to goods but to the conduct of taking more or less or the state of affairs of having more or less.

49. The language is taken from David Keyt, 'Aristotle's Theory of Distributive Justice', in *A Companion to Aristotle's Politics*, D. Keyt and F. D. Miller (eds), Oxford: Basil Blackwell (1991). I am relying considerably here on Keyt's clear-headed exposition of Aristotle's theory of justice. Since Keyt does not take up the issues I am discussing, his exposition may be regarded as neutral on these issues; I do not know whether he would agree with my teleological interpretation of Aristotle.

50. The suggestion is found in Keyt.

51. See Keyt, op. cit., 247–9.

52. One could argue that the use of virtue here introduces circularity, though not necessarily the circularity Sidgwick had in mind: a just distribution of shares of offices is a distribution in proportion to the possession of free birth, wealth and virtue. If the virtue in question includes justice, we have circularity if a just person is defined by reference (eventually) to a just constitution. Perhaps. What Aristotle appears to have in mind, though, is the virtue of practical wisdom or political excellence. See, for example, *Politics*, Book VII, Chapters 11, 12.

53. We may have a reference back to virtue here, because Aristotle holds the view, as old as Socrates in Plato's *Gorgias*, that the end of the state, and so the end of a constitution and the laws, is also and above all the promotion of living well, which includes living virtuously (*Politics*, III, 9, and Keyt, op. cit.). Here it is instructive to note that in lesser constitutions, such as oligarchy or democracy or tyranny, there is no circularity. In an oligarchy, for example, offices are distributed on the basis of wealth, and the promotion of wealth is the end of the oligarchic city; there is no circularity here between justice and the good; nor is there any circularity in having wealth in both places, but just an economic principle, true or false, that wealth best begets wealth. But, to return to Aristotle's account of the best constitution: the best constitution distributes offices on the basis of virtue, as well as on the basis of freedom and wealth; and it promotes a good life and a life of virtue for all the citizens, as well as the goods of defence, property, and so on. In both occurrences of 'virtue', the term presumably refers to all the virtues, and this would include justice. So if by the best constitution Aristotle means the most just constitution, we seem to have a circle.

54. Keyt explicitly raises the question of content and gives a convincing positive answer, op. cit., 243ff.

55. The case of temperance, though, is instructive. For healthy nutrition and exercise, two of the ends of temperance, a mathematical formula – relativised to such things as body weight, height, age and fat content – may now be possible, thus diminishing the need for individual models. Here the relativity of the mean is not necessarily to an individual, but rather to a body type. Apparently, there are indeed many variables, but their number is finite and their relations discoverable. Some try to give rules even for generosity, e.g., a percentage of one's income as the proper amount to give.

56. This is a slightly revised version of an article in *Philosophical Inquiry*, Vol. XV, 1993. I want to thank Gary Watson, Mike Martin, Graig Ihara and Roger Wertheimer for helpful comments on the original version, though none of them might agree with the views expressed here.

# 16

# KANT'S VIRTUE ETHICS

## *Robert B. Louden*

Among moral attributes true virtue alone is sublime.

[I]t is only by means of this idea [of virtue] that any judgment as to moral worth or its opposite is possible . . .

Everything good that is not based on morally good disposition . . . is nothing but pretence and glittering misery.[1]

In recent years we have heard much about the revival of virtue ethics, of normative theories whose primary focus is on persons rather than decision-making in problematic situations, agents and the sorts of lives they lead rather than discrete acts and rules for making choices, characters and their morally relevant traits rather than laws of obligation. Contemporary theorists are often motivated by a sense of the impoverishment of modern moral traditions, for in placing primary weight on the agent rather than the act (much less the act's consequences), virtue theorists set themselves off against what are often viewed as *the* two options in modern ethics – utilitarianism and deontologism. The traditional whipping boy in the latter case is Kant, for he is widely regarded as deontology personified, the first moral theorist to place a non-derivative conception of duty at the centre of the philosophical stage, the first to establish a non-consequentialist decision procedure through his universalisability test, etc. In addition, virtue theorists also seem to have more historical reasons for disapproving of Kant, for the rise of quandary ethics is often associated with Enlightenment efforts to escape from tradition and the pull of local communities, and a consequent yearning for an ahistorical and universalistic conception of morality. Kant, as spokesman for the Enlightenment, is a natural target of criticism here.

For conceptual as well as historical reasons then, Kantian ethics has suffered badly under the current revival of virtue campaign. Alasdair MacIntyre writes: 'In Kant's moral writings we have reached a point at which the notion that morality is anything other than obedience to rules has almost, if not quite, disappeared from sight'.[2] Philippa Foot chastises Kant as one of a select group of philosophers whose 'tacitly accepted opinion was that a study of the topic [of the virtues and vices] would form no part of the fundamental work of ethics'.[3] On her view, Kant should bear a sizeable part of the responsibility for analytic philosophy's neglect of virtue. And Bernard Williams is equally critical in his insistent claims that Kantian moral theory treats persons in abstraction from character, and thus stands guilty of misrepresenting not only persons but morality and practical deliberation as well.[4] The underlying message is not simply that Kant is an illustrative representative of the deontological rule ethics perspective, but that his ethics is the worst possible sort of deontological rule ethics, one which is primarily responsible for the eclipse of agent-centred ethics.

Yet some readers of Kant feel that the conceptual shape of his ethical theory has been distorted by defender and critic alike, that his ethics is not rule ethics but virtue ethics. This reading of Kant has had its defenders in the past (he did after all write *The Doctrine of Virtue*), but Onora O'Neill has recently placed it in the context of the contemporary virtue ethics debate. In 'Kant After Virtue' (a reply to MacIntyre's book), she states confidently that 'what is not in doubt . . . is that Kant offers primarily an ethic of virtue rather than an ethic of rules'.[5] So whose Kant is the real Kant – hers or the more familiar one of MacIntyre & Co.?

The real Kant lies somewhere in between these two extremes. He sought to build an ethical theory which could assess both the life plans of moral agents and their discrete acts. This is to his credit, for an adequate moral theory needs to do both.

## THE SHAPE OF VIRTUE ETHICS[6]

What qualifies an ethical theory as virtue ethics rather than rule ethics?

### *Agents vs Acts*

One hallmark of virtue ethics is its strong agent orientation. For virtue theorists, the primary object of moral evaluation is not the intentional act or its consequences, but the agent. Utilitarians begin with a concept of the good – here defined with reference to states of affairs rather than persons. Duty, rights, and even virtue are all treated by utilitarians as derivative categories of secondary importance, definable in terms of utility maximisation. Similarly, deontologists take duty as their irreducible starting point, and reject any attempt to define this root notion of being morally bound to do something in terms of good to be achieved. The good is now a derivative category, definable in terms of the right. The good that we are to promote is right action for its own sake – duty for duty's sake. Virtue also is a derivative notion, definable in terms of pro-attitudes towards one's duties. It is important, but only because it helps us to do our duty.

Virtue ethics begins with a notion of the morally good person which is primitive in the sense that it is not defined in terms of performing obligatory acts ('the person who acts as duty requires') or end-states ('the agent who is disposed to maximise utility through his acts'). On the contrary, right and wrong acts are now construed in terms of what the good agent would or would not do; worthy and unworthy ends in terms of what the good agent would or would not aim at. It is by means of this conceptual shift that 'being' rather than 'doing' achieves prominence in virtue ethics.

## Decision Procedures vs Good Character

Agent-ethics and act-ethics also diverge in their overall conceptions of practical reasoning. Act theorists, because they focus on discrete acts and moral quandaries, are interested in formulating decision procedures for making practical choices. Because they have derivative and relatively weak conceptions of character to lean on, the agent in a practical choice situation does not appear to them to have many resources upon which to draw. He or she needs a guide – hopefully a decision procedure – for finding a way out of the quandary. Agent ethics, because it focuses on long-term characteristic patterns of action, downplays atomic acts and choice situations in the process. It is not as concerned with portraying practical reason as a rule-governed enterprise which can be applied on a case by case basis. Virtue theorists do not view moral choice as unreasoned or irrational; the virtuous agent is also seen as the practically wise agent. But one often finds divergent portraits of practical reason in act and agent ethics.

## Motivation

A third general area where we are likely to see differences between agent and act ethics is in their respective views on moral motivation. This complex issue is particularly important in any reading of Kantian ethics as virtue ethics. For the duty-based or deontological theorist, the preferred motive is respect for the idea of duty itself, and the good man is the one who does his duty for duty's sake. This does not entail that the agent who does his duty for duty's sake does so grudgingly, or only in spite of inclinations to the contrary, but simply that the determining ground of the motive is respect for duty. For the goal-based or utilitarian theorist, the preferred motive is a steady disposition to maximise utility.

In virtue ethics the preferred motivation factor is not duty or utility but the virtues themselves. The agent who acts from dispositions of friendship, courage or integrity is held higher than the person who performs the same acts but from different motives. For instance, a virtue theorist might call a man courageous only if, when in danger, it was clear that the man did not even want to run away (and thus showed signs of being 'directly moved' to act courageously), while the duty-based theorist would only call a man courageous if he did not run away out of sense of duty (but perhaps wanted to anyway – although the 'want' is here irrelevant). As the example suggests, matters become troublesome when we bring in reason and inclination. I have not said that one theory asserts we are motivated by reason, another by desire. However, reason and inclination do enter into the motivation issue (particularly in debates over Kant) in the following way. Virtue ethics, with its 'virtue for virtue's sake' position on motivation, is also committed to the claim that our natural inclinations play a necessary role in many types of action done from virtue. Acting from the virtue of friendship, for instance, would require that one possess and exhibit certain feelings about friends. Kant, on the other hand, holds (from the *Foundations* on) that the sole determining ground of the will must be respect (*Achtung*) – a peculiarly non-empirical feeling produced by an intellectual awareness of the moral law. Kant thus appears to deny natural inclinations any positive role in moral motivation, whereas virtue ethics requires it.

## VIRTUE AND THE GOOD WILL

Kant begins his ethical investigations with a powerful but cryptic proclamation about the good will: 'Nothing in the world – indeed, nothing even beyond the world – can possibly be conceived which could be called good without qualification except a good will'.[7] From the perspective of virtue ethics, to what extent should Kant's position on the good will be construed as evidence of an agent- rather than an act-centred ethics?

As Robert Paul Wolff remarks, it is 'noteworthy that the philosopher most completely identified with the doctrine of stern duty should begin, not with a statement about what we ought to do, but rather with a judgment of what is unqualifiedly good'.[8] And what is unqualifiedly good, according to Kant, is not an end-state such as pleasure or the performance of certain atomic acts in conformity to rules, but a state of character which becomes the basis for all of one's actions. To answer the question: 'Is my will good?' (a question which can never be answered with certain knowledge, due to the opacity of our intentions), we must look beyond atomic acts and decisions and inquire into how we have lived. A man cannot be 'morally good in some ways and at the same time morally evil in others'.[9] Similarly, he cannot, on Kant's view, exhibit a good will one moment and an evil one the next. Steadfastness of character must be demonstrated.

So Kant's opening claim concerning the unqualified goodness of the good will means that what is fundamentally important in his ethics is not acts but agents. But what is the relationship between 'good will' and virtue? Kant defines virtue (*Tugend*) in the *Tugendlehre* as 'fortitude in relation to the forces opposing a moral attitude of will in us'.[10] The Kantian virtuous agent is thus one who, because of his 'fortitude', is able to resist urges and inclinations opposed to the moral law. Kantian fortitude is strength (*Stärke*) or force (*Kraft*) of will, not in the sense of being able to accomplish the goals one sets out to achieve, but rather in the sense of mastery over one's inclinations and constancy of purpose.[11]

A good will is a will which steadily acts from the motive of respect for the moral law. But human beings, because they are natural beings, always possess inclinations which may lead them to act against reason. Their wills are thus in a perpetual state of tension. Some wills are better than others, but only a holy will (who has no wants that could run counter to reason, and who can thus do no evil) possesses an absolutely good will. This is why Kant holds that 'human morality in its highest stages can still be nothing more than virtue'.[12] Virtue is only an approximation of the good will, because of the basic conflict or tension in human wills. Kant's virtuous agent is a human approximation of a good will who through strength of mind continually acts out of respect for the moral law while still feeling the presence of natural inclinations which could tempt him to act from other motives.

Now if virtue is the human approximation to the good will, and if the good will is the only unqualified good, this does imply that moral virtue, for Kant, is foundational, and not (as one would expect in a deontological theory) a concept of derivative or secondary importance. ('Everything good that is not based on a morally good disposition . . . is nothing but pretence and glittering misery.') As Harbison notes: 'the essence of [Kant's] moral philosophy is quite different from what it has commonly been supposed to be, for on the basis of this enquiry one must conclude that it is the concept of the good will that lies at its foundation'.[13]

But there remains a fundamental problem for this particular argument in favour of a virtue ethics reading of Kant. Both the good will and virtue are defined in terms of obedience to moral law, for they are both wills which are in conformity to moral law and which act out of respect for it. Kant begins with the good will in order to uncover 'the supreme principle of morality' – the categorical imperative. Since human virtue is defined in terms of conformity to law and the categorical imperative, it appears now that what is primary in Kantian ethics is not virtue for virtue's sake but obedience to rules. Virtue is the heart of the ethical for Kant, in the sense that it is the basis for all judgments of moral worth. But Kantian virtue is itself defined in terms of the supreme principle of morality. The conceptual commitment to agency and long-term characteristic behaviour rather than atomic acts and decision procedures for moral quandaries is evident here, as one would expect in virtue ethics. But what Kant prizes most about moral agency is its ability to act consistently from respect for law, not in the sense of following specific rules for specific acts, but in the more fundamental sense of guiding one's entire life by respect for rationally legislated and willed law.

Kantian virtue therefore is subordinate to the moral law, and this makes him look more like an obedience-to-rules theorist. However, it is obedience to rules not in the narrow-minded pharisaic manner for which rule ethics is usually chastised by virtue theorists, but in the broader, classical sense of living a life according to reason. The two perspectives of agent and rule are thus both clearly present in Kant's account of the good will. The virtuous agent is one who consistently 'follows the rules' out of respect for the idea of rationally legislated law. But 'the rules', while they do serve as action-guides, are intended most fundamentally as life-guides.

## RE-READING MAXIMS

A second argument for a virtue ethics interpretation of Kant comes from a re-reading of what he means by a maxim. This strategy is particularly prominent in some of the recent work of Onora O'Neill and in a piece of Otfried Höffe.[14] Kant defines a maxim rather tersely as a 'subjective principle of volition',[15] and from this one can infer that a maxim is (among other things) a policy of action adopted by a particular agent at a particular time and place. Because the principle is subjective rather than objective, it must tie in with the agent's own intentions and interests. So why not simply view Kantian maxims as the agent's specific maxims for his discrete acts? This is a common understanding of maxims, but it is also one that easily lends itself to a rule reading of maxims, since here a maxim becomes, in effect, a rule which prescribes or proscribes a specific act. O'Neill rejects the specific intention reading and argues instead that 'it seems most convincing to understand by an agent's maxim the *underlying intention* by which the agent orchestrates his numerous more specific intentions'.[16] Suppose I have invited a guest to my house, and that my underlying intention is to make him feel welcome. On most such occasions, I will have numerous specific intentions by means of which I carry out the underlying intention: I may offer him a beer, invite him to put a record on the stereo, show him my vegetable garden etc.

O'Neill offers two arguments in support of the underlying intention interpretation of maxims. 1. Usually we are aware of our specific intentions for the future, yet Kant frequently asserts that we never know the real morality of our actions. This suggests that maxims and specific intentions are not the same. 2. Sometimes we act without a specific intention (e.g. when we act absent-mindedly), but Kant holds that we always act on some maxim. All action is open to moral assessment. This again suggests a difference between maxims and specific intentions.[17]

Now if Kantian maxims are best seen as underlying rather than as specific intentions, we do have a strong argument for a virtue reading of Kant's ethics. For our underlying intentions tie in directly with the sorts of persons we are and with the sorts of lives we lead. And the sort of person one is obviously depends upon what virtues and vices one possesses. One's specific intentions, on the other hand, are not always an accurate guide to the sort of person one is 'deep down inside'. This connection between underlying intentions and being a certain sort of person is stressed by both O'Neill and Höffe.[18] However, two basic problems confront this interpretation. First, O'Neill's use of the phrase 'underlying intentions' is ambiguous. At one point, she states that adopting maxims is a matter of 'leading a certain sort of life, or being a certain sort of person'; elsewhere she asserts that maxims (or underlying intentions) 'need not be longer-term intentions, for we remain free to change them'.[19] This distinction between underlying and longer-term intentions does not sit well with the asserted identification between underlying intentions and being a certain sort of person. For becoming a certain sort of person is a long-term process. One cannot decide at noon on Monday to be courageous and saintly, and then suddenly become so by Tuesday. And in what sense do we 'remain free to change' the sort of person we have become? I believe there is a strong sense in which such a change can be undertaken, but the effort and time required to carry it out are certainly much greater than are the effort and time required to change one's specific intentions at any given moment. In short, the more 'underlying' intentions are untied from 'longer-term' intentions, the less plausible it becomes to assert that maxims (in the sense of underlying intentions) have to do with leading a certain sort of life and with virtue. For the latter are long-term ventures. One does not initiate, abandon or change them on a daily basis.

One reason for O'Neill's odd insistence on the underlying/long-term intention distinction is perhaps traceable to Kantian texts. In several places, Kant warns that we must not construe virtue as a 'mere aptitude (*Fertigkeit*) or . . . a long-standing habit (*Gewohnheit*) of morally good actions'.[20] His point is that human virtue is an extremely precarious achievement of pure practical reason which must constantly be on guard against heteronomy and empirical inclinations. In making this claim he is unfortunately led into some rhetorical skirmishes against Aristotle which reflect a poor understanding of Aristotle's own analysis of virtue.[21] What Kant wants is a moral disposition 'armed for all situations' and 'insured against changes that new temptations can bring about'.[22] As O'Neill suggests, Kant is aiming at a distinctively modern conception of virtue here, one which is a response to the fragmentation of modern life and the breakdown of communities and institutions. Furthermore, behind his opposition to construing virtues as long-standing habits lies an acute awareness of our powers of rationalisation and self-deception in repressing our sense of guilt. Kant might seem to have read his Freud, but nothing in these texts implies that long-term intentions must necessarily turn into mechanical habits, for we have seen already that cultivating a good will is, on Kant's view, an achievement of pure practical reason. So O'Neill's reservations about long-term intentions do not appear to be well-founded.

The second problem with the underlying intentions reading of maxims is that it contradicts several of Kant's own examples of maxims. What he sometimes means by maxims are not life plans or even underlying intentions, but simply specific intentions for discrete acts. Furthermore, the testing of such maxims does not require that they be related to the life plan or underlying intention of the agent. The maxim of the agent who feels forced to borrow money but knows he can't repay it is very specific, and applies only to restricted dire circumstances which may never even arise. Similarly, the maxim which reveals a perfect duty to refrain from suicide is again a specific intention which is not necessarily related to a life plan.

For these two reasons then, the underlying intentions reading of maxims must be taken with a large pinch of salt. O'Neill's use of 'underlying' is ambiguous, vacillating between specific and long-term intentions. Second, Kant's own examples of maxims indicate that what he sometimes means by the term is specific intentions for atomic acts. But because 'maxims' for Kant can mean both short as well as long-term intentions, we see again that he possesses and employs the conceptual tools to evaluate an agent's discrete acts as well as his or her course of life. This is to Kant's credit, for both enterprises are essential for an adequate ethical theory.

## SELF-PERFECTION AND THE DOCTRINE OF MORALLY NECESSARY ENDS

Yet there is one fundamental use of 'maxims' in Kant's texts which unequivocally concerns underlying intentions and the sort of life one leads. This is what Kant calls maxims of ends rather than of dutiful actions – maxims to pursue general, long-term goals (which allow for many different ways of pursuing them), rather than maxims to perform narrowly prescribed acts. The strongest argument for the prominence of virtue in Kantian ethics is to be gleaned from his doctrine of morally necessary ends as presented in the *Tugendlehre*.

Section 3 of the Introduction to the *Tugendlehre* is entitled: 'On the Ground for Conceiving an End which is at the Same Time a Duty'. The core of Kant's argument runs as follows: all acts have ends, for action (by definition) is a goal-directed process. Ends, however, are objects of free choice. We do of course have many desires, wants and inclinations which are biologically and/or culturally imposed, and nearly all ends that we do eventually adopt are also objects of desires, wants and inclinations. But ultimately ends are chosen, for we cannot be forced to make anything an end of action unless we ourselves choose to. People can and do renounce even the biological desire for life in extreme circumstances. The adoption of ends is a matter of free choice, and this brings them under the purview of pure practical reason rather than of inclination.

But why assert that ends (which are freely chosen) are also morally necessary? Why claim that there exist ends which agents have a duty to adopt? Isn't this merely a way of implying that all conceptions of the good are not created equal, that reason can discriminate among ends as well as among means – isn't it dangerously unmodern and illiberal? Perhaps, but Kant's position is clear: we must assume that there are morally necessary ends, for if we don't, 'this would do away with all moral philosophy'.[23] His reasoning is that if all ends are contingent, then all imperatives become hypothetical. If we are free to accept or reject any goal put before us whenever we are so inclined, then all commands prescribing maxims for actions are likewise open to rejection once the goal is dismissed. In other words (by contraposition), if there is a categorical imperative, there must be at least one morally necessary end. We cannot accept the claim that reason categorically requires us to do certain things unless we accept the companion claim that reason categorically requires us to adopt certain ends.

As is well known, Kant goes on to argue in the *Tugendlehre* that there are two ends which agents have a duty to adopt: their own perfection and the happiness of others. The former, for Kant, is the more fundamental of the two, and its connection to moral character is also more direct.

The duty which Kant asserts all agents have to promote their own perfection includes as its most important component the obligation to cultivate one's will 'to the purest attitude of virtue'.[24] We saw earlier that the good will is the only unqualified good in the world or beyond it, that it in turn is the condition for the goodness of every other thing. Our highest practical vocation as finite rational intelligences is to produce a will good in itself as an unconditional end, for such a will is the supreme good and ordering principle for all human activities. We saw also that moral virtue, as Kant understands the concept, is a human approximation to the good will. Humans, because of their biological and cultural make-ups, always have inclinations which may run counter to the moral law.

The duty to develop an attitude of virtue is obviously a duty to oneself rather than to others. And it is also an ethical rather than a legal duty, that is, a duty in which the motive for action is the thought of the law itself rather than threats of external compulsion. But what is most important to note for our purposes is that the duty to develop one's moral character is the linchpin of Kant's entire system of duties. As he remarks in his discussion of duties to oneself: 'if there were no such duties [viz. duties to oneself], then there would be no duties whatsoever, and so no external duties either. For I can recognize that I am under obligation to others only in so far as I, at the same time, obligate myself'.[25]

Without duties to oneself, there would be no duties whatsoever. Why would Kant make such a claim? His chief contention is that what is basic to all duties – legal, moral, or otherwise – is the concept of binding oneself. Take first the familiar notion of a legal duty to others, say, a loan taken out with a lending institution to help pay for one's graduate education. In one sense I am clearly bound to another party (the bank). But Kant's view is that this is so only because I first choose to bind myself to the laws of the government under which I am accountable to the terms of the contract. If I don't first choose to view myself as being obligated to obey my government's laws, it is not likely that I will consider myself to have any duty towards the bank. Similarly, consider a moral duty to others, e.g. the Kantian duty to promote others' welfare. Here I am not even accountable to any specifiable others, as was the case in the previous example, but only to my own conscience. We 'owe it to ourselves' to do all we are capable of in fulfilling our moral duties to others.

Once Kant's argument concerning morally necessary ends is considered, it becomes strikingly evident that virtue does indeed have a pre-eminent position in his ethics. Our overriding practical vocation is to realise a state of virtue in our own character as the basis of all action. Without fulfilling such a duty to ourselves, other duties are not possible. Virtue is not only the heart of the ethical for Kant; it also has priority in morals considered as a whole (that is, in *Recht* and *Tugend* taken together). For if there were no ethical duties to oneself, there would be no duties whatsoever.

But again virtue itself is posterior to the supreme principle of morality. Virtue remains conceptually subordinate to the moral law. Kant presents us with a virtue ethics in which the 'rule of law' nevertheless plays the lead role, and in which the theory is designed to assess not only ways of life but discrete acts as well. However, as noted earlier, the priority of the moral law in Kantian ethics does not entail the pharisaic qualities which virtue critics have usually attributed to it. It does not mean that what dominates Kantian ethics is the attempt to construct a decision procedure for all acts, or even to devise determinate rules for a limited set of specific acts. Yet such attempts are generally conceded to be prominent in rule ethics approaches to practical reasoning. Instead, what we do find in Kant's ethics is the categorical command of reason to cultivate a way of life in which all of one's acts (whatever they may be) are in complete harmony with the idea of lawfulness as such. The moral will is subordinate to law in Kantian ethics and is defined in terms of it. But the result is not a legistic conformity-to-rules morality, current interpretations to the contrary. It is a conception of a life lived according to reason.

## VIRTUE AND EMOTION

While virtue has far greater prominence in Kant's ethics than many of his readers suppose, it is nevertheless overstating matters to assert baldly that Kantian ethics is virtue ethics. Significant aspects of both the agent and act perspectives are present in his ethical theory, though the former does dominate. Kantian ethical theory seeks to assess not only atomic acts but also agents' ways of life. And while the sort of person one becomes (rather than the specific acts one may perform and the short-term intentions one may adopt) is central in Kantian ethics, his conception of moral personhood is defined in terms of obedience to law. The Kantian agent commitment is inextricably fused to a law conception of ethics. Each of the three arguments outlined earlier points to these same conclusions, which is not surprising, since they are closely related to begin with. The later material from the *Tugendlehre* regarding morally necessary ends (of which the duty of moral self-perfection is the most important) restates and deepens the earlier material from the *Grundlegung* concerning the good will. The section on maxims establishes that while not all Kantian maxims refer to underlying intentions and agents' life plans, the most significant ones in ethics (maxims of ends) do.

One notorious roadblock to a virtue interpretation of Kantian ethics remains, and it requires an unconventional but (I believe) Kantian reply. Virtue theorists part ways with their deontological and teleological opponents over the issue of moral motivation. In virtue ethics agents are expected to act for the sake of virtue; in deontology, for duty's sake; in utilitarianism, for utility's sake. Now at first glance it would seem impossible to argue that Kant espouses a virtue ethics position with respect to motivation, since he holds that only action from duty can have moral worth. However, as my earlier arguments indicate, Kant's notion of action *aus Pflicht* means in the most fundamental sense not that one performs a specific act for the sake of a specific rule which prescribes it (and likewise for other specific acts one performs) but rather that one strives for a way of life in which all of one's acts are a manifestation of a character which is in harmony with moral law. Action *aus Pflicht* is action motivated by virtue, albeit virtue in Kant's sternly rationalist sense.

But it is precisely on the issue of rationalism and moral motivation that Kant has come under such severe criticism. The motivation problem has been a favourite target of Kantian critics from Hegel onward, and to cover all of its dimensions is far beyond the scope of this chapter. The following brief remarks focus instead on Kant's position regarding the role of emotion in action from virtue.

It is generally acknowledged that, from a moral perspective, the most praiseworthy acts are often those which agents truly want to perform. As Foot remarks:

> Who shows most courage, the one who wants to run away but does not, or the one who does not even want to run away? Who shows most charity, the one who finds it easy to make the good of others his object, or the one who finds it hard? . . . The man who acts charitably out of a sense of duty is not to be undervalued, but it is the other [i.e. the one who is directly moved and who thus wants to act charitably] who shows most virtue and therefore to the other that most moral worth is attributed.[26]

The sense of 'wants' here needs to be clarified, and I will attempt to do so in a moment. But first, a restatement of the underlying anti-Kantian argument: acting from virtue is (at least sometimes) action motivated by altruistic emotion or desire. Kant, however, holds that action *aus Pflicht* must be defined independently of all natural emotions and desires. Therefore, there is no place in Kantian ethics for acting from virtue.[27]

Now back to 'wants'. Does Foot's agent who does 'not even want to run away' act this way by nature or because he knows (in addition, perhaps, to being naturally inclined in this direction) that it is noble to do so? In Aristotelian terminology, does he act courageously out of 'natural virtue' or from 'virtue in the strict sense', the latter of which involves *phronēsis*, a rational understanding of what one is doing? Aristotle and Kant agree on his fundamental point: acting from virtue in the strict sense means acting rationally. But Aristotle also holds that practical choice is 'reason motivated by desire (*orektikos nous*) or desire operating through reason (*orexis dianoētikē*)'.[28] Desire and reason are both necessary factors in moral choice, but neither on its own is sufficient. How about Kant? Does acting from virtue, as he understands it, entail acting from desires (in addition to reason)?

Kant has so often been tagged as enemy-of-the-emotions that it may seem foolish even to ask the question. On most interpretations, Kant allows room for one (and only one) desire in his account of moral choice – respect or reverence (*Achtung*) – a unique '*a priori* feeling', generated by a pure judgment which acknowledges the claim of the moral law, and then in turn acts as the phenomenal spring to action from appreciation of that law. But the role of emotions and natural inclinations in Kant's understanding or moral motivation is trickier than is often assumed. On the one hand, he does assert unequivocally that 'what is essential in the moral worth of actions is that the moral law should directly determine the will'.[29] This way of talking is often construed as meaning that reason is not only a necessary but also a sufficient ground for moral choice, and that natural emotions (with the sole exception of *Achtung*, which again is an *a priori* feeling and thus not natural) have no positive role to play whatsoever. But while determination of choice through reason is obviously necessary in Kantian ethics, it is not sufficient for the attainment of virtue. There are a host of phenomenal emotions (the most important of which are joy, sympathy and love) which, while not the direct *Bestimmungsgrund* of the will, must be present in a virtuous disposition. These emotions are phenomenal effects which, as Karl Ameriks puts it, have 'noumenal backing', and find their ultimate source in a noumenal acceptance of pure duty.[30] In less Kantian but more Aristotelian terms, these emotions are ones that have been trained *by* reason to work in harmony *with* reason. They are secondary in importance to respect, but they are nevertheless essential components in a morally virtuous life.

Granted, it is difficult to see this if one does not read past the *Grundlegung*. In that work, Kant is engaging in a form of analysis which he compares with a chemical experiment. He discriminates elements in a compound by varying the circumstances, and wants to break the compound into its base elements in the most effective manner. His assumption there is simply that it is easier to determine accurately whether an act was performed from duty if the agent had an inclination to perform the 'opposite' act (e.g. feel antipathy rather than sympathy towards the suffering of others) than it would be if the agent were also inclined to perform the same act that duty requires. (Of course, even when natural inclination seems to be ruled out as an incentive, we still can't determine with certainty what ultimately motivated the agent. Kant holds that our moral intentions remain opaque to us.) In a similar vein, Kant states in the second *Critique* that it is 'risky' to view altruistic emotions as 'co-operating' with the moral law in motivating moral behaviour.[31] The reason, again, is that it becomes all the more difficult to ascertain the true motives of action when, in addition to acting out of respect for the law, one also has a natural desire to act in the same manner as duty requires. Nevertheless, while it may indeed be risky to enlist the emotions, this does not rule out the possibility that proper cultivation of them may still be necessary for human beings who aspire to a truly virtuous life. And Kant explicitly asserts that the emotions have a necessary and positive role to play in moral motivation in his later writings. In the Ethical Ascetic of the *Tugendlehre* (which deals with the cultivation of virtue), he writes: 'what we do cheerlessly and merely as a compulsory service has no intrinsic value for us, and so also if we attend to our duty in this way; for we do not love it but rather shirk as much as we can the occasion for practising it'.[32] Here and elsewhere Kant addresses the need to cultivate an 'habitually cheerful heart', in order that the *feeling* of joy accompanies (but does not constitute or determine) our virtue. A parallel passage occurs near the beginning of the *Religion*: 'Now if one asks, what is the *aesthetic character*, the temperament, so to speak, of *virtue*, whether courageous and hence *joyous* or fear-ridden and dejected, an answer is hardly necessary. This latter slavish frame of mind can never occur without a hidden *hatred* of the law. And a heart which is happy in the performance of its duty (not merely complacent in the recognition thereof) is a mark of genuineness in the virtuous disposition.[33]

These and other related passages state explicitly that the enemy-of-the-emotions reading of Kant favoured by so many is a gross misunderstanding. Kant's position is clear: pure practical reason needs to be always 'in charge' of the emotions in a truly virtuous life. The *Bestimmungsgrund* of moral choice must be reason, not feeling. But an integral part of moral discipline or what Kant calls 'ethical gymnastic' is training the emotions so that they work with rather than against reason. Acts in which empirical inclinations of any sort are the *Bestimmungsgrund* lack moral worth, but it doesn't follow that a harmonising sentiment must cancel all moral worth. On the contrary, Kant insists that it is a good thing.

Kant then would agree with Foot's claim that the agent who does not even want to run away shows more courage than the one who wants to run away but does not, provided that the 'want' in question is a rational want with which the agent's desires are trained to be in harmony. More generally, acting from virtue, on Kant's view, does entail disciplining the emotions through reason so that one comes to want to perform the same external act that reason commands. But again, as Kant warns, there is a risk, for in training the emotions in such a manner it becomes more difficult to assess one's motives for action. One is perpetually flirting with the possibility that one's conduct is not autonomously willed but merely a product of heteronomy, but cultivation of virtue requires that the risk be taken.

Kant's position on the emotions and their role in action from virtue is not inconsistent with a virtue ethics view. It is remarkably close to Aristotle's view, the major difference being that Kant was much more aware than Aristotle of the dangers of self-deception by emotional enthusiasm pretending to be moral inspiration.

\* Earlier versions of this chapter were presented at the Johns Hopkins University in August 1983 (in conjunction with the Council for Philosophical Studies Summer Institute – 'Kantian Ethics: Historical and Contemporary Perspectives'), and at the 1984 Northern New England Philosophy Association meeting at Plymouth State College in New Hampshire. I would also like to thank Marcia Baron, Ludwig Siep, Warner Wick and the Editor of *Philosophy* for valuable criticisms of earlier written drafts.

## ENDNOTES

1. The first quotation is From Kant's *Observations on the Feeling of the Beautiful and the Sublime*, trans. John T. Goldthwait, Berkeley and Los Angeles: University of California Press (1965), 57; the second from the *Critique of Pure Reason*, trans. Norman Kemp Smith, London: Macmillan (1963), A 315/B 372; and the third from the essay, 'Idea for a Universal History from a Cosmopolitan Point of View', in *On History*, Lewis White Beck (ed.), Indianapolis: Bobbs-Merrill (1963), 21, Ak. 26.
2. Alasdair MacIntyre, *After Virtue*, Notre Dame: University of Notre Dame Press (1981), 219. Cf. 42, 112.
3. Philippa Foot, *Virtues and Vices and Other Essays in Moral Philosophy*, Berkeley and Los Angeles: University of California Press (1978), 1.
4. Bernard Williams, *Moral Luck: Philosophical Papers 1973–1980*, Cambridge, Cambridge University Press (1981), esp. pp. 14, 19.
5. Onora O'Neill, 'Kant After Virtue', *Inquiry* 26 (1984), 397. Cf. 396. For an earlier interpretation which also stresses the prominence of virtue (but in a less either/or manner), see Warner Wick, 'Kant's Moral Philosophy', in *Kant's Ethical Philosophy*, trans. James Ellington, Indianapolis: Hackett (1983). (Originally published as the Introduction to *The Metaphysical Principles of Virtue* by Bobbs-Merrill in 1964.)
6. For a more detailed look at this issue, see my essay, 'On Some Vices of Virtue Ethics', *American Philosophical Quarterly* 21 (1984), 227–36.
7. Kant, *Foundations of the Metaphysics of Morals*, trans. Lewis White Beck, Indianapolis: Bobbs-Merrill (1959), 9, Ak. 393.
8. Robert Paul Wolff, *The Anatomy of Reason*, New York: Harper & Row (1973), 56–7.
9. Kant, *Religion Within the Limits of Reason Alone*, trans. Theodore M. Green and Hoyt H. Hudson, New York: Harper Torchbooks (1960), 20.
10. Kant, *The Doctrine of Virtue*, trans. Mary J. Gregor, Philadelphia: University of Pennsylvania Press (1964), 38, Ak. 380.
11. On strength and virtue, see *The Doctrine of Virtue*, 49–50, Ak. 389, 54/393, 58/397, 66/404, 70–1/408–9. See also *Anthropology from a Pragmatic Point of View*, trans. Mary J. Gregor, Netherlands: Nijhoff (1974), 26–7, Ak. 147, and the *Lectures on Ethics*, trans. Louis Infeld, New York: Harper Torchbooks (1963), 73. On the accomplishment of goals, see the *Foundations*, 10, Ak. 394.
12. Kant, *The Doctrine of Virtue*, 41, Ak. 382. See also the *Critique of Practical Reason*, trans. Lewis White Beck, Indianapolis: Bobbs-Merrill (1956), 86–7, Ak. 84–5, and the *Foundations*, 30–1, Ak. 414.
13. Warren G. Harbison, 'The Good Will', *Kant-Studien* (1980), 59.
14. Onora O'Neill, 'Kant After Virtue', and 'Consistency in Action', in *New Essays on Ethical Universalizability*, N. Potter and M. Timmons (eds), Dordrecht: Reidel (1984), and Otfried Höffe, 'Kants kategorischer Imperativ als Kriterium des Sittlichen', in O. Höffe (ed.), *Ethik und Politik*, Frankfurt: Suhrkamp (1979), esp. pp. 90–2.
15. Kant, *Foundations*, 17, Ak. 401, n. 1; 38/420, n. 8.
16. O'Neill, 'Kant After Virtue', 394.
17. O'Neill, 'Kant After Virtue', 393–4.
18. O'Neill, 395; Höffe, 91.
19. O'Neill, 394, 395.
20. Kant, *The Doctrine of Virtue*, 41–2, Ak. 383, 69/407. Cf. *Anthropology*, 26–7, Ak. 153.
21. Kant, to the contrary, believes Aristotelian virtue is not a mechanical habit but rather a state of character determined by a rational principle (*Nicomachean Ethics*, 1107a1).

22. Kant, *The Doctrine of Virtue*, 42, Ak. 383.

23. Kant, *The Doctrine of Virtue*, 43, Ak. 384.

24. Kant, *The Doctrine of Virtue*, 46, Ak. 386. Other components of the duty of self-perfection include the cultivation of one's 'natural powers' – powers of 'mind, soul, and body'.

25. Kant, *The Doctrine of Virtue*, 80, Ak. 416. Cf. 17/218: 'All duties, merely because they are duties, belong to ethics'.

26. Foot, *Virtues and Vices*, 10, 14.

27. Two recent examples of this view include Lawrence A. Blum, *Friendship, Altruism and Morality*, London: Routledge & Kegan Paul (1980), and Lawrence M. Hinman, 'On the Purity of Our Motives: A Critique of Kant's Account of the Emotions and Acting for the Sake of Duty', *Monist* 66 (1983), 251–66.

28. *Nicomachean Ethics*, VI. 13, 1139b4–5.

29. Kant, *Critique of Practical Reason*, 74, Ak. 72.

30. Karl Ameriks, 'The Hegelian Critique of Kantian Morality', 11. (MS read at the 1984 American Philosophical Association Western Division Meeting.)

31. Kant, *Critique of Practical Reason*, 75, Ak. 73. Here I am following Ameriks, 12.

32. Kant, *The Doctrine of Virtue*, 158, Ak. 484.

33. Kant, *Religion*, 19, n.; cf. *Anthropology*, 147, Ak. 282, and *Education*, trans. by Annette Churton, Ann Arbor: University of Michigan Press (1960), 120–1.

# INDEX

*Utilitarianism* (Mill), 211
utopianism, 190–1

value maximisation, 83
van Inwagen, Peter, 21
VE *see* virtue ethics
vegetarianism, 25
virtue ethics (VE),
  act VE and rule VE, 199
  and act-appraisals, 21, 27
  agents vs acts, 183–7
    causality and applied ethics, 183–4
    character change, 185–6
    intolerable actions, 185
    moral backsliding, 186–7
    tragic humans, 184–5
  and Aristotle, 26–8
  commonsense, 140, 141, 142
  and communitarianism, 17–18
  contemporary VE and Aristotle, 245–56
  and culture, 15
  defined, 260–6
  difficulties in, 18–22
    applicability, 20–1
    justification, 19–20
    moral status of acts, 21–2
    universality, 20
  and the emotions *see* emotions
  establishing who is virtuous, 187–9
  extreme version, 8–9, 30
  rowing attraction of, 2, 128, 180
  ant as the assumed enemy of, 26, 28
  derate version, 8, 9, 30
  moral dilemmas, 13
  moral education, 13
  moral luck, 14
  oral motivation, 12
  ion issue as main point of disagreement
    DE, 12
    listic', 15–16
    logical, 11, 19
    rian character of, 11
    osition, 11–12
    on of the voluntary, 14–15
    , 167–70
    uiding objection, 169–70
    ncy objection, 170
    edness objection, 169
    tic character, 10, 18
    aracter, 7–8
    ss story, 194–203
    orality', 14
    ficant moral concepts, 9
    tions, 22–6, 171–8
    objection, 174–7

the contingency argument, 177–8
  justification and universality, 22–3
  the self-centredness objection, 171–4
reverses the order of justification, 7
revolutionary nature of, 7, 14, 16, 22, 30
the six dimensions of, 213–17
style over substance, 189–90
teleological view of, 11, 19
as a theory of moral worth, 9–10
and utilitarianism, 11
utopianism, 190–1
and virtuous persons, 23
*see also* under Aristotle
virtue theory, 227–34
virtues
  'actional', 200, 201, 202
  argument for studying, 53
  and business, 217–24
  Christianity and, 15
  defined, 25, 56, 229
  'feminine', 17, 213
  the Homeric era and, 15
  intellectual, 12, 22
  other-regarding, 132–3, 141
  and right behaviour, 7, 8
  self-regarding, 132, 133, 141
  substantive, 45
  von Wright on, 48
  and wellbeing, 8, 48
*Virtues and Vices* (Foot), 101–4, 181, 183
virtuous agent, 229, 232
virtuous persons, 64
  act first and foremost out of virtues, 11–12
  Aristotle and, 10, 57
  features praised in, 23
  learning to be virtuous, 13, 156
  and more than one right answer, 13
  and right behaviour, 9, 21, 44
virtuousness of traits, 47, 49, 51
von Wright, G. H., 42, 48, 50, 53, 260, 265

*Walden Pond* (Thoreau), 18, 159
Wallace, James D., 49, 201–2
Warnock, Geoffrey, 48, 49, 52
Watson, Gary, 6, 7, 9, 10, 13, 82, 260–5
wellbeing, 8, 47, 48, 88, 94, 133, 135, 137,
    138, 171–2
Wettstein, Howard K., 42, 43, 48, 49
Williams, Bernard, 5, 9, 14, 16, 45, 94, 111, 112,
    114, 188, 287
wisdom, 132, 141, 188–9, 231, 232, 269, 273,
    274, 275, 281
Wolff, Robert Paul, 289
women's rights, 234–5, 238, 240

Xenophon, 185–6